Fault Tolerance
in Distributed Systems

Fault Tolerance in Distributed Systems

PANKAJ JALOTE

Department of Computer Science and Engineering
Indian Institute of Technology, Kanpur

P T R Prentice Hall
Upper Saddle River, New Jersey 07458

Jalote, P.
    Fault tolerance in distributed systems / Pankaj Jalote.
      p. cm.
    Includes bibliographical references and index.
    ISBN 0-13-301367-7
    1. Fault-tolerant computing. 2. Electronic data processing-
-Distributed processing. I. Title.
QA76.9.F38J35 1994

004'.36–dc20

Editorial/production: *bookworks*

Acquisitions editor: *Gregory G. Doench*

Artist: *Clovis L. Tondo*

Cover designer: *Design Source*

Cover photo credit: © *Reginald Wickham*

Copy editor: *Henry Pels*

Manufacturing manager: *Alexis R. Heydt*

The publisher offers discounts on this book when ordered
in bulk quantities. For more information, contact:
  Corporate Sales Department
  P T R Prentice Hall
  Upper Saddle River, NJ 07458

  Phone: (201) 592-2863   FAX: (201) 592-2249

Printed in the United States of America
10 9 8 7 6 5 4 3 2 1

ISBN   0-13-301367-7

Prentice-Hall International (UK) Limited, London
Prentice-Hall of Australia Pty. Limited, Sydney
Prentice-Hall Canada Inc., Toronto
Prentice-Hall Hispanoamericana, S.A., Mexico
Prentice-Hall of India Private Limited, New Delhi
Prentice-Hall of Japan, Inc., Tokyo
Pearson Education Asia Pte. Ltd., Singapore
Editoria Prentice-Hall do Brasil, Ltda., Rio De Janeiro

Dedicated
to my Father
Sri Ram Jalote

Contents

Preface

The increased use of computers in almost every aspect of modern life has led to a need for highly reliable computer systems. Fault tolerance is an approach by which reliability of a computer system can be increased beyond what can be achieved by traditional methods. Fault tolerant systems employ redundancy to mask various types of failures.

Fault tolerance is not a new area. Some concepts for fault tolerance were proposed by von Neumann himself. The premiere conference in the area — IEEE's International Conference on Fault Tolerant Computing Systems (FTCS) — started over two decades ago. However, early work on fault tolerance focused almost exclusively on hardware-supported fault tolerance. The area of software/system fault tolerance is relatively new.

Fault tolerance is generally considered as consisting of two subareas: hardware fault tolerance, and software fault tolerance. Though the boundary is not precisely defined, generally speaking, software fault tolerance encompasses those methods in which fault tolerance against different types of failures is largely supported in software, while hardware fault tolerance is where fault tolerance is supported largely in hardware. Whereas hardware fault tolerance activity usually comes under the purview of the electrical engineering community, the topics under software fault tolerance are largely of interest to the computer science community.

This book is an attempt to organize the body of knowledge in the area of software fault tolerance. As most of the proposed techniques in this area use distributed systems as the basic platform, the book focuses on fault tolerance in distributed systems. However, wherever appropriate (e.g., software design faults), the uniprocess case is discussed as a special case of distributed systems.

The book treats a fault tolerant distributed system as consisting of levels of abstraction. The different levels provide different fault tolerant services. At the lowest level are the abstractions which are so frequently needed by techniques for fault tolerance at higher levels that we consider them as "basic building blocks." These are the abstractions of fail-stop processors (implementation of which requires Byzantine agreement protocols), stable storage, reliable communication, synchronized clocks, and failure detection. For supporting fault tolerant services, a distributed system is generally assumed to provide these abstractions. The next level is the abstraction of reliable and atomic broadcast, which is also a building block for many techniques for fault tolerance, but requires the reliable point-to-point message delivery and fail-stop processor abstractions for implementation. Reliable and atomic broadcast abstractions are useful for supporting fault tolerant services where one-to-many communication is required. These lowest two levels provide "building blocks," which by themselves are of limited use, but are employed to support fault tolerant services.

The next five levels deal with fault tolerant services. Perhaps the simplest fault tolerant user service is recovering a distributed system to a consistent state, if any error occurs. The next level of a fault tolerant user service is ensuring the atomicity of actions. While consistent state recovery simply ensures that a consistent state of the system is reached, with atomic actions there are user-defined actions or transactions that need to be executed atomically, even if failures occur during the execution of the action. The focus of the services of these two levels is on ensuring consistency under failures.

With atomic actions, an action is generally aborted if a failure occurs while the action is executing. Clearly, the next desirable fault tolerant service is to ensure that the actions always complete, even if failures occur. For this, the data on which the actions or processes operate should be accessible even if failures occur. In addition, the processes themselves have to be made resilient. These form the next two levels of fault tolerant services.

Methods and protocols in the levels discussed above aim to make some user service fault tolerant against node and communication failures. Even with these, a system may fail due to the presence of software design faults in the user application. Hence, at the highest level we consider software design faults. At this level the goal is to provide an abstraction in which the software masks its own faults. The various levels are shown in Figure P.1.

The book is organized as follows. Each level of abstraction is discussed in a separate chapter. For each abstraction, its precise definition and motivation is given, along with a survey of the important methods for supporting the abstraction. Chapter 2 describes the general distributed system and its properties. Chapter 3 contains the "basic building blocks." For each of the abstractions discussed in this chapter, one or two important methods for supporting the abstraction are described. Chapter 4 discusses the abstraction of reliable broadcast and its variations. Protocols

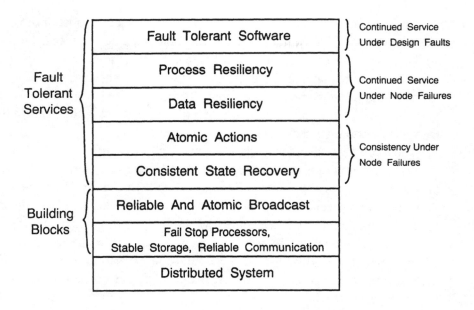

Figure P.1. Levels in a fault tolerant distributed system.

for supporting the different types of broadcast are described. Chapters 5 to 9 discuss the fault tolerant services. Chapter 5 describes the two approaches for recovering a consistent state and some methods for doing so. Chapter 6 discusses how actions can be made atomic in a distributed system. Recovery and commit protocols needed for this are also discussed. Data resiliency is discussed in Chapter 7. Various approaches for managing data replication to provide a "one-copy view" are described. Chapter 8 discusses resilient processes. Methods for supporting resiliency for different communication methods are described. Finally, Chapter 9 discusses the methods for making a software fault tolerant against its own design faults. The uniprocess case is discussed as a special case of distributed systems. Though the commercial and experimental fault tolerant systems that have been built have not been discussed separately, many of the techniques used by such systems have been covered in the various chapters.

This book can be used as a textbook for a graduate/senior level course on fault tolerance in a Computer Science department, or for a professional course in fault tolerance. It can also be used as a reference by researchers/practitioners working in this area. It may also be used as a reference or a co-text for a course on fault tolerance in an Electrical Engineering department, and can also be used as a reference or a co-text in a course on distributed systems.

The area of fault tolerance is very wide. Hence, though most of the important topics have been covered in the book, some topics have been left out. Furthermore, all the topics have not been discussed in great detail, as some of the topics covered in the book have a large body of literature and a comprehensive treatment of these topics would make the book voluminous. Throughout the book, emphasis has been placed on techniques and algorithms rather than formalism, as the focus of the book is to survey important techniques for various abstractions.

There are many people who have helped me in writing this book. I would like to express my gratitude to all of them. Students in my fault tolerance course, both at the Indian Institute of Technology Kanpur and at the University of Maryland College Park, deserve a special thanks, as interaction with them has greatly influenced this book. I am thankful to all the people who responded to my e-mail queries and who readily copied and mailed articles that were not accessible to me. I am also thankful to students and others who helped in critical reading of various portions of the book.

Comments or suggestions about the book will be welcome and can be sent to me by e-mail at jalote@iitk.ernet.in.

Pankaj Jalote

Chapter 1

Introduction

The increased use of computers and our increased reliance on them have led to a need for highly reliable computer systems. There are many areas where computers perform life-critical tasks. Some examples of these are flight control systems, patient monitoring systems, missile guidance and control systems, and air traffic control systems. In these systems, failure of the computers can lead to catastrophe, maybe even loss of human life. There are other application areas, which critically depend on computers, where failures can cause great financial loss, or loss of opportunity. The prime examples of this are banking and stock markets. It is clear that in such applications, highly *dependable* systems are needed. It is also clear that the need for these systems will continue to grow.

Dependability is defined as the trustworthiness of a computer system such that reliance can justifiably be placed on the service it delivers [Lap85, Lap92]. The service delivered by a system is its behavior as it is perceived by its users, where a user is another system (human or physical) which interacts with the computer system [Lap85, Lap92]. Dependability is a general concept, and depending on the application, different attributes can be emphasized. The most significant attributes of dependability are *reliability, availability, safety*, and *security* [Lap85, Lap92]. Reliability deals with *continuity of service*, availability with *readiness for usage*, safety with *avoidance of catastrophic consequences on the environment*, and security with *prevention of unauthorized access and/or handling of information* [Lap85, Lap92]. The attribute of most significance for fault tolerance is reliability (and to some extent availability).

A system failure occurs when the system behavior is not consistent with its specifications. Failures are caused by faults in the components of the system. The more the number of components, the more things there are that could be faulty.

1

Similarly, the more complex a component, the more chances there are of it being faulty. The sheer complexity and number of components that are present in a modern day computing system enhance the likelihood of one of the components being faulty.

Since failures are caused by faults, a direct approach to improve the reliability of a system is to try to prevent faults from occurring or getting introduced into the system. This approach is called *fault prevention* [Lap85, Lap92]. The second approach for increasing reliability is *fault tolerance*. The goal of this approach is to provide service despite the presence of faults in the system. It is assumed that fault prevention techniques will never be able to eliminate all possible faults, and any real system is likely to have or develop faults in it. To increase the reliability of a system beyond what can be achieved by fault prevention techniques, systems have to be designed such that they can provide the service in spite of faults.

In the traditional approach of fault prevention, high reliability is achieved by eliminating as many faults as possible before the system is put in regular use. A system employing only fault prevention has no redundancy, and all components must work correctly, without failing, at all times for the system to work correctly. Since all possible faults cannot be anticipated and eliminated before deployment of the system, fault avoidance assumes that system failures will occasionally take place. For this, manual maintenance methods are devised to repair the system when failure takes place.

Hence the key characteristics of a system that relies on this approach are [Avi76]: (1) lack of any redundancy in the system to mask failures, (2) systems fail occasionally when any of the components fail, (3) manual maintenance procedures are used to repair the system when failures occur. For such systems, occasional failure and manual repair are taken as necessary. The main consequence of these characteristics are that such a system is inaccessible when it is under repair after failure and no operation can be performed during this time. In other words, the jobs being performed by the computer system will, periodically, not be performed for the repair interval. For applications where this is acceptable, computer systems employing only fault prevention will suffice.

However, there are applications where this major consequence of using only fault prevention is not acceptable. The major reasons why this may not be acceptable are [Avi76]: (1) unacceptability of the real-time delays caused by manual repair, (2) the inaccessibility of systems for manual repair, and (3) the excessive high costs of lost time and maintenance. The first reason will exist for any system having real-time constraints. Examples of these are process control applications, guidance systems, air traffic control, and fly-by-wire. The second reason is predominant for systems that have to be unmanned (or manned by persons who are not qualified for repairing computer systems) continuously. A prime example of this is unmanned space exploration. The third reason predominates in applications like banking, life-critical support systems, and defense systems.

To alleviate many of the shortcomings of the traditional approach of fault prevention, fault tolerance can be used. Fault tolerance uses *protective redundancy* to mask failures. That is, the system contains components that are not needed if no fault tolerance is to be supported. These redundant components are used to avert system failure in case some components fail. Essentially, redundancy is used to replace manual repair by automated "repair and reconfiguration," which, in turn, enhances the reliability and availability of the system.

The two approaches — fault prevention and fault tolerance — are complementary in nature. Employing fault tolerance without using the fault prevention techniques for building the components does not make much sense. For fault tolerance to be successful, it is desirable that the components of the system be individually reliable. That is, fault prevention techniques should be used for building the components that will be used for building the fault tolerant system. In addition to using fault prevention methods for making components reliable, prevention methods are also needed to verify and validate the fault tolerant system. Even with highly reliable components, the fault tolerant system will be of no use if it is designed incorrectly or uses the components in an improper manner. Thus, methods have to be used to validate that the fault tolerant system is indeed fault tolerant, capable of masking various types of faults.

The fault prevention methods focus on methodologies for design, testing, and validation; whereas fault tolerant methods focus on how to use components (built using fault avoidance methods) in a manner such that failures can be masked. The theory and techniques for building fault tolerant distributed systems is the subject of this book.

1.1 Basic Concepts and Definitions

Before we embark on discussing any aspect of fault tolerant systems, we have to define what we mean by a system, error, fault, failure, and fault tolerance. These terms have been used in a variety of ways in different contexts, and the terms *fault*, *failure*, and *error* have often been used interchangeably. Now some agreement exists on the definitions of these terms and what concepts they represent. In this section, we give general definitions to these terms following the concepts presented in [AL81, Rob82, Lap92].

1.1.1   System Model

First we must ask what a system is in order to discuss fault tolerant systems. The concept of a system is quite general and exists in other disciplines too. Even in computing, the concept is quite general and represents various things in different contexts. Hence a fairly broad and general definition of a system is needed.

We define a *system* as an identifiable mechanism that maintains a pattern of behavior at an interface between the system and its environment [AL81]. This definition implies that a system must interact with its environment, and that an environment of the system is necessary for defining a system. Essentially, specification of the environment defines the boundaries of the system of interest. The "pattern of behavior" at the interface, then, is the external behavior of the system, which is observed by the environment.

The environment can be partitioned into "sub-environments" with each partition having its own pattern of behavior toward the system. This partitioning is typically done to manage the complexity of defining the behavior of a system, and focus attention on those sub-interfaces that are of primary interest. By doing this, for example, we can ignore, if desired, the interface of a computer system with the air around it and its heat generation behavior at that interface (though this might be the sub-interface of interest to the designer of heat sinks for the boards and chips). A system *user* can be considered a "sub-environment," or that part of the environment whose main aim is to use the service provided by the system. For this, it actively interacts with the system, provides inputs to it, and receives outputs from the system. The user can be a human or another system.

Note that the term interface, in the definition of the system, is a concept rather than an entity. In computer systems, often, the term interface represents identifiable hardware or physical entities. Such entities, with this definition of the system, can themselves be considered as a system with their conceptual interfaces. In the definition of the system, interface is used only to identify a boundary between the system and its environment.

This definition of the system is from the point of view of its external behavior. Though it is needed to identify what a system is, it does not offer any help in specifying the internal structure of a system. More is needed for that. Most engineering disciplines use a system/subsystem hierarchy to define a system structure. We follow the definition in [AL81, Rob82].

A system is considered as being composed of a number of components or subsystems, which interact under the control of a design. Each of the subsystems is a system in its own right, with its own external behavior and its own internal structure. If a system under consideration is one of the systems at level N, then each system at level

N is a subsystem at level (N+1). Each system at level N is itself composed of a number of subsystems at level (N-1), and each system at level (N-1) is composed of a number of subsystems at level (N-2), and so on. This system/subsystem hierarchy continues till a level beyond, which it is either not possible or not desirable to further specify the details of the system. Subsystems at this last level are called "system components" or "atomic components." The level at which the components are considered as atomic is typically application or problem dependent. For example, if we are interested in the behavior of each gate in a computer system (perhaps to consider the faults at gate level), then this hierarchy will continue till we come down to the gates. On the other hand, if we are only interested in the behavior of major components, like memory, CPU, secondary storage, and interconnection network (as is typically the case in distributed systems), then our hierarchy need not look at the detailed structure consisting of boards, chips, or gates.

The external behavior (or the external state) of a system is an abstraction of its internal state. The internal state of the system comprises the external states of its components. During execution, the internal state of the system goes through a sequence of changes, determined by the interaction between its components. Some of the changes in the internal state are reflected as changes in the external state of the system.

For deciding whether the behavior of a system is correct or not, we must have some basis of comparison, which tells the correct behavior of the system. Traditionally, the expected or correct behavior of a system is given by its *specifications*. The specifications include the expected service, which includes the outputs as well as the interactions of the system, and conditions under which the service has to be provided.

Ideally, we want the specifications to be complete, consistent, and correct. Completeness implies that the full behavior of the system is specified under all possible situations. Consistency implies that the specifications do not contradict each other such that it is impossible for a system to implement them. Finally, correctness implies that the specifications specify what was "really intended."

If specifications are suspected to have faults in themselves, then we cannot say whether the behavior of a system is "incorrect" or whether the specifications are faulty. In such situations, usually some external authority is employed to adjudicate. Overall, with the arbitration process, we can assume that the specifications are *authoritative*. This concept of authoritative specifications can also be formalized using the concept of Authoritative System Reference [Rob82], in which, the Authoritative System Reference (ASR) for a system symbolizes the authority process that determines whether or not a proposed interpretation of a specification, or the specification itself, is correct. We will use the term specifications to refer to authoritative specifications, or an ASR.

1.1.2   Failure, Error, and Fault

For the system model defined above, given the specifications of the system, the failure of a system can be defined. A *failure* of the system occurs when the behavior of the system first deviates from that required by its specifications [AL81]. That is, a system fails when it cannot provide the desired service. An *error* is that part of the system state which is liable to lead to subsequent failure [Lap85, Lap92]. If there is an error in the system state, then there exists a sequence of actions which can be executed by the system and which will lead to a system failure, unless some corrective measures are employed. The cause of an error is a *fault*.

Since error is a property of the state of the system, it can be observed and evaluated. Failure, in contrast, is not a property of the system state, and cannot be observed easily (unless special mechanisms are employed to record the occurrence of some types of events). Typically, the occurrence of a failure is deduced by detecting some error in the system state. For example, if the external state of the system is monitored, and if the monitored state forms a part of the expected system behavior, then if an error is detected it implies that a failure has occurred.

Since failure is essentially observed by detecting the error at the output, it will be detected only if the error is actually observed. For example, if the state is not being monitored continuously but is evaluated at fixed intervals, then a failure may not be observed at all. Similarly, a failure may also go undetected if the complete output state is not being monitored and an error occurs in a part that is not being monitored. Since it is typically not feasible to evaluate the entire state to determine an error, it is important that the state to be evaluated is chosen carefully if we want to "catch" most failures.

In general, whenever something goes wrong we attribute it to some fault. We say that a system is not behaving correctly due to the presence of a fault. Fault is associated with a *notion of defect*. A faulty system is the one with defects. We define *fault* as the defects that have the potential of generating errors.

Though a fault has the potential for generating errors, it *may not* generate any errors during the period of observation. In other words, the presence of fault does not ensure that an error will occur. The reverse, however, is true. An error in the system state implies the presence of faults in the system. For example, if a memory cell is such that it always returns the value 0 regardless of what is stored in it, then it contains a fault. However, this fault may not manifest itself until that faulty memory cell is used and a value of 1 is stored in it, before retrieval. As long as the faulty memory cell is not used, or a value of 0 is stored in it, the fact that the memory contains a fault will not be manifested.

Faults can be characterized as transient or permanent. *Transient* faults are faults of limited duration, caused by temporary malfunction of the system or due to some external interference. Transient faults can cause a failure, or an error, only in the duration for which they exist. The error caused by transient faults may also exist only for a short duration. This makes detecting such faults very hard. If a transient fault occurs rarely and the damage caused can be rectified, then its detection is not required. However, if the transient fault is *intermittent* and occurs repeatedly (but always for a short duration), then its detection is desirable. Detecting such faults is quite hard and expensive.

Permanent faults are those in which once the component fails, it never (or for a long period of time) works correctly again. Many techniques for fault tolerance assume that the components fail permanently. In distributed systems also, we will largely be interested in permanent faults causing permanent failures.

Faults can also be characterized by the phase in which they are introduced [Lap92]. *Design faults* are those which arise during the system design or during modification of the system. *Operational faults* are ones which appear during the system lifetime and are caused due to physical reasons. Generally, design faults are much harder to tolerate than operational faults. Except for the last chapter of the book, which deals with software design faults, the rest of the book deals with operational faults only.

1.1.3   Fault Tolerance

Finally, we define what is meant by fault tolerance, the subject of this book. A system is *fault tolerant* if it can mask the presence of faults in the system by using redundancy. The goal of fault tolerance is to avoid system failure, even if faults are present.

The system, as a whole, cannot be made fault tolerant against its own failures. That is, once the system fails there is nothing that can be done, as the failure has already occurred. However, a system can be made fault tolerant against the failure of its components. And that is the goal of fault tolerance: to avoid the failure of the overall system when some of its subsystems fail. In other words, it masks the failure of a subsystem at higher levels.

A system is considered fault tolerant if the behavior of the system, despite the failure of some of its components, is consistent with its specifications. So, if some component of a system is faulty, then the system is fault tolerant if the failure of the component (and the presence of fault in the component) is masked, that is, is not reflected in the external behavior of the system.

Often, it is not required that the entire system behavior be maintained as it is (indeed it may be impossible, since the masking of the failure of the component by the use of redundancy will have some effect on the external behavior, at least in performance), even if some of the components fail. There are some services or properties of particular interest (to the application for which the fault tolerant system is being designed), and it is these properties that have to be preserved despite the failure of some defined components. In fact, as we will see in the course of the book, most of the problems for which solutions have been proposed can be characterized by the property or functionality of the system to be preserved, and the types of faults to be handled. The goal of most of the specific techniques proposed is to preserve some desired property under the face of some set of failures.

Redundancy is the key to supporting fault tolerance; there can be no fault tolerance without redundancy. *Redundancy* is defined as those parts of the system that are not needed for the correct functioning of the system, if no fault tolerance is to be supported. That is, the system works correctly without redundancy, if no failures take place. Redundancy in a system can be hardware, software, or time [Avi76].

Hardware redundancy comprises the hardware components that are added to the system to support fault tolerance. *Software redundancy* includes all programs and instructions that are employed for supporting fault tolerance. A common technique for fault tolerance is to execute some instruction (or sequence of instructions) many times. This technique requires *time redundancy*, that is, extra time for performing tasks for fault tolerance.

In distributed systems, frequently, all three forms of redundancy are used. Hardware redundancy is employed in the form of extra processors, memory, or communication links. Software redundancy is employed for managing these extra hardware components and using them correctly for providing continued service, in case some components fail. Extra time is also usually required by the methods for fault tolerance in distributed systems.

1.2   Phases in Fault Tolerance

As defined above, a fault tolerant system attempts to prevent the failure of the system in spite of the failure of some of its components. By nature, the implementation of fault tolerance in any particular system will be closely linked with the system and its architecture and design. Just like designing a system is dependent on the properties/requirements of the system, designing a fault tolerant system is also a function of the needs and functionality of the system. Clearly, no general technique can be proposed for "adding" fault tolerance to a system. However, some general principles can be identified that are useful in designing fault tolerant systems. Here we specify some general activities that most systems employing fault tolerance have to perform.

In providing fault tolerance, four phases can be identified: error detection, damage confinement, error recovery, and fault treatment and continued system service [AL81]. *Error detection* is the phase in which the presence of a fault is deduced by detecting an error in the state of some subsystem. Once an error has been detected, it implies that failure of the component has occurred. Any damage caused due to the failure has to be identified and delimited in the second phase of *damage confinement*. Often, the system design has to incorporate mechanisms to help limit the spreading of errors in the system, thereby confining the damage to predetermined boundaries. These two phases really are the detection phases, which are necessary for starting the activities for tolerating the failure. After these, the error in the state has to be corrected. This is done in the *error recovery* phase. Since there is an error in the system state, it is necessary to remove the error such that it does not get propagated by future actions. With error recovery, the system will reach an error-free state. So far, the activities have centered around error in the system state. In the final phase of *fault treatment and continued system service*, the fault or the faulty component has to be identified, and the fault tolerant system has to function such that the faulty components are not used, or used in a different manner or configuration such that the fault does not again cause failures.

These are the four general activities that are typically carried out in any scheme for supporting fault tolerance. In some situations, some of these phases may be done implicitly or may be straightforward, but the general sequence of activities is as specified by these phases. In the rest of this section we will discuss these phases in more detail.

1.2.1 Error Detection

The starting point of any fault tolerance activity is error detection. As discussed in the model above, faults and failures cannot be directly observed, but have to be deduced from the presence of errors. Since error is defined by the state of a system (or subsystem), checks can be performed to see if there is an error or not. From the presence of errors, failures and faults can then be deduced. Hence, error detection mechanisms are often referred to as "failure/fault detection," and the presence of an error in the output of a component is declared as failure of the component. How effective a fault tolerance scheme is will clearly depend on the effectiveness of the error detection mechanism employed. Ideally, we would like the error detection mechanism to detect any possible error caused by those faults that the fault tolerance scheme intends to handle. However, such exhaustive mechanisms for error detection are often not practically feasible.

Due to the importance of error detection, let us first determine what is an ideal check for detecting errors. There are some important properties that an error detection check should satisfy [AL81]. First, an ideal check should be determined solely from the specifications of the system and should not be influenced by the internal design of the system. Any influence of the system on the check can cause the same error in the check as is present in the system. Hence, for purposes of designing a check for detecting errors, the system should be treated as a "black box."

Secondly, an ideal check should be *complete and correct*. This implies that the check should be able to detect all possible errors in the behavior of the system that can occur from the presence of those faults that the fault tolerant system aims to handle, and that it never declares an error when there is no error present. With a complete and correct check, it can be asserted that if no error is detected, then there are no faults (of interest) in the system, and if an error is detected, then an error (and therefore a fault) is present in the system. Clearly, if the check is not complete, some errors may go undetected, thereby later causing a failure of the system.

Thirdly, the check should be *independent* from the system with respect to susceptibility of faults. Real checks will sometimes fail (due to the failure of its components). If we have a check that also fails when the system fails, then the check is of no practical value. We would like a check to have an independent failure mode, that is, it fails independently of the system. If this is satisfied, the probability that the check will fail at the same time as the system is minimized.

In real systems, these criteria can rarely be satisfied fully. Only approximations are possible. Typically, it is not feasible to perform a complete check on the output state, since such a check may itself be very complex and therefore more likely to be faulty. Furthermore, a complete check may impose financial and performance constraints that are impractical. Similarly, practical checks are not likely to be performed on all possible outputs at all possible times; to place such a check, information about the structure of the system is often used. Such information is typically used to ensure a larger "coverage." Finally, even the independence of the check from the system cannot be fully obtained, since finally the check and the system must share some environment (power supply, same box, same room, etc). And anything going wrong with the environment will then cause both to fail (e.g., if there is radiation that causes all hardware to perform incorrectly, a hardware-based check will also fail along with the hardware system).

In view of the practical limitations, checks for *acceptability* are often employed for error detection rather than ideal checks. An acceptable check is not an ideal check, but an approximation. The goal of acceptance checks is to keep the cost of error detection checks low, and at the same time maximizing the errors that are detected. Such checks do not guarantee that there are no undetected errors, but try to catch the majority of errors of interest, particularly the ones that are more likely to occur. The errors that occur rarely may be ignored while designing such checks. For such checks, the designer will try to anticipate errors based on some assumptions about the environment of the system, and design checks to catch the errors that are most likely to occur.

The error detection checks that are employed in computer systems can be of different types, depending on the system and the faults of interest. However, there are some general types of checks that are most frequently employed. We will now briefly discuss these [AL81].

Replication Checks. Replication checks are one of the most common and powerful checks. Replication checks can be fairly complete and can be implemented without the knowledge of the internal structure of the system being replicated. As the name suggests, such a check involves replicating some component of the system. The results of different components are compared, or voted, to detect errors. Due to this, it is also one of the most expensive methods of error detection.

The type and quantity of replication depends on the application. If it can be assumed that the design of the system is correct and failures occur due to physical causes, and failures of components are independent, then a component can be replicated many times. This form of replication is used often in hardware. Triple modular redundancy (TMR), which is discussed later in the chapter, uses this method.

Replication using identical copies of a component works if the design of the component is correct. Such replication checks will clearly not work if the design of the system can itself be faulty. For handling design faults, replication can be used, but the replicated components should be different in design also. That is, all the replicated components implement the specifications of the component but in an independent manner. If the failures caused due to errors in design are independent, fault tolerance against design faults can be achieved. We will discuss this later in the context of software faults.

Replication is also used in systems for purposes other than error detection. For example, in distributed systems, replication is used extensively, though not for the purpose of error detection. Typically, data or processes are replicated in a distributed system on different processors such that the failure of some components of the distributed system can be handled. The failure detection is typically done by timing checks (discussed next). Replication is used largely for continued service and fault isolation.

Timing Checks. If the specifications of a component include timing constraints, then timing checks can be used to check if those constraints are being met or not. Timing checks typically set a timer with a value determined from the specifications of the component. If the timer "times out," it means that the timing constraint of the component is violated. A timing violation often implies that the component is behaving incorrectly and its other outputs may also be in error. Hence, indirectly, a "timing error" also signifies an error in the state of the system.

Timing checks are frequently used both in hardware and software systems to detect "problem situations." The timers set for detecting timing problems are sometimes also called "watchdog timers." Most hardware systems employ timing checks to detect problems in memory access or bus access. In software, operating systems, for example, use timers extensively for detecting situations that can lead to more problems.

In distributed systems, timing errors play a central role. One of the most common component failures that fault tolerant techniques try to mask is the "node failure." A node is a component in a distributed system. The distributed system often specifies a timing constraint that a working node must respond within some defined time. This time is typically calculated based on the delays involved in the communication network. If a node does not respond within the timeout period, its behavior is declared erroneous and the node is assumed to have failed. This is the most common form of check for detecting the failure of nodes.

Structural and Coding Checks. On any data, two general types of checks are possible: semantic checks and structural checks. Semantic checks try to ensure whether the value is consistent with the rest of the system. Structural checks just consider the data and ensure that internally the structure of the data is as it should be. If redundancy is built into the representation of the data itself, then structural checks can be used to identify erroneous data.

The most common form of structural check, used extensively in hardware, is coding. In coding, extra bits are added to the data bits, such that the value of these extra bits is always related to the value of the data bits. The checking mechanisms are based on coding checks if this relationship holds. If the coding bits or the data bits are corrupted, this relationship is violated, and the error is detected. We will further discuss coding later in this chapter.

Structural checks, though used more extensively in hardware, can also be employed in software systems. In software systems, structural checks can be devised for data structures, particularly if there is some redundancy in the data structures. Data structures that use redundancy in order to facilitate structural checks are called *robust data structures* [TMB80a, TMB80b]. In robust data structures, if the data structure becomes corrupt, then using the redundancy and structural checks, it is possible to detect and even correct the corrupted part of the data structure. However, since the instance of data structure corruption is very infrequent, as compared to the corruption of data at lower levels in the hardware, robust data structures have a limited use, but more so if the underlying hardware is very reliable.

Reasonableness Checks. Reasonableness checks determine if the state of some object in the system is "reasonable." A common example of reasonableness is the range check, where it is determined that a certain value is within a specified range. These tests for reasonableness do not ensure that the value is correct, only that the value is within a range (which includes the correct value as well). Since checks cannot be devised for the correctness of the value, ranges are used. The range of the acceptable values is determined from the application. Another variation of this is to monitor the rate of change of some value; the rate of change should be within some bounds. This form can be of particular use in control systems, where the change in values has to be continuous, and hence the rate of change of parameters becomes limited.

One of the most common forms of range check that is frequently used is the run-time range checks performed by the system. Many languages, like Pascal, use the declarations of data structures (and the limits on their sizes) given by the user to automatically generate run-time range checks. If the value is outside the range, or if the range check fails during execution, the execution of the program is aborted and necessary signals are generated. These checks are automatically generated from the redundancy that is built into Pascal programs in the form of explicit data and type declarations.

Another possible reasonableness check is to have *assertions* about the state of the system. An *assertion* is a logical expression on the value of the different variables in the system which will evaluate to true if the state of the system is consistent, otherwise it will evaluate to false. Assertions are sometimes used in detecting errors in software.

Diagnostics Checks. In diagnostics checks, a system employs some checks on its component to see if the component is working correctly. Unlike other forms of checks, where the check is part of the system to detect an error in its state, here the check is performed by the system on its component. Diagnostics checks are typically special input values for which correct values are known to the system from previous use. For each of the input values the output is compared with the stored correct value to determine if there is an error.

Diagnostics checks are frequently used in systems at power-up time. In this context they are usually called "self checks." Diagnostic checking usually requires that the system and the component stop performing user operations. This restriction makes it of limited use in many environments. However, as mentioned above, it is used frequently for initial checking of the system when it is turned on. At this time, since there are no users on the system, performing a diagnostics check is feasible.

1.2.2   Damage Confinement and Assessment

By detecting an error in the state of a system, we know that somewhere in the system faults are present and failures have occurred. However, there could be a time delay between the failure and the event of error detection. This delay can occur because the system state is not being continuously monitored for errors. Due to interaction between components during this delay, an error may propagate and spread to other parts of the system.

Hence, by the time an error is detected at the output of a component, the error could have spread to other parts of the system state as well. Therefore, after detecting an error, before the erroneous state of the system can be corrected, we need to determine exactly the boundaries of corruption, or the parts of the state that are corrupt. This is the goal of this phase.

Errors spread in a system through communication between components of the system. Hence, for assessing the amount of damage in the system after an error has been detected, the flow of information between different components of the system has to be examined. Some assumption has to be made about the source of the error, or when the error originated. Then, all information flow after that could potentially spread the error elsewhere. The goal is to identify boundaries in the state beyond which no information exchange has occurred. The damage is then limited to this boundary.

The boundary can be identified *dynamically* by recording and examining the information flow. However, this method is likely to be complex. A better way is to design the system such that "fire walls" are *statically* incorporated in the system. These walls ensure that no information flow takes place across these walls. If an error is detected within this statically defined area, then there is a high probability that the error has not spread beyond the fire walls (unless the failure had occurred before the computation entered the walled area).

In most systems, the static structure is used to assume the spread of damage. Often the damage assessment activity is not performed explicitly, and the system structure is used in the later phase of error recovery to decide the amount of recovery, indirectly making assumptions about the damage confinement.

1.2.3 Error Recovery

Once the error has been detected and its extent identified, it is time to remove the error from the state. Unless the error is removed, the erroneous state may cause failure of the system in the future. In this phase of error recovery, the system state is made error-free. This is one of the most important activities and has been stressed a lot in earlier works on fault tolerance. In fact, in some systems, proper error recovery is an acceptable goal, that is, all such systems want is that in case failures occur, the state should be restored to a consistent state. There are two general techniques for error recovery: backward recovery and forward recovery.

In *backward recovery*, the system state is restored to an earlier state, in the hope that the earlier state is error-free. This method requires that the state of the systems be periodically *checkpointed* on some stable storage that is not affected by failure. When some error or failure is detected, the system is *rolled back* to the last checkpointed state. If the failure occurred after the checkpoint was established, the checkpointed state will be error free and after this rollback, the system state will also become error-free.

Backward error recovery is one of the most commonly used forms of error recovery. It is quite general, and does not depend too much on the nature of the failure or fault. It can recover from arbitrary faults, whether transient or permanent. In fact, for transient faults it is very suitable, as after recovery nothing else needs to be done. The fault would hopefully have gone by then, and restarting the system from the checkpoint will not produce the error again. The main drawback of this form of recovery is the overhead required. First, checkpointing has to be done frequently on the stable storage. This affects the normal execution of the system even if no failure occurs. Then there is a rollback involved if a failure occurs, which causes some wastage of the system computation. Despite the overhead, due to its general nature and the simplicity, it is used frequently.

In *forward recovery*, no previous state is available, and the system does not roll back. Instead, the attempt is to "go forward" and try to make the state error-free by taking the necessary corrective actions. Conceptually, the concept is exciting, since it is likely to be efficient in terms of overhead. However, by the very nature of forward recovery, it requires that an accurate assessment be made of the damage to the state, and assumptions are required about the nature of the damage or error. Only if the exact nature of the error is known can the error be removed by corrective actions. Hence, good diagnosis of the reason for failure and damage caused has to be performed. This diagnosis has to be application and system dependent. This makes forward recovery a system- and application-dependent approach. Due to this, it is not used as commonly as the backward recovery.

In distributed systems, backward recovery is employed in most cases.

1.2.4   Fault Treatment and Continued Service

In the first three phases, the focus is on errors. The error is first detected, its extent assessed, and then removed. After this, we have the system in an error-free state. This may be enough if the error was caused by some transient fault. After error recovery, the system can be restarted (from an error-free state), and no errors will occur, since the fault no longer exists.

However, if the faults are permanent, then the one that caused the failure and the error still remains in the system, even after error recovery. If we restart the system after error recovery, then the same fault will cause the same failure and error again. In order to avoid this, it is essential that the faulty component be identified and not utilized in the computation performed after recovery. That is, in some manner the faulty component has to be "bypassed," without jeopardizing the computation. This is the goal of this phase.

This phase has two important subphases: fault location and system repair. In *fault location*, the component that contains the fault has to be identified. Unless the faulty component is known, no mechanism can be employed to repair the fault or make sure that the fault does not cause a failure again. Typically, after error detection and assessment, the faulty component is identified as the component closest to the source of error.

In *system repair*, the system is "repaired" such that the faulty component is not used or used in a different configuration. A key point to be noted is that this repair is *on-line* and is assumed to be without manual intervention for fault tolerant systems. If manual repair is utilized, then it is not a fault tolerant system. This repair is done by *dynamic system reconfiguration*, such that the redundancy that is present in the system is used to perform the task of the faulty component. One of the simplest strategies for system repair is the *standby spare* strategy. In this, there is a redundant standby component in the system. If the main component fails, the standby is utilized and the faulty component is bypassed.

Once the system is repaired, normal service can continue, as if nothing had happened. Due to this, overall, the effect of fault tolerance is at most some minor discontinuity in service or some performance degradation. But the system is not unavailable for user services.

In distributed systems, for node failures, the detection of a faulty node can be done on the basis of failure detection itself. Since nodes are treated as a complete entity, and typically a faulty node cannot make another node behave incorrectly (i.e., the possibility of propagated errors is remote), failure detection identifies the faulty node. System repair is done by using other nodes in the system to perform the task of the failed node.

1.3   Overview of Hardware Fault Tolerance

Fault tolerance can be, and is, applied at various levels in a computer system. We can treat a computer system as a layered system, with the applications in the topmost layer and gates (or even a smaller unit) at the lowest level. Different layered models are possible for representing a computer system. The lower layers of this model will be considered as the "hardware," while the upper layers will be considered as the "software of system (software)."

It is hard to define what constitutes hardware fault tolerance and what constitutes software/system fault tolerance. Intuitively, we will consider all techniques that aim to provide fault tolerance largely in hardware, to mask failure of components, as hardware fault tolerance methods.

The goal of this book is to focus on principles and techniques for software/system-level fault tolerance, where fault tolerance is supported largely in software. For the sake of completeness, we present a brief overview of the techniques for hardware fault tolerance in this section. This is a vast area and complete books can be written on some of the subjects regarding hardware fault tolerance. Our aim here is just to familiarize the reader with what hardware fault tolerance is and what the basic techniques are. For details, the reader may refer to [Lal85, Joh89].

1.3.1   Process of Hardware Development

Modern hardware undergoes many stages during its development. We first give a brief overview of a typical process of hardware development [AA86]. Initially, many integrated circuits (ICs) are fabricated on a single silicon wafer. These ICs are called *dies* at this stage. Testing is performed at this stage to detect the faulty dies, which are then marked. The wafer is then sliced into individual dies. The marked dies are thrown. The percentage of dies in a wafer that are not faulty is called the *yield* of the fabrication process at this stage. For large-scale integration (LSI) and very large scale integration (VLSI), the yield is often very low (50% or lower). This is due to the complexity of these circuits and the large number of gates that are present in one IC. The precision required here is high; even a particle of dust on a die causes the die to fail the test.

The dies that pass the test are mounted in a package for the IC, and wire bonds between the *pads* on the dies and the pins of the package are made. This again is a very high-precision activity. The packaged chip is then tested. This is a major test which often requires complicated high-speed systems. The testing equipment is typically loaded with a sequence of inputs and the correct outputs to be expected from the IC for these inputs (for details on testing, the reader may refer to [ABF90]). The testing equipment "runs" these test cases at very high speed. For high reliability applications, the chips may be "burned" at high temperatures to accelerate failures, and then tested again. The chips that fail the test are discarded.

The chips are then mounted on printed circuit boards (PCBs), and then the PCBs are tested. Here also typically input/output testing is done, and specialized equipment is employed. Probes are often put at various points in the PCB to obtain the "intermediate outputs."

The PCBs are put together to form a system. The system is tested before being shipped. This assembling of the PCBs into a system may be done in phases, first forming the subsystem and then forming the complete system. The testing here may require running the system in a manner similar to its expected usage. When the system passes the testing it is shipped for usage in the field by customers.

1.3.2   Fault and Error Models

Unlike software, which has no physical properties and therefore no physical causes of failure, hardware failures have their origin in physical causes. Faults in hardware can either be introduced during manufacturing or occur with the passage of time. The two are not independent, and problems in manufacturing can have effect on time-dependent faults.

Physical failures that occur during fabrication include faulty devices, break in connections, shorts between lines, improper doping, and impurities in packaging that affect the functioning of the chip. Failures that occur with the passage of time include breaks, shorts, and shift in threshold voltages. Most of the physical failures are shorts and opens.

Though physical failures are the basic causes of failures for a chip, in most cases, one is not interested in the micro-level physical failure that causes some piece of hardware to malfunction. We are only interested in knowing whether a fault is present or not, that is, we are interested in the consequence of the physical failure. One method of doing this is to describe the effect of physical failures at some higher level. This higher level may be at the level of gates and logic circuits, functional block level, chip level, etc. Such an abstract model is called a *fault model*. A fault model specifies the effect of physical failures. The hope is that a few faults in the fault model will accurately describe most of the physical failures of interest. If this can be done, then, for supporting fault tolerance, only faults in the fault model need to be considered. Typically, many physical-level failures can be modeled by the same fault at the higher level.

The fault model can be defined at a very high level (say a board or subsystem level) or at a low level (transistor level). If we go down to a very low level, then the fault model will contain the physical failures themselves, and if we go to a very high level the fault model may not be able to cover all the lower-level faults. Here we will describe some of the common fault models.

Gate-Level Fault Models. Gate-level fault models are used very frequently in hardware fault tolerance. The classical gate-level fault model is the *stuck-at* fault model, which assumes that physical failures will result in some lines of logic gates to be permanently stuck at 0 or 1. It can be shown that this model captures the bonding failures and circuit breaks, which are the most common failures in small ICs. Another fault model, which is a subset of the stuck-at model, is the *pin-fault* model. In this, only the pins of the chips are considered as stuck-at 0 or 1. A generalization of the stuck-at model is the multiple stuck-at faults, where multiple lines are stuck at some value. A related model, though it is frequently characterized as an error model, is the *unidirectional error model*. In this, in a set of lines either all 0s become 1s, or all 1s become 0s. Such cases typically occur when some lines get shorted.

Though the stuck-at fault model accurately reflects the physical failures in small ICs, in large ICs, made from MOS technology, some of the physical failures cannot be modeled. A break in a line of a CMOS transistor often makes it behave as if it has memory, and it can be detected only if the output of the CMOS gate is properly initialized. This makes even a combinational circuit behave like a sequential circuit. The model that captures this memory property in case of some cuts is called the *stuck-open* fault model [JK90]. On the other hand, defects which cause a transistor to permanently conduct are modeled by the *stuck-on* fault model.

With the ever-increasing density of integrated circuits, shorts between adjacent lines have become quite common. Such defects are modeled by the *bridging fault model*. Another fault model which is considered important is the *delay fault model* [JK90]. This models degradation in the delay of a gate or a path in the circuit. Such a degradation may cause an incorrect logic value to be latched in the output latch.

Function-Level Fault Models. The gate-level fault models reflect the physical failures quite accurately. However, they are too detailed, as one has to consider the gate-level structure of a circuit. For providing fault tolerance, since it is more likely that a chip or a module will be "discarded" if found faulty, one is often simply interested in knowing if a chip or a functional module is working. Functional-level fault models try to model failures at the level of functional modules. It is clearly desirable if the fault model includes effects of most of the physical failures of faults at the gate level.

A very *general fault model* for functional blocks is to assume that a function with N inputs, under faults, can be transformed into another function with N inputs. Such a fault model does not characterize the faulty behavior at all, and is consequently of limited use for fault tolerance. There seems to be no general fault model at functional block level. However, models for specific functional modules have been proposed. For example, in an N input decoder with 2^N outputs, normally only one line is activated corresponding to the input address. It has been shown that all the failures at lower levels in a decoder can be described by a set of three faults [AF86]. These faults are (1) an incorrect line is activated, (2) more than one line is activated, and (3) no line is activated. Similarly, models have been proposed for multiplexer [AF86], and other small functional modules. Functional fault models are also extensively used for testing of iterative logic arrays, in which a faulty cell is assumed to change its function in an arbitrary way.

Memory Fault Models. The main memory (the Random Access Memory, RAM) in computer systems is conceptually an array of memory cells. For access, the main memory also should contain an address decoder, read/write logic, and data registers to transfer data. A widely used set of functional faults for memory contains the following faults: (1) one or more cells are stuck at 0/1, (2) some cells are coupled and when a cell i changes its value, other coupled cells also change their value, and (3) state of a memory cell changes as a result of some state of the other memory cells.

Now we discuss some of the common techniques that are used to support fault tolerance in hardware. This is also a very vast area in which constant progress is being made. Our aim is not to give a complete picture or a tutorial of all techniques, but introduce some of the most commonly known ones. For further details, the reader may refer to [Lal85, Joh89, SW82].

1.3.3   Triple Modular Redundancy (TMR)

The most commonly known hardware fault tolerance technique is *triple modular redundancy* (TMR), which has been used in many fault tolerant systems. The concept was originally suggested by Von Neumann. In TMR, the hardware unit (represented by M in Fig. 1.1) is triplicated, and all three units work in parallel. The outputs of these three units are given to the *voting element* (represented by V in Fig. 1.1). The voting element accepts the outputs from the three sources and delivers the majority vote as output.

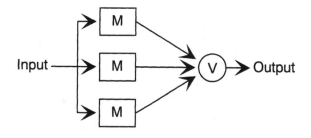

Figure 1.1: Triple Modular Redundancy (TMR)

Clearly, the TMR organization can completely mask the failure of one hardware unit. One of the nice features of TMR is that no explicit actions need to be performed for error detection, recovery, etc. TMR is particularly suitable for transient faults, since in the basic TMR the voter does not "remove" the faulty unit after an error occurs.

It is also evident that this scheme cannot handle the failure of two units. In fact, once one unit fails, it is essential that *both* units should continue to work correctly (so that the voter can get a majority). Due to this, the reliability of the TMR system becomes lower than a simplex system (i.e., one without any redundancy) once a failure occurs (we revisit this point later in the chapter). However, from a practical standpoint, double failures can also be handled in TMR in many cases. For example, if the voter performs bit-wise voting and two units fail such that their outputs are incorrect in disjoint bit positions, the "double failure" can be masked. Similarly, if two units are faulty, such that one output line of one unit is stuck at 0, and the same output line of the other unit is stuck at 1, then this "double failure" can also be handled. In other words, there are situations where the errors are "compensating" in nature, or disjoint. In these situations, failure of two units can also be handled by TMR.

The TMR scheme depends critically on the voting element. However, the voting element is typically a simple circuit and highly reliable circuits of this complexity can be built. Another implementation aspect of TMR is that it requires tight synchronization between the different units. This has been frequently achieved by using a single clock. This requires the clock to be very reliable. A generalization of the TMR approach is the NMR approach, in which the unit is replicated N times.

1.3.4   Dynamic Redundancy

A system with dynamic redundancy consists of several units but with only one operating at a time [Lal85]. The other units are essentially "spares." If a fault is detected in the operating unit, then it is "switched out" and a spare unit is "switched in" by a switching circuit.

A key problem in this approach is how to detect if a unit has failed. The common approaches for detection of failure of a unit are:

1. Periodic tests

2. Self-checking circuits

3. Watchdog timers

Dynamic redundancy schemes can be classified as *cold-standby system* or *hot-standby system* depending on the manner in which its spares are kept. In a cold-standby system, one unit is powered up and operational, the spares are not powered (i.e., they are "cold"). A faulty unit is replaced by turning off its power and powering up a spare. In a hot-standby system, all the units are operating simultaneously, and their outputs are matched. If the outputs are the same, one is selected arbitrarily. If not, the faulty unit is detected and the system is reconfigured so that the system output comes out from one of the nonfaulty units. (A key difference of this approach from TMR is the manner in which the faulty unit is detected and removed.)

The most common arrangement for a hot-standby system is to operate two units in parallel. This is called a *duplex* system [Lal85]. A matching circuit continuously compares the results of the two. If a mismatch occurs, diagnosis programs are run to locate the fault. On locating the fault, reconfiguration is performed through switching circuits.

1.3.5   Coding

Coding is one of the most important techniques for supporting fault tolerance in hardware. It is also used extensively for improving the reliability of communication. Coding has been used in many systems. The basic idea behind coding is to add check bits to the information bits such that errors in some bits can be *detected*, and if possible, *corrected*. The process of adding check bits to information bits is called *encoding*. That is, the information is encoded by addition of the check bits. The reverse process of extracting information from the encoded data is called *decoding*. Hence, coding essentially provides structural checks, in which the error is detected by detecting inconsistency in the structural integrity of the data. Coding is also an area where a vast amount of work has been done [RF89]. Here we give a very brief introduction to coding and some common codes used in hardware fault tolerance.

Detectability/Correctability of a Code

A code defines a set of words that are possible for that code. That is, for a coding scheme, there is a valid set of words that satisfy that scheme. The *Hamming distance* of a code is the minimum number of bit positions in which any two words in the code differ. If *d* is the Hamming distance, *D* is the number of bit errors that the code can detect, and *C* is the number of bit errors it can correct, then the following relation is always true.

$$d = C + D + 1, \quad with \ D \geq C.$$

In the regular binary code, the Hamming distance is 1 (the code for two consecutive numbers often differs in one bit), and so its detectability and correctability are both 0. The common method of adding a parity bit to a word increases the Hamming distance to 2 (if the binary word differs in one position, then the parity bit will also be different, creating a distance of 2). With d=2, we can only detect single bit errors (i.e., D=1). Higher values of D or C do not satisfy the relation above. This relation specifies the fundamental limitation of a given code.

Hamming Codes

Addition of a parity bit, though a common method, can only detect 1-bit errors. A more general method is used in Hamming codes in which multiple parity bits are added such that each parity bit is a parity of a subset of information bits. The code can detect and also correct errors. It is widely used in semiconductor memories.

In Hamming codes, the parity bits occupy the bit positions 1, 2, 4, ... (power of 2) in the encoding. The remaining are the data positions. If we refer to the number of parity bits by k, and the number of data bits by m, then for m=4, and k=3, the word length of the encoded word is 4+3=7 bits. Out of these 7 bits, bits in positions 1, 2, and 4 are the parity bits, and bits in positions 3, 5, 6, 7 are the data bits, as shown below. The parity bits are labeled c1, c2, and c3, and the data bits are labeled d1, d2, d3, and d4.

1	2	3	4	5	6	7
c1	c2	d1	c3	d2	d3	d4

The value of parity bits is defined by the following relations:

$$c1 = d1 \oplus d2 \oplus d4$$
$$c2 = d1 \oplus d3 \oplus d4$$
$$c3 = d2 \oplus d3 \oplus d4$$

A parity bit (or a check bit) is Exclusive-OR (XOR) of some subset of data bits. It is worth noting how these relationships are obtained. For $c1$, which is the parity bit in position 1, all the data bits, whose position in the encoded word, when represented as binary, has the least significant bit (LSB) as 1, are included in $c1$. Similarly, all those data bits whose positions' binary representation contains a 1 in the second position will be included in $c2$. So, $c1$ includes data bits 1, 3, and 4, since they occur in positions 3, 5, and 7 in the encoded word, and the binary encoding of these numbers contains a 1 in the LSB (these are odd numbers). The data bit $d3$ is not included, since it occurs in position 6, whose binary encoding has a 0 in the LSB. Similarly, for $c2$, data bits $d1$, $d3$, and $d4$ are taken, since they occur in positions 3, 6, and 7, and binary encoding of these has a 1 in the next LSB.

This Hamming code is capable of detecting and correcting single errors. The Hamming distance of this code is 3. By adding another parity bit, which contains the parity of the Hamming code word, one can obtain a code with a Hamming distance of 4. Such codes can detect double errors and correct single errors. Many commercial semiconductor memory chips employ these codes.

The detection of erroneous bits can be done as follows. From the received code word, obtain the value of check bits using the relation given above. If the check bits obtained match the check bits that are there in the encoded word, then there is no error. Otherwise, there is an error in the encoded word; either the data bits or the check bits are corrupted.

To correct a single bit error, the location of the bit that is in error has to be determined. This is done as follows. The check bits obtained from the relationship given above are XORed with the actual check bits obtained from the code. From this, we get the error location bits. For the above example, we will get three bits: $e1$, $e2$, and $e3$. If there is no error, then all of these will be 0. If there is an error, then the error location bits specify the location of the bit in error. Correction is done by simply complementing the bit. In the above example, if bit number 3 is in error (i.e., data bit $d1$), then we will have $e1=1$, $e2=1$, and $e3=0$. From this, we get the address of the erroneous bit as 011 (i.e., the 3rd bit). This scheme for error correction works as long as there is a single bit error, and it can correct errors even in check bits.

The use of Hamming codes becomes more efficient, in terms of number of bits needed relative to the number of data bits, as the word size increases. For example, if the data word length is 8 bits, the number of check bits will be 4, and so the overhead is 50%. On the other hand, if the word length is 84 bits, the number of check bits will be 7, giving an overhead of 9%.

Cyclic Redundancy Codes (CRC)

These codes are applied to a block of data, rather than independent words. CRCs are commonly used in detecting errors in data communication. They are also called *polynomial codes*.

In this code, a sequence of bits is represented as a polynomial; if the kth bit is a 1, then the polynomial contains x^k. For example, the polynomial for the bit string 1100101101 is $x^9 + x^8 + x^5 + x^3 + x^2 + 1$. There is a *generator polynomial G(x)* of some degree k. For example, the generator polynomial could be $x^4 + x^3 + 1$, corresponding to the bit sequence 11001.

The *encoding* is done as follows. To the data bit sequence, add (k+1) bits in the end. This extended data sequence is divided (modulo 2) by the generator polynomial. Whatever is the final remainder is added to the extended data sequence to form the encoded data (this adding really replaces the (k+1) bits added to the data bits). *Decoding* is easy if there are no errors; the extra (k+1) bits are just discarded to obtain the original data bits. To check for an error, the data bits are again divided by the generator polynomial, and the final remainder is checked with the last (k+1) bits of the obtained data. If there is a difference, an error has occurred.

CRCs can detect all single bit errors, but cannot correct errors. They can also detect all burst errors of a length less than k. A burst error is where consecutive bits are corrupted. Many other errors also have a high probability of getting detected. Only those errors that are divisible by G(x) will slip by.

Berger Codes

In this code, the number of 0s are counted in the data word, and the count is appended as check bits to form the code. If the word size is k bits, this coding scheme requires $log_2(k)$ extra bits. Berger codes can detect all unidirectional errors, including those that corrupt the check bits. In a unidirectional error, either all the bits in error change from 1 to 0, or from 0 to 1. If the error is of the form 1 to 0, then the number of 0s in the data bits will increase, but the count (whose bits may also change from 1 to 0) will decrease. Hence, a discrepancy will occur. Similarly, if the bits change from 0 to 1, the number of 0s will decrease, but the count will increase.

Berger codes are known to be optimal for detecting unidirectional errors among all codes in which the information and check bits can be separated. An alternative Berger code can be obtained by counting the number of 1s in the data word and appending its bit-by-bit complement as check bits.

1.3.6 Self-Checking Circuits

We have discussed a variety of coding techniques above. All coding techniques work by producing a code, say of length n, such that the valid words (ones that are consistent with the coding method) are a subset of the possible words of length n. That is, out of the possible 2^l words, only a subset of them are considered as valid. The rest represent the situation in which some error has occurred. The error is detected by checking if the word is valid or not. This "redundancy" is essential for a coding scheme to work. If all the possible words were valid, then an error would convert a valid word into another valid word, and hence will stay undetected.

Error detection with a coding scheme requires that a *checker* circuit be employed for detecting if a word is valid or not. If a functional circuit produces an encoded output y, which is to be checked for the presence of an error by a *checker*, then the situation can be represented as shown in Fig. 1.2 [Toh86]. The output checker checks if the output of the functional circuit is valid or not, as per the coding scheme employed. If y is not a valid encoded word, then the output of the checker z will be 1, denoting an error.

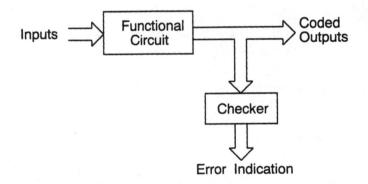

Figure 1.2: Output checker

The above scheme for coding assumes that the error checker is working correctly, such that even if the functional circuit does not work correctly, the correctly working checker will detect the error. If there is a fault in the checker circuit itself, then the coding scheme may fail to provide the error detection capability. It is possible for the faulty checker to be such that if there is no error in the input to the checker, it does not declare an error, but if there is an error, it does not catch the error. That is, some of the errors may go undetected due to the presence of faults in the checker circuit. It is clearly desirable to have the capability of checking the occurrence of a fault within the checker, in addition to the capability of checking the error in the input to the checker. This is the goal of *self-checking circuits.*

We will give some definitions to formally specify what is meant by self-checking circuits [CS68, AM73, Lal85]. Let F be the set of faults for which the circuit is to be self-checking.

A circuit is *fault-secure* with respect to a set of faults F, if for any fault in F, the circuit never produces an incorrect code word at the output for any code word at the input.

A circuit is *self-testing* with respect to a set of faults F, if for any fault in F, the circuit produces a non-code word for at least one input code word.

A circuit is *totally self-checking* with respect to a set of faults F, if and only if it is fault-secure and self-testing with respect to F.

A circuit is said to be *code-disjoint* if any input code word (non-code word) produces an output code word (non-code word).

A circuit is a *totally self-checking checker* if and only if it is self-testing, fault-secure, and code-disjoint.

With a totally self-checking checker, it is possible to detect a fault in the functional circuit or the checker. However, in general, it is not possible to say which is faulty. As an example, consider a self-checking parity checker [Toh86]. Suppose that $(x_8, ..., x_0)$ represents a code word for the odd parity scheme. Divide the set of variables into two groups, say, the even numbered bits, and odd numbered bits, and connect them to the tree of XOR gates as shown in Fig. 1.3 [Toh86].

In the normal operation, the number of 1s in one group is odd, and the other group is even. Therefore the output $Z = (z_2, z_1)$ will take (0,1) or (1,0) but never (0,0) or (1,1). It can be seen that if any gate is faulty, then one of the two outputs will be different, resulting in Z being (0,0) or (1,1).

There are no general techniques for designing self-checking checkers. Specific methods have been proposed for different types of codes. However, there are some techniques for synthesis of general self-checking combinational and sequential circuits [JW91].

1.3.7 Fault Tolerance in Multiprocessors

A multiprocessor system is one which consists of multiple processors connected by some interconnection network. The processors typically work together for solving a single problem, and are usually tightly coupled, in contrast to distributed systems where the different processors are largely independent. The processors communicate with each other by passing messages through the interconnection network. The basic motivation for multiprocessors is the need for high-speed computing. Recent

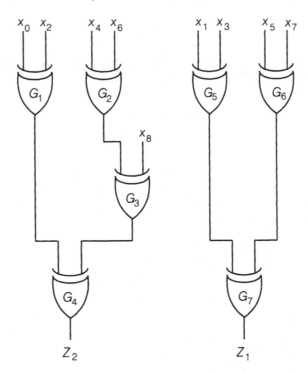

Figure 1.3: Self-checking parity checker

advances in VLSI technology permit the building of multiprocessor systems cheaply. Since there are more components in a multiprocessor system that can fail, there is considerable interest in the area of hardware fault tolerance for multiprocessor systems.

A multiprocessor system is considered fault tolerant if in spite of the failure of one or more processors, a number of active processors remain connected according to the original topology for which they were designed. There are various approaches for supporting fault tolerance in multiprocessors. One is the TMR approach, which we have discussed above. Here we will briefly discuss some of these approaches.

A newer approach to fault tolerance in multiprocessor systems is *algorithm based fault tolerance*, in which fault tolerance is achieved by tailoring the fault tolerance scheme to the algorithm that is to be performed on the multiprocessor [HA84, B+90]. In this approach, the data is encoded at a high level (as opposed to byte/word level as is done frequently). The algorithm to be performed is then redesigned to work on encoded data to produce encoded output. Finally, the computation steps in this modified algorithm are distributed among the processors in the multiprocessor such that the failure of a module affects only a portion of the data, which can be re-created by the redundancy present in the encoded data.

As an example of this approach, consider matrix operations [HA84]. For a matrix A, a column check-sum matrix A_c is one that is obtained from the original matrix by adding a check-sum row. In the check-sum row, each element is the sum of elements of that particular column. Similarly, a row check-sum matrix A_r can be defined. The full check-sum matrix C_f is one which has one extra row and one extra column, which are the check-sum row and check-sum column. With this encoding, if the $C = A * B$ matrix operation is to be performed, then it can be easily seen that $C_f = A_c * B_r$. That is, the matrix multiplication algorithm has to be redesigned to work on A_c and B_r. Similarly, we have $C_f = A_f + B_f$. Similar relations can be defined for transpose and other operations as well.

Now the matrix data has been encoded and the matrix algorithm has been redesigned. Error detection is done in a simple manner. Compute the check-sum for the information elements in the final matrix, and then compare it with the check-sum row and column produced by the redesigned algorithm. The intersection of the inconsistent row and column elements will locate the error. The error can also be corrected.

Another approach to fault tolerance in multiprocessors is to employ redundancy dynamically [Agr88]. A processor is assumed to produce the result of the computation and a signature. The signature is a good representative of the processor outcome, and can be obtained by using data compression techniques. The approach is as follows. Assume that the processors are numbered. Initially, an incoming task is scheduled to a pair of processors, say P_1 and P_2. These produce results R_1 and R_2 and signatures S_1 and S_2. The two signatures are compared, and if they match, then one of the results is returned. If the signatures do not match, then the job is scheduled on another processor, say P_3. The signature S_3 is compared with the earlier signatures S_1 and S_2. If a pair of matching signatures is found, then the result R_3 is returned. Otherwise, the job is scheduled on another processor, until a matching pair of signatures is found.

There are approaches for fault tolerance specifically designed for some common architectures. Here, we will briefly discuss the methods for tree and hypercube architectures. A hypercube multiprocessor consists of 2^n processors that are connected by direct links according to the binary n-cube interconnection pattern [Pra86]. Hence each processor is directly connected to n other processors, and the maximum internode distance (in terms of number of hops or links between them) is only $log(n)$. In one technique, two spare processors are used for every eight processors. Each node is assumed to have $n + 2$ ports. By adding these extra processors, the dimension of the hypercube is increased by one. When the failure of a normal processor is detected, it is replaced by a spare processor (say S), and the links from the spare processor to the faulty processor and the link diagonally opposite to it are disabled. S sends its address and the address of the failed processor to all spare processors connected to it. This information is then used to reset the link connectivities such that the hypercube structure is maintained.

For hierarchically organized multiprocessors, tree networks provide a natural interconnection network. But, an inherent disadvantage of these networks is that any single failure can disconnect the network. Different approaches have been proposed to make such a network fault tolerant [Pra86]. One approach is to augment the tree with extra links such that the tree stays fully connected in spite of single node or link failure. Another approach is to design the tree structure to be redundant by using extra nodes and links. The objective is to preserve the original tree structure in spite of failures by reconfiguring the tree using these extra nodes and links.

1.4   Reliability and Availability

The basic goal of fault tolerance is to increase the reliability of a given system. By employing fault tolerance, many potential failures are averted, thereby increasing the reliability. Another goal of fault tolerance is to increase the system availability, that is, increase the time for which the system is available for user services (as opposed to performing internal bookkeeping tasks). Unless a fault tolerance strategy can increase the reliability or availability of a system, it is of no interest.

A considerable amount of work has been done on performance evaluation of fault tolerant systems, that is, evaluating the reliability, availability, or some other performance measure of systems that employ fault tolerance. It is beyond the scope of this book to do performance analysis of the various schemes for fault tolerance. However, it is important to understand the two key concepts — reliability and availability — that are the driving forces behind fault tolerance. In this section, we give a brief description of these concepts based on [Tri82]. For more details the reader may refer to [Tri82]. During the course of the book, where feasible, we will discuss these for some of the proposed schemes.

1.4.1   Preliminaries

Most of the work done in performance evaluation of computer systems has foundations in probability theory. Probability theory is useful in situations where the outcome of an experiment is not certain. Such an experiment is called a *random experiment*. A classic example of randomness is the tossing of a coin. A random experiment could be "toss the coin n times." The totality of all possible outcomes of a random experiment is called the *sample space* of the experiment. For example, for the experiment "toss the coin 2 times," there are 4 possible outcomes: HH, HT, TH, and TT (where T represents the occurrence of "tail" and H represents the occurrence of "head"). An **event** is a subset of the sample space. An event is more frequently specified by the conditions that define the subset for this event. As an example, consider the event "at least one head occurs." Three of the four points in the sample space will be included in this event. The **probability** of an event represents the "relative likelihood" that a performance of the experiment will result in the occurrence of that event. The probability of an event e is referred to as $P(e)$. We now give some definitions based on [Tri82].

Definition. A **random variable** X, on a sample space S, is a function that assigns a real number $X(s)$ to each sample point $s \in S$. We are more interested in *continuous* random variables, in which for every real number x, the set $\{x | X(s) \leq x\}$ is an event.

Continuous random variables are the starting point in most reliability models. For example, in reliability modeling, the "lifetime of a system" or the "repair time of a system" are frequently modeled as random variables. Random variables could be discrete also. However, in reliability modeling, mostly continuous random variables are employed.

Definition. The **distribution function** F_X of a random variable X is defined to be the function:

$$F_X(x) = P(X \leq x), -\infty < x < \infty.$$

The distribution function is often called the cumulative distribution function, or the CDF. The subscript X of F shows that this is the distribution function of the random variable X. Where clear from the context, the subscript will be omitted. Unlike a distribution function of a discrete random variable, the distribution function of a continuous random variable (which is what we are using) is a continuous function for all values of x. There are a few things to be noticed about the distribution function: (1) Since $F(x)$ is a probability, its value lies between 0 and 1, (2) $F(x)$ is a monotonically nondecreasing function; that is, if $x_1 \leq x_2$, then $F(x_1) \leq F(x_2)$, and (3) $F(x)$ tends to 0 as $x \to 0$, and tends to 1 as $x \to \infty$.

Definition. For a continuous random variable X, $f(x) = d(F(x))/dx$ is called the **probability density function** (pdf) of X.

The following hold for a pdf: (1) $f(x) \geq 0$ for all x, and (2) $\int_{-\infty}^{x} f(t)dt = 1$.

The CDF can be obtained from the pdf by integrating it:

$$F_X(X) = P(X \leq x) = \int_{-\infty}^{x} f_X(t)dt, \quad -\infty < x < \infty.$$

The distribution function, or the density function, completely characterizes the behavior of a random variable, and probabilities of various events can be determined from this. Frequently, we do not need such detailed characterization and are interested only in the **mean**, or the **expectation** of a random variable X, which is denoted by $E[X]$. This reflects the expected value of the random variable X.

Definition. The **expectation**, $E[X]$, of a random variable X is defined by:

$$E[X] = \int_{-\infty}^{\infty} xf(x)dx,$$

provided that the integral is absolutely convergent, that is, $\int_{-\infty}^{\infty} |x| f(x)dx < \infty$.

Expectations are also commonly used in reliability evaluation. One method to characterize reliability of a system is to specify mean time to failure, which is the expectation of the lifetime of the system (a random variable).

1.4.2   The Exponential Distribution

We are now ready to discuss one particular distribution, called the *exponential distribution*, that is very frequently used in reliability evaluation of computer systems. In evaluation of computer systems, often things like time between two successive arrivals of jobs at a computer system, service time at a CPU or I/O device, time to failure of a component or system, time required to repair a failed component or system etc. are modeled as random variables with exponential distribution.

The *exponential distribution function* is given by:

$$F(x) = \begin{cases} 1 - e^{-\lambda x}, & \text{if } 0 \leq x < \infty, \\ 0, & \text{otherwise.} \end{cases}$$

The distribution function is shown in Fig. 1.4 [Tri82].

If a random variable X is exponentially distributed, then the pdf is given by:

$$f(x) = \begin{cases} \lambda e^{-\lambda x}, & \text{if } x > 0, \\ 0, & \text{otherwise.} \end{cases}$$

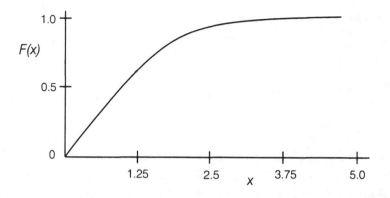

Figure 1.4: The CDF of an exponentially distributed random variable with parameter $\lambda = 1$

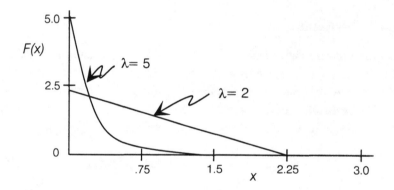

Figure 1.5: The pdf of an exponentially distributed random variable

While specifying the pdf usually only the nonzero part is stated. The pdf of an exponentially distributed random variable is shown in Fig. 1.5 [Tri82].

The exponential distribution is popular in analytic analysis because it possesses the **memoryless**, or **Markov**, property. What the memoryless property means is that if we determine the distribution of an exponentially distributed variable after some time t has elapsed, the distribution is again exponential. For example, suppose that X represents the lifetime of a system, which is exponentially distributed. Suppose that the system is still alive after a time t, then the residual lifetime of the system will also have the same distribution function. Let $Y = X - t$ represent the residual lifetime. Let the conditional probability of $Y \leq y$, given that $X > t$, be denoted by

$G_t(y)$. $G_t(y)$ is a conditional probability:

$$G_t(y) = P(Y \leq y | X \geq t).$$

This expression finally becomes [Tri82]:

$$G_t(y) = 1 - e^{-\lambda y}.$$

Hence, $G_t(y)$ is identical to the original distribution of X, and is independent of t. In other words, if X represents the lifetime of a system, then the distribution of the remaining lifetime of the system at any time t has the same distribution as the original lifetime. That is, the system "forgets" how long it has been alive, or keeps no history. This is the memoryless property of exponential distribution. It frequently simplifies analytic analysis.

1.4.3 Reliability

Let the random variable X represent the life of a system. That is, X represents the time to failure of the system. The time to failure is modeled as a random variable, as it cannot be predicted with certainty. Assume that the variable X has a distribution F. The **reliability** of the system is a function $R(t)$, which represents the probability that the system survives till time t (i.e., it has not failed till t).

$$
\begin{aligned}
R(t) \quad &= \text{probability that the system is alive at time } t \\
&= P(X > t) \\
&= 1 - F(t)
\end{aligned}
$$

As we can see, the definition implies that $R(t = 0) = 1$, meaning that the system is initially working. It also has $R(t = \infty) = 0$, implying that no component has an infinite lifetime. If the lifetime of a system is exponentially distributed, then the reliability of that system is:

$$R(t) = e^{-\lambda t}.$$

The parameter λ is called the **failure rate** of the system.

This notion of reliability represents reliability as a function of time. From this we can compute the **mean time to failure (MTTF)**, or **expected life**, of the system. MTTF is a commonly used measure to specify the reliability of a system, and is given by:

$$E[X] = \int_0^\infty t f(t) dt = - \int_0^\infty R'(t) dt.$$

From this expression we get:

$$E[X] = \int_0^\infty R(t)dt.$$

If the system lifetime is exponentially distributed with parameter λ, then $R(t) = e^{-\lambda t}$, and we get the expected life, or MTTF, of the system as:

$$MTTF = \frac{1}{\lambda}.$$

In most reliability analysis, the life of a system, or component, is assumed to be exponentially distributed, and throughout this book, unless otherwise mentioned, we will use this assumption.

The expression above gives the MTTF of a single system, working in isolation. Often, a system can be considered as a combination of many independent components, each having an exponentially distributed life. Let us consider a *series system*, where different components are connected in a series to form the complete system. Suppose that the lifetime of the ith component in the series is exponentially distributed with parameter λ_i. Since a series system fails if any one of the components in the series fails, the reliability of the overall system is given by [Tri82]:

$$R(t) = \prod_{i=1}^n R_i(t).$$

When the life of each component is exponentially distributed, then this evaluates to a system with an exponentially distributed life with parameter $\lambda = \sum_{i=1}^n \lambda_i$. Therefore, the MTTF of the series system is:

$$MTTF_{series} = \frac{1}{\sum_{i=1}^n \lambda_i}.$$

This says that the MTTF of a series system is smaller than MTTF of any of its components. That is to be expected, since failure of any component causes the failure of the series system, and hence the series system has a lower reliability than its individual components.

A system may be a *parallel system* in which the components of the system are connected in parallel. In this organization, the system fails when *all* the components fail. If X is the life of the system and X_i represents the life of a component i, we have:

$$X = max\{X_1, X_2, ..., X_n\}.$$

This implies that the reliability of a parallel system is larger than the reliability of its components. With exponential assumption, the MTTF of the system turns out to be [Tri82]:

$$E[X] = \frac{1}{\lambda} \sum_{i=1}^{n} \frac{1}{i} \simeq \frac{ln(n)}{\lambda}.$$

Another organization for a system, which is often used in fault tolerance, is *standby redundancy*. In this, one component (often called the *primary*) operates, and others act as standby. When the primary fails, the standby component is switched in and starts operating. In this configuration, if X is the lifetime of the system, and X_i is the life of a component:

$$X = \sum_{i=1}^{n} X_i.$$

With exponential distributions we get the MTTF of the system as:

$$E[X] = \frac{n}{\lambda}.$$

Hence the gain in reliability depends on the number of components. With 2 components having exponentially distributed lifetimes, the life of the primary standby system is twice that of an individual component.

We have seen that in hardware, TMR is a widely used method for supporting fault tolerance. In TMR, three systems are connected in parallel, and their outputs are voted. The TMR system can mask the failure of one component. If $R(t)$ is the reliability of the triply replicated component, then by considering the different combinations of failures under which a TMR system continues to operate, we get [Tri82]:

$$R_{TMR}(t) = 3R^2(t) - 2R^3(t).$$

With exponential distributions $R_{TMR}(t) = 3e^{-2\lambda t} - 2e^{-3\lambda t}$. The function R_{TMR} is not always larger than the function $R(t) = e^{-\lambda t}$, which is the reliability of an individual component. For smaller t, R_{TMR} is larger than R, and for larger t it is the other way around. We can compute t_0, the "threshold" time beyond which the reliability of TMR is lower than that of its components. At t_0 we have:

$$3e^{-2\lambda t_0} - 2e^{-3\lambda t_0} = e^{-\lambda t_0}.$$

Solving this, we get $t_0 = \frac{ln2}{\lambda} = \frac{0.7}{\lambda}$. Hence, TMR configuration provides higher reliability only if the "mission time" of the system employing TMR is less than t_0. This seemingly anomalous behavior occurs because when all three components are working, then TMR can handle the failure of any one component. However, when one component fails, then TMR requires that *both* of the remaining components should work correctly for the system to work correctly. The MTTF of a TMR system is $E[X] = \int_0^\infty R_{TMR}(t)dt$. This reduces to:

$$E[X] = \frac{5}{6\lambda}.$$

Thus, the MTTF of a TMR is actually *lower* than the MTTF of its components. This clearly shows that working with means or MTTF has its pitfalls. The reliability function for TMR gives a clearer picture, namely that TMR is more reliable for short durations, but is less reliable if mission durations are large.

1.4.4 Availability

In a real system, if a component fails, it is *repaired* or replaced by a new component. When this component fails, it is replaced by another one, and so on. The repaired component is new with its own distribution. Over a long period of time, a component can be considered as being in one of the two states: "working" or "under repair." The state of "working" reflects that the current component is operational, and the state of "under repair" means that it has failed and has not yet been replaced by a new component. On failure, the system goes from "working" to "under repair," and when replacement is done, it goes back to the state of "working." In such situations, *availability* is a measure that is frequently used for describing the behavior of the system.

Definition. The **instantaneous availability**, $A(t)$, of a component is defined as the probability that the component is functioning correctly at time t.

In availability, we are interested in probability at a certain instance of time. In the absence of repair or replacement, availability is simply equal to reliability. That is, availability at time t is nothing but $R(t)$. However, with replacement, the life of a component can be viewed as a sequence of independent random variables each representing the life of the component till the next failure (and repair). A component can be represented by a sequence of random variables: T_is and D_is. The random variable T_i represents the duration of the ith functioning period, and D_i represents the downtime for the ith repair or replacement.

In availability analysis, we are often interested in the steady state availability, or availability after a sufficiently long period of time. For this we define *limiting availability* as the limit of $A(t)$ as t approaches infinity. The limiting availability is what is commonly referred to as **availability** of a system. Note, unlike reliability whose limiting value as t tends to infinity is zero, limiting availability is typically nonzero. If the mean time to failure of a component is MTTF (i.e., each T_i has MTTF as the mean), and the mean time to repair of the component is MTTR (i.e., each D_i has MTTR as the mean), then the availability, α, is given by [Tri82]:

$$\alpha = \frac{MTTF}{MTTF + MTTR}.$$

This is a general expression for limiting availability and is not dependent on the nature of distributions of lifetimes and repair times. In other words, this expression holds for distributions other than exponential distribution as well.

Often, in analyzing systems employing fault tolerance, availability is defined as the fraction of time the system is available for "useful" work. If it is assumed that all the time the system is operational it is available for useful work, the above expression of availability holds. However, many fault tolerant schemes require that the system perform many extra activities to support fault tolerance. These activities do not need to be performed if no fault tolerance was implemented. In such situations, these extra activities are overhead in supporting fault tolerance, and are not considered work that is useful. Availability analysis becomes more complicated in such situations, as these overheads use some part of the time when the system is operational in performing activities that are not considered useful.

1.5 Summary

This chapter has introduced the topic of fault tolerant computing. Fault tolerance is useful in systems where high reliability is required. As unreliability is caused by the presence of faults in the system, the goal of fault tolerance is to avoid system failure despite the presence of faults. This is complementary to the fault prevention approach, in which the goal is to minimize the presence of faults in the system. Since fault prevention techniques can never remove all the faults in the system, to increase the reliability of a system beyond what can be achieved by fault prevention techniques, fault tolerance is employed. Fault tolerance techniques are based on the use of redundancy to mask the effect of faults in the system.

A system is defined as consisting of many components, each component being a system in its own right. At the lowest level are atomic or system components which cannot be further divided or whose internal structure is of no interest. The specifications of the system define the correct behavior of the system. A failure of a system occurs when the system cannot provide the desired (specified) service. An error is that part of the system state which can lead to system failure, and a fault is the cause of an error. By definition, a system cannot mask its own failure; if a failure occurs in a system then the system has failed. The goal of a fault tolerant system is to mask the failure of some of its components at higher levels. That is, a fault tolerant system is one which avoids the system failure when some of its components fail.

There are many phases that a system typically undergoes for supporting fault tolerance. These phases are error detection, damage confinement, error recovery, and fault treatment and continued service. In the first phase, the presence of a fault is determined by detecting an error in the system state. Since error detection is the starting point of supporting fault tolerance, a fault tolerance strategy can be, at most, as good as its error detection method. Some of the common error detection methods are replication checks, timing checks, structural and coding checks, reasonableness checks, and diagnostics checks.

As the error may be detected sometime after the failure has occurred, the next step in supporting fault tolerance is to determine the extent of damage to the system state by the failure. This is done in the *damage confinement phase.* For damage assessment, interaction between different components will have to be examined or structured because it is by interaction that errors can propagate. The goal is to identify some boundaries within which the spread of the error is confined. These boundaries can be dynamically determined after the error has been detected by examining the component interactions, or the component interaction can be constrained in such a manner that the error spread is limited to some predefined boundaries.

The next step is *error recovery.* Once the spread of an error has been identified, the error has to be removed from the system. This is done by error recovery. The two major techniques are *backward error recovery* and *forward error recovery.* In backward error recovery, during normal computation the state of the system is periodically checkpointed. For recovery, the checkpointed state of the system is restored. If the failure occurred after the checkpoint, this rollback will remove the error. In forward recovery, on the other hand, no previous system state is available. The goal is to make the system state error-free by taking some corrective actions. While backward recovery is a general technique, forward recovery requires a good diagnosis about the nature of the error.

The last phase is *fault treatment and continued service.* In the earlier phases, the focus was on error and error removal. But the root cause of any error is fault. Though in some cases, particularly with transient faults, just error recovery may suffice, in others, after error recovery, we must remove the fault that caused the error in order to avoid future failures. This is done in this phase. First the fault is located by identifying the faulty component. Then the system is "repaired" by reconfiguring the system by using the built-in redundancy such that either the failed component is not used or is used in a different manner.

Since the book deals with software fault tolerance activities, a brief overview of fault tolerance in hardware was also provided in the chapter. The overview describes the process of hardware development, some fault models, and some common techniques for providing fault tolerance in hardware. Though hardware failures are frequently caused by physical reasons like improper doping, electron migration, line breaks or shorts, these manifestations are frequently quite similar. These are called fault models. The most common fault model is the stuck-at fault model, in which some output of a gate is considered as stuck at either 0 or 1. Fault models are the starting point of supporting fault tolerance in hardware. For the fault models which are to be handled, techniques are used to avoid system failure. The common methods for fault tolerance in hardware are triple modular redundancy, coding, dynamic redundancy, and self-checking circuits. A brief introduction about fault tolerance techniques in multiprocessors is also given.

Since the goal of any fault tolerant system is to increase the reliability and/or availability of a system, we also formally defined what is meant by these terms. For random variables, which are frequently used in reliability and availability analysis, we restrict attention to exponential distribution, which is usually assumed for any analysis. Exponential distribution has the "memoryless" property, in that after some time the distribution of the "remaining part" is the same as the original distribution. For defining reliability, the lifetime of a system is considered as a random variable. The lifetime is the time to failure. *Reliability* of a system at a time is defined as the probability that the system is operational at that time instance. From the reliability function, the *expected life* of the system can be obtained by taking the expectation. This is also called the *mean time to failure (MTTF)* of the system and is a common measure of reliability. For exponential distribution, we also obtained expressions for the reliability of a series system in which components are connected in series and the system fails if any one of the components fails, and a parallel system in which the components are connected in parallel and the system fails only when all fail.

When a component fails, it is generally repaired or replaced by a new component. Hence, over a long period of time, a system can be considered as being in two states: "working" or "under repair." *Instantaneous availability* of a system at a time is defined as the probability that the component is working correctly at that time. Availability is different from reliability only because of system repair. If there was no repair, instantaneous availability will be the same as system reliability. *Steady state availability* (frequently called the *availability*) is the limit of instantaneous availability as time tends to infinity. It represents the fraction of the time the system is operational. If $MTTF$ is the mean time to failure of the system, and $MTTR$ is the mean time to repair of the system, then the availability of the system is $MTTF/(MTTF + MTTR)$, and is independent of the distributions of the lifetime and repair times.

Problems

1. Can fault tolerance be used to replace fault prevention, or vice versa? Explain.

2. Consider a stand-alone computer as a system. Define its interface and its structure (up to a few levels only).

3. Define the system-subsystem hierarchy for a distributed system for 3 levels.

4. Define error, failure, and fault. Can a system be made fault tolerant against its own failures?

5. What are the different phases in supporting fault tolerance? How is error detection done in a distributed system?

6. Show that the Hamming distance of a Hamming code is 3. How can you modify the Hamming code such that it becomes single error correcting and double error detecting?

7. What is the Hamming distance of a CRC code with a generator polynomial $x^4 + x^3 + 1$?

8. What is the Hamming distance of a Berger code?

9. Just as you might define fault models for hardware, define some fault models for software programs.

10. Design a self-checking checker for Berger codes.

11. Consider a general algorithm for a multiprocessor. Identify some canonical sets of primitives that can be used for a range of algorithms, and then design fault tolerance schemes for this.

12. If there is no repair of a system, then what is the relationship between $R(t)$ and $A(t)$ for the system?

13. Consider a system with standby redundancy in which the service is provided by the backup if the primary fails. Assume that there are n components (with (n−1) backups organized in a chain), each has a lifetime with exponential distribution, and the switching circuit is error-free. What is the MTTF of this system?

14. Consider a TMR system in which once a component fails, then one of the remaining failure-free components is also discarded and the system operates in a simplex mode (such a system is called a TMR/Simplex system). Show that the MTTF of this system is actually longer than that of TMR or Simplex systems.

15. Consider a system with n components, each with a MTTF of m and MTTR of r. What is the availability of the system if (a) the components are connected in series, (b) the components are connected in parallel?

References

[AA86]   J. A. Abraham, and V. K. Agarwal. "Test Generation for Digital Systems." In D. K. Pradhan, editor, *Fault-Tolerant Computing Theory and Techniques*. Englewood Cliffs, NJ: Prentice Hall, 1986, pp. 1–94.

[ABF90] M. Abramorice, M. A. Breuer, and A. D. Friedman. *Digital Systems Testing and Testable Design*. New York: Computer Science Press, 1990, p. 1.

[AF86]   J. A. Abraham, and W. K. Fuchs. "Fault and Error Models for VLSI." *Proceedings of the IEEE*, 74(5):639–654, May 1986.

[Agr88] P. Agrawal. "Fault-Tolerance in Multiprocessor Systems Without Dedicated Redundancy." *IEEE Transactions on Computers*, 37:358–362, March 1988.

[AL81]   T. Anderson, and P. A. Lee. *Fault Tolerance Principles and Practice*. Englewood Cliffs, NJ: Prentice Hall, 1981.

[AM73]   D. A. Anderson, and G. Metze. "Design of Totally Self-checking Circuits for M-Out-Of-N Codes." *IEEE Transactions on Computers*, C-22:263–269, March 1973.

[Avi76] A. Avizienis. "Fault-Tolerant Systems." *IEEE Transactions on Computers*, C-25(12):1304–1312, December 1976.

[B$^+$90] P. Banerjee et al. "Algorithm-based Fault-Tolerance on a Hypercube Multiprocessor." *IEEE Transactions on Computers*, 39:1132–1142, September 1990.

[CS68]   W. C. Carter, and P. R. Schneider. "Design of Dynamically Checked Computers." *Proceedings of the IFIP*, pp. 878–883, Edinburgh, August 1968.

[HA84]   K. H. Huang, and J. A. Abraham. "Algorithm Based Fault-Tolerance for Matrix Operations." *IEEE Transactions on Computers*, C33:518–528, June 1984.

[JK90]   N. K. Jha, and S. Kundu. *Testing and Reliable Design of CMOS Circuits.* Norwell, MA: Kluwer Academic Publishers, 1990.

[Joh89] B. W. Johnson. *Design and Analysis of Fault Tolerant Digital Systems.* Addison-Wesley, 1989.

[JW91]   N. K. Jha, and S.J. Wang. "Design and Synthesis of Self-checking VLSI Circuits and Systems." *IEEE International Conference on Computer Design*, Cambridge, MA, 1991.

[Lal85] P. K. Lala. *Fault Tolerant and Fault Testable Hardware Design.* London: Prentice Hall, 1985.

[Lap85] J. C. Laprie. "Dependable Computing and Fault Tolerance: Concepts and Terminology." *15th International Symposium on Fault Tolerant Computing Systems*, pp. 2–11, Ann Arbor, Michigan, June 1985.

[Lap92] J. C. Laprie. *Dependability: Basic Concepts and Terminology — In English, French, German, and Japanese.* Vienna: Springer-Verlag, 1992.

[Pra86] D. K. Pradhan. "Fault-Tolerant Multiprocessor and VLSI-Based System Communication Architectures." In D. K. Pradhan, editor, *Fault-Tolerant Computing Theory and Techniques.* Englewood Cliffs, NJ: Prentice Hall, 1986, Chapter 7.

[RF89]   T. R. N. Rao, and E. Fujiwara. *Error-control Coding for Computer Systems.* Englewood Cliffs, NJ: Prentice Hall, 1989.

[Rob82] A. S. Robinson. "A User-oriented Perspective of Fault Tolerant System Models and Terminologies." *12th International Symposium on Fault Tolerant Computing Systems*, pp. 22–28, 1982.

[SW82]   D. P. Siewiorek, and R. Wsarz. *The Theory and Practice of Reliable System Design.* Bedford, MA: Digital Press, 1982.

[TMB80a] D. J. Taylor, D. E. Morgan, and J. P. Black. "Redundancy in Data Structures: Improving Software Fault Tolerance." *IEEE Transactions on Software Engineering*, SE-6(6):584–594, November 1980.

[TMB80b] D. J. Taylor, D. E. Morgan, and J. P. Black. "Redundancy in Data Structures: Some Theoretical Results." *IEEE Transactions on Software Engineering*, SE-6(6):595–602, November 1980.

[Toh86] Y. Tohma. "Coding Techniques in Fault-Tolerant, Self-checking, and Fail-safe Circuits." In D. K. Pradhan, editor, *Fault-Tolerant Computing Theory and Techniques*. Englewood Cliffs, NJ: Prentice Hall, 1986, pp. 336–415.

[Tri82] K. S. Trivedi. *Probability and Statistics with Reliability, Queuing, and Computer Science Applications*. Englewood Cliffs, NJ: Prentice Hall, 1982.

Chapter 2

Distributed Systems

Since our focus is on fault tolerance in distributed systems, in this chapter we define precisely what we mean by a distributed system. We give the model of the distributed system that is assumed for the rest of the book.

We will first define the physical and logical structures of a distributed system, and identify the major components of it. These components are typically treated as atomic, and their internal structure is not considered in distributed systems. Hence, for fault tolerance, only the failures of these components need to be considered. The different failure modes that are possible in a distributed system are also discussed.

We also discuss the important communication constructs in a distributed system, and define the semantics of distributed programs. The ordering of events in a distributed system and the execution semantics of such systems are defined. It is necessary to understand the behavior of a distributed system in order to understand many of the schemes for fault tolerance in such systems.

2.1   System Model

There are two ways of viewing a distributed system: as defined by the physical components of the system, and as defined from the point of view of processing, or computation. We call the former the *physical model* of the system, and the latter the *logical model*. The computation viewpoint is important, as that is what a user sees, and the services that are defined in this perspective are the ones for which reliability is desired. The model of the physical network is important, since the computation is performed on the physical network, and the components of this physical network are the ones that fail. The goal of fault tolerance in distributed systems is often to ensure that some property, or service, in the logical model is preserved despite the failure of some components in the physical system.

2.1.1 Physical Network

The physical network of a distributed system consists of many computers (frequently referred to as *nodes*) that are geographically at different locations, but are connected by a communication network. All the nodes are *autonomous*, and communicate with each other through the communication network. A key property of distributed systems is the geographical separation and autonomous nature of various nodes.

Distributed systems are different from *parallel* systems, where nodes are *closely coupled*, i.e., they are not autonomous. In contrast, the computational elements of a distributed system are *loosely coupled*. Another important feature of distributed systems is the absence of shared memory between different nodes. That is, there is no memory in the system that can be accessible by more than one node. A memory location belongs to a node and only that node can access it. In contrast, some parallel systems have shared memory. In such systems, different nodes can communicate through the use of this shared memory. Though there are parallel systems that do not have shared memory, for distributed systems, lack of shared memory is essential.

Another difference between parallel and distributed systems is that distributed systems do not have a global clock driving all the nodes, while it is likely that the parallel system has a single clock in the system. In distributed systems, each node has a clock of its own, which can be used to control the instructions executed at that node. But a clock at one node cannot directly control the instructions at another node. A parallel system may have a global clock which is used for controlling instructions at the different processing elements in the system.

We can say that a distributed system consists of several nodes. Each node consists of a *processor*, which has some private volatile memory that is inaccessible to all other nodes, and a *private clock* that governs the execution of instructions on this processor. Each node also has a network interface, through which it is connected to a *communication network*. Two nodes in a system communicate with each other by passing messages over the communication network. In addition, we assume that each node has some *nonvolatile storage* like a disk. Finally, there is the *software*, that governs the sequence of instructions to be executed on a node. Hence, the major components of a distributed system are processor, communication network, clocks, software, and nonvolatile storage. In a distributed system, we consider these as the atomic components, and rarely consider the structure of these components. It is the failure of some of these components that a fault tolerance scheme aims to mask, such that the entire distributed system does not fail. Frequently, a distributed system is modeled as having nodes and a communication network as the basic components, without considering the internal structure of the nodes. In this model, the failure of a node and the failure of the communication network are the main component failures.

In a *point-to-point network*, the communication network consists of a set of links, each link connecting two nodes through their respective network interfaces. In this model, a distributed system can be represented as a graph, where nodes in the graph represent nodes in the system, and edges in the graph represent these communication links in the system. For communication, a node sends messages through the communication links. The manner in which the different links are connected to different nodes is called the network *topology*. Various topologies are possible. Some common ones are shown in Fig. 2.1.

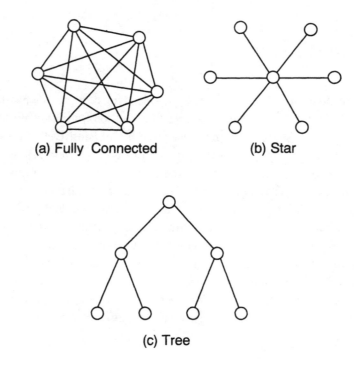

(a) Fully Connected   (b) Star

(c) Tree

Figure 2.1: Some common topologies

Sending messages in a point-to-point network requires *communication protocols*. Protocols are needed due to the autonomous nature of the nodes and the geographical separation between them. Since the nodes may be far apart, the data sent on a link between two nodes may be lost due to transmission and other errors. And since the nodes do not share any clock and can work at different speeds, without a protocol, a sender node can flood a receiver node. Many communication protocols like TCP/IP,

OSI, etc. have been proposed to ensure reliable communication between nodes in the network. Typically, some part of the protocol is executed by the hardware in the network interface, and the remainder is performed by system software.

There is another topology of distributed systems that is quite popular. Here, instead of a point-to-point communication network, the network is a *bus* to which all the different nodes of the network are connected. This is shown in Fig. 2.2. The

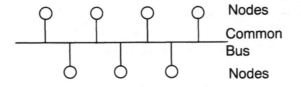

Figure 2.2: A bus topology

communication protocols in such topologies also tend to be somewhat different from the protocols for a point-to-point network. One method for designing such networks is to use a Carrier Sense Multiple Access with Collision Detection (CSMA/CD) protocol [Tan88]. A popular example of this type of network is the Ethernet [Tan88, MB76, SDR82, Sta87]. In Ethernet, any node wishing to transmit a message to another first senses the channel (the common bus to which all nodes are connected) and if there is no message being transmitted currently, starts its own transmission. If multiple nodes start transmitting simultaneously, then a *collision* occurs which garbles the message. The nodes monitor the message transmission. If a collision occurs, the sender finds out about it by sensing the channel. The current transmission is aborted and the transmission is repeated after waiting for a random period of time.

In this book, we will mainly consider a distributed system as consisting of a point-to-point network. In some cases, we will also consider the CSMA/CD type network.

2.1.2 Logical Model

Above we discussed the physical network, consisting of autonomous computing systems connected by a communication network. The distributed system thus formed can be used for *distributed applications*. Often, a distributed system can be viewed from the applications viewpoint, without worrying about the physical system. Here, we discuss the model of distributed applications that we will follow.

A distributed application (or a distributed system from the application point of view) consists of a set of *concurrently executing processes* that cooperate with each other to perform some task. A *process* is the execution of a sequential program, which is a list of statements or instructions. Concurrent processes can be executed on a single processor by allowing the different processes to share the processor. This approach is known as *multiprogramming*. We are, however, more interested in the case where the different processes execute in parallel on different nodes in the system.

For understanding a distributed application we have to understand the behavior of individual processes and how they interact with each other. A set of concurrent processes can be classified into three categories, namely *independent, competing*, and *cooperating* [AL81]. Concurrent processes are said to be *independent* if the sets of objects accessed by them are disjoint. Since the activity of each process must be completely isolated from any other process, this case is conceptually the same as having multiple physically separate sequential processes. Concurrent processes are said to be *competing* if they share resources but there is no information exchange between them. Conventional multiprocessing operating systems support competing processes. Since there is no information flow between processes, competing processes can be treated as a set of independent processes. The last category is the most interesting and imposes no restriction on information flow. *Cooperating processes* exchange information either by using shared data objects or through message passing. In distributed systems, only message passing is possible, as no shared data is allowed. In this book we will largely assume that the processes are cooperating processes.

In a distributed system, since the processes execute on different processors, we cannot make any assumptions about the relative speeds of different processes. The one assumption we can make is that each process has a positive rate of execution. This is called the *finite progress assumption*. Though multiple processes of the distributed application may run on a single processor, in most cases we will assume that each process is executed on a processor of its own.

At the logical level of applications, the underlying network is treated as a fully connected network (if the physical network is connected). That is, if a node is connected to all other nodes, then it means that a message can be sent from that node to any other node. This is ensured by the communication protocols that are there to support communication between different nodes in a network. Hence, the network can be treated as fully connected for the purposes of communication. Due to this, the topology of the network is not considered at this level.

At a logical level, we consider a distributed system as consisting of a finite set of processes and channels between the processes. Channels represent the logical connection between the processes. So long as the underlying network is such that any node can send messages to any other node, at a logical level, channels exist between any two processes. A channel between two processes exists if the processes interact with each other through messages. Hence, at a logical level, the distributed system can be represented as a directed graph in which the vertices represent processes in the system, and a channel from a process P to another process Q represents the fact that P can send messages to Q.

Channels are assumed to have infinite buffer and are assumed to be error-free. A message sent by a process P to another process Q over the channel between P and Q is delivered to Q without any errors. Furthermore, we assume that channels deliver the messages in the order in which they are sent. That is, if P sends multiple messages to Q via the channel from P to Q, then the messages arrive at Q in the order in which they are sent by P. Both these assumptions are not typically satisfied by real communication lines. However, most communication protocols provide a service that satisfies these assumptions. At a logical level, communication is performed by using the services provided by the underlying communication protocols.

Note that the ordering assumption about messages only states that the order of messages is preserved on a particular channel. It does not say anything about the order of messages that are received by a process from different channels incident on it (i.e., that are sent by different processes). That is, if different processes send messages to a process p, then the order in which the messages will be received by p cannot be specified. In other words, there is no total ordering of messages, but only a partial ordering. The general assumption about delays is one of the reasons why even if the "times" of sending messages by different processes to a given process p are known, still the order of receiving messages cannot be predicted.

At the logical level, frequently assumptions are also made about the time bounds on the performance of the system. The existence of such time bounds in a system is frequently necessary for practical reasons. A system is said to be *synchronous* if, whenever the system is working correctly, it always performs its intended function within a finite and known time bound; a system is said to be *asynchronous* otherwise [MS92]. A *synchronous communication channel* is one in which the maximum message delay is known and bounded, whereas a *synchronous processor* is one in which the time to execute a sequence of instructions is finite and bounded [MS92]. The main advantage of a synchronous system is that the failure of a component can be deduced by the lack of response within some defined time bound. Hence, if the distributed system is synchronous, a timeout-based scheme for detecting node failures or message losses can be employed. For example, a node failure can be detected by sending a message to a system and not getting a reply back during the "timeout" duration. Such a scheme cannot be relied upon if the distributed system is asynchronous. We will assume, unless specified otherwise, that the distributed system is synchronous, that is, its channels and the nodes are synchronous.

This is the general model of a distributed system at a logical level that will be considered in this book. Note that failures in the physical system cause the failure of components in the logical system. For example, failure of a node in the physical network may cause "failure" of some of the nodes (i.e., processes) in the logical network. Similarly, failure of a communication line in the physical network may (or may not) cause some logical channels to fail. The goal of fault tolerance is to preserve some properties in the logical model despite some failures in the physical model.

2.1.3   Failures and Fault Classification

We have seen that a distributed system can be defined from the point of view of the physical network or logically from the point of view of the distributed application. From the user's point of view, it is the latter view that is more relevant. For fault tolerance, it is the user's perspective that is important. Hence, we would like the distributed application to continue despite failures.

Failures occur in the physical system. We have seen that the major components in a distributed system are: processors, communication links, clocks, nonvolatile storage, and software. That is, in the system model for a distributed system, these are the atomic components, and their structures are typically not considered for supporting fault tolerance. It is the failure of these components that is usually of interest for supporting fault tolerance in distributed systems. Except software, all the others are physical components, and their failures may have underlying physical causes. The focus of most fault tolerance schemes in distributed systems is on the failures of physical components, particularly those of nodes and communication networks.

One possible way to classify the faults in a distributed system is based on how the faulty component behaves when it fails. Such a classification specifies what assumptions can be made about the behavior of the component when it fails. One such classification is given in [CAS86], which classifies failures as belonging to one of the four categories: crash, omission, timing, and Byzantine.

Crash fault. The fault that causes the component to halt or to lose its internal state. With this type of fault, a component never undergoes any incorrect state transition when it fails.

Omission fault. A fault that causes a component to not respond to some inputs.

Timing fault. A fault that causes a component to respond either too early or too late is called a timing fault. This is also sometimes called a *performance fault*.

Byzantine fault. An arbitrary fault which causes the component to behave in a totally arbitrary manner during failure.

These faults form a hierarchy, with the crash fault being the simplest and most restrictive (or well-defined) type and Byzantine being the least restrictive. They have an inclusion relationship as shown in Fig. 2.3 [CAS86]. This relationship follows directly from their definitions.

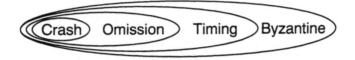

Figure 2.3: Fault classification

There is another class we can add, and that is the *incorrect computation fault*. Clearly, it is a subset of the Byzantine fault, but is different from others. With this type of fault, a component does not have any timing fault, but simply produces an incorrect output in response to the given inputs.

For a processor, most frequently a crash fault or a Byzantine fault is assumed. That is, for a processor, typically it is assumed that its failure is a crash when the processor stops executing, or no assumption is made about its failure behavior.

A communication network, on the other hand, is often considered to have all the different types of faults. It may have a crash fault, in which case it does nothing (i.e., does not receive or deliver any message), it may corrupt messages (incorrect computation fault), it may lose messages (omission fault), it may deliver messages after an inordinately long delay (timing fault), or it may behave in a totally arbitrary manner (Byzantine fault). For providing fault tolerance, Byzantine faults of the communication networks can be considered as Byzantine faults of processors, as a receiver of a message cannot distinguish between the two situations.

For a clock, typically, the failure of interest is the one where the clock runs either too fast or too slow. That is, one commonly considered fault of a clock is the timing fault. In addition, another failure mode that has been considered is the Byzantine fault, in which the behavior of the clock (i.e., the time the clock represents) is totally arbitrary. A clock that stops and shows the same time always can be considered as having an omission fault.

A storage media may have a crash fault, in which the storage is totally inaccessible for reading or writing. It may also show timing (data arriving late) or omission (some data inaccessible) faults. In addition, it may also corrupt data, which can be considered as an incorrect computation fault.

Software components can also have most of the faults defined above. However, the fault of most interest in software is the incorrect computation fault. In the presence of this, the software performs wrong computations. These are also called software design faults.

2.2   Interprocess Communication

In order to cooperate with each other, processes in a distributed application must communicate with each other. Communication allows processes to share information. In other words, it allows one process to influence another process.

Communication between processes often require some synchronization between processes. Since processes progress with unpredictable speeds (recall that we make only the finite progress assumption), synchronization is necessary for controlled communication. For example, suppose a process wants to receive information from another process. Typically, such information is needed at some defined place in program text of the process. Since a process cannot make any assumption about the speed of the sender process, in order to ensure that information exchange takes place at defined points, synchronization is needed. Synchronization between processes can also be viewed as constraints on the ordering of events in the distributed system.

For communication and synchronization, some primitives are needed that can be used by a process. In a distributed system, where there is no shared memory, synchronization and communication are both achieved by *message passing* primitives. In shared memory systems, where different processors share some common memory, communication can be achieved by the use of the shared memory (one process writes it and the other reads it). Different primitives have been proposed for synchronization in shared memory systems. These include semaphores, conditional critical regions, and monitors. Since we are focusing on distributed systems, we will not discuss the shared memory synchronization primitives here. The interested reader is referred to [And83]. In the rest of the section we discuss primitives for synchronization and communication in distributed systems (which do not have any shared memory).

Before we discuss synchronization and communication, a note on process creation is in order. Processes are created in a system by the use of some operating-system-provided *system call*. At the language level, processes are created by the use of some language primitives (that is, compiled into the necessary system call). Two common language primitives for process creation and destruction are *fork and join* and *cobegin-coend statement*.

With a fork and join statement, when the fork statement is executed by a process, another process is created that executes the specified program. The program that contains the fork statement must also have a join statement. At join, the process created by the fork statement and the process executing the original program synchronize. The new process is destroyed and the original process continues. This is shown in Fig. 2.4.

program P1   **program P2**

          ....

    fork P2;   ....

          ....

    join P2;   **end**

          ....

Figure 2.4: Fork and join primitive

In this example, the execution of P2 is initiated (or a process is created which executes the program P2) when P1 executes the fork statement. Then P1 and P2 both execute concurrently. After P1 reaches the join statement *and* P2 terminates, P1 executes the statement following the join statement.

Another common language construct, which is more structured than the fork and join statement, is the cobegin/coend construct. An example of the use of the construct is:

$$\textbf{cobegin } S_1||S_2||...||S_n \textbf{ coend}.$$

The execution of this statement causes n different processes to be created, each executing a different statement S_i. Execution of the cobegin statement finishes when the execution of all the S_i's has terminated.

2.2.1 Asynchronous Message Passing

In shared memory systems, communication and synchronization between processes is treated separately. Communication is done through reading and writing shared variables. For synchronizing access to shared data, different methods are employed. These methods include semaphores and monitors.

In a distributed system, where there is no shared memory, message passing is used both for communication and synchronization. Communication is achieved by a process which sends some data to another process which receives that data. Synchronization is achieved, since message passing implies that the receiving of the message is done after it has been sent. A message is sent by a process by executing the *send* command. A send command is of the form:

$$\textbf{send}(data, destination),$$

where *data* is the data being sent by the process and *destination* specifies the process to which the data is being sent.

Receiving of a message is done by a *receive* command. In the receive command there are different ways in which the *source* of the message is specified. We consider two types here. One is where the source process is directly specified by name. In this case, the receive command will receive a message only from the specified process. This command is of the form:

$$\textbf{receive}(data, source),$$

where *data* is the data received and *source* is the name of the process which will send this data. This form of receive command where the source is explicitly specified is useful in some communication situations like the *pipeline* in which one process sends to another, which in turn sends to the next one, and so on. In general, in situations where the sender is unique and clearly defined, this form of receive command is useful.

There are other situations where this form of receive command is too restrictive. One particular example is the *client-server interaction*. In the client-server model, there is one server (though multiple servers are possible, for simplicity we will focus on the single server case) which provides certain service. There are many client processes, and any of them can request the service from the server process. Clearly, in this situation, the server process cannot know beforehand the identity of the client which will request the service and so cannot specify it in its receive command (to receive the message requesting the service). In this type of situation the receive command can be of the form:

$$\textbf{receive}(message).$$

No source is specified in the receive command. The source is extracted from the message itself. In this model, messages sent to a process from all other processes are kept in a buffer, forming a queue of messages. At each receive command, the first message in the buffer is given to the process, regardless of the source of the message. If there is no message in the buffer, the receiving process *blocks* until some message arrives in the buffer. This form of receive command serves a similar purpose as the receive command based on *ports* [And83].

Message passing requires some *buffer* between the sender and the receiver process. The sender process puts the message in the buffer, from where the receiver process retrieves it. If the message passing is *asynchronous message passing*, then it is assumed that there is infinite buffer to store messages. In other words, with asynchronous message passing, senders can continue to send messages which will be saved in a buffer for the receiver process to consume. In this, the sender *never* blocks, that is, a send command always succeeds immediately and a sender can be arbitrarily ahead of the receiver. However, the receiver process is not non-blocking. It will have to block if there is no message in the buffer waiting for it.

In reality, there cannot be pure asynchronous message passing because the buffer sizes are always finite. With finite buffers, the sender also may have to block, if there is no buffer space left. This form is called *buffered message passing*. However, in many situations, for all practical purposes the buffer can be considered as unbounded and the message passing as asynchronous.

Note that asynchronous and synchronous message passing is different from asynchronous and synchronous distributed systems. The former refers to communication primitives and the size of the buffer between the sender and the receiver, while the latter deals with bounds on message delays. As stated earlier, we assume that the system is synchronous. In a synchronous distributed system, both synchronous and asynchronous message passing can be supported.

Failure of a node on which a process is running, or the failure of the communication network, will have a direct impact on the interprocess communication. If the communication network fails (with a crash fault), such that the source and the destination are disconnected, then the behavior of an asynchronous communication system depends on the underlying implementation. If the implementation has a built-in "timeout" mechanism, then after the timeout, the sender will know that the destination is inaccessible (note that by use of timeout, the synchronous nature of the distributed system is being used). In asynchronous communication, the receiver does not become aware of the failure or disconnection of a sender process. Any messages on the link are lost due to this failure. If there is no timeout, then the communication protocols will keep trying. If the failure of the communication network is temporary, then the messages will get delivered when the network becomes connected. This situation will, at most, cause a timing failure (since the message may get inordinately delayed).

If the node on which a process is executing fails, then in a crash type of fault, a process executing on the node will stop executing (and will not send or receive further messages), and will lose any messages that it had in the buffer. In a Byzantine fault, nothing can be said about the process behavior. The process may even send spurious messages to other processes.

2.2.2 Synchronous Message Passing and CSP

In contrast to asynchronous message passing, synchronous message passing has *no buffering*. In this form, the execution of a send command is delayed till the corresponding receive command is executed. Hence, every execution of a communication command represents a synchronization point where both the sender and the receiver process synchronize. Both the send and the receive command are blocking, and both the sender and the receiver have to block till the corresponding receive or send command is executed.

The main advantage of synchronous message passing is that due to synchronization at each communication command it is easier to make assertions about processes. For example, in the sender process, when the send command finishes, the sender process can make some assertions about the state of the receiver process (e.g., that the message just received is the same as the one sent). This helps in understanding programs and proving their correctness.

Synchronous message passing has been employed in *Communicating Sequential Processes (CSP)*, a notation proposed for specifying distributed programs. CSP has also been used for specifying some fault tolerance schemes. We will briefly describe CSP here, so that these schemes described in later chapters can be readily understood. But before we do so, let us give a brief description of *guarded commands*, which are used in CSP.

Guarded Commands

Guarded commands were proposed by Dijkstra [Dij75] as a construct that will facilitate the systematic development of programs. A *guarded command* is a statement list that is prefixed by a Boolean expression called a *guard*. It has the form

$$guard \rightarrow statement\_list.$$

The statement_list is eligible for execution only if its guard evaluates to true, i.e., the guard *succeeds*. The evaluation of the guard is assumed to have *no side effects*, that is, the evaluation of the guard does not alter the state of the program in any manner. The alternative construct is formed using a set of guarded commands as follows:

$$
\begin{array}{lll}
[& G_1 & \rightarrow & S_1 \\
\square & G_2 & \rightarrow & S_2 \\
& & \vdots & \\
& & \vdots & \\
\square & G_n & \rightarrow & S_n \\
], & & &
\end{array}
$$

where each $G_i \rightarrow S_i$ is a guarded command. The execution of this alternative command aborts if all the guards evaluate to false (or fail). If any guard evaluates to true, then the corresponding statement is eligible for execution. Since multiple guards may evaluate to true, the statement to be executed is *selected non-deterministically* from the statements eligible for execution.

A repetitive command from the guarded command has a similar structure. The start of the construct is prefixed (i.e., before the [) with a * indicating repetition. In a repetitive command, the alternative command is executed repeatedly every time one of the eligible statements is executed. When all the guards fail, the repetitive command terminates.

Guarded command notation allows for non-determinism within a program. The concept of guard, along with non-determinism, makes it quite useful for specifying event-based computation. In such situations, an event is specified as a guard and when the event occurs, the corresponding guard evaluates to true and the statements that should be executed for that event are executed. Non-determinism says that if multiple events occur simultaneously, then one of them is selected non-deterministically for further processing. The concept of guarded commands is used in CSP, a notation proposed for specifying distributed programs.

Communicating Sequential Processes (CSP)

Communicating Sequential Processes [Hoa78] is a programming notation for expressing concurrent programs. It employs synchronous message passing, and uses guarded commands to allow *selective communication* [And83]. We briefly mention the relevant aspects of CSP here.

A CSP program may consist of many concurrent processes. A process P_i sends a message, *msg*, to a process P_j by an output command of the form:

$$P_j!msg.$$

A process P_j receives a message from a process P_i by the input command of the form:

$$P_i?m.$$

A process executing an input (output) command blocks till the corresponding process (i.e., the process specified in the command) is ready to perform the output (input) command. After communication, both processes unblock and proceed independently. The code of each process is essentially a guarded command [Dij75]. For a process P_j the overall code is the form:

$$P_j :: \text{Initialize}; *[G_1 \rightarrow C_1 \square G_2 \rightarrow C_2 \ldots \square G_n \rightarrow C_n].$$

A guard G_i in CSP may contain at most one input command, besides the Boolean expressions. A guard *succeeds* if the Boolean expression is true and the message-passing command in the guard can be satisfied immediately (i.e., the corresponding sender process is ready to send); the guard *fails* if the Boolean expression is false or the process mentioned in the input command in the guard has either terminated or failed; the guard neither succeeds nor fails if the Boolean expression is true but the message-passing statement cannot yet be successfully executed without causing delay (because the process mentioned in the communication command is not yet ready to send the message).

As send commands are not allowed to appear in guards in the original proposal of CSP (extensions were proposed later to allow output commands to also appear in a guard [Sil89]), *selective communication* can be easily supported, which is useful in implementing a client-server type of interaction. In this, if a message can arrive from a number of processes (as would be the case with a server), then each guard can contain an input command from one potential sender (a client in a client-server case). The receiver (the server) can then receive the message from any of the sender processes.

Due to synchronous message passing in CSP, the sender and the receiver processes synchronize at each communication. Another property of synchronous communication in CSP is that a process P_i cannot send a message to another process P_j, until the previous input/output commands of P_i and P_j have been successfully completed. That is, the handshake protocol has been fully executed and the destination process has received the message. This property does not hold for asynchronous communication where the process P_i can send a message to the process P_j, even if P_j has not received the previous message sent by P_i (the messages are buffered by the system for P_j).

The failure of a node or communication network in synchronous communication has similar effects as in asynchronous communication. However, unlike in asynchronous communication, if a node or a communication network fail, the receiver of a message will also detect the failure (if "timeout" is used).

2.2.3 Remote Procedure Call

The send/receive primitives are sufficient to program any type of message-based interaction between processes. In the client/server type of interactions, programs using send/receive primitives will require a send followed by a receive by the client process and a receive followed by a send by the server process. In this interaction, the client process is blocked till the service is complete, even though it uses asynchronous message passing, since the client cannot proceed until it receives the result.

Since the client/server type of interaction is very common in computer systems, a higher level primitive that directly supports this type of interaction has been proposed, called *remote procedure call (RPC)*. In RPC, the service to be provided by the server is treated as a procedure that resides on the machine on which the server is. A client process that wants the service simply makes "calls" to this procedure. The implementation of the RPC takes care of the underlying communication (which may be implemented using sends and receives).

An RPC is an extension of the procedure call mechanism available in most sequential programming languages. A client interacts with the server by means of the **call** statement, as is done in a sequential language. A call statement is of the form:

$$\textbf{call } service(value\_args, result\_args),$$

where *service* is name of the remote procedure, *value_args* are the arguments that provide the parameter values to the remote procedure, and *result_args* are the arguments in which the results of the remote procedure are returned. When the call statement is executed, the value_args are sent to the server (by a send command). The calling program waits till the called procedure finishes and returns the results. After that, it proceeds to the statement following the procedure call. It is a synchronous form of communication, where the client cannot proceed until the server has finished the service and returned the results.

In this client-server type of interaction, after each call to the server by the client, the state of the server and the state of the client changes from some initial state (i.e., the state just before the call) to some final state (i.e., the state just after the call). In general, the states of both the client and server may change as a result of the call. However, there is one particular type of remote procedure that is used in many applications in which the state of the server does not change. These are called *idempotent* procedures. With idempotent servers, the state of the server after a call is the same as before the call. An idempotent server simplifies the task of supporting fault tolerance.

There are two basic approaches to specifying the server side of an RPC [And83]. In the first, the remote procedure is just like a sequential procedure, which is implemented as a single process which executes the procedure as calls are made to the procedure. In this form, the different calls to the remote procedure are executed sequentially. The second approach is to create a new process every time a call is made. These processes could execute concurrently, synchronizing their access to shared variables, if any.

There are many other details that have to be worked out for supporting RPC. Various implementations of RPC have been proposed. The reader may refer to

[BN84, Nel81, PS88, RC89, SP82] for further details about the implementation methods.

Since often two different processes are involved in an RPC — one executing the client, the other executing the server — new issues relating to fault tolerance arise that did not exist in the standard procedure call systems. Of specific interest is the question of what happens if the node executing the RPC fails (or if the node executing the client fails), or if the communication network fails (by losing the messages, or reordering the messages) during the execution of a RPC. We assume that if no failures occur during the execution of the RPC, it terminates normally, otherwise it terminates abnormally.

Under failure conditions, the semantics of the RPC cannot be like that of the simple procedure in a sequential program, in which the failure of a node means the failure of the caller as well as the callee, and the failure of the communication network has no effect. Hence, we have to specify the semantics of the RPC that are suitable for an environment that is prone to failure. The following classification has been proposed for the semantics of remote calls [Nel81, PS88]:

- *At least once:* The remote procedure has been executed one or more times if the invocation terminates normally. If it terminates abnormally, nothing can be said about the number of times the remote procedure has executed. It may have executed partially, zero, one, or multiple times.

- *Exactly once:* The remote procedure has been executed exactly once if the invocation terminates normally. If it terminates abnormally, then it can be asserted that the remote procedure has not been executed more than once.

- *At most once:* This is the same as exactly-once semantics if the invocation terminates normally. If it terminates abnormally, then it is guaranteed that the remote procedure has been executed completely once, or has not been executed at all.

Communication or processor failures during an invocation often cause unwanted executions of remote procedures. These unwanted executions are called *orphans*. For example, a client that crashes during an RPC call and restarts on recovery may reissue the call to the server even though the earlier call is still being executed by the server. In this situation, the first invocation is an orphan. A similar situation occurs if the client "times out," maybe due to inordinate delays in the communication network (a timing fault). In this case, again, the client will resend the request to the server, thereby creating an orphan.

There are many other situations in which orphans are created. Orphans are fundamental to RPC. As shown in the preceding example, even without a crash failure of a communication network or node, performance or timing failure can also cause orphans. The presence of orphans can easily violate the semantics (particularly if the goal is to achieve at most once semantics) of RPC, and lead to inconsistency.

Another property that needs to be preserved by an RPC mechanism is *call ordering*. This property requires that a sequence of invocations generated by a given client result in computations being performed by the server in the same order. Due to the synchronous nature of the RPC, this criteria is automatically satisfied if there are no failures. However, due to the possibility of orphans caused by failures, more needs to be done to satisfy this. Call ordering is not a strict requirement if the server is idempotent.

2.2.4   Object-Action Model

Like remote procedure calls, an object-action model is another high-level communication paradigm which is gaining popularity. In this paradigm, the system consists of many objects, each encapsulating some data and having some well-defined *methods* (operations) on that data. The encapsulated data can be accessed or modified only through the methods defined on the object. The objects themselves are typically instances of a general *class*. This method of organizing a system is often called the object-oriented approach.

Many components, or entities, in a system can be considered as objects. Files are a good example. A particular file is an instance of the general file class. On each file, some well-defined operations are defined through which the file is accessed. These methods typically are open, read, write, close, etc. Most systems do not allow files to be accessed in any manner other than through these well-defined operations. In a traditional system, where the system is not organized or implemented in an object-oriented manner, these operations may be system calls. In an object-oriented system, these will be methods defined on a file object.

In an object-oriented system, an object typically exports some of its methods. These are the methods that are available to other objects or processes outside this object. This model renders itself suitable for distributed systems. The objects may reside on different nodes. A process, when it wants to execute a method on a particular object, sends a message to that object, which performs an *action* by executing the method (if the method is accessible from outside) and returns the results. In a distributed system, this becomes a remote procedure call, except that the procedure is a method on a particular object and works on that object only. Invocation of a method on an object may change the state of that object.

The execution of a method on an object may invoke methods on other objects. This leads to nested remote procedure calls, in which a remote call makes a call to another remote call. Also, in a distributed system it is possible that methods on objects may be executing in parallel. This leads to the possibility that concurrent calls may be made to the same method, or to the same object.

The object-action model is being increasingly used and has been found to be very useful for supporting fault tolerance. The issues with node failures are similar to that of remote procedure calls. If a node fails, the requirement may be that the effects of the partly executed method be undone. Concurrent requests may require some restrictions on how they are resolved. Objects also naturally provide a unit for replication. Objects may be replicated to make an object fault tolerant. During the course of this book we will see some examples of how this model has been used in supporting fault tolerant systems.

2.3   Ordering of Events and Logical Clocks

In many schemes and algorithms in distributed systems, it is important to be able to specify whether an event occurred before another event or not. As defined earlier, a distributed system consists of a collection of autonomous computer systems that are spatially separated and communicate with each other through message passing. Another property of distributed systems is that there is no single global clock; each system has its own independent clock. This fact makes the problem of defining relative timings of different events in the system difficult.

When we say that an event e has occurred before another event f, we mean that the time of occurrence of the event e is *before* the time of occurrence of the event f. It also implies that the timings of the events e and f were measured by the *same* clock. Clearly, if the timings of different events are measured by different clocks, since different clocks may have different times, we cannot ascertain whether an event has occurred before or after another just by looking at the timings of the events. In a distributed system, since there is no global clock, we cannot define a *happened-before* relation in a straightforward manner.

In this section, we discuss how events can be ordered in a distributed system. Since physical clocks cannot be directly used for determining the ordering of events, we define logical clocks in the system and discuss how they are related to the ordering of events.

2.3.1 Partial Ordering of Events

With each node in the network having a clock of its own, actions taking place at that node can be ordered using the clock of the node. In distributed systems, the problem occurs when we try to define an ordering relation between events at different nodes. Here we describe a simple scheme to define a "happened before" relationship between the different events in the distributed system. This scheme was proposed by Lamport [Lam78].

A distributed system consists of many processes and each process consists of a sequence of events. We can consider an event as the execution of an instruction. Since a process is a sequence of events, we can define the *happened-before* relation for events of a particular process. We denote the "happened before" relation by $\rightarrow$. An event a, performed by a process, is considered as having "happened before" another event b, performed by the same process, if the event a occurs before the event b in the sequence of events performed by the process. In such case, we can say $a \rightarrow b$.

The "happened before" relationship can be extended, in some cases, to events of different processes. First, it should be noticed that in a message passing system, a receive of a message cannot occur before the sending of that message. That is, we can say that the sending of a message "occurred before" the receiving of that message. This ordering of events performed by different processes (send is executed by one process and receive is executed by another) is the basic mechanism for ordering events of different processes. The relation "occurred before," or $\rightarrow$, is formally defined as follows [Lam78].

Definition. The relation $\rightarrow$ on a set of events in a distributed system is the smallest relation satisfying the following three conditions: (1) If a and b are events performed by the same process, and a is performed before b, then $a \rightarrow b$. (2) If a is the sending of a message by one process and b is the receiving of the same message by another process, then $a \rightarrow b$. (3) If $a \rightarrow b$ and $b \rightarrow c$, then $a \rightarrow c$. Two distinct events are said to be *concurrent* if neither $a \rightarrow b$, nor $b \rightarrow a$.

The relation $\rightarrow$ defines a partial relation between the events of the distributed system. It *does not* define a total order. That is, there are events (the concurrent events) in the system that are not ordered by the relation $\rightarrow$. Hence, for two events a and b it is possible that $a \not\rightarrow b$ and $b \not\rightarrow a$.

Another way to view the relation $\rightarrow$ is to say that if $a \rightarrow b$, it implies that the event a can causally affect the event b. If the events are concurrent, it implies that neither can causally affect the other.

2.3.2 Logical Clocks

We have defined the relation "happened before" without any notion of clock or time. The basis for the relation is the order of occurrence of events in the sequence of events executed by a process, and the dependence of the event for receiving a message on the event corresponding to the sending of the message. Now we discuss a system of logical clocks, with each node having one logical clock, such that the timings of events by these logical clocks will be consistent with the relation → [Lam78].

A logical clock is just a means of assigning a number to an event (the "timing" of the event). The value of the clock has no direct bearing with the physical time. The logical clock C_i, for a process P_i, is a function which assigns a value $C_i(a)$ to an event a of the process P_i. The entire system of clocks of all processes together can be represented by a function C, which assigns values to events of a process as assigned by the logical clock of that process.

The system of logical clocks is considered to be "correct" if it is consistent with the relation →. That is, a system of logical clocks is considered as correct if it satisfies the following *clock condition* [Lam78]:

For any events a, b, if $a \rightarrow b$ then $C(a) < C(b)$.

The clock condition ensures that the values assigned to the events is consistent with the relation →. Note that the reverse condition need not hold for logical clocks. The use of logical clocks is to "timestamp" an event such that the ordering preserves the partial ordering imposed by the relation →.

The system of logical clocks can be easily implemented. We assume that when a message is sent by a process P_i, the timestamp of the sending event is included in the message m, and can be retrieved by the receiver. Let T_m be the timestamp of the message m. There are two conditions that a system of logical clocks should satisfy in order to be "correct" [Lam78]:

1. Each process P_i increments C_i between any two successive events.

2. Upon receiving a message m, a process P_j sets C_j greater than or equal to its present value and greater than T_m.

The first condition ensures that the events of a process are ordered by the clock as they are ordered by the relation →, and an event that occurs before another in the sequence of events being performed by a process will indeed have the smaller timestamp by the logical clock. The second condition ensures the second condition of the relation →. It ensures that the timestamp by the logical clock of the event corresponding to the receiving of a message is more than the timestamp of the event corresponding to the sending of that message. Both of these together ensure that the clock condition is satisfied. Hence, if we have, say, a counter associated with each process in which any value can be loaded by the process, then this implementation can be realized easily.

It should again be pointed out that the logical clocks have no relationship to the actual clocks and their "times" have no relationship with physical time. As we discussed earlier, it is not possible to assign timestamps that will be consistent with the relation $\rightarrow$ purely by physical clocks. In other words, physical clocks need not satisfy the clock condition by themselves, the clocks have to be synchronized if they have to satisfy the clock condition. We will discuss this issue of "clock synchronization" later.

2.3.3 Total Ordering of Events

We can use logical clocks that satisfy the clock condition to place a total ordering on the events in a distributed system [Lam78]. A simple method is to order the events by the timestamps assigned to them by the logical clock system. Since the logical clock system consists of many logical clocks, events may be assigned the same timestamp by this clock system. To break ties, we can use any order on the processes. An easy way of doing this is to order the processes according to the lexicographic ordering of their names. With this, if two events have the same timestamp (such events must be from different processes, since different events of the same process must have different timestamps), the event of the process that occurs before in the lexicographic ordering is considered as having happened before.

Hence, we define a relation $\Rightarrow$ on the set of events as follows [Lam78]: for two events a and b of processes P_i and P_j respectively, $a \Rightarrow b$ if and only if either (i) $C_i(a) < C_j(b)$, or (ii) $C_i(a) = C_j(b)$ and P_i comes before P_j in the ordering (e.g., lexicographic) of the processes. It is clear that the relation $\Rightarrow$ defines a total ordering and it is consistent with the clock condition, or the relation $\rightarrow$, that is, if $a \rightarrow b$ then $a \Rightarrow b$. This total order is thus obtained by extending the relation $\rightarrow$.

This total ordering depends on the system of logical clocks (and how we order the processes), and is not unique. Since the logical clocks have no relationship with real time, they can behave in any manner as long as they continue to satisfy the clock condition. Essentially, this method of totally ordering the events preserves the order specified by the relation $\rightarrow$, but those events that are concurrent by the relation $\rightarrow$ can be included in the total order in different ways, depending on the logical clock system.

Being able to order the events totally can be very useful in designing distributed applications. Total order by the timestamp ensures that different nodes in the system order the events in the same manner. This, in turn, ensures that a decision function, executing at different nodes, will give the same value if it is based on the order of events. This facilitates synchronization of distributed programs.

2.4 Execution Model and System State

Now we describe how we can model the computation or execution of a logical system. It is important to understand the execution model to understand the behavior of the system under failures and with strategies for fault tolerance. The model we use is based on the models proposed in [CL85, OL82].

As defined earlier, at a logical level, a distributed system can be modeled as a directed graph with nodes representing processes and arcs representing channels between processes. The *state* of a channel in this model is the sequence of messages that are still in the channel, that is, the sequence of messages sent along the channel excluding the ones that have already been delivered by it.

A process can be considered as consisting of a set of states, an initial state, and a sequence of events (or actions). A process typically consists of many variables that are local or internal to the process (i.e., they cannot be accessed by any other process, as there is no shared memory in our distributed system model). The state of a process is an assignment of a value to each variable of the process, along with the specification of its *control point* which specifies the event that has been executed last (essentially the value of the program counter).

Each action or event of a process is assumed to be atomic, which is executed indivisibly by the underlying hardware. An event e of a process p can change the state of p and *at most one* channel c that is incident on p. The state of a channel is changed by a process by either sending a message along c or by receipt of a message along c. Each event has an *enabling condition*, which is a condition on the state of the process and the channels attached to it. An event e can occur only if its enabling condition is true. The simplest example of the use of an enabling condition for specifying an event e is "when the program counter has a specific value," then the event corresponding to the execution of the statement pointed to by the PC can occur (i.e., the statement can be executed).

The *global state* of a distributed system consists of states of each of the processes in the system and the states of the channels in the system. The *initial global state* is one in which each process is in its initial state and all the channels are empty. The global state of a distributed system is also called the **system state**. The occurrence of an event e can change the global state of the system by changing the state of the process that executes e (and maybe changing the state of one channel). An event e can occur in a system state S if its enabling condition is satisfied in S.

We define a function *ready(S)* on a global state S [OL82], which is a set of events for which the enabling condition is satisfied by S. These are the events that can occur in S. The events in $ready(S)$ may belong to different processes. However, only one of these events will take place. The event that occurs is "selected" non-deterministically. That is, which of the events in $ready(S)$ will actually occur cannot be predicted. We define another function *next*, where $next(S, e)$ is the global state immediately following the occurrence of the event e in the global state S. Clearly, e must belong to $ready(S)$.

The computation of a distributed system can now be defined as a sequence of events. Let the initial state of the system be S_0, and let $seq = (e_i, 0 \le i \le n)$ be a sequence of events. Suppose that the system state when the event e_i occurs is S_i. The sequence of events *seq* is a *computation of the system* if the following conditions are satisfied:

1. The event $e_i \in ready(S_i), 0 \le i \le n$.

2. $S_{i+1} = next(S_i, e_i), 0 \le i \le n$.

That is, a sequence of events is considered as a computation of the system if, starting from the initial state, each event is one which was enabled in the system state in which it occurs, and the state after the event is determined entirely by the event, as specified by the function *next*.

As an example, consider the concurrent program shown in Fig. 2.5 [OL82]. This is a shared memory program, which is chosen to illustrate the concept of execution of a distributed system. Assume that each assignment statement or condition checking is executed indivisibly by the hardware (i.e., is the unit of interleaving).

Suppose that the state of the system before the execution of the program was started was $x = 2$, and $y = 7$. One possible computation (i.e., one possible sequence of states) of this program is given below. We represent each state by the value of the two variables x and y, and the value of the *ready* function; the arrow represents the transition from one state to another due to the execution of an atomic action. The atomic action responsible for the transition is mentioned above the arrow representing the transition. We represent an atomic action corresponding to the execution of a statement by the label of that statement. One possible execution sequence of this system is shown in Fig. 2.6.

This is just one computation of the system. Many such computations are possible for this program, depending on which of the events from the *ready* set is selected

a: x := 0
b: **cobegin**
    c: y := 0
    d: **cobegin**
        e: y := 2 * y
        || f: y := y + 3
    coend
  || g: **while** y=0 **do**
      h: x := x + 1
coend
j: x := 2 * y

Figure 2.5: An example concurrent program

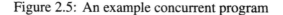

$S_0 : [(2, 7); \{a\}] \xrightarrow{a} S_1 : [(0, 7); \{c, g\}] \xrightarrow{c}$
$S_2 : [(0, 0); \{e, f, g\}] \xrightarrow{g} S_3 : [(0, 0); \{e, f, h\}] \xrightarrow{h}$
$S_4 : [(1, 0); \{e, f, g\}] \xrightarrow{f} S_5 : [(1, 3); \{e, g\}] \xrightarrow{e}$
$S_6 : [(1, 6); \{g\}] \xrightarrow{g} S_7 : [(1, 6); \{j\}] \xrightarrow{j}$
$S_8 : [(12, 6); \{\}]$

Figure 2.6: An execution sequence

for execution in a given state. All of these sequences are valid computations of this program.

The possible states of the system can also be represented as a tree with its root as the initial state and each event in the ready set producing a child of a node. Such a tree is sometimes called a "reachability tree," as it shows all the possible states that can be reached by the system. In this tree, each node represents a state, and the number of children of a node equals the cardinality of the *ready* set at that state. Part of the reachability tree for the example above is shown in Fig. 2.7.

In a reachability tree, the path from the root to a leaf node represents one possible execution sequence of the system. And all such paths represent an execution. The set of all paths together represent all possible executions of the system. Hence, from a given initial state, any of the states in the reachability tree can be "reached"

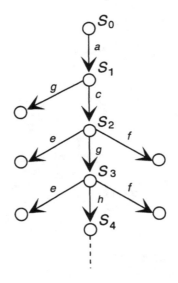

Figure 2.7: Reachability tree

in an execution of the system. These states of the system are called *consistent* or *valid*. Note that the user has no control over the path in the tree that is followed by a particular execution of the system.

In this model, the execution of a system is considered as a sequence of events and has no notion of concurrent events. The model also permits the actions of different processes to interleave; any action from any process can occur in a system state provided its enabling condition is satisfied. This model is usually called the *interleaving model*, and is one of the most commonly used execution models for a distributed system. It must be pointed out that in a distributed system, where multiple processes execute simultaneously, the events do occur concurrently. In this model, the concurrent execution of events is modeled by non-deterministic interleaving of events.

2.5 Summary

In this chapter, we have specified our model of a distributed system that would be used in this book. Physically, a distributed system consists of autonomous nodes that are connected to each other by a communication network. Each node consists of a processor, some private memory which is inaccessible to all other processors, and a private clock. The nodes are *loosely coupled*, do not have shared memory, and communicate via message passing. The communication network may be point-to-point, in which case the *topology* of the network determines the set of nodes to which a node is connected. Various topologies are possible. *Communication protocols* are used for sending messages from one node to another. The communication network may also be *bus based*, in which there is a common communication medium shared by all nodes. Special protocols are used to manage communication in this. A common protocol is Carrier Sense Multiple Access with Collision Detection (CSMA/CD).

The logical model of the system views the system from the point of view of applications. The logical model consists of processes and channels between processes. Processes are nodes in the model, and channels are the links that connect them. If the underlying physical network is connected, the network is treated as fully connected at the logical level. Processes communicate with each other by sending and receiving messages. A logical system is said to be *synchronous* if, whenever the system is working correctly, it always performs its intended function within a finite and known time bound; a system is said to be *asynchronous* otherwise. A synchronous system has synchronous communication channels, in which the maximum message delay is known and bounded, and synchronous processors, in which the time to execute a sequence of instructions is finite and bounded. In a synchronous system, timeout-based scheme can be used for detecting failures. We assume that the distributed system is synchronous.

For supporting fault tolerance in distributed systems, the components whose failure is generally of interest are the processor, storage, clock, communication links, and software. The faults of these components can be classified as belonging to one of the four categories: crash, omission, timing, and Byzantine. A *crash fault* causes the failed component to just halt, an *omission fault* causes a component to not respond to some inputs, a *timing fault* causes a component to respond too early or too late, and a *Byzantine fault* causes the component to behave in a totally arbitrary manner. These faults form a hierarchy. The simplest failure mode is the crash fault in which the component behaves in a most benign manner on failure. The most general is the Byzantine fault in which no assumption can be made about the behavior of the component during failure. Besides this, the failure of the software can also display an *incorrect computation fault*, in which the component produces incorrect output.

The processes running in a distributed system communicate with each other via message passing, since no shared memory is available. Message passing can be done through asynchronous *send* and *receive* primitives. In asynchronous message passing, the receive primitive does not specify any source and consumes the message that is first in the queue of waiting messages. The communication is called *asynchronous*, since a send never has to block and can be arbitrarily ahead of the receivers. Communication can also be through synchronous message passing where the receiver and sender synchronize at each message exchange. CSP is one proposed language notation that employs synchronous message passing. Another method of communication between processes is through remote procedure call, which is an extension of the procedure-call primitive of sequential programming languages to distributed systems. Remote procedure call is a higher level communication construct, which is synchronous in nature, though it may employ asynchronous message passing for implementation. Finally, there is the object-action model in which the system is viewed as a collection of objects, each providing some operations. A request for operations is sent to the object, which performs the operation and sends the results back. The operations themselves can be considered as remote procedure calls.

In a distributed system many processes execute concurrently. Each process performs events. Since there is no global observer, and since the different nodes in the system have different clocks, it is not always easy to specify if an event "happened before" another. Based on a message exchange between processes, a partial order can be specified between events of different processes. The relation $\rightarrow$ captures the "happened before" notion for events. If a and b are events, then $a \rightarrow b$ if both are performed by the same process, and a is performed before b, or if a is the sending of a message by one process and b is the receiving of the same message by another process, or for some event c if $a \rightarrow b$ and $b \rightarrow c$, then $a \rightarrow c$. Two events are said to be *concurrent* if neither $a \rightarrow b$, nor $b \rightarrow a$.

The relation $\rightarrow$ defines a partial order on the set of events in a distributed system. It is clearly desirable to have clocks in the system which will attach times to events in the system such that the timestamps they assign to events are consistent with the partial ordering defined by $\rightarrow$. A system of independent clocks will not automatically satisfy this. Hence *logical clocks* are needed. One such logical clock can be formed from counters, with one counter for each process. To ensure that the clocks are consistent with $\rightarrow$, each process must increment its clock between two successive events, and upon receiving a message, a process must set its clock to a value greater than or equal to its present value and greater than the value of the timestamp of the incoming message.

Total order on a set of events is frequently desired. The partial order defined by $\rightarrow$ can be extended to a total order, but that total order will not be unique. One way is to use the logical clocks to timestamp events. The events are ordered according to their timestamps. If the timestamps are the same, then they are ordered according to a predefined ordering on the names of the processes.

Finally, we discussed the execution model of the distributed system. Because of multiple processes which are loosely coupled, the execution of a distributed application is inherently different from the execution of a single process application.

The global state of the system (or the system state) is defined as the state of each of the processes and each of the channels. The execution of a distributed system is modeled as a sequence of actions, each action being performed by a process. This sequence of actions represents a computation of the system, which makes a transformation on the system state. Hence, the execution can also be modeled as a sequence of states, with state transitions occurring due to the occurrence of events. In distributed systems, unlike sequential systems, the event that can be performed in a given state is not unique. At any state there could be multiple events that can occur. Which of the events will actually occur depends on the particular execution and cannot be fixed. This leads to non-determinism. That is, even if a distributed system starts from the same initial state and the same inputs are given to it, in different executions it may follow a different sequence of states, and each of these sequences is a valid execution of the system. A system state is defined to be *valid* or *consistent* if it occurs in one of these possible executions of the system. These are the *reachable states* of the system, that is, the states that the system *can* reach during its execution.

Problems

1. The finite progress assumption is needed to argue about a distributed application. How can it be ensured that for a distributed system this assumption holds?

2. Suppose there are four processes in the system $P_1, ..., P_4$. P_1 sends m_1, m_2 to P_4, P_2 sends m_3, m_4 to P_4, and P_3 sends m_5, m_6 to P_4. What are the different orders in which $m_1, ..., m_6$ can be received by P_4?

3. In the Venn diagram showing the relationship of different failures in a distributed system (Fig. 2.3), add the "incorrect computation fault" set.

4. Implement call and return RPC primitives using the asynchronous message-passing primitives.

5. Suppose there are three different systems, each having the same procedure, but supporting different RPC semantics. If a call is made to the RPC on each of these, how will the state of the systems differ if (a) no failures occur while the RPC is executing, and (b) if the nodes fail while executing the RPC?

6. Implement the CSP type of communication using the RPC primitives.

7. We say that $m_1 \rightarrow m_2$ if $s(m_1) \rightarrow s(m_2)$ and $m_1||m_2$ if $s(m_1)||s(m_2)$, where $s(m_i)$ is the event of sending the message m_i. Consider the

execution of a system shown in Fig. 2.8. What is the relationship between (m_1, m_2), (m_1, m_3), (m_5, m_7), and (m_7, m_8)?

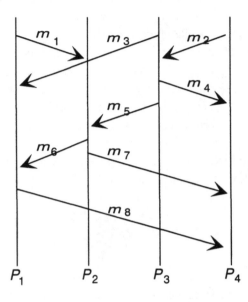

Figure 2.8: An example execution

8. Consider a clock which assigns a timestamp to a message which is the number of messages sent or received by the node before sending this message. Does this clock satisfy the clock condition?

9. Suppose that the clocks of different nodes which are used to timestamp messages are always within β of each other's time as well as the real time. What conditions should be satisfied by the network such that this set of clocks satisfies the clock condition? If the partial order relation is extended to total order and any tie is broken by using the ordering on node identifiers, is this total order unique?

10. For the example shown in Fig. 2.5, give another execution sequence.

11. The granularity of the primitive actions — the ones that are executed indivisibly — is crucial in determining the set of consistent states. Suppose there are n parallel components in a cobegin-coend statement, and each is executed indivisibly. What are the possible execution sequences and the consistent states for such a system?

References

[AL81] T. Anderson, and P. A. Lee. *Fault Tolerance Principles and Practice.* Englewood Cliffs, NJ: Prentice Hall, 1981.

[And83] G. R. Andrews. "Concepts and Notations for Concurrent Programming." *ACM Computing Surveys*, pp. 3–44, March 1983.

[BN84] A. D. Birrell, and B. J. Nelson. "Implementing Remote Procedure Calls." *ACM Transactions on Computer Systems*, 2(1):39–59, February 1984.

[CAS86] F. Cristian, H. Aghili, and R. Strong. "Clock Synchronization in the Presence of Omissions and Performance Faults, and Processor Joins." *16th International Symposium on Fault Tolerant Computing Systems*, June 1986.

[CL85] K. M. Chandy, and L. Lamport. "Distributed Snapshots: Determining Global States of Distributed Systems." *ACM Transactions on Computer Systems*, 3(1):63–75, 1985.

[Dij75] E. W. Dijkstra. "Guarded Commands, Nondeterminacy, and Formal Derivation of Programs." *Communications of the ACM*, 18(8):453–457, August 1975.

[Hoa78] C. A. R. Hoare. "Communicating Sequential Processes." *Communications of the ACM*, 21(8):666–677, August 1978.

[Lam78] L. Lamport. "Time, Clocks, and Ordering of Events." *Communications of the ACM*, 21(7):558–565, July 1978.

[MB76] R. M. Metcalfe, and D. R. Boggs. "Ethernet: Distributed Packet Switching for Local Computer Networks." *Communications of the ACM*, 19(6):395–404, July 1976.

[MS92] S. Mishra, and R. D. Schlicthing. *Abstractions for Constructing Dependable Distributed Systems.* Technical Report TR 92-19. Tucson, Arizona: Department of Computer Science, University of Arizona, 1992.

[Nel81] B. J. Nelson. "Remote Procedure Call." Ph.D. Thesis, Department of Computer Science, Carnegie-Mellon University, Pittsburgh, Pennsylvania, 1981.

[OL82] S. Owicki, and L. Lamport. "Proving Liveness Properties of Concurrent Programs." *ACM Transactions on Programming Language and Systems*, 4(3):155–495, 1982.

[PS88] F. Panzieri, and S. K. Shrivastava. "Rajdoot: A Remote Procedure Call Mechanism Supporting Orphan Detection and Killing." *IEEE Transactions on Software Engineering*, 14(1):30–37, January 1988.

[RC89] K. Ravindran, and S. T. Chanson. "Failure Transparency in Remote Procedure Calls." *IEEE Transactions on Computers*, 38(8):1173–1187, August 1989.

[SDR82] J. F. Shoch, Y. K. Dalal, and D. D. Redell. "Evolution of the Ethernet Local Computer Network." *IEEE Computer*, pp. 896–901, August 1982.

[Sil89] A. Silbershatz. "Communication and Synchronization in Distributed Programs." *IEEE Transactions on Software Engineering*, SE-5:542–546, November 1989.

[SP82] S. K. Shrivastava, and F. Panzieri. "The Design of a Reliable Remote Procedure Call Mechanism." *IEEE Transactions on Computers*, C-31(7):692–697, July 1982.

[Sta87] W. Stallings. *Local Networks, an Introduction*. MacMillan Publishing Company, 2nd edition, 1987.

[Tan88] A. S. Tanenbaum. *Computer Networks*. Englewood Cliffs, NJ: Prentice Hall, 1988.

Chapter 3

Basic Building Blocks

The goal of fault tolerant systems is to continue to provide services despite the failure of some of its components. The major components of a distributed system are its nodes and the communication network. Different methods exist to provide fault tolerant services in a distributed system. Most of these schemes make implicit and explicit assumptions about the behavior of the system and its components, and their failure modes. These assumptions are made frequently, and many methods for supporting fault tolerance depend critically on these assumptions. That is why we consider these assumptions and the methods for supporting them as the "basic building blocks."

Assumptions are most frequently made about the relationship between the clocks of the different processors, the availability of data beyond failures, the behavior of nodes during failures, and the reliability of the communication network. In many cases, the clocks of the different processors are assumed to be synchronized. As we shall see, synchronizing clocks is not a trivial problem and special protocols are needed for it, particularly if failures can occur in the system. Another assumption often made is that some data is available even after failures occur. That is, there is some storage that is immune to failures in the system. Along with this, it is frequently assumed that the processors fail in a "nice" manner and do not corrupt existing data or behave arbitrarily while failing. Both these assumptions ordinarily do not hold, and extra hardware, along with protocols, is needed to satisfy these assumptions. In addition, many fault tolerant schemes also assume that if a node fails in a "nice" manner its failure can be detected by other nodes in the system. This failure detection requires fault diagnosis protocols. It is also typically assumed that the network provides a reliable message service between two nodes, as long as the network is connected. Supporting this also requires protocols.

In this chapter we discuss the abstractions that are commonly assumed to be provided by a distributed system, and discuss how these abstractions can be supported. We consider each of these abstractions a "building block," upon which fault tolerant applications can be constructed. For each of the "building blocks" we first specify the problem, and then discuss some methods to implement a system from existing components (that typically do not provide the desired property) that support the property of the "building block."

3.1 Byzantine Agreement

Often it is assumed that when a component in a computer system fails, it behaves in a certain well-defined manner, though its behavior may be different from its failure-free behavior. Examples of these types of failures are a component always showing a 0 at the output (stuck at 0), or simply stopping execution. However, in the most general case, when a component or a system fails, its behavior can be totally arbitrary. In particular, the faulty component/system may send totally different information to the different components with which it communicates. With such types of failures, reaching agreement between different components is quite complex. The problem of reaching agreement in a system where components can fail in an arbitrary manner is called the *Byzantine generals problem*. As defined earlier, the failure mode in which a component behaves totally arbitrarily and may even send different information to different components is called a Byzantine failure. We will refer to protocols that are used to reach agreement with Byzantine failures as the *Byzantine agreement protocols*.

Byzantine agreement is an important problem, since the failure mode considered in this problem is most general, and if we can handle it satisfactorily, we can be sure that most types of failures can be masked. Also, real computer systems/components often behave arbitrarily when they fail. Hence, if we want the components to fail in a certain manner, we have to construct such a system from systems that can fail in any manner. In other words, if we want a component with a "nice" failure mode on which a fault tolerant system can be built to mask the failure, we have to build it from ordinary components that may fail in an arbitrary manner. We will see later how a solution to the Byzantine generals problem is used to support fail stop processors, which are frequently assumed in protocols for fault tolerance in distributed systems. A Byzantine agreement protocol is therefore a building block for other building blocks.

3.1.1 Problem Definition and Impossibility Results

The Byzantine generals problem needs a careful definition. We will consider a system with many components in which components exchange information with each other. We will consider a distributed system in which nodes are the components and information is exchanged by message passing. The components (nodes) may be faulty and may exhibit Byzantine failures. That is, a faulty node may send different values to different nodes (for the same data).

The basic goal to be achieved is to obtain a consensus among all nonfaulty nodes in this context. Each node has to make a decision based on values it gets from the other nodes in the system. We require all nonfaulty nodes to make the same decision. Hence, the goal is to ensure that all nonfaulty nodes get the same set of values. If all nonfaulty nodes get the same set of values from different nodes, consensus can easily be achieved by all nodes using the same procedure for making the decision. The problem is complicated by the possibility that a faulty node may send different values to different nodes. So a simple message exchange method for transmitting values of different nodes will not work (this can suffice in a failure-free environment, or in some situations with simpler failure modes).

To ensure that each nonfaulty node receives the same set of values, we can state a simpler requirement that is equivalent. The requirement is that every nonfaulty node in the system uses the same value for a node i for decision making. Clearly, if this property is satisfied for all nodes, we can say that the set of values at each nonfaulty node is the same. Hence, the general problem of consensus is reduced to agreement by nodes in a system on the value for a particular node. This solution can then be used to disseminate values of all the nodes in the systems. This is stated formally as the following two requirements [LSP82]:

1. All nonfaulty nodes use the same value $v(i)$ for a node i.

2. If the sending node i is nonfaulty, then every nonfaulty node uses the value i sends.

This problem is also called the *interactive consistency* problem. Note that this formulation allows any type of behavior during failure, and that the sending node (node i) may itself be faulty. Any solution to this problem should take this into account. In particular, a solution to this problem must consider the possibility of a faulty node acting "maliciously" and sending messages that will thwart the consensus process.

Given a protocol to solve this problem, the protocol can be used by each node to send its value to other nodes. Then each node can use the same procedure to take its decision based on the values obtained from the different nodes, thereby achieving consensus.

The Byzantine agreement problem is hard because the information sent by a node to another cannot be trusted. Hence, to agree on a value sent by a node, besides getting the value from that node, the value as received by other nodes is also needed to verify the original value. The problem becomes complex, since these "forwarding" nodes may also be faulty (and may behave arbitrarily or maliciously). The problem can be solved only if the number of faulty nodes in the system is limited.

If the distributed system is asynchronous (i.e., there is no bound on the relative speeds of nodes or the communication delays), then it can be shown [FLP85] that agreement is impossible if even one processor can fail, and even if the failure is a crash failure, which is much more benign than Byzantine failure. This is because in such systems the failure of a node to send a message (because it is faulty) cannot be distinguished from the situation where the node and the communication network are extremely slow. In such a situation, a node can never detect the absence of a message with certainty. Consequently, a faulty node can block the consensus algorithm merely by not sending a message. Hence, most of the algorithms proposed for solving the Byzantine generals problem are for synchronous distributed systems where the message delays and the differences in the relative speeds of processors are bounded.

For the rest of this section we assume that the distributed system is synchronous. Let us first see that in a three node system, if one node is faulty, this problem cannot be solved if ordinary message passing is employed by nodes [LSP82]. Suppose the nodes need to agree to a Boolean value: true (1) or false (0). Let us consider the two scenarios shown in Fig. 3.1 with one of the three nodes as faulty [LSP82].

In the first scenario, one of the receiving nodes j is faulty, and though the sender sends it a 1, it transmits to node i that a 0 was sent by the sender. In the second scenario, the sending node itself is faulty, and it sends a 1 to node i and a 0 to node j, which the node j faithfully forwards to i. Both these situations are indistinguishable to node i, and it cannot decide whether the value sent by the sender should be considered as correct, or the value forwarded by node j. If it decides to accept the value sent by the sender (i.e., 1), then in the same scenario node j will accept the value 0. This will violate the second requirement.

It has been shown [LSP82, PSL80, FLM86] that with ordinary messages it is impossible to solve this problem unless more than two-thirds of the nodes are nonfaulty. That is, the number of faulty nodes has to be less than one-third of the total number of nodes. To cope with m faulty nodes, at least $3m + 1$ nodes are needed to reach consensus.

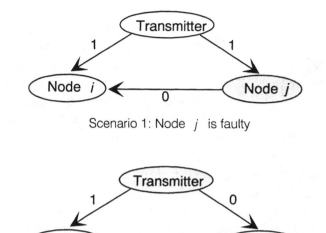

Figure 3.1: Two scenarios

The problem is simplified if the messages can be "signed." That is, a node can attach a "signature" to each message it sends. The message with a signature is such that no node can tamper with the message contents of a nonfaulty node without the alteration being detected by other nonfaulty nodes. Hence, when a nonfaulty sender sends a message to other nodes, a faulty node cannot tamper with its message and forward it to other nodes. If it attempts to do that, the tampering will be detected. In this situation, an arbitrary number of faulty nodes can be tolerated [LSP82]

3.1.2 Protocol with Ordinary Messages

Let us now discuss a protocol for solving the Byzantine generals problem in a distributed system, where ordinary messages are employed. As mentioned above, consensus can be reached in the presence of m faulty nodes only if the total of the nodes is at least $3m + 1$. We assume that a fault-free node executes the protocol correctly; a faulty node can behave in any manner. First, let us define more precisely the assumptions we are making about the message passing system [LSP82].

A1. Every message that is sent by a node is delivered correctly by the message system to the receiver.

A2. The receiver of a message knows which node has sent the message.

A3. The absence of a message can be detected.

Assumption A1 ensures that a faulty node cannot interfere with communication between other nodes. A2 ensures that a faulty node cannot masquerade as another node. This assumption has some implications for the underlying network. It essentially means that there is a dedicated physical channel between two nodes, and no message switching is used. With switching, an intermediate faulty node in the path can corrupt the message. The practical implication of these two assumptions is that the physical communication network must be fully connected, i.e., there must be a direct physical line between any pair of nodes. A3 ensures that a faulty node cannot foil the consensus attempt by simply not sending messages as required by the protocol. This assumption is typically implemented using timeouts, and requires clocks at different nodes to work at the same rate. It also implies that the message delays and the differences in the relative speeds of processors are bounded.

The algorithm presented here will work only if the message passing system satisfies the assumptions A1 through A3. It was proposed by Lamport, Shostak, and Pease in [LSP82]. This algorithm will be referred to as *interactive consistency algorithm, ICA(m)*, for all nonnegative integers m. The integer m represents the number of faulty nodes. Let n represent the total number of nodes. For this algorithm to achieve consensus, we must have $n \geq 3m + 1$. One node is designated as the *transmitter*, whose value has to be agreed upon by other nodes. Other nodes are *receivers*. If a node does not send a message it is supposed to send (recall that our assumption ensures that this will be detected by a receiver), the receiver node uses a *default value*. We take this default value to be 0. The algorithm is specified inductively, and is given in Fig. 3.2 [LSP82].

This algorithm works in rounds, each round consisting of message exchanges between nodes. In round 1, the transmitter sends values to other $n - 1$ nodes. The receiver nodes cannot trust the values they receive from the transmitter, since the transmitter may be faulty. Hence, a receiver node first determines from other nodes the value they received from the transmitter. A node takes the majority values it gets from other nodes and the value it got from the original transmitter. This majority value is taken to be the value sent by the transmitter.

In other words, each receiver has to communicate the value it receives from the transmitter in round 1 to others (or an arbitrary value, if it has failed) in round 2. In this round, each of the receivers acts as a transmitter, and sends messages to nodes other than the transmitter (and itself). That is, we can consider it as a system of $n - 1$ nodes, in which each node sends $n - 2$ messages. Messages sent by a node i in this round essentially aim to inform other nodes about the value it received from the transmitter. However, since a receiver cannot trust a transmitter in this round (since a node which is "forwarding" the message of the original transmitter may be faulty), by the same argument as used after round 1, now the version of values as received by other nodes is needed to determine the value sent by a node. For this, messages

Algorithm ICA(0).

1. The transmitter sends its value to all the other $n - 1$ nodes.

2. Each node uses the value it receives from the transmitter, or uses the default value, if it receives no value.

Algorithm ICA(m), m > 0.

1. The transmitter sends its value to all the other $n - 1$ nodes.

2. Let v_i be the value the node i receives from the transmitter, or else be the default value if it receives no value. Node i acts as the transmitter in algorithm $ICA(m - 1)$ to send the value v_i to each of the other $n - 2$ nodes.

3. For each node i, let v_j be the value received by the node j ($j \neq i$). Node i uses the value $majority(v_1, ..., v_{n-1})$.

Figure 3.2: Interactive consistency algorithm

are sent in round 3. Once again, for a node i, a majority of the values (one received from the node i as a message in round 2, and $n - 3$ messages received from other nodes from round 3) is taken to determine the value sent by a node i. This value is taken as the value sent by the original transmitter to the node i. A majority of these values was taken after round 1 to determine the transmitter's value.

This distrust in round 2 requires round 3 of message exchange. In round 3, the system can be considered as consisting of $n - 2$ nodes, and each node will send, for each message it receives in round 2, its version to the remaining $n - 3$ nodes. Again, a majority is taken as the value. However, again due to the possibility of faulty nodes, messages of this round cannot be trusted, and hence the next round is needed to agree on the value sent on this round, which requires another round, and so on.

Eventually, in round $m + 1$, ICA(0) will be called. In this case, the recursion ends, and a node, for each message it gets in round m, simply transmits it (if the node is faulty, it may transmit any value). A majority of the values directly received in the messages is taken to be the value sent by a node in round m. This value then percolates up the recursion chain.

To better understand the protocol, consider a system with 1 faulty node and a total of 4 nodes [LSP82]. First consider the case where the transmitter is reliable, and one of the receivers (node 3) is faulty. In this case, the transmitter during its execution of $ICA(1)$ will send the same value (say x) to the three remaining nodes (one of which is faulty). During execution of $ICA(0)$, the two reliable nodes will forward the value they received from the transmitter (x) faithfully to other nodes. However, the faulty node can send any value to others. Suppose it sends y to nodes 1 and 2. In this case, node 2 (and node 1) will get the values (x, x, y). The majority of this is x. Hence, the value agreed to by node 2 is the same as the one sent by the reliable transmitter node. This situation for node 2 is shown in Scenario 1 of Fig. 3.3.

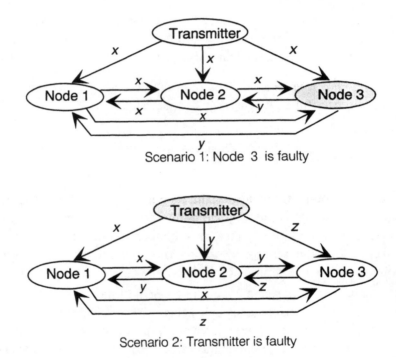

Scenario 1: Node 3 is faulty

Scenario 2: Transmitter is faulty

Figure 3.3: Algorithm $ICA(1)$

Now let us consider the case where the transmitter itself is faulty, and the receivers are reliable. This is shown in Scenario 2 of Fig. 3.3. Suppose the faulty transmitter sends x to node 1, y to node 2, and z to node 3 during $ICA(1)$. Since the nodes 1, 2, and 3 are reliable, during $ICA(0)$ they will transmit faithfully to others the value they received from the transmitter. Hence, each one of them will get the values (x, y, z). Since each executes the same *majority* algorithm, they will agree on the same value, regardless of the actual values of x, y, and z, thereby satisfying the requirements.

Now let us try to understand intuitively why taking a majority works, and why this algorithm can only handle m faulty nodes in a system of $3n + 1$ nodes. A formal proof can be found in [LSP82]. For $ICA(m)$, in the last round, the system for this round of message exchanges consists of $(3m + 1) - m = 2m + 1$ nodes, as there are originally $3m + 1$ nodes, and in each new round, the original transmitter is not included in the system. In the worst case, all the faulty nodes are still in the system. That is, all the transmitters were reliable, and the faulty nodes are receivers in the mth round. The value sent by these nodes in the $m + 1$ round (with $ICA(0)$) will be used to determine the majority. Since there are, at most, m faulty nodes, and a total of $2m + 1$ nodes, a majority of nodes are fault-free. Since each fault-free node takes a majority, all the fault-free nodes will agree on the same value, since a majority of nodes are fault-free and a fault-free node faithfully "forwards" a message. If there were more faulty nodes, then a majority agreement may lead to different nodes agreeing on different values in round m (since faulty nodes may send a different value to different nodes), which will then affect the values in earlier rounds.

It is clear that with the protocol described by $ICA(m)$, different nodes in the system can reach an agreement on the value for the transmitter node, as long as there are no more than m nodes that are faulty (and there are a total of at least $3m + 1$ nodes). Clearly, this can be used by all the nodes to reach an agreement on their values. Hence, by executing $ICA(m)$ for each node, each node in the system will have the same value for every node. Clearly then, all the nonfaulty nodes will reach the same decision, if the decision is based on the values from the different nodes. In other words, a consensus can be reached by different nodes in a distributed system using an $ICA(m)$ protocol.

3.1.3 Protocol with Signed Messages

The protocol $ICA(m)$ is complicated because it has to handle the case that a faulty receiver node may "forward" a different value from the one received by it from the repeater. And a receiver of this message has no way of determining whether the sender node has tampered with the original message. The problem becomes easier if we restrict the ability of nodes to tamper with messages. This can be achieved by a transmitter sending a "signed" message. That is, a node adds a digital signature to its message. The signature is such that if any node changes the contents of the message it receives from the transmitter and then forwards the altered message, this change can be detected by the receiver. The signature can be obtained using encryption techniques.

With signed messages, the impossibility result of being able to tolerate m faults in a $3m + 1$ node system does not hold. Agreement can be reached for an arbitrary number of faulty nodes.

We present here a protocol for satisfying the interactive consistency conditions in a system where a node can send signed messages. This protocol was presented by Lamport et al. in [LSP82]. In this algorithm, a transmitter node sends a signed message to other nodes. A node adds its signature to the message it receives, and transmits it in the next round of message exchange to other nodes. If the receiver node is not faulty, its message will have the same content as the message it received from the transmitter. If the receiver node is faulty, it must also send the message containing the same value, or not send the message at all (the case that it alters the message and then gets caught by the receivers can be modeled as its not sending the message).

Let the set of values received by a node be V. Note that this is the set of values, not the set of messages (many messages may contain the same value). If the transmitter node is fault-free, then the set of values received by a node will contain a single value, the one sent by the transmitter. Only if the transmitter is faulty can multiple values be received by a node. From the set of values, to obtain a single value, the function $choice(V)$ is used. If V consists of a single value v, then $choice(V)$ is v; if V is empty then $choice(V)$ is some default value, say 0. In other cases, the choice could be the median or some other value. The important thing is that all nodes use the same function for selecting the final value.

If a node i sends a value x to some node, then the node appends its signature to the message and this is represented as $x : i$. When a node j receives this value and then further passes it on to another node, the message is represented as $x : i : j$. The protocol $SM(m)$ reaches agreement with up to m faulty nodes, where nodes send only signed messages. $SM(m)$ is shown in Fig. 3.4 [LSP82] (we assume that the transmitter is the node 0).

In step 2, a node ignores a message that contains a value v that it had received earlier, and does not forward this message to other nodes. Similarly, it ignores any message that does not have the correct sequence of signatures. Timeouts are used to determine when no more messages will arrive.

If the transmitter is not faulty, then it will send the same value v to all the other nodes. Since its signature cannot be forged, no node can receive any other value in step 2(B) of the algorithm. Hence, any nonfaulty node i will have a single entry in V_i, namely v. By definition, $choice$ will select that value.

If the transmitter is faulty, then it can send different values to different nodes. To ensure that each nonfaulty node selects the same value by applying $choice$, we have to ensure that whenever a nonfaulty node i adds a value v to V_i, then another nonfaulty node j also adds value v to V_j. If i receives the value from the transmitter in step 2(A), then it sends it to j, and j will add it to V_j. If i got it as a sequence of

Algorithm SM(m)

Initially $V_i = \phi$

1. The transmitter signs its value and sends to all other nodes.

2. For each i:

   (A) If node i receives a message of the form $v : 0$ from the transmitter then
       (i) it sets V_i to $\{v\}$, and (ii) it sends the message $v : 0 : i$ to every other
       node.

   (B) If node i receives a message of the form $v : 0 : j_1 : j_2 : ... : j_k$ and v is
       not in V_i, then (i) it adds v to V_i, and (ii) if $k < m$ it sends the message
       $v : 0 : j_1 : j_2 : ... : j_k : i$ to every node other than $j_1, j_2, ..., j_k$.

3. For each i: when node i will receive no more messages, it considers the final
   value as $choice(V_i)$.

Figure 3.4: Agreement with signed messages

signed message $v : 0 : j_1 : j_2 : ... : j_k$, then if j is in the sequence $j_1, j_2, ..., j_k$, it
implies that j already has v. If j is not in $j_1, j_2, ..., j_k$, then if $k < m$, i will send
him a message containing v in step 2(B)(ii). If $k = m$, then since the transmitter is
faulty, at most $m - 1$ of the remaining nodes are faulty. This implies that at least one
of the $j_1, j_2, ..., j_m$ nodes is nonfaulty. This nonfaulty node must have sent v to j.
Hence, in all situations j gets the value v, which ensures that all nonfaulty nodes get
the same set of values, and therefore select the same value.

3.1.4   Discussion

The algorithms described above work in rounds, and are quite expensive in terms
of the number of rounds and the number of messages needed to reach agreement.
Algorithm $ICA(m)$ requires $m + 1$ rounds of message exchange. It has been shown
that no deterministic algorithm for Byzantine agreement can reach an agreement in
less than $m + 1$ rounds [FLM86]. Hence, in terms of the number of rounds, $ICA(m)$
is optimal. However, the number of messages required by $ICA(m)$ is exponential,
since each invocation of $ICA(m - i)$ involves $n - i - 1$ invocations of $ICA(m - i - 1)$,
making the number of messages proportional to $(n - 1)(n - 2)...(n - m - 1)$. Since
m can be $(n - 1)/3$ we obtain the exponential message complexity $O(n^m)$. Clearly,

this algorithm is a quite expensive in terms of number of messages. Like $ICA(m)$, the algorithm $SM(m)$ (for signed messages) requires $m+1$ rounds, which is optimal. $SM(m)$ also requires an exponential number of messages.

Other, more efficient, algorithms have also been proposed. A deterministic algorithm which requires $2m + 3$ rounds but only $O(t^3 log(m))$ messages for $n = 3m + 1$ has been presented in [DFF$^+$82]. Its extension to handle the general case of $n \geq 3m + 1$ requires $2m + 3$ rounds and $O(nm + m^3 log(m))$ messages. An algorithm for signed messages that uses only $m + 1$ rounds and $O(nm)$ messages has been proposed in [DS83]. A simple and efficient solution that uses a broadcast primitive has been proposed in [STS87]. This broadcast primitive uses ordinary messages to provide properties of authentication. The number of messages required by the protocol is $O(nm^2)$.

For $ICA(m)$ and $SM(m)$ we assumed that the communication network was fully connected, so that any two processors could communicate directly. The problem clearly becomes more complicated if the network is not fully connected. It has been shown [LSP82] that with minor modifications $ICA(m)$ and $SM(m)$ will still be able to achieve agreement in a network that is not fully connected. Another assumption made by most deterministic protocols is that all the processors begin the protocol simultaneously. In an actual distributed system this condition is hard to satisfy and we need algorithms to solve the associated synchronization problem. This problem is called the Distributed Firing Squad (DFS) problem [CDDS85]. Any algorithm for this problem must satisfy the following two conditions: (1) If any correct processor receives a message to start a DFS synchronization, then at some future time all correct processors will "fire," and (2) all correct processors fire at the same time. Algorithms for this problem have been proposed in [CDDS85].

The proposed solutions mentioned above are all deterministic and guarantee agreement at a certain cost in terms of the number of rounds and the number of messages. The impossibility of having deterministic agreement protocols in an asynchronous distributed system has led to randomized solutions (for example, [Ben83, Rab83, Bra87]). These randomized protocols require "coins" that can be tossed with fairness. The value of these coins are used by all nodes to try to reach agreement. Like deterministic protocols, these protocols also work in rounds. However, there is no strict bound on the number of rounds needed to reach agreement. Generally, the randomized algorithms work with the expected number of rounds needed to reach agreement. The advantage of randomized protocols is that their expected running time (or the expected number of rounds needed to reach agreement) is often considerably less than that of deterministic algorithms.

3.2 Synchronized Clocks

As defined earlier, a distributed system consists of a number of autonomous nodes that are connected by a communication network and which have their own separate clocks. Clocks being physical processes, they naturally differ from each other. They can show different "times" from each other, and can also drift from the external accepted reference time. We have seen in the previous chapter that with logical clocks we can define a partial order on the set of events. Though this order can be extended to a total order, that total order may not have any relationship with ordering based on global time. Without synchronizing the clocks, it is not possible to say for every pair of events which event "occurred before" the other in time.

Synchronized clocks is a requirement for some applications in distributed systems. The total order that can be imposed with synchronized clocks is sometimes needed by applications. Even if fault tolerance is not required, synchronized clocks are frequently needed. As we shall see, even approaches for implementing some of the "building blocks" assume that the clocks of the different nodes are synchronized. Hence, it is desirable that the clocks of the different nodes are synchronized with each other.

Synchronization may be *external* or *internal*. External clock synchronization requires maintaining processor clocks within some given maximum deviation from an external time reference, which keeps real time. Internal clock synchronization requires that the clocks of different processors be kept within some maximum relative deviation of each other. Externally synchronized clocks are also internally synchronized, though the reverse is not true. Whereas internal synchronization may be needed to measure duration of distributed activities within the system, external clock synchronization may be needed in real-time systems where the real time of occurrence of events may be specified.

The problem of clock synchronization has various aspects. Not only may the clocks of different nodes have different times, they may also be running at different speeds. An attempt to synchronize clocks will require different processors to get the value of other clocks. Since communication is possible only through the communication network, there will be a delay between the sending of a message by one node and the receipt of the message by another. This implies that the network delay has to be assessed properly if the clock values of other nodes are to be determined. And network delays can vary randomly.

Perhaps the biggest problem in clock synchronization is the possibility of faulty clocks. If some of the clocks are faulty, then the clock synchronization protocols should try to ignore the values of these faulty clocks. If we allow faulty clocks to behave in an arbitrary manner, the problem gets even more complex. Specifically, a clock may be "dual-faced." That is, the faulty clock may give different values of time to different processes. This clearly makes the task of synchronizing the clocks of different processors more difficult.

3.2.1   Problem Definition and Background

We assume that there is a hardware clock in each node, which is controlled by a process at that node. Since the controlling process is the one that informs others about the time shown by the clock, the failure of a clock can be viewed as the failure of its process. For clock synchronization, we consider a failure model which can capture the failure of the process as well as the failure of physical clocks. The processes are numbered $1, 2, ..., i, ...$, and are assumed to be connected by a communication network.

Let $C_i(t)$ denote the reading of a clock C_i (i.e., the value returned by the process controlling this clock if an attempt is made to read this clock) at the physical time t. Let $c_i(T)$ denote the real time when the ith clock reaches a value T. For synchronized clocks, we want the values of different clocks to be very close to each other, and close to the real time as well. For explanation purposes, we assume that a clock is continuous (even though physical clocks are discrete).

The clocks may be faulty or nonfaulty. If a clock is nonfaulty, we assume that the time it shows is close to physical time. That is, it runs at a rate close to the physical time, and its drift is bounded by some constant. For a nonfaulty clock C_i, this can be specified as:

$$|d(C_i/dt) - 1| < \rho.$$

For a typical crystal controlled clock, ρ is of the order of 10^{-5}. We make no assumptions about the faulty clocks. Specifically, a faulty process (representing the clock) may be malicious and send different values to different processes requesting the value of the clock.

We assume that a process can read a clock only by sending a message to the process controlling that clock. This is important, as it implies that when a process wants to read some clock, it will have to send a message, which will take some amount of time to reach the destination. Then the process will respond by sending a message, which will also take some time to reach the requester. These delays make the problem of estimating the value of a clock difficult, but are intrinsic to the problem of clock synchronization.

We now specify the requirements of clock synchronization. There are two basic requirements [LM85].

S1. At any time the value of all the nonfaulty processors' clocks must be approximately equal. That is, for some constant β:

$$|C_i(t) - C_j(t)| \leq \beta.$$

S2. There is a small bound Σ on the amount by which a nonfaulty processor's clock is changed during each resynchronization.

The first condition is the basic condition stating that the clocks be close to each other. However, that condition can be satisfied trivially by setting each clock to some value (say 0) at each resynchronization. To disallow these trivial solutions, the second condition is required. Also, with the assumption that the nonfaulty clocks run at approximately the same rate as a reliable clock keeping physical time, this requirement ensures that the clock values never become too far from the real time.

The goal of clock synchronization protocols is to satisfy these two conditions. The protocols can broadly be classified as falling into two general categories: deterministic and probabilistic. In deterministic protocols, the clock synchronization conditions and the bounds are guaranteed. However, these protocols often require some assumptions about message delays. Probabilistic clock synchronization does not require any assumption about maximum message delays, but guarantees precision only with a probability.

3.2.2   Deterministic Clock Synchronization

In deterministic clock synchronization protocols, a required precision is guaranteed. Most of the deterministic clock synchronization protocols assume some maximum bound on message delays. This bound is used to detect the absence of messages (since faulty processes may not send messages). Various protocols have been proposed [CAS85, LM85, LL88]. Here we will describe one particular protocol in some detail.

First, let us see the similarity of this problem with the Byzantine generals problem discussed above, and some bounds and limitations. One approach to synchronization is that a process reads all the clocks in the system and then sets its value to the median of these values. If only a minority of processes are faulty, this approach can work. However, due to the possibility of dual-faced clocks, the directly read value of a clock cannot be used. For this approach to work, we require that:

1. Any two nonfaulty processes obtain approximately the same value of a clock C_i.

2. If C_i is nonfaulty, then all nonfaulty processes obtain approximately the correct value of C_i.

These conditions are similar to the interactive consistency conditions discussed above. This shows that the clock synchronization problem has a close similarity with the Byzantine generals problem. In fact, the solutions proposed in [LM85] use this similarity to extend the interactive consistency algorithms described in [LSP82] to achieve clock synchronization.

Just like in the Byzantine generals problem, there are some possibility and impossibility results. We state some of them here, without giving proofs. For details, the reader is referred to [DHS84]. A deterministic solution to the problem of clock synchronization can exist only if the number of faulty clocks is less than $n/3$ in a system that has n clocks and that employs ordinary messages. However, if there is a bound on the rate at which messages can be generated, or if unforgeable signed messages can be sent by processes, then clock synchronization can be achieved as long as the fault does not disconnect the network. If max is the maximum time delay for message delivery, and min is the minimum time delay, and there are n processes, then for a deterministic clock synchronization protocol, the closeness of synchronization that can be attained is roughly $(max - min)(1 - 1/n)$ [LL88]. Stronger results on the closeness of synchronization can also be proved.

Now we describe the solution proposed by Lundelius-Welch and Lynch [LL88]. This solution can handle all types of failures, assuming that the number of faulty processes is less than $n/3$ for an n process system. It requires only n^2 messages in a synchronization round (as compared to the exponential number of messages used in [LM85]), and the size of the adjustment made to clocks in each round is independent of the number of faulty processes.

It is assumed that the hardware clock is never altered, and that the drift of a correct clock is bounded by ρ. The value of the logical clock, or the value returned by the process reading the clock, is obtained by applying a correction to the value provided by the hardware clock. That is:

$$C(t) = H(t) + CORR(t),$$

where $H(t)$ is the time shown by the hardware clock at time t, and $CORR(t)$ is the adjustment function, whose value changes with time. At each resynchronization, the value of $CORR(t)$ is changed. The logical clock value is changed by changing the value of this function.

No assumption is made about the behavior of a faulty process. However, it is assumed that the number of faulty processes is at most f, such that the total number of processes in the system is at least $3f + 1$.

All clocks are assumed to be initially synchronized to approximately the same value. That is:

$$|c_i(T_0) - c_j(T_0)| < \beta.$$

This says that the difference between the real times when the two clocks i and j reach a value T_0 is at most β. The time T_0 is the time when the processes are supposed to start the clock synchronization protocol. The clock synchronization algorithm discussed below can also, with some minor modifications, be used to ensure this initial condition.

Each process can communicate directly with any other process. If a process sends a message to another at real-time t, and that message is received at real-time t', then the *message delay* is $t' - t$. It is assumed that there is a bound on the message delay. A message is delivered in $[\delta - \epsilon, \delta + \epsilon]$ time, for a fixed δ and ϵ, with $\delta > \epsilon$. Conceptually, the message system is viewed as a global message buffer in which the sender puts the message, and from which the receiver process takes the message. A message is received when the *receive* event occurs. It is also assumed that when a process sets a timer for time t, then a TIMER message is sent to the process at local clock time t (i.e., at local time t the message is put in the buffer).

The algorithm executes in rounds as follows [LL88]. The ith round is triggered when the clock of a process reaches some predefined time T_i. After a round, the next round is started when a time ΔT has elapsed. This ΔT is predecided, and the same for each process. Initially, it is assumed that a START message arrives at each process when the logical clock of the process reaches T_0, and starts the clock synchronization algorithm. When the local clock of a process j reaches T_i, then the process broadcasts a message containing T_i. It also collects the similar ith round messages of as many other processes as it can within a bounded amount of time and records their arrival times according to its own local clock. This waiting period is chosen to ensure that if a correct process has sent a message, it will be received by a nonfaulty process within its waiting period.

The bounded waiting time can be determined by the parameters described above. By assumption, when a process j's clock reaches T_i, another process k's clock will reach this value within a time β. At that time k will broadcast T_i to all processes. This message can take up to $\delta + \epsilon$ real time to arrive at process k. Hence, the process j will surely receive k's message containing T_i within the real time $\beta + \delta + \epsilon$ after its own clock reaches the value T_i. Since clock rates may differ by ρ from the real time, the bounded time, as measured by j's clock, within which j should receive the message of k containing T_i is:

$$(1 + \rho)(\beta + \delta + \epsilon).$$

Once this time has elapsed on the local clock of a process after its own clock reaches T_i, the process can be sure that it has received the messages from all the nonfaulty processes.

A process calculates the correction function from the set of arrival times of the messages it receives, thereby switching its logical clock to a new value. It then waits for ΔT time to execute the next round. That is, the next round is initiated when its clock reaches $T_i + \Delta T$.

From the set of arrival times (by local clock) of the messages that a process receives, it has to determine the average value of other nonfaulty clocks, which is then used to reset its own logical clock. However, due to the possibility of faulty clocks, a simple averaging function will not work. Since a faulty clock may send different values to different processes, if a simple average is taken, the averages at different nodes can differ by arbitrary amounts, which will cause the clocks of the processes to differ arbitrarily. Hence a fault tolerant averaging function is required.

To prevent dual-faced clocks from misleading different processes, the averaging function works as follows. Since there are, at most, f faulty clocks, the averaging function throws away the top f and the bottom f values from the set of values (i.e., the arrival times of the messages the process receives), and then takes the midpoint of the remaining values. The idea is that in the worst case when the faulty processes represent very high or very low values, all the values of the nonfaulty processes will be in the middle. Hence by discarding the top and bottom f values, we make sure that these values are not considered. In the average case, when some of the values for the faulty clocks also lie in the middle, then there can be no harm in considering these values too for determining the midpoint, and the midpoint will still be close to the midpoint of the values of the correct clocks. This property has been proved formally in [LL88].

We now present the algorithm formally. The main parameters of the algorithm are ρ (bound on the clock drift), β (bound on how far apart the clocks are initially), δ, ϵ (bound on message delays), and ΔT (period between rounds). In addition to these parameters, the algorithm uses the following variables and conventions [LL88]:

- CORR — correction variable, initially empty.

- ARR — array containing the arrival times of the most recent messages. For a process k, ARR[k] is the arrival time of the message from k.

- NOW — represents the current logical clock time.

- *reduce* — a function that is applied to an array and returns the middle values with the f highest and the f lowest values removed.

- *mid* — returns the midpoint of a set of values.

The algorithm is given in Fig. 3.5 [LL88].

do forever

    /* in case messages are received before the process reaches T_i */

        while $u = (m, k)$ from some message m and sender k **do**
           ARR[k] = NOW

    /* fall out of the loop when u = START or TIMER and begin round */
        T := NOW
        broadcast(T)
        set-timer($T + (1 + \rho)(\beta + \delta + \epsilon)$)
        while $u = (m, k)$ for some message m and sender k **do**
           ARR[k] = NOW

    /* fall out of the loop when u = TIMER; end round */
        AV := *mid (reduce (ARR))*
        ADJ := $T + \delta$ - AV
        CORR := CORR + ADJ
        set-timer($T + \Delta T$)
enddo

Figure 3.5: Clock synchronization algorithm

This algorithm is relatively simple. Basically, it collects the arrival times of messages from other processes until its local clock reaches T_i and a TIMER message is generated (which takes the algorithm into its second part). It then broadcasts its clock value, but continues receiving messages from others and waits for a maximum time. These messages are sent by other processes in the second part of their algorithm when their clocks reach T_i. At the expiry of this time it times out, stops collecting the messages, and reaches the last part. For each message it receives, it records the local time of the arrival of the message in the array ARR. All these messages carry the message T_i (the local clock value when the message was sent), though their arrival times may be different. On the arrival times of these messages, it applies the reduce function to remove the highest and the lowest f values. That is, it removes the earliest f and the last f messages it receives. Of the remaining values, it takes the midpoint, represented by AV.

Now let us intuitively see how clock synchronization is achieved. Let us consider a process j. AV is the arrival time of the message that j is going to consider for synchronization. Suppose this message was sent by the process m. When m sent the message, its clock was T_i, and on an average it takes δ time for the message to travel. Hence, when the message arrives at j (i.e., at local time AV), the expected clock value of m is $T_i + \delta$. Hence the clock of j differs from the clock of m by $(T_i + \delta) - AV$. This is the adjustment which j must apply to its local clock in order to set it close to the expected value of the process m. It is referred to as ADJ in the algorithm (the variable T in the algorithm has the value T_i as it is set in the second part of the algorithm, which is initiated when the local clock reaches T_i and the TIMER message is generated). Hence, j sets its clock to what it expects to be the value of the clock at m by adjusting its logical clock by ADJ. This adjustment is done by adding ADJ to the variable CORR which determines the logical clock value.

The formal proof that clock synchronization conditions are satisfied by this protocol is very complex, and is given in [LL88]. Let us get an intuitive feel of how clock synchronization is achieved. By throwing the smallest and the largest f values from ARR, a correct process is left with $n - f$ values. If $n > 3f$, it ensures that of the values left, at least one of them belongs to a nonfaulty clock, and the other values are close to this nonfaulty clock value. Since nonfaulty clocks send correct values to all processes (and at correct times) it ensures that the estimates of the clocks representing the mid value of the reduced ARR at each nonfaulty process will not differ too much. This has been formally proved in [LL88]. It guarantees that when the clocks are set, clocks of nonfaulty processes are close to each other. If the condition $n > 3f$ is not satisfied, then there is no guarantee that after applying the function reduce, ARR will be left with any value belonging to a nonfaulty process. This, in turn, implies that the estimate of values by nonfaulty processes of their respective mids may not be close to each other.

The algorithm works for given values of the parameters. Generally, the parameters ρ, δ, and ϵ are fixed, but the designer has some freedom in the selection of β and ΔT. We may want β to be small to keep the clocks closely synchronized. There is a lower bound on the value of ΔT. The value of ΔT should be such that the local time at which a process j schedules its next broadcast should be greater than the local time of the clock at the moment it is reset, and a message from another nonfaulty process k for a round should arrive at j after j has set the clock for that round. This leads to a bound on ΔT which is [LL88]:

$$\Delta T \leq \beta/4\rho - \epsilon/\rho - \rho(\beta + \delta + \epsilon) - 2\beta - \delta - 2\epsilon.$$

Any combination of ΔT and β that satisfy this inequality will work for the algorithm. If ΔT is fixed, then the closeness of synchronization, in terms of real time, is approximately [LL88]:

$$\beta \approx 4\epsilon + 4\rho\Delta T.$$

In each round the adjustment ADJ is bounded by [LL88]:

$$ADJ \leq (1 + \rho)(\beta + \epsilon) + \rho\delta.$$

The number of messages needed in a round is n^2, where n is the number of processes (clocks) in the system. This is independent of the number of faulty processes.

3.2.3 Probabilistic Clock Synchronization

We now discuss a probabilistic approach to clock synchronization which can only ensure that the clocks will be synchronized with a very high probability, unlike deterministic protocols which always guarantee synchronization (as long as the number of failures is bounded). The advantage of the probabilistic approach is that it does not need any assumption about maximum message delay (which a deterministic protocol needs). That is, message delays are random and unbounded. It can also achieve closer synchronization between clocks. The probabilistic clock synchronization approach that we discuss here was proposed by Cristian [Cri89]. The method assumes that "dual-faced" clocks do not exist, and hence the faults it can handle are not as general as in the algorithm discussed above.

The basic aim of this approach is to synchronize clocks despite arbitrary message delays in the network. Hence the clocks are assumed to be correct. The message delays are unbounded, though there is a minimum delay *min* that exists. This *min* can be computed by considering the minimum time needed to prepare, transmit, and receive a message in the absence of any load or transmission errors.

To read the clock of a process i, a process j sends a message (time = ?) to i. When i receives this message, it replies with a message (time = T), where T is the time on i's clock. The round trip delay for receiving i's clock value, as measured by j's clock, is 2D. With the round trip delay, the time in the received message, and the value of *min*, a process j can make some estimation of the time at node i.

Let t be the real time when j receives a reply from i, and let $2d$ be the real-time round trip delay. Since *min* is the minimum real-time delay, the time of receipt of message, according to i's clock, has to be more than $T + min(1 - \rho)$, where ρ is the bound on the drift of the clocks. Since $2d$ is the total real-time round trip delay, the maximum delay of the return message is $2d - min$. In clock time it can be at most $(2d - min)(1 + \rho)$. Since $2d \leq 2D(1 + \rho)$, the maximum clock time delay is $2D(1 + \rho)(1 + \rho) - min(1 + \rho)$. Ignoring the higher powers of ρ, the delay can be at most $2D(1 + 2\rho) - min(1 + \rho)$. From this, j can infer that at the time j receives the (time = T) message from i, i's clock is in the range:

$$[T + min(1 - \rho), T + 2D(1 + 2\rho) - min(1 + \rho)].$$

Hence from the values of the round trip delay as measured by the local clock, the value of the timestamp in the received message, and the system constants, a node j can estimate the value of the clock at node i within a particular range. Now j has to take some value in this interval as i's clock value. The value taken should be such that it minimizes the error. The error is minimized if the midpoint value is selected. With this, the estimate by i of the value of clock at i at the time it receives the (time = T) message is $C_i = T + D(1 + 2\rho) - min * \rho$. The maximum error possible with this estimation of time is $e = D(1 + 2\rho) - min$.

The maximum error value e can be taken as the precision with which j can read the value of clock of i. Clearly, the shorter the actual round trip delay, the better the precision of reading a clock. It follows from the expression for e that if a process j wants to read the clock of another process i with a specified precision ε, it must discard all reading attempts in which the round trip delay is greater than 2U, where:

$$U = (1 - 2\rho)(\varepsilon + min).$$

If the round trip delay is less than or equal to twice this value, then the required precision can be achieved. Hence, for a given precision, a process may have to make many attempts to read the clock of another process until the round trip delay of an attempt is within the limit. Since the delay is arbitrary and unbounded, there is no guarantee that a small enough round trip delay will be achieved within a finite number of tries. It is due to this that the method is probabilistic. It cannot guarantee that a process can read the clock of another process. However, the probability of failure can be made arbitrarily small by increasing the number of attempts a process makes to read a clock.

Note that in this approach of attempting to read the clock of i, a process j, when it succeeds, knows the precision with which it has read the clock. The best possible precision that is achievable can also be determined. Since min is the minimum delay, U must be greater than min. In clock time we have $U_{min} = min(1 + \rho)$. From this we get $e_{min} = min(1 + \rho)(1 + 2\rho) - min$. By expanding this expression and ignoring all higher powers of ρ, we get $e_{min} = 3 * \rho * min$. This gives the best possible precision that can be achieved using this method.

This method of reading the clock of a process by another process is the basic idea behind probabilistic clock synchronization. A master-slave synchronization protocol was also proposed in [Cri89], in which external synchronization is also achieved. It is assumed that the system has some clocks that are externally synchronized by some other means (e.g., listening to nationally broadcast time). These clocks become the masters, while the rest are slaves. The slaves read the clock of a master using the reading method described above and then synchronize. Clearly, this synchronization is probabilistic. As the slaves synchronize, they achieve internal synchronization as well.

Most deterministic clock synchronization protocols require that a process estimate the value of other clocks. These values are then used to reset the local clock. Any such protocol can be used for synchronizing clocks by using the method described above for reading a remote clock.

3.3 Stable Storage

Techniques for supporting fault tolerance frequently require that some state of the system be available after the failure occurs. That is, it is assumed that the computer system has some *stable storage* whose contents are preserved despite failures. The contents of stable storage are not destroyed or corrupted by a failure. Often it is assumed that a secondary storage system like a disk provides stable storage. Though the data on the disks is non-volatile and usually survives node failures and power outages, disks are not too reliable a form of stable storage. For fault tolerant systems, where high reliability is a fundamental goal, the reliability of stable storage offered by a general disk may not be acceptable. In this section we will define precisely what is meant by stable storage, and then describe some techniques to construct stable storage.

Existence of stable storage is essential in many schemes for supporting fault tolerance. Any scheme that depends on some previously saved state being available (and many schemes fall under this category) will not be able to function reliably without stable storage. For example, if a node fails in a distributed system, nothing can be said about that part of the system state that was controlled by the failed node. The presence of stable storage enables some state information (though perhaps old) to be available despite failure. In other words, some state before the failure is available after the failure to those parts of the system that have not failed. This state information is essential in many schemes for supporting fault tolerance.

3.3.1 Problem Definition

The basic problem is to take a physical storage system with its various failure modes, and convert it into a storage device by adding extra hardware/software, such that application programs running on the system can treat the storage as stable storage. No system can handle all possible faults and be completely fault tolerant. The goal of all fault tolerant systems is to make the system resilient to some defined faults, which hopefully cover most of the likely failures, and thus increase the reliability of the system. With stable storage too, the goal is not to handle all possible failures, but some of them.

To understand the problem we should first study the physical system on which the stable storage will be constructed, and the failure modes of this physical system. Stable storage is typically built from disk systems. A physical disk storage system is modeled as a set of pages (or blocks or sectors) that has blocks of data and a *status* (*good* or *bad*) associated with each block. The status of a block specifies whether the data in the block is correct or has been corrupted. If the status of a block is *bad*, reading the block will not be successful. There are two operations with which the processor (or a process) can interact with the disk [Lam81]:

> **procedure** write(addr, data)
> **procedure** read(addr) **returns** (status, data).

The write operation takes two parameters: the address of a sector, and the data to be written to that sector. It does not return any status. The read operation has the address of the sector to be read as the parameter and returns the data. It also returns the status of the operation. The status may be *good* or *bad*, indicating whether the read was successful or unsuccessful.

Various types of failures are possible with a disk storage system. Many errors that occur with a storage system are often taken care of by techniques like coding. However, there are other types of failures that these techniques cannot handle. Some of the common ones are:

- *Transient failures.* These cause the disk to behave unpredictably for a short period of time.

- *Bad sector:* A page becomes corrupted, and data stored in it cannot be read. This could occur due to physical reasons (like dust particles).

- *Controller failure:* The disk controller fails. This could occur due to hardware problems in the controller itself, or due to a crash of the node to which the controller is attached. The contents of the disk are not corrupted, but are unavailable until the controller (or the node) is repaired.

- *Disk failure:* The entire disk becomes unreadable. This type of failure could occur due to hardware faults like a disk head crash. The contents of the disk are unrecoverable.

There are other possible physical failures for the disk. Instead of enumerating all physical reasons for failure and finding ways to tolerate them, we could study their manifestations on the behavior of the disk and then provide methods to support stable storage where these errors are hidden. It is easier to follow this route, since the possible events are easy to enumerate. The events that occur in a disk system can be considered as comprising those events that are a result of a read or a write operation, and some events that are spontaneous [Lam81]. Some of these events are desirable (like *read* returning a correct value and status) and some are undesirable. The undesirable events are caused by some physical failure of the disk. For constructing stable storage, our goal is to mask the undesirable events. The possible undesirable results of a *read (a)* operation are [Lam81]:

1. *Soft read error:* Page *a* is *good*, but *read* returns *bad*. This situation may not persist for long, and is caused by transient failures.

2. *Persistent read error:* Page *a* is *good*, but *read* returns *bad*, and successive reads also return *bad*. This could be caused by a bad sector (or a disk/controller failure).

3. *Undetected error:* Page *a* is *bad* but *read* returns *good*, or page *a* is *good*, but *read* returns different data.

If a write is successful, then the data of the page *a* will be changed to *d*. However, the write can be unsuccessful. The undesirable effects of a *write(a, d)* operation are [Lam81]:

1. *Null write:* Page *a* is unchanged.

2. *Bad write:* Page *a* becomes (*bad, d*).

Besides these events that occur with read and write operations, there are *decays* that model some other failures of the disk. Each such event damages some set of pages called a *decay set* [Lam81]. Two pages are *decay related* if there is some event in which both pages are in the same decay set. To implement an approximation of stable storage with one disk unit, we assume that it is possible to partition the disk into pairs of pages which are not decay related. That is, in each pair, even if one page becomes *bad* due to some failure, then the other page remains *good*. We assume that decay events occur infrequently. We consider the following decay events [Lam81]:

1. *Corruption:* A page goes from $(good, d)$ to (bad, d).

2. *Revival:* A page goes from (bad, d) to $(good, d)$.

3. *Undetected error:* A page changes from (s, d) to (s, d') with $d \neq d'$.

These events may be caused by transient failures in the disk, disk crashes, or controller crashes (if a disk crashes, all pages become *bad*). In addition to these errors, there are processor *crashes* which also affect the working of the disk. Processor crashes can be modeled as asynchronous events, and can be considered as causing controller failure (assuming that the disk is connected to a node through a controller). A node/controller crash does not corrupt the disk, and the data is available after the node/controller recovery/repair. However, the results of any ongoing operation will be unpredictable. If a crash occurs when some operation is being performed on the disk, the result of the operation should be assumed to be undesirable.

The goal of a stable storage system is to take one or more disk storage systems, which can fail in the manner described above, and construct a system where the abstract operations of the disk (i.e., read and write) continue to work despite failures and errors.

3.3.2   Implementation

Ideal stable storage is where *read* always returns *good* data (which is also the most recently written data), and the *write* always succeeds. The stable storage has to be implemented on existing hardware and storage systems, which do not by themselves provide this stable storage abstraction. Here we describe a few schemes by which approximations to stable storage can be implemented using disk storage systems. These techniques, like any technique for providing fault tolerance, can only provide approximations to the ideal. A finite amount of resources cannot provide total fault tolerance or complete reliability, since all the components may fail together. Furthermore, not all techniques can handle all types of failures. Most provide only an approximation by handling a few types of faults, which occur most frequently in practice. The techniques described here provide stable storage under some types of failures.

Using One Disk

Here we describe an approximation of stable storage that can work with one disk [Lam81]. First, from an ordinary disk storage system we construct a *careful disk storage* with two operations: *CarefulRead* and *CarefulWrite*. In *CarefulRead*, a *read* is performed repeatedly until it returns the status *good*, or the page cannot be read after a certain number of tries. Similarly, a *CarefulWrite* performs a *write* followed by a *read* until *read* returns the status *good*. This eliminates the *null write* and *bad write* errors.

CarefulRead and *CarefulWrite* cannot take care of decay events and crashes during a *CarefulWrite* operation. More needs to be done for stable storage. A stable storage is represented by an ordered pair of disk pages, such that the pages are not decay-related. The data for a page is replicated in both the pages in this pair. Since the pages are not decay-related, at least one page should have the status *good*.

With this, we can implement the operations called *StableRead* and *StableWrite*. A *StableRead* does a *CarefulRead* from one of the paired pages, and if the result is bad, does a *CarefulRead* from the other one. A *StableWrite* does a *CarefulWrite* to one of the representative pages first. When the operation is completed successfully, it performs a *CarefulWrite* to the other page. This takes care of the decay events, since it is assumed that the two representative pages are not decay-related.

However, crashes during a *StableWrite* may cause the two representative pages to differ. To handle this, another operation called *cleanup* has to be performed on stable storage. This action is performed for every stable page at least at system initialization time and after each crash. The cleanup operation is described in Fig. 3.6 [Lam81].

Do a *CarefulRead* from each of the two representative pages
if both return *good* and the same data **then**
    Do nothing
else if one returns *bad* **then**
    Do a *CarefulWrite* of data from the *good* page to the *bad* page
else if both return *good*, but different data **then**
    {A crash occurred during a *StableWrite* }
    choose either one of the pages and do a *CarefulWrite*
        of its data to the other page

Figure 3.6: The cleanup operation

The implementation of stable storage described above can mask undesirable events like *soft read error*, *null write*, *bad write*, and *persistent read error* (if only one of the representative pages has this error). However, it cannot handle events like a *disk crash*. Also, though inconsistencies caused by node crashes can be handled, the data in the storage is unavailable to any other node until the crashed node is recovered. In many cases, one of the requirements of stable storage is that the data should be available to other nodes even after the node crashes. This scheme will not be suitable for those applications. The scheme can be implemented on one disk by partitioning the disk, though it is quite general and implementations with multiple disks can also be used.

Disk Shadowing

Disk shadowing is another way to implement stable storage which can also handle errors like disk failure. With the help of extra hardware, it can also allow access to data on the disk even after one node/controller fails. Disk shadowing is essentially an implementation of the scheme described above, in which the two representative pages of a stable storage page reside on two different disk units (and therefore satisfy the assumption about not being decay related). However, disk shadowing typically requires some hardware support for implementation.

Disk shadowing is a technique for maintaining a set of identical disk images on separate disk devices [BG88]. Its primary purpose is to increase the reliability and availability of secondary storage. Here, we will consider only the case of two disks. In this case, the disks are called *mirrored disks*. One or more host nodes may be connected to the mirrored disks. When a host *writes* data, the data is written to *both* the disks. A *read* request is executed from either of the disks.

Disk mirroring can be implemented in the disk driver software running on the hosts. This approach is followed in Tandem systems [Bar81]. For reliability and performance reasons, mirrored disks should be "dual-ported" and should be connected to a pair of controllers, as shown in Fig. 3.7 [BG88].

With this configuration, most of the errors described above can be handled. Disk mirroring can also handle disk crashes, and allows access to data on the disk while the failed node is being repaired. Failure of one host, one disk, or one controller (and some combinations) can be masked. That is, despite the failure, data can be written to or read from the mirrored disk. Hence, mirrored disks provide a close approximation to stable storage. It should be clear that even this is not a perfect example of stable storage, since a failure of both disks cannot be handled.

With mirrored disks, a failure of the stable storage system occurs only if both disks fail. Specifically, if one disk fails, and the other disk fails before the first has been repaired, the mirrored disk system will fail. If the mean time to failure of a disk is $MTTF$, and the mean time to repair is $MTTR$, and if the failure time and repair times are exponentially distributed, then the mean time between failures of the mirrored disk system can be given by the expression [BG88]:

$$MTTF_{mirror} = \frac{MTTF}{2} * \frac{MTTF}{MTTR}.$$

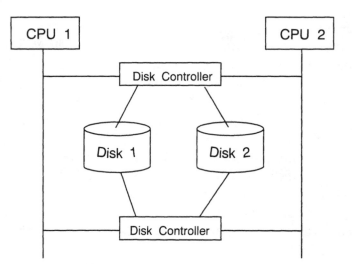

Figure 3.7: Disk mirroring

We do not give the formal derivation of this here. Intuitively, the equation says that on an average, the first failure will occur after $MTTF/2$ time, and $MTTF/MTTR$ refers to the probability that the second disk will fail while the first is being repaired. If the MTTF of a disk is 100 days, and the repair time is 1 day, then the mean time to failure of the mirrored disk is 5,000 days (over 14 years). Clearly, with reliable disks, mirrored disks provide a good approximation of stable storage.

Redundant Arrays of Disks

Another method to approximate stable storage is through the Redundant Arrays of Inexpensive Disks (RAID) [PGK88]. Arrays of inexpensive disks have been proposed as a cost-effective means of simulating high capacity disks. In this, the data is spread over multiple disks by using "bit-interleaving." In bit-interleaving, different bits of a data word are stored on different disks. Bit-interleaving provides high I/O performance, since reading different parts of the data can be done in parallel. However, an array of disks used in this way is not reliable, since the failure of any one of the disks can cause the entire data to become unavailable. The solution is to have some redundant disks in the array, such that the failure of a few disks does not cause the entire data to become unavailable. This approach is called RAID (Redundant Array of Inexpensive Disks).

There are various levels of implementation for RAID [PGK88]. The different implementations provide different levels of cost benefit, reliability, and performance.

Disk mirroring can be treated as the simplest and most expensive method of RAID, since it uses an array of two disks, one of which is redundant. This is the most costly method, as it has a 100% overhead — an extra disk for every disk. Here we describe one particular implementation of RAID that employs one check disk for a group of disks [PGK88].

In this implementation there is a large number of disks partitioned into *groups*. A group of disks is the unit for providing redundancy or for bit-interleaved storing of data. Each group has some data disks and some *check disks*. The check disks are the redundant disks. The data disks and check disks together store the data using some coding technique, such that despite the failure of a few disks in the group, the original data can be obtained from the remaining disks. The number of check disks depends on the coding technique used. In the scheme described here, a single check disk is needed for each group.

The redundant disk stores the parity. The data is bit-interleaved over the data disks in the group, and for each set of bits in the data disks, one parity bit is kept in the redundant disk. Hence, the jth bits from all disks together form the jth code word, as shown in Fig. 3.8.

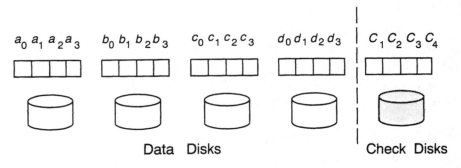

Figure 3.8: Redundant array of inexpensive disks

The failure of any one disk can be fully masked if the failed disk can determine by itself that it has indeed failed (i.e., it does not fail by returning an incorrect value, in which case the failure can only be detected but not masked). This assumption holds for many modern disks which have extra hardware built into the controller and use encoding to detect a disk failure. With this, the data of the failed disk can be reconstructed by calculating the parity of the remaining data disks and comparing it with the parity as stored in the check disk. If the two parities agree, this bit on the failed disk was 0, otherwise it was 1.

It is clear that this method of implementing RAID can handle the failure of a

behaves like a fail stop processor. As has been mentioned before, it is impossible to build a system that can handle the failure of any number of components. This holds true for a fail stop processor too. So we have to approximate a fail stop processor in an implementation. We define a *k-fail-stop processor* as a computing system that behaves like a fail stop processor unless $k + 1$ or more components of the system fail [SS83]. A k-fail-stop processor is an approximation of the ideal fail stop processor. Our goal is to implement a *k-fail-stop processor*.

3.4.2 Implementation

Here we will discuss some implementations of a k-fail-stop processor from ordinary processors. For this, the interaction of the stable storage with the fail stop processor is important. A fail stop processor reads data from the stable storage and writes data to the stable storage. Processors also interact with each other through the stable storage, as the internal state of a processor or its volatile memory is not visible to other processors. Clearly, the functioning of a fail stop processor will depend on the reliability of the available stable storage.

A stable storage is typically a *storage medium* that is controlled by some active device (often the controller, which is controlled by the programs running on the processor) which is capable of executing instructions (for doing read/write, interacting with the main memory or the processor, etc.). We can view this as having a processor which controls the storage medium. We will refer to this processor as the *storage processor*. This processor is responsible for interacting with processors that wish to use the stable storage, and performs all activities needed to manage the storage medium (this includes the software and hardware activities typically performed for secondary storage). Hence, in this model of a computing system, we have processors for running programs, and processors that provide the stable storage. For the rest of the discussion on fail stop processors, we will use the terms *process* and *processor* interchangeably, since we assume that the processor is performing one task.

Earlier, we discussed various methods for ensuring that the storage process provides a close approximation of stable storage to others (by masking various types of failure related to the storage medium). We tacitly assumed that the storage processor worked correctly. Now that we are discussing the working of processors, we have to reexamine this assumption. A stable storage may not function properly if the medium does not work correctly or the storage processor controlling the medium is malfunctioning. Both these situations can easily be modeled as a malfunctioning storage processor. Hence, we will assume that an incorrectly working stable storage means that the storage processor is not working correctly.

If the storage processor is functioning correctly, then the task of implementing a k-fail-stop processor is considerably simplified. However, if the storage processor may not work correctly (i.e., can fail), then the implementation of a k-fail-stop processor must take this into account and must also involve support for reliable stable storage. Here we will describe two implementations of a k-fail-stop processor, one with a reliable stable storage available, and one where reliable stable storage is not available.

Implementation with Reliable Stable Storage

We first consider the case where we have a reliable stable storage. The scheme discussed here was proposed in [Sch83]. This means that the storage process (or s-process) works correctly and does not fail. A k-fail-stop processor is constructed from $k + 1$ ordinary processors (and the stable storage or s-process). The ordinary processors can fail in an arbitrary manner; no assumptions are made about their behavior during failure (except that it is different from the defined semantics). This permits *Byzantine* or *malicious* failures, in which the processor can act in a manner that attempts to thwart any consensus-building exercise. Specifically, it allows the process to give different values for the same variable to different processors requesting the value.

The $k+1$ processors and the s-process are connected by a reliable communication network. It is assumed that the origin of a message can be authenticated by its receiver. This means that a malicious processor cannot change the message of a process and forward it to another without the recipient detecting it. This can be implemented by the use of digital signatures.

It is further assumed that the clocks at all nonfaulty processors and the s-processor are synchronized and run at the same rate. We have seen earlier various methods of synchronizing clocks despite arbitrary failures. One of these techniques can be used to achieve the desired degree of synchronization.

A k-fail-stop processor can be implemented as follows [Sch83]. Each of the $k+1$ processors executes the same program, and accesses the stable storage by sending a message to the s-process. The request can be to read from or write to the stable storage. The non-failed processors will make the same (sequence of) requests to the s-processor. A failure is detected by the s-process if any of the requests from the $k + 1$ processors is different, or any request does not arrive within a specified period of time. In that case, the s-process considers that the k-fail-stop processor being implemented by the $k + 1$ processors has failed, and discards any request for access of stable storage, thereby effectively halting the fail stop processor. Once a failure has been detected (resulting in a variable *failed* being set), all requests for operations are discarded, thereby keeping the fail stop processor in the halt state. Synchronized clocks are needed so that all the copies of a particular request from the nonfaulty p-processors will have the same timestamp and are guaranteed to arrive within some time interval, according to the clock at s-process. This avoids unbounded waiting for requests by s-process, and is needed to detect the absence of messages or incorrect timestamps. Failure in this implementation is detected by the s-process when the processes try to access the stable storage.

Suppose a nonfaulty process make a request to the s-process at time T by its own local clock. Since clocks of all the processes are synchronized, requests of all other nonfaulty processes will also have a timestamp T. These requests will be received by s-process by local time $T + \delta$, where δ is based on the maximum network delay and the maximum difference between clocks of processes and the s-process. The k-fail-stop processor is considered to have failed if any one (or more) of the processes behaves differently from the others, i.e., if there is any disagreement between the different processes. This means that a failure is detected if for a request sent at time T by nonfaulty processes, requests from all the $k + 1$ processes are not received by time $T + \delta$, or if the received requests do not agree. The stable storage is updated only if the k-fail-stop processor is not faulty.

The operation of the s-process, which is responsible for deciding whether the k-fail-stop processor has failed or not, is shown below in Fig. 3.9 [Sch83]. (For simplicity, the timing aspect is not represented in this algorithm.)

R := bag of received requests with proper timestamp
if $|R| = k + 1 \bigwedge$ all requests are identical $\bigwedge$ all requests
        are from different processes $\bigwedge \neg$ *failed* **then**
                if request is a write, write the stable storage
                    else if request is a read, send value to *all* processes
            else /* k-fail-stop processor has failed */
                set variable *failed* in stable storage to true

Figure 3.9: Implementing k-fail-stop processor with reliable stable storage

It should be clear from the implementation that the s-process performs the operation on the stable storage only if the k-fail-stop processor has not failed. If any of the $k + 1$ processes disagrees with the rest, or its request does not arrive in time (i.e., does not have a proper timestamp), then the k-fail-stop processor is considered to have failed and the operation on the stable state is not performed. Instead, a variable *failed* is set, which can be accessed by other fail stop processors to detect that this fail stop processor has failed. Setting of this variable disallows any future operation by the processor.

It should be pointed out that taking a majority of values received from the processes, as is done in replicated systems, will not work in the presence of Byzantine faults. Since the faults can be malicious, if a majority of the processes fail (i.e., more than (k+1)/2 processes), then they can collude with each other and send the same "wrong" value. The s-process, if it takes a majority, will accept this wrong value. A majority works in situations where malicious failures are ruled out (or are considered as highly unlikely).

One practical way in which this scheme can be implemented (as in Stratus fault-tolerant systems) is to build a 1-fail-stop processor, with the part of the s-process that decides whether a failure has occurred separated from the stable storage, and replaced by an interface or voting hardware, which is assumed to be reliable. The comparison of the results is done by this hardware. The stable storage itself is a passive device, implemented by disk mirroring. Two processors are used (2 are needed to handle 1 failure), along with voting or interface hardware, for implementing the fail stop processor. The interface hardware compares the results of the two processes for each operation. If it gets different values from the two processors, it does not send the result outside the processor and halts the processors. (In Stratus, a backup 1-fail-stop processor is switched in to continue the processing.)

Implementation Without Reliable Stable Storage

Now we describe an implementation that does not assume that the s-process is reliable. This approach was proposed in [Sch84]. In this case, to implement a k-fail-stop processor, we have to implement a reliable stable storage processor as well. So we need multiple s-processors. Just as for processors, we assume that the s-processors can fail in an arbitrary (perhaps malicious) manner. For implementing a fail stop processor, in addition to the $k + 1$ processors needed to replicate the computation, we need $2k + 1$ different s-processes to implement the stable storage, each running on a different processor. During the discussion we assume that each of the $k + 1$ processors is modeled as a process called p-process. Hence, we have [Sch84]:

1. $k + 1$ *p-processes* (p for program).

2. $2k + 1$ *s-processes* (s for storage).

The p-processes are for supporting the fail stop processor. Each of the p-processes executes the same program. The s-processes support a reliable stable storage and are also used for detecting failure of the fail stop processor. A copy of all the variables to be kept in the stable storage is stored by each s-process. At each variable update, all nonfaulty s-processes update their variables. The failures that should cause the fail stop processor to stop, i.e., the failure of the fail stop processor, is detected when the p-processes write to stable storage. The fail stop processor is considered to have failed (and hence should halt) if any of the $k+1$ p-processes disagrees in what is to be written on the stable storage (or if their timestamps or arrival times are incompatible). This disagreement is detected by the s-processes. Since there are $k+1$ p-processes, as long as less than $k+1$ p-processes fail, disagreement among the values of the different p-processes will occur, since at least one p-process will send the "correct" value. And, as long as less than $k+1$ s-processes fail, there will still be a majority of s-processes that will not have failed. Hence, as long as only up to k processes fail in all, we can be sure that at least one p-process is working correctly, and the majority of s-processes are working correctly.

We assume that all the processes are connected by a reliable communication network, which delivers a message to the destination without any error. Furthermore, we assume (as was done in the previous implementation) that the origin of a message can be determined by a receiver. We also assume that the clocks of all the non-failed processes are synchronized and run at the same rate.

A k-fail-stop processor is implemented as follows [Sch84]. Every request for an update to a variable in the stable storage is sent by a p-process to *every* s-process. If the k-fail-stop process has not failed, we want the update operation to be performed by all the nonfailed s-processes. Otherwise, the s-processes should "declare" that the k-fail-stop processor has failed and inform all the p-processes to "halt." Since the $k+1$ p-processes are executing the same program (and the clocks are synchronized) each of the non-failed processes sends the update request at approximately the same time to each of the s-processes. That is, each s-process receives messages from at least each of the non-failed p-processes. Since we want each s-process to make the same decision regarding the update, it is important that each s-process agrees on the values it gets from the p-processes. This can be stated as the following requirements [Sch84]:

- If p_j is nonfaulty, then every nonfaulty s-process receives the request of p_j.

- If s-processes s_k and s_l are nonfaulty, then both agree on every request received from p_j.

This problem of agreeing on the values being sent by a process becomes complex because of the possibility of the malicious failure of p-processes (which may send different values to different s-processes) and s-processes. Hence, a simplistic method in which each p-process sends its request to each s-process will not work. The problem of agreement in the presence of arbitrary and malicious failures is called the *interactive consistency problem* or the *Byzantine agreement problem*. A number of protocols have been developed for reaching this agreement. Earlier in the chapter we discussed the problem and some protocols. Such a protocol will have to be used for updating a variable in the s-processes.

With this, the activities of the different processes to implement a k-fail-stop processor can be described as shown in Fig. 3.10 [Sch84]. (For simplicity, we are ignoring timing errors.)

1. For writing the stable storage, a p-process p_j initiates a Byzantine agreement with all s-processes.

2. For reading the stable storage, a p-process p_j:

   (a) Broadcasts the request to s-processes.

   (b) Uses the majority value (i.e., obtained from at least $k + 1$ s-processes).

3. An s-process s_i, on receiving a request from all the p-processes:

> M = bag of requests received
> **if** the request is a read **then**
> > send requested value to all p-processes whose request is in M
> **if** request is write **then**
> > **if** $|M| = k + 1 \bigwedge$ all requests are identical $\bigwedge$ all requests
> > > are from different processes $\bigwedge \neg$ *failed* **then**
> > > > write the value
> > **else**
> > > set variable *failed* to true
> > > send message "halt" to all p-processes

Figure 3.10: Implementation of a fail stop processor

Note that in this implementation, as in the previous implementation, the failure of the k-fail-stop processor is detected by an s-process. In this implementation, a failure is detected when all p-processes attempt to update a variable in the stable storage. The update is performed by all s-processes only if the k-fail-stop processor has been determined not to have failed, otherwise no update is done.

With synchronized clocks, timing errors can be detected by an s-process as follows [Sch84]. If a nonfaulty p-process makes a request at time T by its clock, all other nonfaulty p-processes will make a request at time T by their local clocks. If one such request arrives at an s-process s_r at time T_r according to the clock at s_r, then all these requests by nonfaulty p-processes will arrive at s_r by time $T_r + \delta$, where δ depends on maximum network delay. Only those requests that arrive within δ of the first request arriving are considered (i.e., only these requests are added in M — the bag of requests considered by an s-process).

The main difference in this implementation from the earlier one with reliable stable storage is the need for Byzantine agreement whenever some variable in the stable storage is to be updated by a p-process. Also, this implementation requires $2k + 1$ s-processes, which together implement the stable storage, as compared to one s-process that was required in the previous implementation in which an s-process was assumed to be nonfaulty. This implementation assumes that the original sender of a message can be determined by the receiver. If we do not make this assumption, then the Byzantine agreement protocol will require $3k + 1$ s-processes to handle up to k failures. As in the previous implementation, another fail stop processor can determine if this processor has failed by reading the variable *failed* from the stable storage of the processor. Once *failed* is set, no operation is performed thereby keeping the processor halted.

3.5 Failure Detection and Fault Diagnosis

We have seen earlier that a distributed system consists of a few basic components whose failures a fault tolerant application needs to consider. We have described the various failure modes of the different components, and have considered the fail-stop failure mode of a processor in some detail. Once a component of the system fails, the goal of a fault tolerant system is to mask this failure to the application. This implies that other components have to perform some activities beyond their normal activities, in case a component fails. For this, the components first have to identify that a component failure has occurred. That is, the failure of a component has to be detected and diagnosed by other components.

Most fault tolerant applications and methods in distributed systems assume that once a node fails in the system, other nodes find out about the failure within a finite time (and then take the actions specified by the particular algorithm/method). This assumption is easy to satisfy by a brute force method of each node using timeouts to detect failures. However, in a large system, this approach may be too costly and unwieldy. In this section we will discuss the issue of fault diagnosis (or failure detection) in a distributed system, whereby each nonfaulty component detects the failure of other components in a finite time.

Fault diagnosis, in general, is a wide area in which considerable amount of research has been done. The problem of fault diagnosis itself is quite general and is applicable to any system. We make no attempt to provide an extensive survey of the various techniques that have been proposed. Here we will focus mainly on diagnosis in distributed systems, and in that too, we will limit our attention to node failures. For discussing diagnosis in distributed systems, we first provide some background for system-level fault diagnosis.

3.5.1   System-Level Fault Diagnosis

The theory of system-level fault diagnosis has received considerable attention in recent years. Though the initial work was abstract and was motivated by the perceived diagnosis needs for multiprocessors and other hardware systems, recently, work has been done to develop fault diagnosis techniques for distributed systems. Before we discuss diagnosis in distributed systems, we will discuss the basic diagnosis model and provide some background for the area of system-level fault diagnosis.

The basic goal of fault diagnosis is to identify all the faulty units in a system. Clearly, it cannot always be possible to meet this goal. For example, when all the units in a system are faulty, no unit can be utilized to perform diagnosis and achieve the stated goal. A bound on the number of faulty units in a system has to be assumed. As we will see, there are theoretical bounds on how many units, at most, can be faulty if the diagnosis goal is to be met.

For the purpose of determining how diagnosable a system is and for performing diagnosis, a model is used. The first model of diagnosable systems was introduced by Preparata, Metze, and Chien [PMC67] and is known as the PMC model. We begin our discussion with a description of the PMC Model.

PMC Model

In the PMC model, a system S is decomposed into n units, not necessarily identical, denoted by the set $U = \{u_1, u_2, ..., u_n\}$. Each unit is a well-defined portion of the system, which cannot be decomposed further for the purpose of diagnosis. That is, either the complete unit is considered to be working correctly, or the complete unit is considered as faulty. The units have to be powerful enough to test other units in the system and determine if they are faulty or fault-free.

System diagnosis hinges on the ability of units to test the status of other units. It is assumed that the status of a unit is either "faulty" or "fault-free" and the status does not change during diagnosis. A *test* involves controlled application of some stimuli and observation of the corresponding responses. These tests may be diagnosis programs with fixed inputs and known correct outputs. It is also assumed that a fault-free unit always reports the status of the units it tests correctly, while the faulty units can return incorrect results of the tests conducted by them. The output of a test is simply 1 (failed) or 0 (not failed). The test is assumed to be *complete*, that is, if the test is applied by a fault-free node, then it always returns the correct status of the tested node and the test result reflects the condition of the tested unit accurately. The goal of diagnosis is to have some units of the system test other units such that together the test results capture the complete system state.

In the PMC model, each unit belonging to U is assigned a particular subset of U to test (no unit tests itself). The complete set of tests is called the *connection assignment*, and is represented as a graph $G = (U, E)$. In this graph, each node represents a unit, and each edge represents a *testing link*. An edge (u_i, u_j) exists in G if and only if node u_i tests node u_j.

An outcome a_{ij} is associated with each test (u_i, u_j), where a_{ij} represents the outcome of the test. If the testing unit u_i is fault-free, a_{ij} is 0 if u_j is nonfaulty, and 1 if it is faulty. If u_i is faulty, then the result of the test is unreliable and a_{ij} can assume any value, regardless of the status of u_j. The set of test outcomes of a system S is called the *syndrome* of S.

As an example, consider the model of a system shown in Fig. 3.11 [PMC67]. The system consists of five units, and the test assignments as shown in the figure.

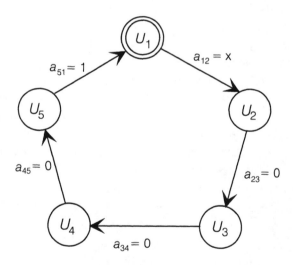

Figure 3.11: A system consisting of five units

That is, unit u_1 tests unit u_2, u_2 tests u_3, and so on. The syndrome of this system is a 5-bit vector:

$$(a_{12}, a_{23}, a_{34}, a_{45}, a_{51}).$$

Suppose that only one unit u_1 is faulty, then the syndrome can only be of the form:

$$(x, 0, 0, 0, 1).$$

Thus u_5 correctly identifies u_1 as faulty, and others, except u_1, also obtain the correct status. The value of a_{12} can be either 0 or 1, since u_1 is faulty, and is represented by x.

In this model, each unit knows only the results of its tests. For diagnosis, the faulty units have to be identified from the results of the test. In the PMC model, the syndrome is assumed to be analyzed by a centralized supervisor, which is an ultra-reliable processor. This supervisor diagnoses the system state, that is, labels each unit as faulty or fault-free. Note that the diagnosis problem of the supervisor is quite difficult since the results of a node which has been declared as faulty by the test of some other node cannot be trusted. We will later discuss an algorithm for diagnosis. But before that, let us discuss the capabilities of such a system.

Definition. A system S is t-fault diagnosable (or t-diagnosable) if, given a syndrome, all faulty units in S can be identified, provided that the number of faulty units does not exceed t.

For a given test assignment, the diagnosability of a system may be limited. For example, the system shown in Fig. 3.11 is 1-fault diagnosable, but is not 2-fault diagnosable. It is one-step 1-fault diagnosable, since the faulty node can always be determined by the following method. If in the syndrome or one of its cyclic permutations a string of 0s is followed by a 1, then the 1 correctly represents the faulty unit. To see that it is not one-step 2-diagnosable, consider the situation where both u_1 and u_2 are faulty, and suppose u_2 returns a 0 (it can return anything). The syndrome of this system is indistinguishable from the syndrome of the system shown in Fig. 3.11 with one faulty unit, and hence cannot be diagnosed correctly.

In t-diagnosable systems, the problem of determining t for a given system, that is, determining the maximum number of units that can be faulty, such that the set of faulty units can be *uniquely* identified on the basis of any syndrome, is called the *diagnosability problem*. And the problem of determining the faulty units from any syndrome, given that there are at most t faulty units, is called the *diagnosis problem*. The diagnosability problem is concerned only with what is theoretically possible. The diagnosis problem is concerned with actually finding an algorithm for diagnosis (provided, of course, the system is diagnosable) from a given syndrome.

A complete characterization of the t-diagnosable systems was first given in [HA74]. In this characterization, it was also shown that if no two units test each other, then the following two conditions form sufficient conditions for a system S with n units to be t-diagnosable:

1. $n \geq 2t + 1$, and

2. each unit is tested by at least t others.

Hence, if it is known that in the system under consideration no two units test each other, then the diagnosability problem can be solved by checking these conditions.

Diagnosis Algorithms

So far, we have just modeled the diagnosis problem and discussed the characterization of the diagnosability problem. Once the test assignment has been decided, and the tests performed, the collection of all test results is called the *syndrome* of the system. The problem of *diagnosis* is to determine from the syndrome the state of the system, that is, which units are faulty and which are fault-free. This is done by diagnosis algorithms. Note that in the PMC model a centralized observer is assumed and it gets all the test results and runs the diagnosis algorithm. Due to this centralized nature, the PMC model and the diagnosis algorithms based on it are not suitable for distributed systems.

Many algorithms have been proposed for diagnosis. One of the earliest algorithms has the time complexity of $O(n^3)$ [KTA75]. In this algorithm, an arbitrary unlabeled unit is guessed to be faulty or fault-free. Based on this guess, and the test results, other units are labeled. If a contradiction occurs, the algorithm must backtrack.

The best-known algorithm for centralized diagnosis has the time complexity of $O(n^{2.5})$ [DM84]. This approach first defines an L-graph, $G_L = (U_L, E_L)$, such that $U_L = U$, the set of units in the system, and $E_L = \{(u_i, u_j) : u_i \in L(u_j)\}$, where $L(u_i)$ is the set of all units in U that may be deduced to be faulty under the assumption that u_i is fault-free. It has been shown that for a t-diagnosable system S, the set of faulty units in S is the unique minimum vertex cover set of G_L. Hence by computing the vertex cover the system can be diagnosed.

Discussion

The PMC model is the first proposal for system-level fault diagnosis. Since then, a large number of models, approaches, and theoretical results have been presented. However, most of them are of theoretical interest only and have had little or no practical impact. Now with the size of computing systems growing, the results of system-level diagnosis are being applied and their use is likely to increase. Here we give a brief background of this area. Interested readers are referred to the survey articles [Dah88, KH87, Kim86].

Many new models have been proposed to represent more complicated relationships between units. The model in [Kim70] represents the case when more than one unit is involved in performing a test. Generalizations of this approach were given in [RK75]. A further generalization was given in [MH76] in which a single test may only be able to isolate a faulty unit to a set of units. This leads to *probabilistically diagnosable* systems. Models have also been proposed which take into account the nature of tests. In such models certain outcomes of tests are considered as extremely unlikely, which leads to simpler models. Other variations have been proposed by taking into account the nature of faults. For example, a model for diagnosing systems where the failure of units may be intermittent was given in [MM78].

Different strategies have also been proposed for performing diagnosis. The definition of t-diagnosable systems implies that all the faulty units are detected together. In some cases, it may be sufficient to detect some, but perhaps not all, of the faulty units. In this situation, typically far fewer total tests are needed to perform diagnosis. Tests are applied in rounds, and in each round at least one faulty unit is detected. After each round, the units that are identified as faulty are replaced by spares, and the testing process continues till no faulty units remain. This approach is called *sequential diagnosis* or *diagnosis with repair*, and is in contrast to the traditional approach of *one-step diagnosis* or *diagnosis without repair*.

There are also variations on how diagnosis is done. The PMC model assumes that a centralized controller exists that supervises testing, collects the results, and decides on the state of the system. Distributed diagnosis approaches have also been proposed [HKR84, BB92], in which each unit arrives at its own diagnosis by testing its neighbors and asking them for their test results. Another approach to diagnosis is *adaptive diagnosis*, introduced in [HN84]. Here diagnosis and testing are interspersed. The next test to be applied is a function of the results collected so far.

3.5.2 Fault Diagnosis in Distributed Systems

Most of the approaches for system-level diagnosis assume a central supervisor. This centralized approach is not suitable for distributed systems. Here we discuss approaches for diagnosis in distributed systems, and describe one particular approach, called *adaptive Distributed System-level Diagnosis (adaptive DSD)*, in some detail. As mentioned earlier, the goal of diagnosis in distributed systems is to ensure that if some nodes fail (or recover), then other nodes in the system find out about the failure (recovery) in a finite time.

An algorithm, called the NEW-SELF, was first proposed for self-diagnosis of distributed systems [HKR84]. This algorithm is distributed in nature, and all fault-free nodes independently diagnose the system state. The algorithm works correctly, provided the number of faulty nodes in the system is no more than t, there is a fixed testing assignment, and a node is responsible for testing a defined subset of its neighbors. The fault-free nodes pass their diagnosis results to their neighbors. The diagnosis node reaches other nodes through intermediate nodes. Each node independently determines the state of the system depending on the results of its tests and the results it receives from its neighbors.

The scheme assumes that a node cannot fail and then recover without its failure being detected. It also requires the number of faulty nodes to be no more than t, such that $2t + 1 \geq n$, where n is the total number of nodes in the system. No assumption is made about the behavior of the faulty nodes, and a faulty node's diagnosis is considered unreliable. For correct diagnosis, each node must receive test reports of all other nodes. This condition is satisfied if each node is tested by at least $t + 1$ nodes. The algorithm requires at least $n(t + 1)$ tests, since each node must be tested by at least $t + 1$ nodes. The number of messages required to transfer the test results reports is $n^2(t + 1)^2$, which can be quite significant for a large distributed system. This algorithm was later extended in [BGN90].

More recently, an algorithm called *adaptive DSD* has been proposed for diagnosis in a distributed system [BB91, BB92]. This approach is based on the SELF-TEST algorithm, and has been implemented for a large distributed system. Adaptive DSD considers only node failures, though the number of failures need not be bounded. It models a system S as a triple $(V(S), E(S), T(S))$, where $V(S)$ is the set of nodes $\{1, 2, ..., n\}$ in the system S, $E(S)$ is the set of edges in S (initially S is assumed to be fully connected), and $T(S)$ is the set of tests (or testing edges) of the system S. Clearly, $T(S)$ is a subset of $E(S)$.

The results of tests performed by a fault-free node are assumed to be accurate; the test results of a faulty node are considered as unreliable. A basic idea in the approach is that a node, besides its own tests, also uses the testing results of other nodes. During the algorithm, a node accepts testing information from a node only if it has determined that the sending node is fault-free. Hence, in adaptive DSD, if a node i tests another node j and finds it to be fault-free, it accepts diagnosis information from j. After this, it checks if j is indeed fault-free. If j is found to be fault-free by i, the node i assumes that the diagnostic information of j is valid and uses it for diagnosis.

The adaptive DSD algorithm is executed by each node in the system. Central to the adaptive DSD algorithm of any node i is the array $TESTED\_UP_i$. $TESTED\_UP_i$ contains n elements, indexed by the node number. Each element of

$TESTED\_UP_i$ contains a node number. The entry $TESTED\_UP_i[k] = j$ means that the node i has received diagnostic information from a fault-free node specifying that the node k has tested j to be fault-free. An entry $TESTED\_UP_i[l]$ may be arbitrary (represented by x) if the node l is faulty.

At a node, the adaptive DSD algorithm first identifies a fault-free node and then updates its local diagnostic information (TESTED_UP) from the diagnostic information of the fault-free node. This is achieved as follows. The nodes are sequentially ordered in a circular list, say as $1, 2, ..., n, 1$. A node i sequentially tests nodes $i + 1$, $i + 2$, ..., till it finds a fault-free node (the addition is modulo n). Diagnostic information from this node is used. The algorithm for a node i is shown in Fig. 3.12 [BB92].

1. $t = i$
2. **repeat**
3. $\quad$ $t = (t + 1) \bmod n$
4. $\quad$ request t to forward $TESTED\_UP_t$ to i
5. **until** (i tests t as "fault-free")
6. $TESTED\_UP_i[i] = t$
7. **for** $j = 1$ **to** $n - 1$ **do**
8. $\quad$ **if** ($i \neq t$)
9. $\quad\quad$ $TESTED\_UP_i[j] = TESTED\_UP_t[j]$

Figure 3.12: The adaptive DSD algorithm

Each node i executes this algorithm at predefined testing intervals. In this algorithm, steps 1–5 represent the loop in which i is searching for its first fault-free successor in the sequence of nodes (the addition in step 3 is modulo n, since the successor of node n is node 1). Once a successor node t is determined to be fault-free, node i first sets $TESTED\_UP_i[i] = t$, representing the fact that t has been tested by i to be fault-free. For other elements of $TESTED\_UP_i$, it copies the value of $TESTED\_UP_t$ which it had received in step 4. Thus the diagnostic information contained in the TESTED_UP array is forwarded to nodes in the reverse direction of the test arcs (i.e., $T(S)$).

Consider the example of an 8-node system shown in Fig. 3.13 [BB92]. In this example, assume that the nodes 1, 4, and 5 are faulty, and the rest are fault-free. When node 0 executes its algorithm, it first tests node 1, finds it faulty, and then tests node 2, which is found to be fault-free. It then stops testing. Since node 1 is faulty, we do not worry about its actions. Node 2, when executing its algorithm, starts its

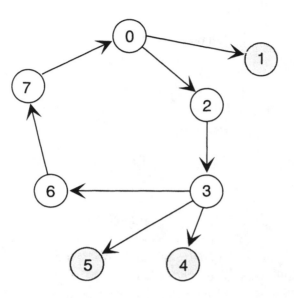

Figure 3.13: Example system and test set

testing with node 3. It finds 3 to be fault-free, and stops immediately. In this system, the set of tests is shown in Fig. 3.13. The number of tests is quite low, and a node stops testing as soon as it finds a fault-free node.

It is intuitively clear that the information contained in TESTED_UP of a node gets transmitted to other nodes. When a node i finds a node t to be fault-free, it saves this information in $TESTED\_UP_i[i]$. In the next round of testing, this test data of i is taken by its first fault-free predecessor (say $i - 1$) in the sequence of nodes, and it sets $TESTED\_UP_{i-1}[i]$ to t. In the next round, this information will reach the first fault-free predecessor of node $i - 1$. In this manner, diagnostic information spreads in the system.

The information about the state of the system is kept in the array $TESTED\_UP$ of a node, though in an indirect manner. From this information, a node i has to diagnose the state of the entire system. A node employs the *Diagnose* algorithm whenever it wants to diagnose the system. The Diagnose algorithm for a node i is shown in Fig. 3.14 [BB92]. The algorithm uses the information in $TESTED\_UP_i$ to determine the system state, which it stores in the array $STATE_i$. The kth element of $STATE_i$ represents the state of the node k, as determined by the node i. The desired goal is that $STATE_i$ will capture the true state of the system (i.e., state that a node is faulty only when it is indeed so) for all nodes i.

The Diagnose algorithm of a node i first initializes the state of all nodes as faulty.

1. Initialize $STATE_i[j]$ to faulty for all j
2. $t = i$
3. **repeat**
4. $STATE_i[t]$ = fault-free
5. $t = TESTED\_UP_i[t]$
6. **until** $(t = i)$

Figure 3.14: The Diagnose algorithm

It then sets its own state (i.e., makes it fault-free) in step 4 during the first iteration of the repeat loop. During the second iteration, it sets the state of the node which i has directly determined to be fault-free. In the next iteration, it sets the state of that node which this one had detected as fault-free. This continues till it reaches the node which has detected i to be fault-free. The loop has been completed and the algorithm terminates.

Let us understand the reasons why this approach works. Formal proofs of correctness are given in [BB91, BB92]. The algorithm works in rounds. A *testing round* is defined as the time period in which each fault-free node has executed one iteration of its testing algorithm. After a testing round, each node i knows exactly one fault-free node (call it j). This testing gives rise to an edge in the testing graph from node i to node j. That is, the edge (i, j) is in $T(S)$. Since faulty nodes are ignored during the execution of an algorithm, no node will set an edge to a faulty node during this testing round. Hence, from each nonfaulty node there is exactly one edge to another nonfaulty node. Furthermore, since nodes are ordered in a circular list, an edge from a fault-free node is to its first fault-free successor in the list of nodes. This ensures that after one testing round, $T(S)$ contains a directed path from any fault-free node to any other fault-free node. It follows then that all the fault-free nodes will be part of a cycle. That is, $T(S)$ contains a cycle that includes all the fault-free nodes.

Now consider the adaptive DSD algorithm again. Suppose a nonfaulty node i detects that j is nonfaulty in one testing round, and sets $TESTED\_UP_i[i] = j$. After two testing rounds, another node k which tests i (and finds it fault-free) will inherit $TESTED\_UP_i$, and will set $TESTED\_UP_k[i] = j$. In the next round, the node that tests k will set its ith element of TESTED_UP to j. In other words, the information about the result of testing of j by i flows backwards in the cycle of fault-free nodes. Since the longest possible path in the cycle is of size n, after no more than n rounds, all fault-free nodes will set their ith element of TESTED_UP to

j. Since this holds for all the test results obtained during the first round, after at most n rounds, the test results in the first round of each fault-free node will be known to every fault-free node. It follows that all nodes, by using the Diagnose algorithm, will reach the same decision regarding the faulty nodes in the system, thereby satisfying the basic goal of distributed diagnosis.

It is clear that there is no bound on the number of faulty nodes in the system for diagnosis to succeed. In an n node system, even if $n - 1$ nodes are faulty, the fault-free nodes will correctly diagnose the state of the system. This is a definite advantage of the algorithm, as it does not require the parameter t (maximum number of faulty units), which needs to be provided to the t-diagnosable algorithms.

An implicit assumption in the above arguments is that no changes (failures or recovery) occur during the n rounds. In other words, the adaptive algorithm is such that after the state of the system changes, the system stabilizes after, at most, n rounds, after which each node will diagnose the correct state of the system. That is, there is a "convergence period" following a change in the system state. During this convergence period, correct diagnosis by all the nodes is not guaranteed. This should be acceptable if failures and recoveries are infrequent.

Finally, let us discuss the "test" that is always the heart of a diagnosis algorithm. The test that has been used in the implementation of the adaptive DSD algorithm is as follows [BB91]. When a node i tests another node j, a separate subprocess is created at the node j. Creation of this subprocess itself verifies that the process scheduler is operational. This subprocess checks several hardware and software facilities, the disk subsystem, and performs some known arithmetic operations. If the results of the test are not provided within a "timeout" period, then the node being tested is also assumed to have failed. This simple test probably suffices for distributed systems, where the node is treated as a complete entity, and detailed analysis is perhaps not needed. No assumption is needed about the failure-mode behavior of nodes, other than that a failed node is unable to perform the test correctly and within the specified time. In the implementation described in [BB91, BB92], all failures of workstations during a 2-year period have been detected. Note that the adaptive DSD method will also work if a node mistakenly considers another node as faulty in a given round. In this case, in a later round it (or some other node) will detect that the node is indeed working and update the state accordingly.

3.6 Reliable Message Delivery

In distributed systems, it is frequently assumed that a message sent by one node to another arrives uncorrupted at the receiver, and that the message order is preserved between two nodes. That is, if a node i sends many messages to another node j, then the node j receives the messages in the same order in which i sent them. Real communication lines sometimes lose messages and introduce errors. Hence, some protocols are needed to satisfy these assumptions.

In most schemes for supporting fault tolerance in distributed systems, it is frequently assumed implicitly that the above two properties are satisfied even if nodes in the network fail, provided the two nodes involved in communication stay connected. Whereas the reliable and ordered communication is a general property, this additional requirement is of particular interest from the point of view of fault tolerance. In this section, we will discuss how these properties are satisfied.

3.6.1 Problem Definition

Consider a network of nodes connected by a communication network. We assume that the graph representing the network is connected. Suppose a node i wants to send messages to another node j. Nodes i and j need not be directly connected to each other by a communication link, though they are connected by some path in the graph representing the network. We want the following properties to hold always:

1. A message sent from i is received correctly by j.

2. Messages sent from i are delivered to j in the order in which i sent them.

Furthermore, we want these two properties to hold even if nodes or links in the network fail. In other words, the reliable delivery and ordering is preserved even if components of the network fail. Ideally, we would like these properties to be preserved even if failures cause a network to get partitioned into two or more disjoint graphs. However, practically, that may require long waiting times for message delivery, since a node cannot send a message to a node in another partition, as there is no path between them, and hence they must wait for the network to get reconnected. Consequently, we limit attention to the case where failures do not cause the network to become partitioned.

The failures of interest here are permanent node and link failures, and transient failures that cause messages to be occasionally corrupted or discarded. Once this abstraction is implemented, then as far as communication between nodes is concerned, transient failures and permanent failures that do not cause the network to be partitioned will be completely masked. In other words, the applications (even fault tolerant applications) utilizing this abstraction do not have to be concerned about the effect of these failures on communication between processes.

3.6.2 Implementation

The two properties described above typically form part of the communication architecture requirement and are usually supported through communication protocols. That is, they are essentially communication issues, and are dealt with by communication protocols and their implementations. We will not go into the details of these protocols or their implementations here. We will only briefly describe how these protocols achieve these goals and then focus on how the properties are preserved even under failures. For further details the reader is referred to [Tan88].

Error Detection

Transmission errors are inevitable. Errors are introduced due to various reasons like thermal noise, signal attenuation, impulse noise (caused by lightning, sparking, etc.), cross talk, and so on. Causes of transmission errors are typically transient, i.e., they exist for a short period of time during which they corrupt the messages being transmitted. That is why we have classified all these under transient failures.

Transmission errors can be detected by a receiver. The basic method employed by most networks is to use some type of coding. As discussed earlier in Chapter 1, coding techniques are very effective for detecting errors. The most common methods are use of parity (used in many modems), error detecting/correcting codes, and Cyclic Redundancy Codes (CRCs). CRCs are used extensively in local area networks, particularly the Ethernet. These codes were discussed earlier in Chapter 1.

If a receiver detects that a message has been corrupted, the message is usually discarded by the receiver, unless an error-correcting code is being used. Hence, most transient failures resulting in data corruption effectively cause the packet to be lost, either by the network itself, or by the receiver which drops a corrupt packet. The communication protocols have to ensure that this does not lead to the message not being delivered. It is typically assumed that the errors are such that they are detected by the error-detection mechanism, and permanent failures of a node are detected by other nodes.

Message Ordering and Guaranteed Delivery

We have seen that in real communication networks some data packets may get lost. A communication protocol ensures, by techniques such as sequence numbering, retransmission, etc., that the desired services are provided to the user of the network, even though the underlying network is unreliable.

A communication protocol can offer two different types of service for communication between two nodes: connection-oriented and connectionless. Connection-oriented service is modeled after the telephone system. A connection is first established and then the data is transferred using the established connection. In a connectionless service, each message carries the full destination address and each message is routed to the destination independently. In connectionless service, it is possible that some data may be lost, or that some data sent later may arrive at the destination before data sent earlier. Clearly, for supporting the reliable delivery and ordering property, connection-oriented service is required.

One popular method of providing connection-oriented service is by the use of sliding window protocols. Sliding window protocols can satisfy both the properties we require. Here we describe very briefly some relevant aspects of these protocols. The reader is referred to [Tan88] for details.

A sliding window protocol is a positive acknowledgement-based scheme (in which a receiver sends an acknowledgement for each message it receives), which makes extensive use of the sequence numbers of messages. In a sliding window protocol, at any time instance, the sender maintains a list of consecutive sequence numbers corresponding to the messages it is permitted to send. This list constitutes the *sending window*. These sequence numbers represent the messages sent but as yet not acknowledged. These are the messages the sender may need to retransmit, in case any of them have been lost. When a new message is to be sent, it is assigned the next highest sequence number and the upper end of the window is advanced by one. When an acknowledgement arrives, the lower end of the window is advanced. If an acknowledgement does not arrive within some time, it is assumed that the message is lost, and is retransmitted.

Similarly, the receiver maintains a *receiving window* containing the sequence numbers it is permitted to accept. Any message it receives whose sequence number does not fall within the window is discarded. When a message with a sequence number equal to the lower edge of the receiving window is received, the window is rotated by one, and an acknowledgement for this message is generated. The messages are delivered in order of their sequence number. Messages received out of order are buffered (the maximum number of buffered messages equals the window size) until the "missing" messages are received.

Sliding window protocols ensure that a message sent by a node is indeed delivered to the receiver, even if the communication channel is unreliable. It also ensures that the receiver gets messages in the order in which they are sent. Hence, it satisfies our two requirements. Besides this, sliding window protocols also perform flow control and have other desirable functions.

Failures

With sliding window protocols, both guaranteed message delivery and message ordering can be supported if no failures occur. Let us now see how these properties are preserved even when nodes or links fail. As mentioned above, we assume that failures do not partition the network. We also assume that the receiver or the sender do not fail.

The key issue in handling failures is *routing of messages*. In most situations, messages will require multiple hops to reach the destination from the source (i.e., the path from source to destination contains many nodes). A *routing algorithm* decides which output line an incoming message (whose destination is specified in the message) should be transmitted on. By means of a routing algorithm, nodes forward messages correctly such that each message reaches its destination. Routing is done by what is called the *network layer* in the communication protocols' architecture. For simplicity, we assume that the network layer provides a connectionless service (in which each packet is independently routed) to higher layers, which convert this service into a connection-oriented service by using appropriate protocols.

Suppose that a routing algorithm is used in a network for routing messages from node i to node j via a node k. If the node k fails (or a link on this route fails), then we want the routing algorithm to be robust and start routing the messages on a different route (since the network is connected, another route must exist). If the routing protocols can do this, then the sliding window protocols at the higher layers (typically the transport layer) will ensure the ordering property for message delivery.

For handling failures, we need *adaptive routing algorithms*, in which the routing decisions change as the topology changes. Many adaptive routing algorithms are known, each with different strengths and weaknesses [Tan88]. Here we will describe one approach that was used in ARPANET, to illustrate how communication networks handle failures based on description in [Tan88].

In this approach, each node maintains a routing table that contains, for each destination node, the preferred outgoing line, and an estimate of the delay (or some other metric like distance) to that destination. Each node is assumed to know the delay to its immediate neighbors (this is achieved by sending "echo" packets to neighbors to estimate the round-trip delay).

Each node periodically sends to each neighbor a list of its estimated delays to each destination (not just the neighbor). Suppose that a node i gets this information from one of its neighbors j, which says that the estimated delay from j to a node k is d_j^k. Since i knows the delay to j (assume it is x_j), it knows that it can send a message to k via j and the estimated delay along this path will be $d_j^k + x_j$. By performing this calculation for each neighbor, the node i can find out which of its outgoing links will result in the least delay for sending to destination k. This entry and the estimated delay for all the nodes constitute its new routing table. If N_i is the set of nodes that are the neighbors of the node i, then for a destination k, the message is routed through a neighbor j such that:

$$(d_j^k + x_j) \leq (d_j^l + x_l), \forall l \in N_i.$$

From this exchange of information, nodes adapt their routing tables to changes in network topology. Consider what happens if a node n goes down. All of its immediate neighbors will detect this failure (because the echo packet will not return), and will set the delay to this node as infinity. Consequently, for any destination for which a neighbor of n earlier had the best path through n, the best path will change to pass through some other node, since the delay through n will not be the minimum. As information about delays spreads through the network by the periodic exchange of routing delay information between neighbors, the network adapts to the new topology, and messages that were earlier routed through n will be routed through alternate paths.

This method of adapting to topology changes may not prevent some messages from getting lost (particularly the ones that were sent to a failed node before the failure was detected). However, this message loss and similar problems will be handled at the upper layers of the communication software (e.g., by using a sliding window protocol).

As an example, consider the network shown in Fig. 3.15. The numbers on the

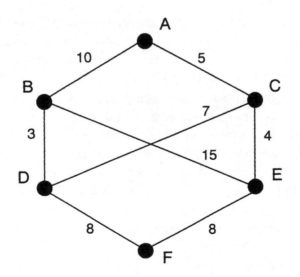

Figure 3.15: An example network

links represent the delays along them. Assuming that the delays of links do not change, and no failures occur, after some time, the routing protocol described above will ensure that the routing table of each node is such that a packet from any node to any other node will be routed along the path of the shortest delay. For example, a packet from node E to node A will be routed through node C and its expected delay will be 9, a packet from D to E will also be routed through C with an expected delay of 11, and a packet from F to A will be routed through E (and consequently through C) with an expected delay of 17.

Now consider the case where the node C fails. Its failure causes the links CD, CE, and CA to fail. The nodes A, D, and E will notice the failure and will set their cost of sending packets to C as infinity. Assume that the delays of other links stay the same. For the destination A, its entry will change from C to B with an estimated delay of 25. Similarly, D will change its entry for destination E. Now its preferred outgoing edge will be to node F, with an estimated delay of 16. In the next round of exchange of tables, the tables of these nodes will be sent to their neighbors. When F computes its new tables, its computation will find that its earlier optimal route to A (which was via E) is no longer optimal, since the cost reported by E for sending to A has increased to 25 (from 9). The new route it will choose will be through D, with an estimated cost of 21.

As we can see from this example, all nodes eventually choose routes that do not go through the failed node. And with more exchanges of routing tables, each node will again choose the path of minimum delay. Clearly, some packets that were sent to C or via C may get lost during the transition of the tables. The loss of these packets will be detected by higher layers and retransmission will be requested. Eventually, the retransmitted packet will be routed through the new route. Ordering is preserved by the use of sequence numbers in higher-level protocols (the higher-level protocol is insensitive to changes in paths, as paths may change even without failures).

3.7   Summary

Most schemes to provide fault tolerant services in a distributed system make implicit and explicit assumptions about the behavior of the system, particularly when the components fail. In this chapter we have discussed some of these common assumptions. We have seen that a system using ordinary components does not satisfy these properties and special hardware/software is needed to convert ordinary components into components/systems that satisfy these assumptions. The goal of the chapter is to precisely specify the abstractions corresponding to each of the major assumptions, and then discuss methods that have been proposed to implement them. Once a distributed system can be built that provides the abstractions described in this chapter, then fault tolerant systems can be built using these abstractions as building blocks.

The first abstraction we discussed was that of *Byzantine agreement*. Byzantine agreement is the problem of reaching agreement between processors that can fail in an arbitrary manner. In the Byzantine failure mode, no assumption can be made about the behavior of the processor during failure. In particular, a processor can send different values to different processors requesting a value. The Byzantine agreement problem is that if a processor has a value to send, then all nonfaulty processors agree on the same value, and if the sender processor is nonfaulty, then the agreed-upon value is the same as the value sent. It was shown that if there are n nodes in the system, then reaching agreement in this environment is possible only if the number of failed nodes is less than $n/3$. For the case where the number of failed nodes is less than $n/3$, two different protocols were discussed. The first protocol works with ordinary messages, and is a recursive algorithm requiring an exponential number of messages. The second protocol assumes that signed messages can be sent and a message by a nonfaulty node cannot be altered without the receiver discovering the alteration. An efficient protocol for this which can handle an arbitrary number of failures was discussed.

The second abstraction that was discussed was that of synchronized clocks. The goal of *clock synchronization* is to keep the clocks of different nodes in a distributed system synchronized with each other. That is, at any time instance, the clock values of two nodes differ by at most a constant β. The clock synchronization approaches can be *deterministic* or *probabilistic*. In deterministic approaches, a guarantee is given about when clock synchronization will be achieved. This problem has similarities with the Byzantine agreement problem, and like the Byzantine agreement protocols, deterministic synchronization is not possible if more than $n/3$ clocks in the system are faulty. We discussed a deterministic protocol for synchronizing clocks that can handle all types of clock failures, and requires only n^2 messages in a synchronization round. We also discussed a probabilistic approach to clock synchronization, in which clocks are synchronized only with a probability.

An extremely common assumption made in many approaches to fault tolerance is that some *stable storage* exists, which preserves data even if nodes in the system fail. Existence of stable storage is essential for many schemes for supporting fault tolerance. A stable storage is one where the read and write operations on the storage are always successful, even if the underlying storage hardware components fail. We discussed a few approaches to implement stable storage. In the method using one disk, the (unreliable) disk read and write operations are first converted into *CarefulRead* and *CarefulWrite* which mask some types of failures. Then, by replicating each page on two disk blocks, such that the two blocks are not related by any failure event, these operations are converted into operations for the stable storage. Other techniques we discussed involve more than one disk. In *disk shadowing*, the entire disk data is replicated on multiple disks and as long as one of them is uncorrupted, the read/write operation succeeds. The approach of Redundant Array of Inexpensive Disks (RAID) is a generalization of the disk mirroring approach. Data is distributed among various disks and some disks keep some redundant data such that even if some disks fail, the data can be re-created from the remaining disks.

One of the most common assumptions made in schemes for fault tolerance is that the processors in a system are fail stop. That is, the behavior of a processor during failure is well-defined, namely, that the processor simply halts. In general, real processors do not provide this type of failure behavior. We have discussed how Byzantine agreement can be used to build an approximation of a fail stop processor from ordinary processors that can fail in an arbitrary manner. Two different techniques were discussed: in one a reliable stable storage was available, and in the second, the reliable storage was not available. In the scheme with reliable stable storage, a process was replicated $k + 1$ times. When a process writes to the stable storage, the (reliable) process controlling the stable storage collects the value from all $k + 1$ processes and writes only if all agree. In the scheme without the stable storage, the process controlling the storage is not assumed to be reliable, and hence the storage processes are also replicated. For writing data, Byzantine agreement protocol is used by a process with all the storage processes. A value is written to the storage only if a storage process gets identical values (using Byzantine agreement) from all the processes. For reading, the value returned by the majority of the storage processors is taken.

Coupled with the fail-stop behavior assumption about processors, it is also commonly assumed, explicitly or implicitly, that the failure of a node is detected by other nodes in the system in a finite time. This assumption is essential for other nodes to perform any activities that may be needed for recovery. Failure detection can be viewed as a fault-diagnosis problem, in which the goal is for the set of nonfaulty system components to detect the set of faulty components by using diagnostic tests and disseminating information of their tests to others. We have discussed the basic formalism of the general fault-diagnosis problem, and have described the *adaptive Distributed System Diagnosis (adaptive DSD)* approach that is suitable for detecting failed nodes in a distributed system. In this approach, each fault-free node runs a diagnosis algorithm in which it tests others' nodes. When a node tests other nodes, it obtains from them their information about the status of nodes in the system. This collected information is compiled into a consistent view of the state of the different nodes in the system. If no failures occur, then after n testing rounds, all the nodes will have the same view of the system, which will be consistent with the actual system state.

Finally, we discussed the assumption of reliable message delivery. Most methods assume that if the network is connected, then even if nodes fail, a node can send a message to another in a reliable manner, maintaining the order of its messages. We have shown that this is a special case in routing, and have described one particular approach to support this abstraction.

For the rest of the book, unless otherwise mentioned, we will assume that by using the techniques discussed in this chapter, the distributed system supports these abstractions. Specifically, we assume that the clocks are synchronized, stable storage is available, processors are fail stop, if a node fails its failure is detected by others in a finite time, and the message delivery system delivers messages reliably.

Problems

1. In a five-node system, with one node being faulty, list the sequence of messages sent and received by the faulty node and one nonfaulty node for the Interactive Consistency Algorithm ICA.

2. Perform the same exercise as above for the protocol SM.

3. Modify ICA and SM such that they can work for networks that are not fully connected.

4. Suppose that the clocks in the system are not dual-faced, but may be faulty in that they may show incorrect times. Design a deterministic clock synchronization algorithm for this system. State the assumptions clearly.

5. For the deterministic clock synchronization algorithm discussed in the chapter, give the arguments for how it achieves the synchronization condition.

6. Use the method for probabilistic clock reading to design an internal clock synchronization algorithm (one which has no external clock). Specify clearly what is meant by "probabilistic" in the algorithm.

7. Disk mirroring is a common method for providing stable storage for fault tolerant systems. An array of disks can be used to improve performance. Design a RAID scheme where each disk is mirrored but there is no check disk. Specify how data is distributed in the scheme. What is the MTTF of this memory system? How does it compare with the RAID scheme described in the chapter?

8. Suppose a mirrored disk storage is connected to the disk controller processor, which is connected to the main processor of the system. Extend this system in such a way that all processors are 1-fail-stop.

9. List some of the important actions of a processor, which are not fail stop, when it fails. Which, in your opinion, are unlikely?

10. Most systems simply assume fail stop behavior but do not actually add hardware to support it. Assuming that actually malicious acts are unlikely during failure, how valid is this assumption if the memory unit employs error correcting codes?

11. A system consists of 6 units, organized as a ring. The connection assignment for the PMC model is that each unit tests its successor and its predecessor in the ring. If, at most, two units are faulty, is this assignment sufficient for diagnosis? What is the syndrome?

12. Suppose all the test results are compiled together. Design a simple (even inefficient) algorithm to diagnose the faulty nodes, assuming that the system is diagnosable. If the system is t-diagnosable, and more than t units are faulty, then how will the algorithm behave?

13. In a distributed system, the main components are links and nodes. Can the adaptive DSD be extended to diagnose link failures also (maybe with a high probability)?

14. Suppose that nodes in a network are fail stop, and a working node can detect a node failure by sending a message and timing out if no response is received within some time. A simple scheme for diagnosis in such a system is for each working node to periodically poll each node in the system and individually determine the status of the system. What are the advantages and disadvantages of this scheme as compared to adaptive DSD?

15. A fully connected system is desired which has synchronized clocks, stable storage, fail stop processors, detection of a node failure by all non-failed nodes, and reliable message delivery. If the system is to be built from ordinary components whose clocks are not dual-faced, and disk processors are reliable, what is the cost of building this system in terms of (a) extra hardware that is needed, (b) extra software/protocols, and (c) extra time and messages, assuming that, at most, one component fails?

References

[Bar81]　J. F. Bartlett. "A Nonstop Kernel." *7th ACM Symposium on Operating Systems Principles*, pp. 22–29, 1981.

[BB91]　R. Bianchini Jr., and R. Buskens. "An Adaptive Distributed System-Level Diagnosis Algorithm and its Implementation." *21st International Symposium on Fault-Tolerant Computing Systems*, pp. 222–229, June 1991.

[BB92]　R. P. Bianchini Jr., and R. W. Buskens. "Implementation of on-Line Distributed System-Level Diagnosis Theory." *IEEE Transactions on Computers*, 41(5):616–626, May 1992.

[Ben83]　M. Ben-Or. "Another Advantage of Free Choice: Completely Asynchronous Agreement Protocols." *2nd ACM Symposium on Principles of Distributed Computing*, pp. 27–30, Montreal, Quebec, August 1983.

[BG88]　D. Bitton, and J. Gray. "Disk Shadowing." *Proceedings of the 14th VLDB Conference*, pp. 331–338, 1988.

[BGN90]　R. Bianchini Jr., K. Goodwin, and D.S. Nydick. "Practical Application and Implementation of Distributed System-Level Diagnosis Theory." *20th International Symposium on Fault-Tolerant Computing Systems*, pp. 332–339. IEEE, June 1990.

[Bra87]　G. Bracha. "Asynchronous Byzantine Agreement Protocols." *Information and Computation*, 75(2), 130–143, 1987.

[CAS85]　F. Cristian, H. Aghili, and R. Strong. "Atomic Broadcast: From Simple Message Diffusion to Byzantine Agreement." *14th International Symposium on Fault Tolerant Computing Systems*, pp. 200–206, 1985.

[CDDS85]　B. A. Coan, D. Dolev, C. Dwork, and L. Stockmeyer. "The Distributed Firing Squad Problem." *17th ACM Symposium on Theory of Computation*, pp. 335–345, 1985.

[Cri89]　F. Cristian. "Probabilistic Clock Synchronization." *Distributed Computing*, 3:146–158, 1989.

[Dah88]　A.T. Dahbura. "System-Level Diagnosis: A Perspective for the Third Decade." In C. S. Tewksbury, B. Dickson, and S. Schwartz, editors, *Concurrent Computations: Algorithms, Architecture, and Technology*. Plenum Press, 1988, Chapter 21, pp. 411–434.

[DFF$^+$82] D. Dolev, M. Fischer, R. Fowler, N. Lynch, and H. Strong. "Efficient Byzantine Agreement Without Authentication." *Information and Control*, 52:257–274, 1982.

[DHS84] D. Dolev, J. Halpern, and R. Strong. "On the Possibility and Impossibility of Achieving Clock Synchronization." *16th ACM Symposium on Theory of Computation*, 1984.

[DM84] A.T. Dahbura, and G. M. Masson. "An O(n$^{2.5}$) Fault Identification Algorithm for Diagnosable Systems." *IEEE Transactions on Computers*, C-33:486–492, 1984.

[DS83] D. Dolev, and H. Strong. "Authenticated Algorithms for Byzantine Agreement." *SIAM Journal of Computing*, 12(4):656–666, November 1983.

[FLM86] M. Fisher, N. Lynch, and M. Merritt. "Easy Impossibility Proofs for Distributed Consensus Problems." *Distributed Computing*, 1:26–39, January 1986.

[FLP85] M. Fisher, N. Lynch, and M. Paterson. "Impossibility of Distributed Consensus with one Faulty Process." *Journal of the ACM*, 32(2):374–382, April 1985.

[HA74] S.L. Hakimi, and A.T. Amin. "Characterization of the Connection Assignment of Diagnosable Systems." *IEEE Transactions on Computers*, C-23:86–88, 1974.

[HKR84] S.H. Hosseini, J.G. Kuhl, and S.M. Reddy. "A Diagnosis Algorithm for Distributed Computing Systems with Dynamic Failure and Repair." *IEEE Transactions on Computers*, C-33:223–233, 1984.

[HN84] S.L. Hakimi, and K. Nakajima. "On Adaptive Systems Diagnosis." *IEEE Transactions on Computers*, C-33:234–240, 1984.

[KH87] S. E. Kreutzer, and S. L. Hakimi. "System-Level Diagnosis: A Survey." *Microprocessing and Microprogramming*, 20:323–330, 1987.

[Kim70] C.R. Kime. "An Analysis Model for Digital System Diagnosis." *IEEE Transactions on Computers*, C-19:1063–1070, 1970.

[Kim86] C. R. Kime. "System Diagnosis." In D. K. Pradhan, editor, *Fault-Tolerant Computing Theory and Techniques, Vol II*, Englewood Cliffs, NJ: Prentice Hall, 1986, Chapter 8, pp. 577–632.

[KTA75] T. Kameda, S. Toida, and F.J. Allen. "A Diagnosing Algorithm for Networks." *Information and Control*, 29:141–148, 1975.

[Lam81] B. W. Lampson. "Atomic Transactions." In B. W. Lampson, M. Paul, and H. J. Siegert, editors, *Distributed Systems — Architecture and Implementation*, Springer-Verlag, 1981, pp. 246–265.

[LL88] J. Lundelius-Welch, and N. Lynch. "A new Fault-Tolerant Algorithm for Clock Synchronization." *Information and Computation*, 77:1–36, 1988.

[LM85] L. Lamport, and P. M. Melliar-Smith. "Synchronizing Clocks in the Presence of Faults." *Journal of the ACM*, 32, January 1985.

[LSP82] L. Lamport, R. Shostak, and M. Pease. "The Byzantine Generals Problem." *ACM Transactions on Programming Languages and Systems*, 4(3):382–401, July 1982.

[MH76] S.N. Maheshwari, and S.L. Hakimi. "On Models of Diagnosable Systems and Probabilistic Fault Diagnosis." *IEEE Transactions on Computers*, C-25:228–236, 1976.

[MM78] S. Mallela, and G.M. Masson. "Diagnosable Systems for Intermittent Faults." *IEEE Transactions on Computers*, C-27:560–566, 1978.

[PGK88] D. A. Patterson, G. Gibson, and R. H. Katz. "A Case for Redundant Arrays of Inexpensive Disks (RAID)." *Proceedings of ACM SIGMOD*, pp. 109–116, 1988.

[PMC67] F.P. Preparata, G. Metze, and R.T. Chien. "On the Connection Assignment Problem of Diagnosable Systems." *IEEE Transactions on Electronic Computers*, EC16:848–854, 1967.

[PSL80] M. Pease, R. Shostak, and L. Lamport. "Reaching Agreement in the Presence of Faults." *Journal of the ACM*, 27(2):228–234, April 1980.

[Rab83] M. Rabin. "Randomized Byzantine Generals." *Proceedings of the IEEE Symposium on the Foundations of Computer Science*, pp. 403–409. IEEE, 1983.

[RK75] J. D. Russell, and C. R. Kime. "System Level Diagnosis, Closure and Diagnosability with Repair." *IEEE Transactions on Computers*, C-24:1078–1089, 1975.

[Sch83] F. B. Schneider. "Fail-Stop Processors." *Digest of Papers, COMPCON83*, pp. 66–70, 1983.

[Sch84] F. B. Schneider. "Byzantine Generals in Action: Implementing Fail-Stop Processors." *ACM Transactions on Computer Systems*, 2(2):145–154, May 1984.

[SS83] R. D. Schlichting, and F. B. Schneider. "Fail Stop Processors: An Approach to Designing Fault-Tolerant Computing Systems." *ACM Transactions on Computer Systems*, 1(3):222–238, August 1983.

[STS87] K. Perry, S. Toueg, and T. Srikanth. "Fast Distributed Agreement." *SIAM Journal of Computing*, 16(3):445–457, June 1987.

[Tan88] A. S. Tanenbaum. *Computer networks*. Englewood Cliffs, NJ: Prentice Hall, 1988.

Chapter 4

Reliable, Atomic, and Causal Broadcast

In the previous chapter, we discussed reliable point-to-point communication as one of the basic building blocks. Though point-to-point communication is sufficient for many applications, there are many other applications where a node needs to send a message to many other nodes. In such applications, a one-to-many form of communication is more useful. There are two forms of one-to-many communication: *broadcast* and *multicast*. Broadcast is the communication paradigm where the sender sends a message to all the nodes in the system. In multicast, the sender sends the message to only a subset of the nodes in the system. In this chapter, for ease of exposition, we will focus on broadcasting.

Since the basic communication primitive supported by a network is a one-to-one communication (except in the case of broadcast networks), this communication primitive has to be used to support broadcast and multicast primitives. This makes the implementation of broadcasting protocols susceptible to node and communication failures. It is possible that a sender may fail while broadcasting a message leading to the possibility of only some of the nodes receiving the message. Though this may be acceptable in some applications, this clearly cannot be accepted when building fault tolerant systems. Just like a reliable one-to-one communication primitive is a basic building block, a reliable broadcast primitive is a building block for those fault tolerant systems that employ broadcasting. In this sense, reliable broadcasting is also an abstraction that is not an end in itself but is needed for building fault tolerant applications.

When messages are being broadcast by different nodes in the system, there are three properties of interest: *reliability*, *consistent ordering*, and *causality*

141

preservation. The reliability property requires that a broadcast message be received by all the operational nodes. The consistent ordering property requires that different messages sent by different nodes be delivered to all the nodes in the same order. Causality preservation requires that the order in which messages are delivered at the nodes is consistent with the causality between the send events of these messages.

These three properties bring in three different types of broadcast primitives: *reliable broadcast*, *atomic broadcast*, and *causal broadcast*. Reliable broadcast supports reliability only, that is, a message that is broadcast is delivered to all alive nodes, even if failures occur in the system. Atomic broadcast, in addition to the reliability property, also supports the ordering property. Causal broadcast ensures that the order in which messages are delivered is consistent with the causal ordering of these messages.

Each of these broadcast primitives has its own applications. If an application sends isolated messages (e.g., an e-mail message, or a news item), reliable broadcast may be enough. However, in database-type applications, it is generally necessary to perform operations in the same order at all the nodes to preserve consistency. Hence, in this case, atomic broadcast would be needed. If the nodes sending the messages also communicate with each other and the contents of the message being broadcast depend on the contents of received messages, then causality must be preserved at the receiving end and so causal broadcast is required. In this chapter, we will discuss all three broadcast paradigms. For each of these we will specify the requirements, and then the methods, for implementing them. We will assume throughout the chapter that failures do not partition the network.

4.1   Reliable Broadcast

In broadcasting, a sender node tries to send a message to all the nodes in the system. Reliable broadcast has one basic property: that a message to be broadcast should be received by all the nodes that are operational. This property should be preserved despite failures. Even if the sender node fails after sending the message to some nodes, this property should be preserved. In this section, we will discuss two protocols that support reliable broadcast.

4.1.1   Using Message Forwarding

We first describe a protocol for reliably broadcasting a message that considers a network as a tree [SGS84]. This tree is used as the basis of disseminating the message to all the nodes. The root of the tree is the original sender (or the initiator) of the broadcast message. If there is an edge from a node P in the tree to another node Q, it implies that during broadcasting the node P will forward the message to node Q. This rooted tree represents a *broadcast strategy* and could be "flat," or a linear chain, or something else.

This tree is a logical structure used to organize the nodes in the network and has no direct relationship with the physical structure of the network. How the structure of the tree is decided is not an issue for this protocol, though it is clear that it will be more efficient if the neighbor of a node in the tree is a neighbor of the node in the underlying physical network also. The tree is statically defined and is known to all the nodes in the system.

A relation *SUCC* is defined on the given tree (V, E). This relation captures the hierarchy of the tree. For a node P, *SUCC(P)* represents the set of successor nodes of P in the tree. For a set of nodes X, *SUCC(X)* is the set of successors of the nodes in X. Let the root of the tree (the broadcast initiator) be node S (source). The protocol has to ensure that if a message m is broadcast by S, then all nodes that have not failed will receive m.

The set of all failed nodes is represented by *FAILED*. If a node fails, we assume that all other nodes find out about the failure in a finite time. We assume that each node has a copy of the set *FAILED*. In the previous chapter, we discussed how this can be achieved by fault diagnosis.

The basic strategy for broadcasting is as follows [SGS84]. Starting from the root of the tree, the message is forwarded along the edges of the tree. A node i, on receiving a message, forwards it to all its successor nodes, which send an acknowledgment back to i. If the node i does not get an acknowledgment from a node j (in *SUCC(i)*), and finds that j has failed, it assumes that j failed before completing its task and that the successors of j may not have received the message. Hence, i takes over the role of j and forwards the message to nodes in *SUCC(j)*. This may result in duplicates, but duplicates can easily be detected by using sequence numbers.

This strategy works well for handling the failures of all nodes other than the root, since the failure of a node is detected by its parent node which completes the task that had to be performed by the failed node. However, the root node has no parent. Hence, a special situation arises if it fails before forwarding the message to all its successors.

If the root node S does not forward the message to any of its successors, then it is all right, since no alive node has received the message. However, if S had failed after sending the messages to some, but not all, of its successor nodes, then something has to be done. Essentially, some other node that has received the message has to complete the task of S to ensure that the reliable broadcast property is satisfied. Multiple nodes performing this does not cause any problem, since duplicate messages can be detected.

For this, a node i, on receiving a message m from S, monitors S until it recognizes that S has failed or that its broadcast has been successful. If i detects the failure of S, it takes over the job of S if the broadcast of S was not successful. To help other nodes detect whether S has completed its broadcast successfully, S informs its successors when its broadcast is successful (i.e., it has received acknowledgments from all its successors). If we assume that a node does not initiate any new broadcast until its previous broadcast is successfully completed, a node i can infer successful completion of a broadcast when it receives a new broadcast message from S, that is, it receives a broadcast message which has a larger sequence number.

Each node i executes the same protocol, except for the root node, whose protocol is slightly different (since it initiates the broadcast). Each node i maintains three sets of nodes: *sendto*, *ackfrom*, and *ackto*. These represent the nodes to which a message must be sent, the nodes from which acknowledgments are expected, and the set of nodes to which acknowledgment has to be sent, respectively. For clarity, we use the operation $send(k, ack(m))$ to signify that a message carrying the acknowledgment for the message m is being sent to node k. Similarly, a primitive $receive(ack(a))$ is used to signify the receipt of a message a that is an acknowledgment. The protocol for a node i is shown in Fig. 4.1.

In this protocol, in the first guard, the protocol sends a message to one of the nodes to which it needs to send a message and updates *sendto* and *ackfrom* appropriately. In the second guard, if it finds that some of the nodes from which it is expecting an acknowledgment has failed, it adds the successors of the failed nodes to its *sendto* and appropriately modifies *ackfrom*. The third guard is straightforward: if an acknowledgment is received, then *ackfrom* is updated. In the fourth guard, if the node finds that it has completed its own broadcast (signified by $ackfrom = sendto = \phi$), and that the root S has failed, then it takes over the role of S. The variable r represents the node whose successors the protocol is trying to cover by broadcasting; usually it is i, but if S fails, it is set to S. The actions the protocol performs upon receiving a new message are shown in the next guard. The actions depend on the sequence number. If the sequence number is the same as the sequence number of the current message, then it is recorded that an acknowledgment also has to be sent to the sender of the message. If the sequence number of the new message is smaller, this means that it is an old message, and an acknowledgment is sent to the sender. If the sequence number of the new message is larger, this means it is a new message, and *ackto* is set to the sender of the message and *sendto* is set to the successors. Finally, in the last guard, if a node i has no message to send and is not expecting any *acks*, but has some *acks* to send, it sends those *acks*.

The protocol given in Fig. 4.1 is for a node i that is not the root of the tree. For

$m.sender := S$
$r := i$
$sendto, ackfrom, ackto := \phi$
$*[$

$\qquad sendto \neq \phi \rightarrow$
$\qquad\qquad$ from $sendto$ chose a node i
$\qquad\qquad sendto := sendto - \{i\}$
$\qquad\qquad send(i, m)$
$\qquad\qquad ackfrom := ackfrom \cup \{i\}$
$\qquad \Box ackfrom \cap FAILED \neq \phi \rightarrow$
$\qquad\qquad t := ackfrom \cap FAILED$
$\qquad\qquad sendto := sendto \cup SUCC(t)$
$\qquad\qquad ackfrom := ackfrom - t$
$\qquad \Box receive(ack(a)) \rightarrow$
$\qquad\qquad$ **if** $a.seqno = m.seqno$ **then** $ackfrom := ackfrom - \{a.sender\}$
$\qquad \Box S \in FAILED \wedge r \neq S \wedge ackfrom = \phi \wedge sendto = \phi \rightarrow$
$\qquad\qquad r := S$
$\qquad\qquad sendto := SUCC(S)$
$\qquad \Box receive(new) \rightarrow$
$\qquad\qquad$ **if** $new.seqno = m.seqno$ **then** $ackto := ackto \cup \{new.sender\}$
$\qquad\qquad$ **if** $new.seqno < m.seqno$ **then** $send(new.sender, ack(new))$
$\qquad\qquad$ **if** $new.seqno > m.seqno$ **then**
$\qquad\qquad\qquad$ **forall** $p \in ackto$ **do** $send(p, ack(m))$
$\qquad\qquad\qquad m := new$
$\qquad\qquad\qquad r := i$
$\qquad\qquad\qquad ackto := \{m.sender\}$
$\qquad\qquad\qquad sendto := SUCC(i)$
$\qquad\qquad\qquad ackfrom := \phi$
$\qquad \Box ackto \neq \phi \wedge (r = b \vee (sendto = \phi \wedge ackfrom = \phi)) \rightarrow$
$\qquad\qquad$ **for all** $p \in ackto$ **do** $send(p, ack(m))$
$\qquad\qquad ackto := \phi$

$]$

Figure 4.1: The broadcast protocol for a node i [SGS84]

the root node S, the guard beginning with $S \in$ *FAILED* is replaced by another where it accepts a message if its *ackfrom* and *sendto* are empty, prepares the message m, and sets *sendto = SUCC(S)*.

This protocol ensures that if a message sent by the root node S has reached even one node that has not failed, then the message reaches all the nodes that have not failed. Formal proofs of many properties are given in [SGS84]. For messages to be sent by different nodes, copies of the protocols, but with different root nodes, will have to be executed. That is, for each node, a rooted tree is defined, and a protocol for that rooted tree operates at different nodes. However, the different protocols for different trees can be easily combined into a single process that will perform all the tasks.

4.1.2 An Approach by Piggybacking Acknowledgments

Now we describe the *Trans protocol* for reliable broadcasting [MMA90, MSM94]. The Trans protocol uses a combination of positive and negative acknowledgments to achieve the reliable broadcast property. By piggybacking acknowledgments (acks) and negative acknowledgements (nacks) on messages that are being broadcast by nodes, it simplifies the detection of missed messages, and minimizes the need for explicit acknowledgments.

The protocol assumes that when a node broadcasts a message, some nodes receive it and some nodes miss it. This type of physical communication medium exists, for example, in the Ethernet. An underlying unreliable broadcast protocol in a point-to-point network will also have the same effect. The Trans protocol builds a reliable broadcast primitive from the unreliable broadcast primitive which it assumes is available to it.

The basic idea of the protocol is to piggyback acknowledgments and negative acknowledgments on a broadcast message. Each broadcast message carries the identity of the sender node, and a unique sequence number for the message. From the acknowledgments and negative acknowledgments, a receiving node knows which message it does not need to acknowledge, or which messages it has missed and must request other processor to retransmit. The idea behind the protocol is illustrated by this sequence of events in a system consisting of three nodes (or processes): P, Q, and R [MMA90]:

1. Node P broadcasts a message m_1.

2. Node Q receives the message and piggybacks a positive acknowledgment on the next message that Q broadcasts, say, m_2.

3. On receiving m_2:

- If R had received m_1, it realizes that it does not need to send an acknowledgment for it, as Q had acknowledged it.

- If R had not received m_1, it knows about this loss by the acknowledgment on m_2, and requests retransmission by sending a negative acknowledgment in the next message it broadcasts.

From this it is clear that by the effective use of acknowledgments and negative acknowledgments, the Trans protocol can support reliable broadcast efficiently. When a retransmission is requested, any node (not just the original sender of the message) may retransmit it. A retransmitted message is identical to the original message and contains the same contents.

To support the protocol, each node maintains an *ack-list*, a *nack-list*, a *received-list*, and a *Pending Retransmissions list (PR-list)*. The ack-list contains the message identifiers of messages for which this node has to send an acknowledgment; the nack-list contains the message identifiers of messages for which this node has to send a negative acknowledgment. The received list contains the messages that this node has received or has sent recently, which may need to be retransmitted. Messages are deleted from this list when no retransmission of the message could be needed by any processor. The PR-list contains the message identifiers of the messages whose retransmission has been requested by some node.

To support the Trans protocol, special actions have to be performed by a node when sending or receiving a broadcast message. *Sending a message* by a node is straightforward. When a node has a new message m to broadcast, it executes the following steps:

1. Append ack-list to m (as $m.acks$); reset ack-list to empty.

2. Append nack-list to m (as $m.nacks$).

3. Broadcast m.

In addition to sending its own messages, a node also sends messages in its PR-list. Furthermore, if a node does not receive a positive acknowledgment of a message within some time interval, it adds the message to the PR-list (and later broadcasts it again). On receiving a message m, a node performs the actions shown in Fig. 4.2 ($m.id$ refers to the message-id of m).

On receiving a message m, it is saved in the received-list and its id is added to the ack-list, representing that m has to be acknowledged. If $m.id$ is in the nack-list, it is deleted, as the message has been received and there is no need to send any negative

add $m.id$ to ack-list
add m to received list
if $m.id \in$ nack-list **then** delete it.
if $m \in$ PR-list **then** delete it.

for all id, such that $id \in m.acks$ **do**
    if $id \in$ ack-list **then** delete it
    if message corresponding to $id \notin$ received-list **then** add id to nack-list

for all id such that $id \in m.nacks$ **do**
    if message corresponding to $id \in$ received-list
        then add message corresponding to id to PR-list
    else add id to nack-list

Figure 4.2: Receiving a message in the Trans protocol

acknowledgment. Similarly, if m was in the PR-list, it is deleted, since the arrival of the message means that some other node has satisfied the retransmission request, hence this node need not send the message.

After this, the acknowledgments and the negative acknowledgments in the message m are processed. All the messages for which acknowledgments are in m need not be acknowledged by this node now, and hence are deleted from the ack-list. If a message that is acknowledged in m is in the ack-list, it is deleted, as no acknowledgment need be sent by the node. If the message acknowledged in m is not in the received-list, then the node has missed the message and its id is added to the nack-list. If a message is negatively acknowledged in m, then if that message has been received by the node, it is added to the PR-list, as the sender of m has requested retransmission. If the negatively acknowledged message has not been received by the node, its id is added to nack-list.

Besides these actions, if the sequence number $m.id$ of m indicates that messages from the sender have been missed, then the missing sequence numbers are also added to nack-list. Sequence numbers can also be used to detect duplicates, if needed.

Let us consider a few examples to illustrate the working of the Trans protocol. In the examples, we will use A, B, C, D, etc. to represent messages, a, b, c, d, etc. to represent acknowledgments for the messages, and $\bar{a}$, $\bar{b}$, $\bar{c}$, $\bar{d}$, etc. to represent negative acknowledgments for the messages. In the examples, we do not specify the source of a message, as it is not particularly significant. Consider the following sequence of messages that is broadcast [MMA90]:

$$A \quad Ba \quad Cb \quad Dc \quad E\bar{c}d \quad Cb \quad Fec.$$

First message A is sent, which is acknowledged by the sender of B by piggybacking acknowledgment a with B. On seeing this acknowledgment, no other node that receives B will send an acknowledgment for A. The message C carries an acknowledgment for B, and the message D carries an acknowledgment for C. The sender node for the message E has not received C, but by receiving D and seeing the acknowledgment c, it knows it has missed C, and so sends $\bar{c}$ as well as d along with its message E. On receiving this message, some node retransmits C. Note that the retransmitted message is the same as the original message and is not used to acknowledge recent messages. The sender of F acknowledges both E and C in the message. By these acknowledgments it implicitly acknowledges messages D and B (whose acknowledgments came with messages E and C) as well. Thus each message typically contains a few acknowledgments, but implicitly acknowledges many more messages.

This example illustrates how the acknowledgments work and how a message missed by a node is requested and retransmitted. Now let us see what happens if a series of messages is missed. Consider the following sequence of messages [MMA90]:

$$A \quad Ba \quad Cb \quad Dc \quad E\bar{c}d \quad Cb \quad F\bar{b}ec \quad Ba \quad Gfb.$$

In this example, we consider a situation in which the sender of E received neither C nor B, but received D. From the message for D, it detects that it has missed C, but still does not know about missing B. Hence with E, it sends a negative acknowledgment for C. When C is retransmitted and received by this node, the positive acknowledgment for B in this message will alert the node about missing B, a negative acknowledgment which can then be included in the next message (F in this example). Hence, if a sequence of messages is missed, they are not all detected together, but in a transitive fashion. Loss of some messages is first detected by the receipt of acknowledgments on the message that has been received. These messages are then retransmitted. Some other missed messages are detected when these retransmitted messages are received. This transitivity ensures that all messages that are missed are detected and finally retransmitted. In some cases, more than one message may acknowledge a message. But this does not cause any problem in the working of the protocol.

It is clear that for any message, if some working node has received a message and it transmits messages in the future, then all the working nodes will eventually receive it, assuming that all nodes have messages to send or they send dummy messages to transfer information about their ack-list and nack-list to others. This happens, since on the receipt of a message, some missing messages are detected, which causes further detection of missing messages, until all such messages are detected (since for each missed message there is some node that has received it). It should also be clear that the different nodes may receive the messages in a different order (e.g., one node may receive the message in the original transmission, while the other may receive it in a retransmission after receiving other messages). As we will see later, this protocol can be extended to ensure that all operational nodes deliver the messages in the same order.

4.2   Atomic Broadcast

The atomic broadcast paradigm for one-to-many communication is stricter than the reliable broadcast paradigm. Not only does it require that a message sent by a node be received by all the operational nodes, but it also requires that if multiple messages are broadcast by different nodes, then the different messages must be delivered at all the nodes in the same order. Hence, in addition to reliability, the same order of delivery at all nodes is an additional requirement. And both of these requirements should be satisfied even during the occurrence of failures. We have already seen how reliability can be satisfied. The focus in atomic broadcast is ensuring the same ordering of messages at different nodes.

With atomic broadcast, we need to distinguish between a node *receiving* a message and a node *delivering* it. Receiving a message means that the node has received the message using its network interface. Typically, a message sent to a node is meant for some process (probably a user process) running on the node. Hence, after receiving a message, the node (or rather the operating system on the node) has to deliver the message to the process. With reliable broadcast, it was implicitly assumed that when a node received a message, it delivered it to the higher layers for consumption. However, in atomic broadcast, after receiving a message, it is first buffered, and is later delivered. An atomic broadcast protocol has to ensure that the messages are delivered in a consistent order, which may not be the same as the order in which the messages are received. Frequently, a node has no control over the order in which messages are received by it, but it can exercise control on the order in which they are delivered. Hence, in atomic broadcast, the order in which the messages are delivered is significant, and may be different from the order in which messages are received.

Atomic broadcast is frequently needed in managing process groups, replicated data, replicated processes, etc. It is a very useful primitive for constructing fault tolerant systems. Consequently, a large number of protocols have been proposed for atomically broadcasting a message. In this section, we will discuss a few of these protocols.

4.2.1 Using Piggybacked Acknowledgments

Earlier, we discussed the Trans protocol for reliable broadcast. The protocol ensures that a message is successfully received by all operational nodes, but does not guarantee that different messages are received by different nodes in the same order. Here we will see how that protocol can be extended to satisfy the ordering property as well.

In the Trans protocol, since acknowledgments and negative acknowledgments are appended in the message itself, and the message is broadcast, a node can determine if another node has received a message. We define an *Observable Predicate for Delivery*, denoted by $OPD(P, A, C)$, where P is a node, and A and C are messages. We denote the sender of a message A by P_A. If $OPD(P, A, C)$ is true, it states that the node P is certain that P_C has received and acknowledged (directly or indirectly) the message A at the time of broadcasting C. The node P can evaluate the predicate based on the messages it receives. This predicate is true if, and only if, from the sequence of all the messages received, by deleting some of the messages, P can form a sequence S_M of messages such that [MMA90]:

1. S_M commences with message A and ends with message C.

2. Every message of S_M, other than A, positively acknowledges the predecessor in S_M, or is broadcast by the same node as its predecessor.

3. No message in S_M is negatively acknowledged by C.

Essentially these properties say that P has received a sequence of messages (not necessarily consecutively) in which the acknowledgments, starting from the acks in C, transitively acknowledge A. For example, suppose that the sequence of messages that are transmitted by four different processors is [MMA90]:

$$B_1 \quad D_1 \quad A_1 d_1 \quad C_1 \bar{d}_1 b_1 a_1 \quad D_2 \bar{a}_1 c_1 \quad D_1 \quad C_2 d_2 d_1 \quad B_2 \bar{a}_1 c_2.$$

The acknowledgments and negative acknowledgments of the messages can be represented as a graph, where nodes are the messages and arcs represent the acknowledgments of messages. If a message m_1 acknowledges a message m_2, then there is an arc in the graph from m_1 to m_2. Negative acknowledgments are

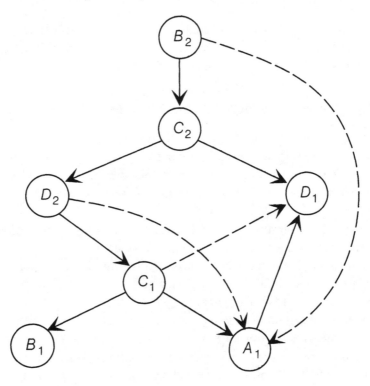

Figure 4.3: Graphical representation of the sequence of messages

represented as dashed arcs. The graph for the sequence of messages given above is shown in Fig. 4.3.

Note that the message D_2 is considered to implicitly acknowledge D_1, as it is sent by the same node. This graph is for the global sequence of messages that are transmitted. At a given time, the graph at a node will depend on the sequence of messages received by that node. However, since Trans supports reliable broadcast, and since a retransmission is exactly the same as the original message, eventually all nodes will have a graph that is the same as the global graph. If a node receives a message m_1 before transmitting m_2, then there will be a path from m_2 to m_1. For example, in the graph in Fig. 4.3, there is a path from the node B_2 to the node C_1. There is an arc from B_2 to C_2, implying that B_2 has acknowledged C_2. But C_2 contains acknowledgments for D_2 and D_1. Hence, at the time of broadcasting B_2, the processor P_B must have received these messages, else it would have included a negative acknowledgment for them. Again, D_2 contains a negative acknowledgment for A_1 and a positive acknowledgment for C_1. Since B_2 does not contain any negative acknowledgment for C_1, P_B must have received it at the time of sending B_2. Since it has not received A_1, a negative acknowledgment is attached to B_2.

$OPD(P, A, C)$ represents that there is a path from C to A in the graph formed by the messages received by P and there is no negative acknowledgment edge from C to any node in the path from C to A. That is, C transitively acknowledges A. OPD can be used to define a partial order on the sequence of messages, as follows.

In the *partial order* constructed by P, a message C *follows* a message B if, and only if, $OPD(P, B, C)$ and for all messages A, $OPD(P, A, B)$ implies $OPD(P, A, C)$.

In the partial order, if C follows A, it implies that C acknowledges (directly or indirectly) the message A and also all the messages that A acknowledges. If C is included in the partial order, it means that at the time of transmitting C, the processor P_C had received and acknowledged, directly or indirectly, all messages that precede C in the partial order. For the graph shown in Fig. 4.3, the partial order is shown in Fig. 4.4.

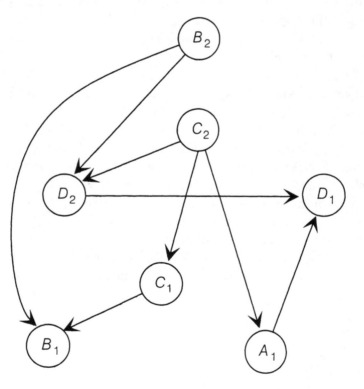

Figure 4.4: Partial order corresponding to the graph

Note that in this partial order, message C_1 does not follow A_1 (even though it contains an ack a_1) because A_1 follows D_1, but C_1 has a negative acknowledgment for D_1. Similarly, B_2 does not follow C_2 because of A_1. However, C_2 follows A_1, since there is a path from C_2 to A_1, and also a path to any node to which there is a path from A_1 (which is only the node D_1).

Since the Trans protocol ensures that all operational nodes eventually receive each broadcast message, all operational nodes will have the same partial order eventually. However, at any given time, the partial orders at different nodes may be different, as they may have received a different set of messages. Typically, the partial orders of nodes will differ only in the recent messages. Node failures can cause further transient discrepancies between the partial orders of different nodes at a given time. This partial order can be converted into a total order by the *Total protocol* [MMA90, MMSA93].

The Total protocol needs no additional messages beyond those required by the Trans protocol. However, a message is not placed in the total order by a node immediately after it is received. A node must wait to receive more messages from other nodes before it can add a message to the total order. That is, the protocol incrementally extends the total order. The Total protocol is also resilient to node failures. Though it can handle multiple node failures, in our discussion we will limit attention to the single-node failure case only.

A message that follows in the partial order only those messages that are already in the total order (or follows no message) is a *candidate* message for inclusion in the total order. Each set of candidate messages (called a *candidate set*) is voted by the messages that precede the candidates in the partial order. This "voting" is not an actual voting involving messages; rather it is an evaluation based on the messages received. Hence the decision of a node about including a message in the total order is only dependent on the sequence of messages it receives.

Voting on a candidate set (CS) takes place in stages. The number of voting stages depends on the candidate set and the partial order. In stage 0, the vote of a message is based on the precedence in the partial order. In stage i ($i > 0$) it also depends on which messages voted in stage $i - 1$. Stage i voting also requires the parameter N_v, which is $(n - 1)/2$ (for a resiliency of 1). A message m votes for a candidate set CS as follows [MMA90]:

Stage 0:

- m votes for CS if CS contains only m.

- m *votes for* CS, if (i) no message from the sender of m that precedes m has voted for CS, (ii) m follows every message in CS, and (iii) m follows no other candidate message. It *votes against* CS if it follows some other candidate message.

Stage i:

- m votes for CS if (i) no message from the sender of m that precedes m has voted for CS, (ii) the number of messages that had voted for CS in stage $i - 1$ that m follows in the partial order is at least N_v, and (iii) it follows fewer messages that voted against CS than voted for CS in stage $i - 1$.

- m votes against CS if the number of messages that had voted against CS in stage $i - 1$ that m follows in the partial order is at least N_v, and it does not vote for CS in stage i.

It is clear from these rules of "voting" that a node can determine its votes from the messages it receives. From these votes a node decides how and when to add messages to the total order. The voting rules and the decision criteria together ensure that all nodes form the same total order from the partial order. The decision criteria for a node P is given below. The decision criteria requires the parameter N_d which is $(n + 2)/2$ (for a 1-resilient system).

The Decision Criteria:
In stage i where $i > 0$

- P decides for CS if the number of messages in its partial order that voted for CS in stage i is at least N_d, and for each proper subset of CS, P has decided against it.

- P decides against CS if the number of messages in its partial order that voted against CS in stage i is at least N_d.

Once a decision is made in favor of a candidate set, the messages of that set are included in the total order in some deterministic order. The whole process is then repeated with the new set of candidate messages. Note that by the way the partial order is constructed, a node can always determine the vote of a message in its partial order, since all messages that precede this message in the partial order must have been received by the node. The Total protocol ensures [MMA90] that: (i) If a node decides for (against) a candidate set, then all nodes decide for (against) that set. (ii) If a node includes a candidate set as its jth extension to its total order, then all nodes include that set as their jth extension. Consequently, the total orders of all nodes are the same. (iii) The total order is consistent with the partial order.

Let us illustrate the Total protocol by use of examples. First, let us consider a 1-resilient, six node system. In this system, four votes are needed for a decision to include a candidate set in the total order. Assume that the transmissions are all reliable and all nodes receive all the transmitted messages. The partial order of such a system is a linear chain, and is shown for five messages in Fig. 4.5.

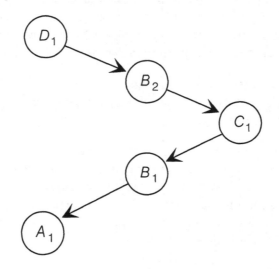

Figure 4.5: A simple partial order that converts easily into a total order

The graph with acknowledgments will also be the same, as there are no negative acknowledgments in the system. At the start, there is only one candidate message, A_1, and so only one candidate set $\{A_1\}$. The messages A_1, B_1, C_1, and D_1 vote for this candidate set (B_2 does not, since B_1 is voting). Four votes are sufficient for a decision. Hence, whenever a node receives the message D_1, it can decide to include A_1 in the total order. Note that until D_1 is received, a node cannot decide on A_1.

Let us now consider the partial order shown earlier in Fig. 4.4. Assume that there are four nodes in the system. Hence, three votes are needed for a decision. The candidate messages are B_1 and D_1 and the candidate sets are $\{B_1\}$, $\{D_1\}$, and $\{B_1, D_1\}$. Only messages C_1 and B_1 vote for $\{B_1\}$, which is not sufficient for a decision. Similarly, A_1 and D_1 vote for $\{D_1\}$, which is not sufficient for a decision. Hence, both these candidate sets are rejected. For the candidate set $\{B_1, D_1\}$, the messages C_1, A_1, D_2 and B_2 vote, which is sufficient to decide. Hence, this candidate set is chosen for inclusion in the total order. After these messages have been added, the candidate messages are A_1, C_1, and D_2. It can be seen that no candidate set of these messages will get the required three votes. Hence, no further addition to the total order will be made till enough new messages are received to obtain the required number of votes.

4.2.2 A Centralized Method

Now we discuss an approach in which consistent ordering of messages is guaranteed by conceptually funneling each message through a centralized message exchange [CM84]. Like the Total protocol, this protocol also assumes that the underlying communication is broadcast. The protocol converts the unreliable broadcast communication available to it into an atomic broadcast primitive.

The basic idea behind the protocol is simple. If multiple nodes broadcast messages, there is no guarantee of the order in which the messages will reach the different destinations. However, if all messages are broadcast through a centralized message exchange, then the order in which the messages will be received at different nodes will be the same as the order in which the centralized message exchange sends them. This order may be the same as the order in which the message exchange receives the messages from the different original senders of the broadcast messages. This centralized approach can guarantee consistent ordering at all nodes, but it is not resilient; the failure of the message exchange can disrupt the process. Hence, in this protocol, the centralized message exchange is rotated between different nodes.

In the protocol, the senders do not actually send the message through the message exchange (called the *token site* in the protocol). Instead, a sender node directly transmits the message using the (unreliable) broadcast primitive available. On receiving these messages, nodes save them in a buffer queue Q_B. The token site, which is one of the receiver nodes, assigns the message a unique global sequence number, *gseq*, and transmits it to all nodes through an acknowledgment message. This global sequence number is used to determine the order in which the messages in Q_B are delivered by nodes, and also to detect missing messages. The token site is rotated among a set of nodes called the *token list*.

Normal Phase

The protocol has two phases: a *normal phase* and a *reformation phase* [CM84]. The normal phase consists of activities performed if no failure occurs, while the protocol gets into the reformation phase when some nodes fail. For the normal phase, each node i maintains the following information:

- $M_i[j]$: The sequence number of the next broadcast message it expects from a node j. A node assigns sequence numbers consecutively, and hence receipt of a message from j with a higher sequence number than expected tells the receiver that it has missed some messages that were earlier sent by j.

- $gseq_i$: The next global sequence number it expects. Again, if a node receives a global sequence number from the token site that is higher than what it expects, it knows that it has missed some global sequence numbers sent earlier.

Initially, all nodes have the same $gseq$ (say 0), and the same sequence number it expects from other nodes (say 0). During the normal phase, there are three major activities that are performed for atomically broadcasting the messages: transmitting, assigning global sequence numbers, and committing [CM84].

Transmitting. A node transmits (i.e., broadcasts) a message. The current token site, if it receives the message, sends an acknowledgment to the sender node. The sender node repeatedly transmits the message until it receives an acknowledgment from the token site. Each broadcast message contains $< j, n >$, where j is the node identifier and n is the sequence number j has assigned to the message. This sequence number represents the number of messages that have been broadcast by node j, hence successive messages from j have sequential numbers.

Assigning global sequence number. The token site acknowledges messages broadcast by nodes. If the token site i receives a message with $< j, n >$ such that $M_i[j] = n$, it assumes that this message has not been acknowledged, and transmits an acknowledgment $ACK(gseq_i, < j, n >)$. Each ACK message, besides acknowledging the sender, also signifies the transfer of the token site to the next node in the token list. After transmitting an acknowledgment, it increments its $gseq_i$ and $M_i[j]$.

The nodes save the messages they receive in Q_B. A node processes the ACK messages $ACK(seq, < j, n >)$ in the order they arrive. An ACK message is processed by a node k only if $seq = gseq_k$ and the message corresponding to $< j, n >$ is in Q_B. When an acknowledgment is processed, $gseq_k$ is incremented, and $M_k[j]$ is set to $n + 1$. If for an ACK message, the node k does not have the message corresponding to $< j, n >$ in its Q_B, it implies that it has missed this message earlier, and it transmits a request for its retransmission. If $seq < gseq_k$, this acknowledgment is a duplicate and is not processed. If $seq > gseq_k$, it means that the node k has missed some previous ACK messages, and it transmits a request for retransmission of messages between $gseq_k$ and seq. All retransmission requests are satisfied by the token site, and a node repeatedly transmits its request for retransmission until it gets the requested message or ACK.

Committing. After the message has been assigned a global sequence number and the token has been successfully transferred L times, it is certain that at least the $L + 1$ token sites have successfully received the broadcast message. At this time, the message is "committed." As long as L of fewer nodes in the token list fail, all committed messages can be recovered. As the token is transferred with an ACK message, a null ACK is sent to transfer the token site in case there are no broadcast messages. The committed messages are delivered by nodes in the order of their global sequence numbers. This ensures that all nodes will deliver the messages in the same order.

In this method, the token site is responsible for acknowledging a message and thereby assigning a global sequence number to it, and also for transferring the token site. Since the token is also transferred as a part of the ACK message, token transfer does not require any additional messages. A token site accepts the transfer from the previous token site, if the global sequence number in the ACK message is the same as the node expects, and the corresponding message is in the queue. Otherwise, it waits till it receives all the required messages. Therefore, when a token site accepts a transfer of token, it has received all the messages and acknowledgments that may be requested for retransmission later. This property makes the token site capable of satisfying a retransmission request.

Reformation Phase

The protocol enters the *reformation phase* when a failure or recovery is detected [CM84]. The token list initially consists of all the nodes. Failure of some of these nodes can disrupt the token-passing mechanism. Hence, the reformation process redefines the token list. The new list will consist of only operational nodes. When a new list is formed, the protocol resumes normal operation.

Any site that detects a failure initiates a reformation, and is called the *originator*. Since there could be different token lists at different times, a *version number* is associated with a token list. A new token list will always have a higher version number than the old token list. Since multiple sites may initiate reformation, the reformation protocol has to ensure that after the reformation there is exactly one *valid token list*. The process also has to make sure that none of the messages that was committed from the old token list are lost.

An originator first asks the other nodes to join in forming a list. The originator also chooses the version number of the new list to be one more than the version number of the previous list. During the reformation, a node can join only one list. The lists formed during the reformation started by a node become the *new token list* only if they satisfy the *majority test* and the *sequence test*.

The *majority test* requires that a valid list has a majority of the nodes. This test ensures that there is only one valid list at a given time. The *sequence test* requires that a site only joins a list with a higher version number than the list it previously belonged to. The originator always passes this test, since it chooses the version number to be one more than its previous version number. If any of the nodes fail this test, it tells the originator its version number. The originator adopts the higher version number, and uses one more than this version number the next time that it tries to form a list. The combination of the majority test and the sequence test ensures that all valid lists have increasing version numbers. This happens because any two valid lists must have some nodes in common, which ensures that a new valid list always has a higher version number than the previous valid list.

In addition to these, the protocol has to ensure that none of the messages that was committed with the old list are lost. It should also make sure that the old list cannot be used by nodes that are unaware of the new list. This is done by the *resiliency test*. In the normal phase, for L resiliency, a message is committed only after the token has been passed L times after the message is acknowledged by the current token site. That is, $L + 1$ sites have the message before it is committed. If the new list consists of any one of these sites for the message that was assigned the highest global sequence number in the old list, then the committed messages cannot be lost.

To ensure this, when a site i agrees to join a list, it tells the originator the next global sequence number that would have been assigned to a message with the old list, and the old list version number. The list with the largest known version number is considered to be the old list.

The reformation protocol of [CM84] is a three-phase protocol. In Phase I, the originator forms a new list. The procedure for forming a list is described above. The originator enters Phase II when all nodes have either responded or have been detected to have failed. To prevent the reformation process from being blocked due to the failure of the originator, a site leaves a list if no messages are received from the originator during some specified timeout period. A node can respond only if it belongs to the list (i.e., has not left it) and has recovered all the missing messages. A site that has missed some messages first requests the missed messages from the new token site.

In Phase II, the new list is formed. The new list consists of all the nodes that have responded. The majority and resiliency tests are applied to the new list. If the list is not valid, the originator aborts the reformation process. If the list is found to be valid, it is announced to all the nodes in the new list. A new token site is elected and the starting global sequence number determined. The new token site has all the messages up to the starting global sequence number of the new list.

In Phase III, the originator generates a new token and passes it to the new token site. The new token site accepts the token and starts acknowledging the message, and the reformation process is complete.

4.2.3 The Three-Phase Protocol

A straightforward way to achieve consistent ordering of messages at different nodes is to assign priorities to messages, and then deliver the messages in the order of priority, say the lowest priority message is delivered first. With different nodes assigning priorities, the problem in this approach is how a node should ascertain that no other message with lower priority will arrive later. This is particularly harder if the communication delays can vary.

The three-phase protocol solves this problem by all the nodes explicitly agreeing to a priority of a message and then only assigning higher priorities to later messages [BJ87]. This agreement protocol for assigning priorities works in three rounds of message exchange. That is why this protocol is called the three-phase protocol. The protocol presented here can work for both multicasting and broadcasting, though we will discuss only the broadcasting case.

Assume that a message is atomically broadcast by a node by using the $abcast(m, p)$ primitive, where m is the message and p is the priority (an integer) assigned to the message locally by the node broadcasting m. Each node maintains a queue, in which it keeps the messages it has received, till it delivers them. Each message is tagged *deliverable* or *undeliverable*. The protocol works as follows [BJ87]:

1. **(Phase I.)** The sender transmits the message (m, p) to all the nodes.

2. **(Phase II.)** Each receiver adds the message to its queue, and tags it as *undeliverable*. It then assigns this message a priority higher than the priority of any message that was placed in the buffer. It then informs the sender of the priority that has been assigned to the message.

3. **(Phase III.)** The sender collects the responses from all the nodes that have not failed. It then computes the maximum value of all the priorities it has received, and sends this value back to the receivers.

4. Each receiver changes the priority of the message to the priority received from the sender, and tags the message as *deliverable*. It sorts the queue in the order of the priority of the messages. Starting from the lowest priority message, it delivers all the messages which have been marked as *deliverable*, in order of priority. The delivery of messages stops at the first encounter of a message that is still not marked *deliverable*.

It is clear how the unique priority is being assigned and how a node determines that it will not receive a message with a lower priority. Consider a message m which a node S wants to atomically broadcast. The final unique priority to m is assigned by S itself in Phase III. Since the initial priority to m was assigned by each receiver and it was higher than any priority the receiver was aware of, in Phase III, the priority that the S assigns to m will be the highest global priority in the system. Since these messages are sent to all the nodes, all nodes will later assign priorities that are higher than the final priority assigned to m. So, if the message m is marked as *deliverable*, any later message will have a higher priority and hence will be delivered after m.

However, an older message with a lower priority may be in the queue, whose final priority has not yet been determined, and whose final priority may finally turn out to be lower than the final priority of m. Since message delays are arbitrary, we cannot make any assumptions about the order in which different messages from different nodes arrive at a node, and this scenario is possible. To avoid this, a message is not delivered if there is any message of lower priority that has not yet been delivered. That is, in the last step of the protocol, the message that is first delivered is the one that has the lowest priority *and* is marked *deliverable*. When one such message is delivered and is removed from the queue, this process repeats itself till either all the messages have been delivered, or till we encounter a message which has the lowest priority but is not marked *deliverable*. Since only the messages that are marked *deliverable* are actually delivered, and the messages are marked *deliverable* only after they have been assigned their final priority, we can see that all nodes will deliver the messages in the same order, which is the order of the final priorities of the messages. This also implies that a message is delivered only after the three phases have been executed for it.

Let us consider an example of messages concurrently being broadcast. Suppose two messages m_1 and m_2 are broadcast by two different nodes. Let us consider two nodes 1 and 2. Suppose node 1 gets m_1; m_2, and sends the initial priorities p and p' back to the senders of m_1 and m_2 respectively (we know that $p' > p$). Suppose node 2 gets m_2; m_1 and sends q and q' to the senders of m_2 and m_1 respectively (with $q' > q$). The sender for m_1 computes the final priority $P_1 = max(p, q')$ and the sender for m_2 computes the final priority $P_2 = max(p', q)$. These priorities are communicated to nodes 1 and 2. Let $P_1 < P_2$. We then want both nodes 1 and 2 to deliver the messages in the order m_1; m_2. If $P_1 < p'$, then as soon as P_1 is received by node 1, its m_1 will be ready for delivery, since it will have the lowest priority and will be marked *deliverable*. Let us see what happens if node 2 gets P_2 before it gets P_1. When it gets P_2, it will set the priority of m_2 to P_2, and mark it *deliverable*. The other message it has is m_1 which is marked *undeliverable* and still has the priority q'. Since $P_1 > q'$, $P_2 > p'$, and by assumption $P_1 < p'$, we have $P_2 > q'$. That is, even though m_2 has been marked *deliverable*, it still does not have the lowest priority, and hence cannot be delivered. When P_1 is received, then both messages can be delivered, but m_1 will be delivered first, as $P_1 < P_2$. Hence, the protocol ensures that even though the messages may be received in a different order, they are actually delivered in the same order at all nodes.

Let us now consider failures. In this protocol, the failure of a receiver node causes no problem. Since the sender only tries to communicate with operational nodes, and since a sender also detects the failure of a node, the failed node is simply ignored by the sender. However, if a sender node fails during the protocol, it can cause problems if at least one of the receivers has its message tagged as *undeliverable*. The presence of an *undeliverable* message implies that the protocol was not completed and some nodes may have the final priority, while others may not. In such a case, a node with the *undeliverable* message takes over the role of the failed sender, on detecting its failure, and becomes the *coordinator*. After becoming the coordinator, it first asks all the nodes the status of their messages. If any of the nodes has a message tagged *deliverable*, it sends the message and its priority. The presence of a *deliverable* message implies that the sender had computed the final priority and had communicated it to some of the nodes before failing. The new coordinator then uses this as the final priority and distributes it to other nodes. If this is not the case, the new coordinator first checks if any node has missed the initial message (sent in Phase I). If so, it sends its copy of the message to those nodes. After this, Phase II and Phase III are executed, as they would have been executed by the original sender. This approach requires that even after a message is delivered by a node, it cannot be actually removed until all nodes have received the message. Hence, the "garbage collection" of unneeded messages is done separately by a separate process.

4.2.4 Using Synchronized Clocks

Now we describe a protocol that employs synchronized clocks to guarantee ordering [CAS85]. Many protocols were presented in [CAS85] to satisfy the ordering property in the face of different types of faults. We will limit our discussion to fail stop failures only. It is assumed that node and link failures do not partition the network.

The protocol assumes that the network delay is bounded. A message m sent by a node P to another node Q takes, at most, δ time to arrive at the destination, if both P and Q remain operational. For a fixed upper bound on the number of node and link failures, the worst-case message delay from one operational node to another can easily be determined for a given network topology [CAS85]. Let this worst-case message delay be D. That is, even in the presence of a maximum number of nodes and link failures, a message sent by a nonfaulty node arrives at another nonfaulty node within D time. This worst-case delay D depends on the maximum transmission delay δ, and the maximum number of nodes and links that can fail.

The clocks of the different nodes are assumed to be synchronized, so that the clocks of different nodes are within β of each other. With this, we can say that if a message is sent by a node P at time t by its clock, the message will arrive at its destination by time $t + D + \beta$, by the clock of the destination node. The *termination time* of the protocol is $\Delta = D + \beta$. The goal of the protocol is to ensure (i) every message broadcast by a node at time t (by local clock) is delivered to every nonfaulty node at time $t + \Delta$ (by the receiver's clock), and (ii) all delivered messages are delivered in the same order to all nonfaulty nodes.

The protocol uses message diffusion to achieve its goals. When a node initiates the broadcast of a message, it timestamps the message with the value of its local clock, and also attaches its own unique node-id. A node sends the message along all outgoing links. When an intermediate node receives the message, it forwards it on all links other than the link on which the message arrived. To satisfy the ordering property, the messages are delivered by all nodes in the order of the timestamps of the messages. If the timestamps are the same, ties are broken based on node-ids of the sending nodes. Bounded message delays and synchronized clocks are used by a node to determine how long it should wait before it can be sure that no message with a smaller timestamp can arrive.

The protocol consists of three tasks. The *start* task initiates the broadcasting by sending a message on all of its outgoing links, the *relay* task forwards the message to adjacent nodes, and the *end* task delivers the message. The start task is given in Fig. 4.6.

> obtain message m to be transmitted
> attach local timestamp and node-id to m
> send m to all neighbors
> append m to history H
> $schedule(End, t + \Delta, t)$

Figure 4.6: The start task

This task is performed by a node whenever it gets a message (from a process) to atomically broadcast. The node attaches the local clock and the node-id to the message and sends it to all the neighbors. The fact that m has been broadcast is recorded in a history variable H. This history H keeps track of ongoing broadcasts. In the end, the task schedules the *End* task to start at time $t + \Delta$, by which m will be received by all nodes. The current time at which the broadcast is initiated (i.e., t) is passed as a parameter to the *End* task when it is executed.

The relay task is shown in Fig. 4.7. This task is initiated by a node when it

receive (m) →
      τ = current time
      if $\tau > m.t + \Delta$ **then exit** /* late message */
      if $m \in H$ **then exit** /* An old message */
      send m on all outgoing links except on which m came
      append m to history H
      $schedule(End, m.t + \Delta, m.t)$

Figure 4.7: The relay task

receives a message. If the current time is more than the time at which the message was sent plus Δ, the message is late and is discarded. Similarly, if the message is already in history H, it is discarded as a duplicate. Otherwise, m is forwarded to other neighbors and is appended to H. The *End* task of this node is scheduled at time $m.t + \Delta$. It should be noted that the *End* task is scheduled based on the time when the message was originated, not based on the time of arrival at the node.

Each message that is broadcast by some node at time t (by its local clock), must be received by all the nodes in the network by time $t + \Delta$ by their local clocks. As messages pass by the nodes, the *End* task is scheduled to execute at time $t + \Delta$, where t is the time at which the broadcast of the message was originated (as this time is recorded in the message, all nodes know about it). When the *End* task is executed, it delivers all the messages whose broadcast was initiated at time t by the local clock of the originator node. If there are multiple such messages, then the messages are delivered in the order of the node-ids of the originator nodes (the node-id of the originator is also appended in the message). All the messages it delivers are also deleted from the local history H.

It is clear that a message that is broadcast by any source node at time t_s is delivered by a node when its local clock is $t_s + \Delta$. It is also clear that all the nodes deliver the messages in the same order. This order is the same as the order of the timestamps of the messages, with those messages sent at the same local time by different nodes being delivered in the order of their node-ids.

4.2.5 A Protocol for CSMA/CD Networks

Now we describe a protocol for atomic broadcast for Carrier Sense Multiple Access with Collision Detection (CSMA/CD) networks that exploits the broadcast and collision detection property of such networks [Jal92]. Consider a system which uses a common, shared medium for communication, and follows the Carrier Sense Multiple Access with Collision Detection (CSMA/CD) protocol [Tan88, Sta87]. Ethernet [MB76] is a prime example of such a network. In such networks, a node in the system usually has the Network Interface (NI) hardware that executes the Medium Access Control layer (MAC layer) protocol for the CSMA/CD network [Tan88]. The NI is usually connected to the common medium through a passive device called a transceiver, whose job is to pass the bits to the NI as they arrive. It also contains the collision detection hardware, and when a transceiver detects a collision, it sends a short jamming signal to enhance collision detection at other nodes.

A packet to be broadcast is given to the NI for transmission. The NI receives/sends a packet bit-by-bit from/to the transceiver and is responsible for all the activities of the MAC layer protocol, such as sensing the channel, transmitting the packet if the channel is free, aborting the transmission and later retransmitting a packet if a collision occurs, buffering of packets, etc. Above the NI are the communication software for higher-level communication protocols and user processes.

Even though the medium in such networks is inherently a broadcast medium, it does not guarantee that all the nodes will receive a broadcast message. Some of the nodes in the network may not receive a broadcast message. This can happen due to transient problems of buffer, network connection, etc. resulting in *missed messages*. Even though such networks are very reliable, this rare event where some nodes might miss some messages requires a special protocol for supporting reliable broadcasts. The protocol makes the following assumptions about the network:

1. The number of nodes that miss a broadcast message is less than half of the total nodes. This assumption is likely to be satisfied for most LANs.

2. The NI of a node can cause a collision at any time, even while receiving a message being transmitted by some other node, by sending a "jamming signal." Current network interfaces of CSMA/CD protocols do not provide this facility, since it is not needed, and the logic of NI has to be extended to support this. However, since the NI receives a packet bit-by-bit as it arrives on the cable, it can send a jamming signal, if needed, during the receiving of the packet. Further details about how to satisfy this assumption are given in [Jal92].

The NI of each node maintains a counter, initialized to 0. The counter at a node i, is referred to as C_i. When the NI transmits an atomic broadcast message, it attaches the *current value* of the counter as the sequence number of the message (for a message m, the sequence number is represented by $m.seq$). If no collision occurs (i.e., the broadcast is successful), then the counter is incremented.

On receiving a message, if the sequence number of the message is greater than or equal to the counter value of the node, the counter is set to one more than the sequence number of the incoming message. If the sequence number is less than the counter value, the counter remains unchanged. Proper use of sequence numbers is central to the scheme. Only atomic broadcast messages have sequence numbers and affect the counters. Other messages, such as messages to particular destinations, or control messages, have no effect on the counters.

If there are no missed messages, all the counters will have the same value, and the messages will be sequentially numbered in the order in which they are actually transmitted. A *global sequence number* is defined as the number of broadcast messages that have been successfully transmitted. The counter of a node is said to be *correct* if its value is the same as the global sequence number. Due to missed messages, the counter value of some nodes may be less than the global sequence number. This property is used for detecting missed messages. At any given time, the set of alive nodes can be partitioned into two sets: a set of nodes whose counter value is the same as the global sequence number, and a set of nodes whose counter value is less than the global sequence number. No node can have a counter value greater than the global sequence number. Note that a node does not know by itself which set it belongs to. A node knows that it has missed some messages if it receives a message with a sequence number greater than its counter value. However, if a node receives a message whose sequence number is the same as its counter, it does not imply that the node has not missed any messages. If a node that has missed some messages transmits a message to others, other nodes which have also missed the same number of messages will have a counter value that is the same as the sequence number.

This creates the possibility that a node that has missed some messages may broadcast a message which can be received and delivered by another node. This will make the order of delivering the messages by this receiving node different from, say, a node that has not missed any messages. If we can ensure that a node with an incorrect counter is not allowed to successfully broadcast a message, then if the counter value at a node is the same as the sequence number at a node, it implies that the node has the correct counter value.

The problem is to stop a node with an incorrect counter from broadcasting. In the protocol, a simple approach is used. If, while receiving a message, the NI of a node discovers that the incoming message has a sequence number less than its counter value, *it immediately sends a jamming signal, thereby causing a collision.* This collision has the same effect as it does in a regular CSMA/CD protocol; the message is not successfully received by any node. This checking of the sequence number and jamming has to occur while the message is being received and before the transmission ends. For this reason, it has to be done in the NI. The communication software above the NI will not be able to do this, as the NI passes the packet only after it has successfully received the entire packet. The effect of this feature on timing and minimum packet size is discussed in [Jal92].

The sending and receiving procedures at a node have to be modified to accomplish all this. The modified procedures for a node i are given in Fig. 4.8 [Jal92].

The sending procedure (lines 1–7) is similar to a regular procedure for sending a message in a CSMA/CD network. The only difference is the addition of the sequence number, and the management of the counter.

In the receiving procedure, different actions are taken depending on the relation of the sequence number of the incoming message to the counter value. If $m.seq = C_i$ and the previous message in the buffer is marked (i.e., has been delivered), then the message is immediately delivered and marked, the counter is incremented, and the messages are buffered (lines 12–18). If the previous message is not marked (i.e., has not yet been delivered), the message is simply buffered and is not delivered (lines 17–18). The jamming by a node of any incoming message m for which $m.seq < C_i$ (lines 10–11) ensures that when $m.seq = C_i$, then all the messages with a sequence number less than $m.seq$ have either been received or have been requested. If $m.seq > C_i$, a retransmit_request for the messages with the sequence number $C_i + 1$ through $m.seq - 1$ is broadcast, and the counter is set from the sequence number of the message (lines 19–23). Note that retransmit_request is not an atomic broadcast message, and may not be received by all the nodes. Also, it has no effect on counters.

If a retransmit_request is received by a node, it transmits any message in the requested sequence that it has in its buffer (lines 24–25). Sending of messages in response to a retransmit_request is considered as a reliable point-to-point, positive-acknowledgment-based scheme. Counters are not modified for these messages. Many nodes may respond to a retransmit_request, and the requesting node may receive many copies of the message from many different nodes. However, all these will have the same sequence number and the duplicates can easily be discarded. Once all the messages have been received, the node marks and delivers all the unmarked messages (lines 26–30).

The protocol uses the fact that a message is received by more than half of the nodes (the set of nodes that receive a message is called the *receiving set* of that message). Consequently, the intersection of the receiving sets of any two messages is non-empty. The protocol ensures that after any successful broadcast, more than half the alive nodes have counter values which are the same as the global sequence number, and any node with a counter value less than the global sequence number is

1. $send(m) \rightarrow$
2. $m.seq = C_i$
3.   Attempt broadcast
4.   **if** successful
5.   Increment C_i
6.   Buffer m
7.   **else** wait for random time and try again

8. $receiving(m) \rightarrow$
9.   **if** m is a ordered broadcast message
10.   **if** $m.seq < C_i$
11.   Jam the transmission
12.   **if** $m.seq = C_i$
13.   Receive the entire message
14.   **if** msg with seq $C_i - 1$ is marked
15.   Mark m
16.   Deliver m
17.   Increment C_i
18.   Buffer m
19.   **if** $m.seq > C_i$
20.   Receive the entire message
21.   Buffer m
22.   Send retransmit_request $[C_i + 1..m.seq - 1]$
23. $C_i = m.seq + 1$
24.   **if** m is a retransmit_request
25.   Send requested messages from buffer to sender
26.   **if** m is a retransmitted_message
27.   Buffer m
28.   **if** all requested messages received
29.   Deliver all unmarked messages in order
30.   Mark all these messages

Figure 4.8: Modified send and receive procedures

prevented from successfully transmitting any message. This leads to the property that if a node receives two messages numbered s and s+1, then it has not missed any message between these two messages.

Due to the non-null intersection of the receiving sets of different messages, all the nodes that receive the retransmit_request together have all the messages a node has missed. Hence, every retransmit request is satisfied. There are other properties of the protocol which can be used to reduce the number of messages that need to be stored in the buffer by a node [Jal93]. Further details about implementing this protocol are also given in [Jal93].

4.3   Causal Broadcast

In atomic broadcast, the order in which messages are delivered is not important. Though this is sufficient in many applications, it is not strong enough in others. In some situations there are some restrictions on the order in which different requests sent by different nodes should be delivered to the resource. For example, consider the situation of a distributed database system in which a node i broadcasts a request, and then sends a message to another node j. After receiving this message, node j sends its own request for some operation on the database. It is conceivable that the request made by j uses the information given to it by i, and may depend on the fact that i has already performed some operation on the database. In such a situation, it is desirable that the request made by j be performed on the copies of the database after the request by node i has been performed. With atomic broadcast, this restriction cannot be enforced. For this, we require *causal broadcast* in which the causal ordering of messages is preserved.

As we have seen in Chapter 2, a "happened before" relation (represented by $\rightarrow$) can be defined by the events in a distributed system. This relation defines the potential causality between events in a distributed system. That is, $e_1 \rightarrow e_2$ means that the event e_1 can causally affect the event e_2. This relation specifies a partial ordering of the set of events in the system. We will also refer to the ordering defined by $\rightarrow$ as *causal ordering*. Causal broadcast requires that the order in which the messages are delivered by a node is consistent with the partial ordering defined by $\rightarrow$ on the events corresponding to the sending of the messages. Let the event corresponding to the sending of a message m be represented by $s(m)$. Causal broadcast requires that if $s(m_1) \rightarrow s(m_2)$, then m_1 is delivered before m_2 by all nodes. In the rest of this section, $m_1 \rightarrow m_2$ means that $s(m_1) \rightarrow s(m_2)$.

The causal ordering of messages can be preserved by two different approaches, leading to two different sets of requirements for causal broadcast. The weaker requirement only states that the causality should be preserved. The stricter requirement states that the consistency with the causal relationship is over and above the total ordering requirement. That is, the messages should be delivered in the same order at all the sites, but the order should be such that it preserves the causal relationship between messages. We will discuss two different protocols for causal broadcast, one for the weaker requirement, and one for the stricter requirement.

As in atomic broadcast, we distinguish between a node *receiving* a message and *delivering* a message. A message is received by a node when it arrives over the network and the node has no control over the order in which messages are received. A received message is delivered (to the processes executing on the node) whenever the node wishes to do that. Hence, the order of delivery is entirely in the control of a node. Causal broadcast protocols have to ensure that the order in which the messages are delivered is consistent with the causal ordering.

4.3.1 Causal Broadcast without Total Ordering

We first discuss a protocol that delivers messages to nodes in the system in an order that preserves the causal ordering. However, it does not guarantee the same total ordering of all messages at all nodes. That is, if two messages m and m' are such that $m \rightarrow m'$, then m is delivered before m' at all nodes. However, if there is no causal relation between m and m', that is, $m \not\rightarrow m'$ and $m' \not\rightarrow m$, then m and m' can be delivered in any order, and that order may not be the same at different nodes.

The protocol described here is distributed, and can support causal multicasting also [BJ87]. For causally broadcasting a message, a process executes the broadcast primitive $CBCAST(m, l, dests)$, where m is the message, l is a label, and $dests$ is the set of destination nodes to which the message is to be sent (where not needed, we will ignore the last two parameters). The label is a timestamp based on logical clocks (discussed earlier in Chapter 2) which preserve causal ordering. Hence, two labels l and l' are comparable if there is a causal relationship between the sending of the corresponding messages m and m', and $l < l'$ if $CBCAST(m) \rightarrow CBCAST(m')$. If there is no causal relationship between $CBCAST(m)$ and $CBCAST(m')$, then the labels l and l' are not comparable. We say that a message m *precedes* another message m' if $CBCAST(m) \rightarrow CBCAST(m')$.

For supporting $CBCAST$, a node P contains a buffer BUF_P which contains all messages sent to and from P, as well as copies of messages that arrive at P *en route* to other destinations. From the buffer, messages are put on a *delivery queue* from which the application processes can receive the messages. The protocol for $CBCAST$ ensures that the messages are added to the delivery queue in an order which is consistent with the causal order of messages.

When a node P performs a $CBCAST(m, l, dests)$, the message m (along with other related information) is added to BUF_P. If P is one of the destination nodes, then m is added to the delivery queue of P. Messages in BUF_P are later scheduled for transmission so that they can reach other destinations. It is assumed that each message in the buffer is transmitted in a finite amount of time.

When a message m is to be transmitted from P to Q, only m is not sent. P sends all messages in BUF_P that precede m. In other words, when P wants to send m to Q, it sends a *transfer packet* consisting of a sequence of messages $m_1, m_2, \ldots$. This transfer packet includes all messages in BUF_P that precede m. The messages are kept in a sorted order in the transfer packet so that if $m_i \rightarrow m_j$, then m_i comes before m_j in the transfer packet (i.e., $i < j$).

When a node Q receives a packet $m_1, m_2, \ldots$, it processes each message m_i in the transfer packet in the order in which it appears in the packet. For an m_i, Q first checks if this message is a duplicate (this is done easily by use of sequence numbers). If it is a duplicate, the message is discarded. If Q is one of the destination nodes of the message m_i, then m_i is put on the delivery queue of Q. Otherwise m_i is simply added to BUF_Q.

Let us see how this supports causal broadcasting. Suppose a message m was sent by a node P and a message m' was sent by a node Q (nodes Q and P also could be the same). If m precedes m', it implies that there is a sequence of broadcasts $m_0, m_1, \ldots, m_n$, such that $m = m_0$ and $m' = m_n$, and for all $i, 0 < i \leq n, m_{i-1}$ is received by the sender of m_i before m_i is sent. Since in each broadcast, besides the message, all messages in the buffer that precede the message are also sent to the destination, it is clear that when m_n is sent, the transmission packet will contain all messages $m_0, m_1, \ldots, m_{n-1}$. Each node that receives this packet will deliver m before delivering m', since a node processes the messages in the packet in the order they appear. Hence, the causal broadcast property is satisfied. Failures do not affect this as long as the network does not get partitioned.

4.3.2   Causal Broadcast with Total Ordering

Now we describe a protocol that delivers messages to the different nodes in the same order, such that the order preserves the causality between messages [Jal93]. The protocol is based on the primary site approach. One of the nodes in the system is designated as primary, and k other nodes are designated as backups for a k-resilient system. If the primary fails, a backup takes over the role of the primary site. If a node wants to broadcast a message, it sends it to the designated primary site (PS), which then broadcasts it to other nodes. This approach can easily satisfy the atomic broadcast properties. However, supporting causal broadcast is not straightforward, since messages sent by two different nodes, regardless of any causal dependency between them, can arrive at the PS in any order. For causal broadcasting, the PS has to order the incoming messages in a manner consistent with the causal ordering between them. This approach uses a method based on sequence numbers and counters for capturing and disseminating information about dependency between nodes.

Each node i keeps a counter C_i which represents the number of messages that this node has sent to PS for broadcast (initialized to 0). The counter is used to assign sequence numbers to messages whose broadcast is requested by node i. A node i also maintains an array $seq[]$. This array keeps a sequence number for each node, such that $seq[j]$ is the sequence number of the last message sent by the node j to PS for broadcasting, as known by the node i. Clearly, for a node i, $seq[i]$ represents the sequence number assigned by the node i (i.e., the value of C_i) to the last message it sent to PS for broadcasting.

Whenever a node j sends a message to another node i, it sends a copy of the array $seq[]$ along with the message. On receiving a message, a node sets its $seq[]$ such that each element is the maximum of its local value and the value received in the message. That is, if a node receives a new message m it sets:

$$\forall j : seq[j] = max(seq[j], m.seq[j]).$$

At a node i, at a given time, the array seq[] represents the sequence number of the last message from each node on which events of this node causally depend. In other words, any send command executed by the node i causally depends only on those broadcast messages of node j which were assigned by j a sequence number less than or equal to seq[j] at the node i.

The sequence number assigned by the PS to a broadcast message is represented as $gseq$, and is different from the sequence numbers assigned by the nodes using their local counters. The sequence number $gseq$ is used for globally ordering the delivery of messages. Each node maintains a variable *last-msg*, initialized to zero, which is the sequence number of the last broadcast message received by this node from the PS. This is used to identify and discard duplicate messages.

The major logical participants in the broadcast protocol are a simple node which is a sender and receiver of messages, the primary site, and a backup site (these are logical sites; a node may act as a simple node as well as the PS). Here we specify the actions that need to be performed by these different parties to support atomic broadcast. The actions performed by a simple node are shown in Fig. 4.9. When the node i has a message to broadcast, it assigns to seq[i] the value of the local counter C_i, adds seq[] to the message, and sends it to the PS. The message is also saved in the buffer, in case it is needed for retransmission later on.

Node i:

> msg-to-send(msg) $\rightarrow$
> > $seq[i] = C_i$
> > $C_i = C_i + 1$
> > msg.seq[] = seq[]
> > send(PS, msg)
> > save msg in buffer
>
> $\square$ request-to-resend(n) $\rightarrow$
> > PS = sender
> > send(PS, messages numbered n .. C_i - 1)
>
> $\square$ receive(msg) $\rightarrow$
> > PS = msg.src
> > if (msg.gseq $\leq$ last-msg) then ignore the message
> > else if (msg.original-src = i) delete msg from buffer
> > > last-msg = msg.gseq
> > > deliver(msg)

Figure 4.9: Actions of a sender/receiver node

If the primary site fails and a backup takes over as the primary, the backup may have missed some messages sent by the node to the primary site. In that case, when the backup assumes the role of the primary and detects that it has missed some messages, it sends a request for resending the missed messages. If that request comes, the sender retransmits the missed messages to the new primary site (second guard).

Finally, if the node receives a broadcast message (the node is also one of the recipients), and if the sequence number assigned to the message by the PS (*gseq*) is less than or equal to the sequence number of the last message received by the node from the PS, it implies that this message is a duplicate, and is discarded by the node. The primary site is identified as the source of the coming message (represented by *msg.src*). If the original source of the message is this node, then the copy of the message is deleted from the buffer, since it will not be needed for retransmission. In Fig. 4.9, msg.original-src represents the originator of the message.

Now let us consider the actions that need to be performed by the primary site.

Primary Site:

    receive(msg) →

        if expected[msg.src] > msg.seq[msg.src] →

            discard the message as duplicate

        else save *msg* in buffer

    □∃*msg* in buffer such that ($\forall j \neq msg.src$: expected[j] > msg.seq[j])

            and (expected[msg.src] = msg.seq[msg.src]) →

        add *msg* to Q_B

        increment expected[msg.src]

    □Q_B not empty →

        take *msg* at the head of Q_B

        msg.gseq = Ctr

        to backups in sequence, send (msg and expected[])

        to other receivers, send(msg)

        Ctr = Ctr + 1

Figure 4.10: Actions performed by the primary site

The primary site keeps an array called *expected[ ]*, where *expected[i]* is the expected sequence number of the next message to be received from the node i. In other words, the PS has already received messages numbered 0 .. i (expected[i] - 1) from the node i for broadcasting. In addition, the PS maintains a counter Ctr, which is used to assign sequence numbers ($gseq$) to the broadcast messages. The primary site maintains a queue Q_B, in which the messages to be broadcast are kept in order. It takes the messages from Q_B and broadcasts them to other sites. It also has a buffer in which messages are kept till they can be added to Q_B. The actions of the PS are shown in Fig. 4.10.

    When the PS receives a message from a node for broadcasting, it compares its sequence number from what it expects. If the sequence number is less than expected, it means that this message is a duplicate (which may arise because of requests to resend messages), and is discarded, otherwise the message is put in a buffer. If at any time there exists some message *msg* in the buffer for which msg.seq[msg.src] is the same as expected[msg.src] (implying that all previous messages from this node have been received by PS), and msg.seq[j] is less than expected[j] for all other nodes j (implying that messages from all other nodes that were "sent before" this

Primary Site:

    receive(msg) $\rightarrow$

        if expected[msg.src] > msg.seq[msg.src] $\rightarrow$

           discard the message as duplicate

        else save *msg* in buffer

    $\Box \exists msg$ in buffer such that ($\forall j \neq msg.src$: expected[j] > msg.seq[j])

                 and (expected[msg.src] = msg.seq[msg.src]) $\rightarrow$

        add *msg* to Q_B

        increment expected[msg.src]

    $\Box Q_B$ not empty $\rightarrow$

        take *msg* at the head of Q_B

        msg.gseq = Ctr

        to backups in sequence, send (msg & expected[])

        to other receivers, send(msg)

        Ctr = Ctr + 1

Figure 4.11: Actions performed by the primary site

message have been received by PS), then *msg* is added to Q_B for broadcasting, and expected[msg.src] is incremented. Finally, if Q_B is not empty, PS sends the message expected[], first to the backups in order, and then to the other nodes.

Now let us consider the activities which a backup node should do. If the primary site and all earlier backups fail, then this node has to become the primary site. So, first it sets the value of its counter Ctr from the *gseq* of the last message received from the previous PS. The messages that were there in the buffer of the primary site at the time of failure are lost and have to be recovered by the backup. For this, the backup requests every node *j* to resend messages with a sequence number more than or equal to expected[j]. Note that expected[] at the backup is as obtained from the last message by PS to this backup. This ensures that any message from *j* with a sequence number less than expected[j] must have been broadcast by PS earlier. Since the backup does not know whether the PS was able to complete broadcasting of the last message it received (PS must have completed broadcasting of earlier messages), the backup also broadcasts the last message it received from the PS. This may result in duplicate messages, but they will be discarded by the receivers by the use of *gseq*, as discussed earlier. It should be pointed out that any failure during the recovery of a backup poses no problems, as long as the assumption about one alive node with the message holds. Failure during recovery simply means that the next backup will start its own recovery and take over as the primary.

In this protocol, the PS broadcasts messages one by one in the order in which they appear in Q_B. The Ctr value assigned by the PS is incremented at each broadcast. If PS fails, the backup completes the last broadcast in which PS was involved, and starts assigning Ctr values to messages after that. Since the message service ensures ordering between a sender and receiver, and all nodes discard duplicates based on $gseq$, all nodes will receive and deliver the messages in the order defined by $gseq$.

Hence, it is clear that the protocol does deliver the messages in the same order to all nodes. Now let us see how the delivery order of messages is consistent with the causal ordering. Suppose m_i is the message sent by node i and m_j is the message sent by node j. If $m_i \rightarrow m_j$, it means that either the event for sending m_i, or some later send event in i, and some receive event in j before sending m_j are related by a sequence of send-receives. On receiving a message m from another node, since a node j sets $seq[k] = max(seq[k], m.seq[k])$, for all k, it implies that $m_i.seq[i] \leq m_j.seq[i])$. As m_j is added to Q_B only after all messages m from i with $m.seq[i]$ less than or equal to $m_j.seq[i]$ have been added, clearly m_i is added before m_j in Q_B. Since the messages are delivered by the nodes in the order in which the PS broadcasts them, and the PS broadcasts messages in the order they appear in Q_B, the causality condition is satisfied.

4.4 Summary

Just like reliable point-to-point communication is a building block for building fault tolerant systems that require point-to-point communication, reliable broadcast is a building block for those fault tolerant applications that require one process to send a message to multiple destinations. The topic of this chapter is the abstraction of reliably broadcasting a message in a distributed system.

For broadcasting, the three properties of interest are *reliability, ordering*, and *causality*. Reliability requires that a broadcast message reach all the nodes, ordering requires that different messages sent by different nodes be delivered to all the nodes in the same order, and causality requires that the messages be delivered in an order that is consistent with the causality between them. For satisfying these three properties, three different broadcast primitives are needed: *reliable broadcast, atomic broadcast*, and *causal broadcast*. These primitives and the means of supporting them in a system that only supports reliable point-to-point communication, or unreliable broadcast communication, are the topic of this chapter. The protocols for these primitives become more complex because the properties need to be satisfied even if failures occur. We have assumed that nodes and links in a system can fail, but that the failures do not partition the network.

Reliable broadcast has one basic requirement: that a message to be broadcast should be received by all the nodes that are operational. This property should be preserved as long as even one operational node has the message. We discussed two protocols for reliable broadcast. First, one organizes the nodes in a network in a logical tree with the root as the originator of the message. Message diffusion along the tree is used to send messages to all the nodes. Node failures are taken care of by the parents of the node monitoring it, and in case of failure, the parent node performs the message-forwarding task of the failed node. The root node is treated as a special case, as it has no parents, and it is monitored by other nodes. If the root fails before completing its task, any node that has received the message from the root can complete the task of the root.

The second protocol for reliable broadcast that we discussed was the Trans protocol. In this, an (unreliable) broadcast communication medium is assumed. Each message contains positive and negative acknowledgments. Receiving nodes use this additional information to detect any missing messages and request their retransmission, thereby satisfying the reliable broadcast property.

Atomic broadcast, in addition to the reliability property, also requires that the messages broadcast by different nodes be received in the same order at all the nodes. The ordering property is essential in many systems that use replication for supporting fault tolerance. We have discussed many protocols for this. First, we discussed how the Trans protocol can be extended into Total protocol in which ordering is maintained. In the Trans protocol, the messages and their acknowledgments form a partial ordering among messages. This partial ordering is the same for all the nodes that receive the same messages. The partial ordering is extended into total ordering, such that all nodes convert the partial order into the same total order. To handle the situation in which all nodes may not have received all the messages, a voting protocol is used to decide which messages should get added to the total order at a given time instance.

The protocol using the centralized approach also employs unreliable broadcast communication. Messages are broadcast by nodes, but a global sequence number is assigned to each message by a node called the token site. This ensures a total ordering of messages. Missing messages are detected by a node when it detects discontinuity in the sequence numbers of messages it receives. To make the protocol resilient to node failures, the token site is rotated among the set of nodes in the token list. If failures occur, a new token list is constructed. The protocol for this ensures that there is only one valid token list at a given time.

The three-phase protocol for atomic broadcast assumes a point-to-point communication. It is a distributed protocol in which each message is assigned a unique priority, and messages are delivered by all in the order of the priority. To ensure that no message with a lower priority can arrive after a higher priority message is delivered, a three-phase protocol is followed. In this protocol, in the first phase the sender sends the message to all. In the second phase, all receivers assign a priority that is higher than any priority, and send it back to the sender. The sender assigns to the message the final priority as the maximum of these priorities, and sends the final priority back to the nodes in the third phase.

Another protocol we discussed uses synchronized clocks as the basis for ordering messages. The difference between the clocks of different nodes is assumed to be bounded, as is the maximum delay in sending a message from one node to another. From these bounds, for a message whose sending is initiated at time t, the maximum time at a local clock at which this message must arrive is determined. When the local clock reaches this time, all messages that were sent at time t are delivered. If multiple nodes have sent messages at time t by their local clocks, then they are delivered in the order of the node-ids of the sender nodes.

The last protocol that we discussed for atomic broadcast is for a CSMA/CD network. The protocol assumes the underlying broadcast network is reliable and a message that is broadcast is received by more than half the nodes in the network. The protocol orders the messages in the order they are transmitted on the shared medium. Nodes use local counters for assigning sequence numbers to messages they broadcast. A node updates its counter with each message it receives. If it receives a message whose sequence number is more than what is expected based on the local counter value, the node detects that it has missed some messages and requests retransmissions. For the scheme to work, any node that has missed any message has to be disallowed from transmitting a message. This is achieved by a node that has not missed any message jamming the sending of a message whose sequence number is less than its counter value. The protocol is for CSMA/CD networks only and requires hardware support from the network interface.

The last broadcast primitive to be discussed is causal broadcast. Causal broadcast requires that the order in which messages are delivered be consistent with the causal ordering of the sending of these messages. This can be achieved in two ways: by just ordering the messages that have some causal relationship between them, or by having a total order which is consistent with the causal ordering. We discussed two protocols for causal broadcast: one where total ordering is not supported, and another where total ordering is supported. In the first one, when a node sends a message to another node, it sends all the messages in its buffer which it has received and which causally precede the message being sent. This ensures that when a node receives a message, it also receives all the messages that causally precede this message. The messages are then delivered in the causal order.

The second protocol for causal ordering uses a centralized approach. All messages are broadcast through the primary site. This guarantees the total ordering property. Sequence numbers are used for communication between processes. These sequence numbers are used to determine which messages causally precede a message. The primary site, on determining this from the sequence number information on the message it receives for broadcasting, waits to actually broadcast the message until it has received and broadcast all the "earlier" messages. This satisfies the causal ordering property. To support resiliency, backups are used for the primary site, which take over the role of the primary site, if it fails. The primary site periodically checkpoints relevant information on the backups to help the backup restart when it takes the role of the primary site.

In this chapter we have discussed only a few protocols for each broadcast primitive. As atomic broadcast is perhaps the most important primitive for supporting fault tolerant applications, we have discussed a wider range of protocols for that. However, many other protocols exist, mostly for atomic broadcasting. Protocols for reliable broadcasting have also been proposed [MPM83, PL79, SA83]. The protocol discussed in [PBS89] for delivering messages in order is somewhat similar to the Total protocol discussed above. In this protocol also, a partial ordering is first constructed which is later converted into a total ordering of messages. A protocol based on a two-phase commit protocol is presented for token bus networks in [VRB89]. The protocol presented in [NCN88] uses the centralized approach for ordering broadcast messages, much in the same manner in which ordering was enforced in the second causal broadcast protocol discussed earlier. The centralized approach to ordering messages is also used in [KT91]. The focus of the work in [GS91] is to ensure that consistent ordering is enforced while multicasting messages in those nodes that occur in two or more destination groups. A general source of references for work done in the area of broadcasting can be found in [CNL89].

Problems

1. Consider the Trans protocol for reliable broadcasting. Suppose there are 5 nodes in the system and they send messages in order (i.e., node 1 sends, then node 2 sends,...). If every message is missed by the nodes which are two nodes down (viewing the nodes as being in ring), what is the sequence of messages for the first 8 messages?

2. In the above problem, how will the order be preserved by using the extension

of the Trans protocol? In which order will the first 4 messages be delivered (you may extend the message sequence, if needed)?

3. In the centralized protocol for atomic broadcast, the message is broadcast by a node but the sequence number is assigned by the token site. Suppose that this is modified and the message is sent to the token site which assigns the sequence number and broadcasts the message. How will this compare with the existing protocol?

4. Consider a set of 5 nodes. Suppose that when node 3 is the token site, it fails (while others do not). Explain how reconfiguration will work.

5. Is it possible in the three-phase protocol that there is a tie for delivering messages from two nodes (which can be easily broken by node-ids)?

6. In the three-phase protocol, a node cannot delete a message even after delivering it, in case the message is needed later during failure recovery. Develop a "garbage collection" method to delete messages that are "no longer needed."

7. Consider a CSMA/CD network with 10 nodes, each broadcasting a message in sequence. Assume that if a message is to be retransmitted due to a collision, two transmissions take place between the collision and the retransmission. Suppose that every second message sent is missed by the node that will send its message after two messages. What is the order in which the messages are delivered by the atomic broadcast protocol for CSMA/CD networks?

8. Design a reliable broadcast protocol (or extend one of the existing ones) that will also work with network partitioning. Assume that the network rejoins after a short duration.

9. Design an atomic broadcast protocol that will also handle network partitioning. Make any assumption about the duration of partitioning.

10. Can the centralized approach for causal broadcast be made into a distributed one?

References

[BJ87] K. P. Birman, and T. A. Joseph. "Reliable Communication in the Presence of Failures." *ACM Transactions on Computer Systems*, 5(1):47–76, February 1987.

[CAS85] F. Cristian, H. Aghili, and R. Strong. "Atomic Broadcast: From Simple Message Diffusion to Byzantine Agreement." *14th International Symposium on Fault Tolerant Computing Systems*, pp. 200–206, 1985.

[CM84] J. Chang, and N. F. Maxemchuk. "Reliable Broadcast Protocols." *ACM Transactions on Computer Systems*, 2(3):251–273, August 1984.

[CNL89] S. T. Chanson, G. W. Neufeld, and L. Liang. "A Bibliography on Multicast and Group Communication." *ACM Operating Systems Review (SIGOPS)*, pp. 20–25, October 1989.

[GS91] H. Garcia-Molina, and A. Spauster. "Ordered and Reliable Multicast Communication." *ACM Transactions on Computer Systems*, 9(3):242–271, August 1991.

[Jal92] P. Jalote. *Efficient Ordered Broadcasting in CSMA/CD Networks.* Technical Report TRCS-92-160, Indian Institute of Technology Kanpur, Department of Computer Science and Engineering, Kanpur, India, 1992.

[Jal93] P. Jalote. *Reliable Causal Broadcasting.* Technical Report, Indian Institute of Technology, Department of Computer Science and Engineering, Kanpur, India, 1993.

[KT91] M. F. Kaashoek, and A. S. Tanenbaum. "Group Communication in the Amoeba Distributed Operating System." *11th International Conference on Distributed Computing Systems*, pp. 222–230, Arlingon, Texas, 1991.

[MB76] R. M. Metcalfe, and D. R. Boggs. "Ethernet: Distributed Packet Switching for Local Computer Networks." *Communications of the ACM*, 19(6):395–404, July 1976.

[MMA90] P. M. Melliar-Smith, L. E. Moser, and V. Agrawala. "Broadcast Protocols for Distributed Systems." *IEEE Transactions on Parallel and Distributed Systems*, 1(1):17–25, January 1990.

[MMSA93] L. E. Moser, P. M. Melliar-Smith, and V. Agrawala. "Asynchronous Fault-Tolerant Total Ordering Algorithms." *SIAM Journal of Computing*, 22(4):727–750, August 1993.

[MPM83] D. A. Menasce, G. J. Popek, and R. R. Muntz. "A Locking Protocol for Resource Coordination in Distributed Databases." *ACM Transactions on Database Systems*, 5(2):103–138, 1983.

[MSM94] P. M. Melliar-Smith, and L. E. Moser. "Trans: A Reliable Broadcast Protocol." *IEE Transactions on Communications, Speech, and Vision*, To appear in 1994.

[NCN88] S. Navaratnam, S. Chanson, and G. Neufeld. "Reliable Group Communication in Distributed Systems." *8th International Conference on Distributed Computing Systems*, pp. 439–445, San Jose, CA, 1988.

[PBS89] L. L. Peterson, N. C. Buchholz, and R. D. Schlicting. "Preserving and Using Context Information in Interprocess Communication." *ACM Transactions on Computer Systems*, 7(3):217–246, August 1989.

[PL79] R. Pardo, and M. T. Liu. "Multi-Destination Protocols for Distributed Systems." In *Proceedings of Computer Networking Symposium*, 1979.

[SA83] A. Segall, and B. Awerbuch. "A Reliable Broadcast Protocol." *IEEE Transactions on Communication*, 31(7):896–901, 1983.

[SGS84] F. B. Schneider, D. Gries, and R. D. Schlicting. "Fault-Tolerant Broadcasts." *Science of Computer Programming*, 4:1–15, 1984.

[Sta87] W. Stallings. *Local Networks, An Introduction*. MacMillan Publishing Company, 2nd edition, 1987.

[Tan88] A. S. Tanenbaum. *Computer Networks*. Englewood Cliffs, NJ: Prentice Hall, 1988.

[VRB89] P. Verissimo, L. Rodrigues, and M. Baptista. "Amp: A Highly Parallel Atomic Multicast Protocol." *ACM SIGCOMM'89*, pp. 83–93, Arlingon, Texas, 1989.

Chapter 5

Recovering
a Consistent State

In the previous two chapters we have discussed the building blocks and the communication architectures that are useful for developing fault tolerant distributed applications. We can consider the services that were discussed in the previous two chapters as basic services that are supported either by the hardware or the operating system, and which can be used for constructing fault tolerant services. We now turn our attention to the supporting of fault tolerant services.

Perhaps one of the simplest of fault tolerant services is to restore the system to a consistent state. As we have seen earlier, error recovery, which restores the state to an error-free state, is an essential step in supporting fault tolerance. In some systems, just recovering to an error-free state may be sufficient.

In a uniprocess system, once an error is detected, error recovery is not a difficult task. Backward error recovery is straightforward. *Checkpoints* (or *recovery points*) are established periodically during normal execution of the process by saving all the information needed to restart a process on the stable storage. The information to be saved includes the value of the variables in the process, its environment, the control information, the value of the registers, etc. Saving the information on the stable storage ensures that even if nodes fail, the saved checkpoint will be safe. When an error is detected, the process is rolled back to its previously saved state by restoring the last saved checkpoint of the process. In case of node failures, the state restoration can occur after the failed node has been repaired.

When there are multiple processes in the system, and these processes are communicating, as is the case with distributed systems, checkpointing and rollback of the system is not as simple as in a single-process system. The main difficulty is due

185

to the fact that the state of the system now includes the states of different processes that are executing on different nodes. And the event of "establishing a checkpoint" is an action that can be performed at a node for its local data only (for distributed systems, we consider the checkpoint of a node as containing all the information of all the processes at that node). That is, each node can establish a checkpoint locally at a given time, but there is no direct method for establishing a checkpoint at the same time at all the different nodes to capture the state of the entire system at a particular time instance. This lack of a global observer requires that some other methods be used to establish a system-wide checkpoint.

A naive method would be to let each node independently establish a checkpoint, and a collection of these checkpoints — one of each node — would be taken as the system-wide checkpoint. Intuitively, we can see that in a system with communicating processes, this cannot be taken as a valid system state to which the system can be rolled back, as message exchange between processes may not be appropriately reflected in this state.

In this chapter we consider the problem of taking a distributed system to a consistent state, in case it is desired. Why recovery is initiated is not an issue for this chapter. We discuss only backward-recovery-based methods, where a consistent state is achieved by rolling back the system to a previously recorded state. There are two approaches to this. One is *asynchronous checkpointing*, where the checkpointing by different nodes is not coordinated, but sufficient information is kept in the system, such that when a rollback needs to be performed, the system can be rolled back to a consistent state. The second approach is to coordinate the establishing of checkpoints by different nodes, such that the set of checkpoints together form a consistent system state. This is called *synchronous checkpointing* or distributed checkpointing. Synchronous checkpointing limits the amount of rollback the system has to perform, but increases the cost of establishing the checkpoints, while asynchronous checkpointing keeps the cost of checkpointing low but the amount of rollback may be unbounded. We will discuss both of these approaches in this chapter.

5.1   Asynchronous Checkpointing and Rollback

As mentioned above, the goal of a rollback scheme is to roll back the system to a consistent state. In a distributed system, consisting of a set of communicating processes, a consistent state is not necessarily a state that has existed in the past during the execution. We have defined consistent or valid states earlier in Chapter 2, but discuss it here again for the sake of completeness. As described earlier in Chapter 2, the execution of a system can be considered as a sequence of states, with state transitions occurring when an event occurs (by a process executing some statement). In a uniprocess system with a deterministic process, for a given input state, the sequence of states that occurs during execution is unique. However, in a distributed system, many sequences of states are possible, even for the same initial state. In a given execution, any of these sequences may occur, and different executions of the same system (with the same initial state) may follow different state sequences.

Clearly then, there is nothing special about the states that exist in a particular execution of a system, since in other executions of that system those states may not exist. Hence, we should not define a consistent state as one that has existed during the execution of the system. (In uniprocess systems, the states that exist during the execution are special, since the same states will occur every time the system is executed.) In any case, since it is not possible to directly observe or record the state of a distributed system at a given time instance, the state that exists at a particular time instance has value only for modeling, but has little practical importance.

A more general definition is that a state is *consistent* if it *could* exist in an execution of the system. This includes, besides the states that actually exist in an execution, all the states that are in the state sequences representing other possible executions. Hence, the goal of a rollback scheme is to take the system back to a state that has either existed at some time in this execution, or could have existed in this execution.

Since usually only the state of the processes is recorded during checkpointing, as recording the state of the channels is not always easy, any global checkpoint will comprise the checkpointed state of the processes. For such a global state to be consistent, it is essential that if the recorded state of a process indicates that a message has been sent to another process, then the other process's recorded state must indicate that the message has been received. This requirement is the source of most difficulties in recording a consistent global state of a distributed system.

5.1.1 Rollback and Domino Effect

Now that we have established the goal of rollback, let us take a closer look at the issue of rollback itself. Suppose that each process periodically checkpoints its state on stable storage. Further, suppose that the processes establish checkpoints independently, without any coordination between themselves. Clearly, the global checkpoint of the system will consist of a checkpoint from each process. But the checkpoints of different processes that are taken together to form a global checkpoint have to be such that the state of the system formed by the checkpoints is a consistent system state.

If we ignore the transmission time of messages from one process to another, then clearly a system state cannot be consistent if the following situation exists: the state of a process P is such that it indicates that it has sent a message m to process Q, but the state of process Q is such that it has not yet received the message m. Such a situation represents a *lost message*, and cannot exist in any system execution in which reliable channels are assumed. Similarly, the converse of this situation can also not occur in a consistent system state where the state of process Q is such that it has received a message m from the process P, but the state of the process P is such that it has never sent the message m to Q. Such a message which has been received but has no sender is called an *orphan message*. Clearly, a state in a normal failure-free execution of a system will not have orphan messages. Avoiding orphan and missing messages during rollback imposes restrictions on which collection of checkpoints of different processes form a consistent system state.

These restrictions can be stated as follows. A set of recovery points form a consistent system state if the following conditions are satisfied:

1. The set contains exactly one recovery point for each process.

2. There is no event for sending a message in a process P succeeding its recovery point, whose corresponding receive event in another process Q occurs before the recovery point of Q that is contained in the set. That is, there are no orphan messages.

3. There is no event for sending a message in a process P preceding its recovery point, whose corresponding receive event in another process Q occurs after the recovery point of Q that is contained in the set. That is, there are no lost messages.

The set of recovery points that satisfy these conditions is called a *recovery line*. A rollback scheme has to ensure that the above conditions are satisfied, and that the system is rolled back to a recovery line. As an example, let us consider the system execution shown in Fig. 5.1. This figure shows the executions of the processes P, Q, and R, and the messages sent from one process to another. The small arcs cutting each process indicate the point during the execution of the process where a checkpoint was established.

Suppose that the process P is rolled back to its checkpoint p_3. Since P had sent the message to R after p_3, the state just after the rollback of P is not consistent (it does not satisfy condition 3 above). The process R has to roll back to its previous checkpoint r_4 to "unreceive" the message sent by P. When R rolls back, then it "nullifies" the message it sent after r_4 to Q, hence Q has to roll back to its previous checkpoint q_4. This rollback, in turn, nullifies the message exchange between P and

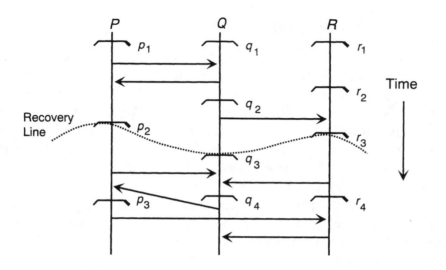

Figure 5.1: Domino effect

Q, and hence P has to roll back farther to its checkpoint p_2, which forces a farther rollback of Q and R. It can be seen that in this particular example, the state formed by the checkpoints p_2, q_3, and r_3 forms a consistent state, or a recovery line. The sets $\{p_2, q_2, r_2\}$, and $\{p_1, q_1, r_2\}$ also form consistent system states. In all these states there are no orphan or missing messages.

As can also be seen that the amount of rollback is determined by the pattern of message exchange between the processes, and their relative placements with recovery points. And there is no bound (other than the initial state) that can be imposed on this rollback. This flurry of rollbacks is called the *domino effect* [Ran75, Rus80], where a rollback by a process can cause an avalanche of rollbacks, which may even lead to the initial state of the system. If the checkpoints of processes are established independently and there is no restriction imposed on the message exchange between processes, then the domino effect is always a possibility during a rollback.

With a checkpoint-based scheme there is one way to avoid a domino effect. And that is to coordinate the establishment of checkpoints by the different processes or restrict communication between processes, such that a defined set of recovery points of processes together forms a recovery line. That is, the recovery line is determined during execution or by the recovery point establishment activity. This is the approach followed by the distributed checkpointing protocols, examples of which we will see later in the chapter.

5.1.2   Occurrence Graph Modeling

Here we present a formal model of system behavior, based on occurrence graphs, that can be used to precisely specify and understand state restoration in distributed systems [MR78]. The *places* in the model (represented by circles) represent a condition. The occurrence of an event is represented by a *bar*. A bar has some input arcs from some places, and some output arcs pointing to some places. The input arcs of a bar indicate which conditions were necessary to generate the occurrence of the event, or the conditions that together caused the event, and the output arcs represent the conditions that hold after the event has occurred.

It is assumed that a condition can influence, at most, one event. Hence, a place from which there is an outgoing arc cannot influence any more events. In other words, a place can have, at most, one outgoing arc. It follows that an event can be generated only by those conditions that have no outgoing arcs. Such conditions are called *active conditions*. Since a condition is created by an event, a place will also have, at most, one incoming arc. From the way occurrence graphs are constructed, it is clear that two places or arcs have a directed path between them only if they are causally connected. Due to this reason, the occurrence graphs are acyclic.

The occurrence graph models the dynamic behavior of a system. It does not represent an algorithm, but represents an execution of an algorithm. The occurrence of events during a system execution and their dependency on conditions is represented by an occurrence graph. An occurrence graph model is generated as the system is executed, and a system may have different occurrence graph models during different executions. In other words, the occurrence graph model is another way to represent the behavior of a concurrent system.

Let us illustrate the occurrence graph model with the example given in [MR78]. Suppose there are two files F1 and F2 at different nodes, and a terminal T. The terminal requests the copies of the files to be sent to a location where they will be merged into a single file F3 which will replace F1. A copy of F3 is also kept at the merging location. The occurrence graph representing this initial condition is shown in Fig. 5.2(a). Place 1 represents the existence of F1, place 2 the existence of F2, and place 3 represents that terminal T is ready to send requests. The first event that occurs in the system is that T sends a request to F1 and F2, which creates two new conditions "Req F1"(place 4) and "Req F2" (place 5). The occurrence graph for this situation is shown in Fig. 5.2(b). After the files F1 and F2 are copied by two independent events — bars 2 and 3 — the presence of the new files is represented by places 7 and 8, while the existence of the old files is represented by places 6 and 9. Merging of the two files is the fourth event, and copying of F3 onto F1 is the fifth event. The complete occurrence graph is shown in Fig. 5.2(c). Note that the graph

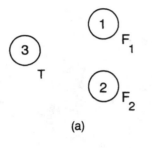

(a)

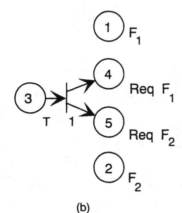

(b)

Figure 5.2: Occurrence graphs

captures the entire history of this execution, as well as the dependencies.

Modeling State Restoration

In the occurrence graph context, establishing a recovery point can be viewed as making some conditions of the system recoverable. Such a condition is called a *recoverable place*, and is represented by a double circle. State restoration is achieved by reactivating appropriate non-active conditions, and deactivating appropriate active conditions [MR78]. In modeling, we are only concerned with understanding what should be reactivated and what should be deactivated. How this is done is not addressed here.

The reactivation of a place can be performed only if the place is restorable (and non-active). When a place is reactivated, we want to ignore the previous effects due to this place. This is done in an occurrence graph by placing a black triangle in the place, replacing its outgoing arc by a dotted arc, and marking the bar to which it is connected by a "*." Such a bar is called an *invalid bar*. A deactivated state that was

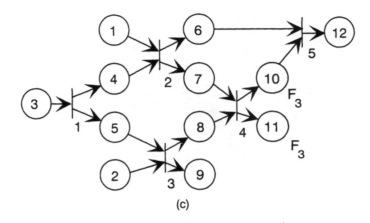

(c)

Figure 5.2: Occurrence graphs (continued)

previously active is also marked by a "*."

A *component* of an occurrence graph is a subgraph that has no outgoing edges, and has no regular incoming arcs. Incoming dotted arcs are permitted. Suppose that such a component does not have any active places. Then this component cannot generate any new bars. And since there are no outgoing arcs, the events in this component have no effect on other parts of the system. With respect to other parts of the system, such a component can be ignored and is called an *ignorable activity*. Ignorable activities can be deleted from an occurrence graph. A *recoverable activity* of an occurrence graph is a subgraph that has no outgoing edges, and whose incoming edges are either dashed or are coming directly from a recoverable place. The set of restorable places from which arcs are going to this recoverable activity form the recovery line for this recoverable activity. If all the places of a recovery line are restored, then the recoverable activity becomes a component of the graph, and can be converted into an ignorable activity by deactivating all its active places. It is clear that only recoverable activities can be turned into ignorable activities.

If some events are made invalid (by some error-detection mechanism, which is considered outside the scope of occurrence graph modeling), then the goal of state restoration is to construct an ignorable activity that contains the invalidated bars.

Consider the occurrence graph of the example discussed above. Let us suppose that some places, as shown in Fig. 5.3(a), are recoverable. Suppose that some error is detected and it is determined that the event represented by bar 5 has caused the error. Hence this bar is declared invalid. This situation is shown in Fig. 5.3(a). Now we have to find an ignorable activity that includes bar 5. This can be done by deactivating places 11 and 12, and reactivating places 6, 7, and 8. Due to the

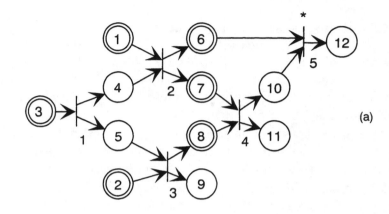

Figure 5.3: State restoration with occurrence graphs (a)

reactivation of places 7 and 8, bar 4 also becomes invalid. The resulting occurrence graph is shown in Fig. 5.3(b). The bars 4, 5 and the places 10, 11, and 12 form an

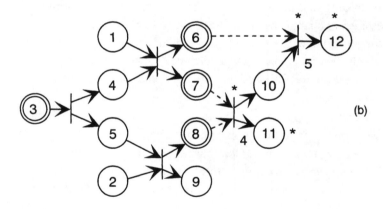

Figure 5.3: State restoration with occurrence graphs (b)

ignorable activity that includes all the invalid elements. This ignorable activity can be deleted from the occurrence graph.

The model presented here is for modeling and understanding the relationship between recovery points, dependence between events (e.g., sending and receiving of the same message), and rollback. By itself it does not present any method for detecting ignorable activities. Some protocols, called the "chase protocols," were also proposed [MR78] for decentralized recovery using this model.

5.1.3   Protocols for State Restoration

Now we will look at a few protocols for restoring a consistent state of a distributed system, in case some processes initiate a recovery. Why the recovery is initiated is not an issue for these protocols. No restrictions are placed on interprocess communication, and the processes establish checkpoints asynchronously on the stable storage, without any coordination between them for establishing the checkpoints. A checkpoint can be *committed* if it is determined that the checkpoint will never be needed in any recovery. Commitment of checkpoints by different processes is also not coordinated. In one of the protocols discussed here, only the checkpoints on the stable storage are used for recovery. The other protocol also logs events on volatile storage. In an event of failure and rollback, the processes that fail can only make use of the checkpoints on the stable storage. However, other processes which have not failed can still have access to their logs in the volatile storage. Since logging in main memory is not expensive, it can be done frequently, unlike checkpointing. This is exploited in the second protocol that we will discuss.

Clearly, in such a system where the establishment of checkpoints is not coordinated and the message exchange is unrestricted, some information about the message exchange between the processes will need to be saved. Based on this information, and the relative positions of checkpoints, a recovery line to which the rollback should go has to be determined. This is done by progressive rollback of the processes involved, based on information about checkpoints and messages during the execution.

The first approach that we discuss was proposed in [Woo81]. In this approach, each process periodically establishes checkpoints. The most recent checkpoint is said to be *active*. For any two checkpoints C and C' belonging to processes P and P', C is a *direct propagator* to C' if, and only if, information flows from P to P' while C and C' are both active. A checkpoint C is an *indirect propagator* to another checkpoint C', if either C is a direct propagator, or recursively, there exists some other checkpoint R'' in some other process that is a direct propagator of C' and C is an indirect propagator of R''. The indirect propagator relationship may be considered as a transitive closure of the direct propagator relation, and is similar to the partial ordering relation discussed in Chapter 2 on events in a distributed system. Note that in indirect propagator relationship, P and P' may actually be the same process. This occurs due to the domino effect, described above. There are two goals of the protocol [Woo81]:

1. The protocol must ensure that the system reverts to a consistent state in the event one (or many) processes initiate recovery.

2. It must support the determination of checkpoint safety.

The first goal is the essential requirement of the protocol. The second is a desired goal; the checkpoints that are determined to be safe, or committable, need not be saved any further. Since there is progressive rollback, a process needs to save multiple checkpoints. A practical rollback system will need to determine when a checkpoint is no longer needed. Here we will just discuss how the correct recovery is ensured. Interested readers are referred to [Woo81] for more details about checkpoint safety.

If a process knows the checkpoints to which each of its checkpoints is a direct propagator, then it can determine the checkpoints that must be recovered. These are the checkpoints which are linked by the direct propagator relationship to those of its own checkpoints that are affected by recovery, namely, the checkpoint to which the process is rolling back to and all its successors. Using this repeatedly, a recovery line can be reached.

Hence, to support recovery, the information about the direct propagator must be recorded. For this, each process in the system maintains a Prop-list, which records the identity of all checkpoints to which its own checkpoints are direct propagators. Whenever a checkpoint is established, the *Prop-list pointer* of the checkpoint is set to the tail of the Prop-list, and is never changed after that.

New entries to the Prop-list are added to the tail of the list. Whenever information flows from P to P', when the respective checkpoints are C and C', the name $P'.C'$ is added at the tail of the Prop-list of P. The Prop-list of a checkpoint is that part of the list that occurs after the Prop-list pointer of that checkpoint.

For performing recovery, *recovery control messages* have to be sent. Whenever a process has to initiate recovery to its current checkpoint, it sends a recovery control message to all names in the Prop-list of its active checkpoint. It then reinstates the state saved at this checkpoint, destroys the Prop-list of this checkpoint, establishes a new checkpoint with a different name, and then continues processing. The same actions have to be performed upon the receipt of a recovery control message. In this case, the process first recovers to the checkpoint mentioned in the recovery control message.

The second protocol we discuss was proposed in [JV90, JV91]. In this protocol, a process uses two types of logs: a *volatile log* and a *stable log*. The volatile log is maintained in the main memory, and is hence faster to access and involves small overhead. But this log does not persist after the failure of the process. The stable log is saved on the stable storage. This is more expensive to establish, since it requires accessing secondary storage and hence cannot be done very frequently. The stable log persists even after the process failure. All the events relating to the message exchange are large in the volatile log. The volatile log of the processes that did not fail is available even after rollback is started, and is used to make rollback efficient.

This protocol considers the computation of a system as event-driven, where a process P_i waits until a message is received, processes the message, changes its state, and sends out a set (possibly empty) of messages to other processes. For explanation, this activity of a process (receiving, processing, and sending) is treated as one event. An event e_{ij} represents the jth local event of the process P_i. A process P_i, after its jth event e_{ij}, records a triple $\{ps_i, m, M\_sent_{ij}\}$ in its volatile log, where ps_i is the state of the process P_i before the jth event, m is the incoming message that triggered the event, and M_sent_{ij} is the set of messages that P_i sends in this event.

From time to time, a process P_i independently saves the contents of its volatile log in the stable storage (and clears the volatile log), thereby creating the stable log or a new checkpoint. The jth checkpoint of a process P_i is represented by c_{ij}. We assume that the new checkpoint does not destroy the earlier ones. Hence, at any given time, conceptually, each process has a record of its complete behavior from the beginning to its latest checkpoint.

If the state of a process P_i is represented by s_i, then we define $SENT_{i \to j}(s_i)$ as the total number of messages sent by process P_i (from the beginning) to process P_j, and $RECEIVED_{i \leftarrow j}(s_i)$ as the total number of messages received by P_i (from the beginning) from process P_j. A process P_j is considered a neighbor of a process P_i, if P_i and P_j have communicated (i.e., there is a logical channel between them).

The rollback algorithm is executed at each process and works in iterations. The first iteration at a process is started after a process restarts after the failure or if a process detects the failure of a process. In this iteration, a process P_i that has failed and recovered, sets its state s_i to the latest event logged in stable storage. A process P_i that starts recovery, since it detects the failure of a process, sets s_i to the latest event that is recorded in the volatile log or the stable log. For each neighbor process P_j, process P_i computes $SENT_{i \to j}(s_i)$ and sends a message $rollback(SENT_{i \to j}(s_i))$ to P_j. It then waits to receive the rollback messages from its neighbors (when they send it).

During an iteration, a process P_i processes all the $rollback$ messages sent by its neighbors in the previous iteration. If P_i receives a message $rollback(c)$ from P_j, it first determines $RECEIVED_{i \leftarrow j}(s_i)$, which represents the total number of messages it has received from P_j in the current state. Clearly, if this number is greater than c, which is the total number of messages sent by P_j according to the local state of P_j, it represents that more messages have been received than sent. That is, there are orphan messages and the current state of P_i is not consistent with the current state of P_j. In this case, P_i rolls back farther, by restoring an older state from its volatile or stable log, such that the two numbers match. That is, it sets s_i to that event in which $SENT_{i \to j}(s_i)$ is the same as c. After processing the $rollback$ messages from all its neighbors, it sends a *rollback* message to its neighbors with the value of $SENT_{i \to j}(s_i)$ in the current state s_i. The algorithm terminates when the number of iterations becomes equal to the number of processes in the system. The algorithm for a process P_i is specified in Fig. 5.4 [JV91]. In the algorithm, N represents the number of processes.

if P_i has failed and recovered **then**
        s_i = the latest event logged in stable log
else s_i = latest event of P_i

for $k = 1$ **to** N **do**
        for each neighboring process P_j **do**
                send $rollback(SENT_{i \to j}(s_i))$ message
        repeat
                $m = rollback(c)$ message received from P_j
                if $RECEIVED_{i \leftarrow j}(s_i) > c$ **then**
                        find the latest event e_{ik} such that $RECEIVED_{i \leftarrow j}(s_i) = c$
                        $s_i = e_{ik}$
        until (a *rollback* message is received from each neighbor)
end for

Figure 5.4: Rollback algorithm for a process P_i

As we can see, the goal of the algorithm is to keep rolling back a process P_i until it is in a state in which the number of messages it received from any other process P_j is less than the number of messages sent by P_j in the state in which P_j is. That is, by rollback, the state of P_i is made consistent with the *current* state of its neighbors. After this, P_i sends information about how many messages it has sent to other processes in its current state. A process P_j, upon receiving this information from its neighbors, may roll back to make its state consistent with its neighbors. This rollback invalidates the consistency that P_i had achieved, and hence P_i must execute another iteration to make its state consistent with its neighbors. That is why the algorithm is iterative. It has been shown that after this has been executed N times, where N is the number of processes, then the state of each of the processes is consistent with that of its neighbors, and hence the global state is consistent [JV91]. It has also been shown that the amount of rollback by this method is the minimum, that is, without this amount of rollback, a consistent system state cannot be reached.

Let us illustrate this algorithm by an example [JV91]. Consider the execution of the system consisting of 4 processes as shown in Fig. 5.5. As mentioned before, e_{ij}

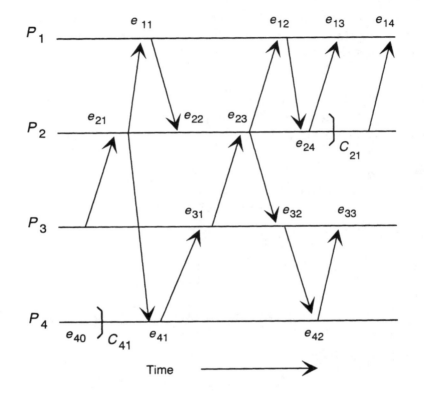

Figure 5.5: An example

represents the jth event of the process P_i, and c_{ij} represents the jth checkpoint (in which the volatile log is appended to the stable log) of process P_i. Let S represent the current state of the system: the state will be represented as a vector with one element for each process. For a process, the state will be represented by an event of the process, meaning that the state of the process is the same as it would be just after that event. Let C_i be the vector containing the contents of the *rollback* messages sent by P_i (i.e., the value of $SENT_{i \rightarrow j}(s_i)$) during the current iteration to different processes.

Assume that P_2 and P_4 fail and both restart from their most recent checkpoints, c_{21} and c_{41}, respectively. In the first iteration, we have $S = [e_{14}, e_{24}, e_{33}, e_{40}]$ (for P_2 P_4, the state is represented by the last event preceding their checkpoints to which they have rolled back), $C_1 = [-, 2, 0, 0]$, $C_2 = [3, -, 1, 1]$, $C_3 = [1, 2, -, 1]$, and $C_4 = [0, 0, 0, -]$. Recall that C_i represents the values sent in the *rollback* messages by P_i. For example, since P_2, in its current state e_{24} has sent 3 messages to P_1, 1 message to P_3, and 1 message to P_4, the vector C_2 is $[3, -, 1, 1]$.

In the second iteration, P_1 processes the $rollback(3)$ message from P_2. Since the value of $RECEIVED_{1 \leftarrow 3}(e_{14})$ is 4 (which is greater than 3), P_1 rolls back to e_{13}, the latest checkpoint in which $RECEIVED_{1 \leftarrow 2}(e_{14})$ is 3. This state of P_1 is then consistent with the current state of all other processes. Similarly, after the first iteration, P_3 will rollback to the state e_{30}, and after the first iteration we have $S = [e_{13}, e_{24}, e_{30}, e_{40}]$, and $C_1 = [-, 2, 0, 0]$, $C_2 = [2, -, 1, 1]$, $C_3 = [0, 1, -, 0]$, and $C_4 = [0, 0, 0, -]$. Similarly, in the third iteration we get $S = [e_{13}, e_{22}, e_{30}, e_{40}]$. In the fourth and final iteration, we get $S = [e_{11}, e_{22}, e_{30}, e_{40}]$. It can be seen easily that this state S is consistent, and in this state the number of messages received by a process from another is greater than or equal to the number of messages sent by that process.

These protocols ensure that a consistent system state is recovered, once a set of processes initiate a recovery. Since the protocols are used with asynchronous checkpointing, the domino effect is possible and the amount of rollback depends on the pattern of message exchanges and checkpoints.

5.2 Distributed Checkpointing

Unlike asynchronous checkpointing, in distributed checkpointing different processes coordinate the checkpointing of their local states. By proper coordination, checkpointing is timed to avoid those situations where message passing and the establishment of checkpoints is such that the domino effect can occur. That is, orphan and missing messages are eliminated by the proper placement of process checkpoints. A distributed checkpointing protocol ensures that the checkpoints taken by the different processes form a consistent system state. In this section, we will see some approaches to distributed checkpointing. But first, let us better understand the problem by examining a method of obtaining a "global snapshot" of a distributed system. This method shows that the problem of recording a consistent system state is not straightforward even if no failures occur, and forms the basis for distributed checkpointing approaches.

5.2.1 Distributed Snapshots

We first describe an approach to record a global state in a distributed system. This is not a distributed checkpointing scheme for the purposes of recovery and rollback, as it does not handle failures. The problem of capturing a global state is difficult even without failures. The approach discussed here was proposed by Chandy and Lamport [CL85].

A distributed system is modeled as a directed graph, where nodes represent the processes in the system, and arcs represent logical unidirectional channels between processes. It is assumed that the channels are reliable and preserve the ordering of messages. The state of the system is the state of all the processes, along with the state of all the channels in the system. An event in a process P can change the state of the process, or at most, one channel to which it is connected. A process can record its own state and the messages it sends and receives; it can record nothing else. Furthermore, it is assumed that the processes do not have access to a common global clock and so all processes cannot record their own local states at precisely the same time instance.

The model of execution is as defined earlier in Chapter 2. An execution of a distributed system is considered as a sequence of states, in which a state transition takes place when an event occurs in the system. There is inherent non-determinism in the system execution, as at any given state, a set of possible events can occur, out of which one actually occurs. As defined earlier, a valid or consistent system state is one which can occur in a system execution. All the states that occur in a given execution are valid; but other states that do not occur in the execution also can be valid.

The goal of the distributed snapshot scheme is to ensure proper cooperation between processes so that the states recorded by different processes together form a valid system state. In other words, this scheme obtains a "snapshot" of the system state in a distributed manner.

Clearly, the timing at which the different processes record their local states have to be coordinated, otherwise, an inconsistent state may be recorded. To see this, consider a "single-token conservation" system [CL85]. This is a distributed system consisting of two processes P and Q and two channels C and C'. The system contains one *token* that is passed from one process to another. Suppose that P records its state when it has the token. It then sends the token along C to Q. After Q gets the token, it also records its state. Assuming that the state of the channels are also recorded at this time (i.e., they are empty), we see that the recorded global state is inconsistent; this state has two tokens, which is never possible in a single-token conservation system. A different scenario in which the recorded state has no token can also be easily constructed.

In general, if n is the number of messages sent by P on a reliable channel C before P's state is recorded, and n' is the number of messages sent along C before C's state is recorded, then a consistent global state will have $n = n'$. Similarly, if m is the number of messages received by Q on C before Q's state is recorded, and

m' is the number of messages received along C before C's state is recorded, then consistency requires that $m = m$'. Since the number of messages received along a channel cannot exceed the number of messages sent along the channel, we have n' $\geq m$', and $n \geq m$.

For recording a consistent state, we want the recorded state of a channel C to be the sequence of messages sent by the sender before the sender's state is recorded, excluding the messages received along the channel before the receiver's state is recorded. If this is the case, then the state of the sender, receiver, and the channel between them form a consistent state. This implies that if n' $= m$', then the recorded state of C must be empty, and if n' $> m$', then the recorded state of C must be the $(m$' $+ 1)st$, ..., n'th messages sent by P along C.

This clearly requires that the different processes must coordinate the recording of their local states, and must cooperate in recording the states of channels in order to record a consistent state such that the above condition is satisfied. This is what the approach of [CL85] does. The state recording in this approach is initiated by one process. A process P initiates state recording by recording its local state and sending a special message, called a *marker*, along each outgoing channel C from P. On receiving this marker message, a process may record its own local state and/or record the state of the channel between the sender of the marker and the receiver, and forward the marker along all its outgoing channels. This is shown in Fig. 5.6.

Let us try to understand how this approach records a consistent global state. If a process Q records its state after it gets the marker from P, then it knows that it must have received all the messages sent by P to Q before P recorded its own state, and that any further messages that may be in the channels must have been sent by P after recording its state. Hence, it records the state of C as empty. This state of P, Q, and C being empty corresponds to a scenario where P has just recorded its state and has halted for some time (since no assumption is made about the relative speeds of the processes, a process can be "made" to wait in any state), and Q is at a point just after recording its own local state. This global state is possible, and in this state, the state of C is actually empty.

In the other case, where Q has already recorded its local state earlier, since it has received the marker message earlier, it records the state of the incoming channel C as the sequence of messages received between recording its state and receiving the marker message. When Q receives the marker message, it knows that it has received all the messages sent by P before P recorded its own local state. Some of these messages sent by P were consumed by Q before it recorded its state, and are reflected in the recorded state of Q. The remainder of the messages sent by P must have been received after the state recording of Q. If Q is considered as being at the point at which it recorded its state, these messages will be regarded as being in the

For the initiator process:
>   record its state
>   ∀ outgoing channels C, send *marker* along C

For a process q:
>   on receiving *marker* message from P →
>   **if** Q has not recorded its state **then**
>   **begin**
> Q records its state
> Q records the state of incoming channel C as empty
>   **end**
>   **else** Q records the state of C as the sequence of messages received
>   along C after Q's state was recorded and before Q received
>   the marker along C
>   **if** Q has not generated *marker* or received it earlier **then**
>   ∀ outgoing channels C, send the *marker* along C

Figure 5.6: The distributed snapshot algorithm

channel C, and are hence recorded in the state of C. This global state (recorded state of P, Q, and C) corresponds to a scenario where P has just recorded its state, Q has just recorded its state, and the messages that P sent to Q which have not yet been consumed are still in the channel C (since delays are assumed to be arbitrary, this is a possible scenario).

Since after a process receives the marker message, it is guaranteed to have recorded its state and the state of the channel along which the marker came (note that even if the marker comes for the second time, the state of the incoming channel is recorded), if the marker traverses all the channels in the system, we can be sure that the state of the entire system has been recorded. The forwarding of the marker by a process ensures this. If the graph representing the processes and channels is strongly connected, then once a process initiates the state recording activity, all processes will eventually receive the marker message.

It is clear that the state recorded by the approach above forms a "snapshot" of the system state, i.e., forms a valid system state. It is also clear that this recorded state is one which need not necessarily exist in the computation during which the state is recorded. It is a state that could exist in an execution with the same initial state as in the current execution. It has been formally shown in [CL85] that if the system started in the initial state S_i, and the state recorded is S^*, then there exists a computation of the system from this initial state whose sequence of states contains S^*, that is, there is a computation of the form $S_i \rightarrow ... \rightarrow S^* \rightarrow ...$.

This algorithm is not suitable for distributed checkpointing, as it makes no attempt to handle failures. In addition, it also records the state of the channels, while in checkpointing typically only the state of the processes is recorded. The problem of the distributed snapshot is discussed here to show the concept of a global state and to motivate the problem of recording a global state. The distributed checkpointing schemes that we discuss have their origins in this work.

5.2.2 A Distributed Checkpointing and Rollback Method

Now we discuss one particular approach to distributed checkpointing, and the corresponding method for recovering a consistent state. This approach has been proposed by Koo and Toueg [KT87], and can also handle failures during the execution of the protocol.

In distributed checkpointing, a process establishes a checkpoint by recording its local state. A set of checkpoints is consistent if the saved states form a consistent global state. There is no recording of channel states here; only local process states are saved. As discussed earlier in the chapter, rollback by a process may cause the system state to become inconsistent. This happens because rolling back a process may also "undo" an event of sending a message. This results in *orphan* messages, that is, those messages that have been received by some process but which the sender has not sent (since the send event has been undone). Similarly, the undoing of a receive event results in a *lost message*.

This protocol only aims to avoid orphan messages from occurring by properly establishing local checkpoints. For lost messages, the protocol assumes that the situation of lost messages is just like the loss of messages in the channels. Hence, the communication protocols will handle it. The consistent state that the protocol ensures will not have orphan messages but may have missing messages.

The algorithm saves two kinds of checkpoints on stable storage: permanent and tentative. A permanent checkpoint cannot be undone, while a tentative checkpoint can be undone or changed to a permanent checkpoint.

The basic idea of the algorithm for recording a global state is similar to the distributed snapshot algorithm. However, unlike the distributed snapshot algorithm, this protocol employs a two-phase protocol to ensure that either all processes checkpoint or none do. For supporting this, the two types of checkpoints are used. A tentative checkpoint is established when the process of state recording is ongoing. If it is found that the recorded state is an acceptable global state, the tentative checkpoints will be converted into permanent checkpoints.

The basic algorithm works in two phases as follows [KT87]. In the first phase, an *initiator* process Q takes a tentative checkpoint and requests all processes to take tentative checkpoints. On receiving this request, a process P establishes the tentative checkpoint. It may also choose not to do so for any local reason. The process P then informs the initiator about its decision, and refrains from any communication with any process until the second phase is over. If the initiator process Q learns that all processes have taken tentative checkpoints, in the second phase it makes its checkpoint permanent and requests others to do so. This ensures that either all processes take permanent checkpoints or none do.

This simple approach ensures that together the checkpointed states of the processes form a consistent state. That is, there are no orphan messages in the recorded state (though missing messages may be present). Let us understand why it is so. An orphan message occurs if a process P receives before its local checkpoint a message for which the corresponding send event in the sender process Q is after the local checkpoint of Q. This situation cannot occur in this protocol. Since a process is not allowed to communicate during the execution of the protocol, once the tentative checkpoint is taken, the process Q can send a message to P only after the second phase is over. The conclusion of the second phase guarantees that other processes, including process P, have established their checkpoints. Hence, any message sent by Q after its checkpoint can only be received by Q after Q has established its checkpoint. Note, however, that missing messages are possible. It is clearly possible that P may send a message to Q before taking its checkpoint, and this message may be in the channels when Q records its checkpoint.

Though in the discussion above we implied that all processes record their states during checkpointing, this is not necessary for obtaining a consistent set of checkpoints. New checkpoints of some processes along with old checkpoints of other processes may also form a consistent set of checkpoints. For example, consider the execution of three processes P, Q, and R, as shown in Fig. 5.7.

Suppose P initiates checkpointing by establishing its checkpoint p_2 and requesting Q and R to follow. Suppose the new checkpoints established by Q and R are q_2 and r_2. Hence, the set $\{p_2, q_2, r_2\}$ forms a consistent set of checkpoints. However, the set $\{p_2, q_1, r_2\}$ is also consistent, since there are no orphan messages in this set either (the set $\{p_2, q_1, r_1\}$ is not consistent, as there will be an orphan message in this checkpoint set). Clearly, the process Q need not take a new checkpoint, as its old checkpoint will suffice.

This idea is used by the protocol to ensure that only a minimum number of processes establish checkpoints, thereby reducing the checkpointing. A process assigns monotonically increasing sequence numbers to each message m sent by it.

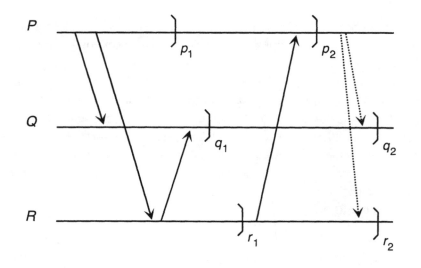

Figure 5.7: An example

This is represented by $m.seQ$. Let $last\_recd_Q(P)$ be the sequence number of the last message that Q received from P after it took its last permanent or tentative checkpoint. Similarly, let $first\_sent_Q(P)$ be the sequence number of the first message that Q sent to P after Q took its last permanent or tentative checkpoint. When Q requests P to take a tentative checkpoint, it appends $last\_recd_Q(P)$ to its request. On receiving the request from Q, a process P gets the $last\_recd_Q(P)$, and takes the checkpoint only if:

$$last\_recd_Q(P) \geq first\_sent_P(Q).$$

This condition says that a checkpoint is established by P only if before establishing its new checkpoint Q has received some messages from P that were sent by P after its last checkpoint. If this condition does not hold, that is, the sequence number of the last message Q received from P is less than the sequence number of the first message P sent to Q, then there will be no orphan message in the state comprising P's last checkpoint and Q's current checkpoint.

Clearly, if a process Q has not received any message from another process P since its last checkpoint, then there is no need for P to establish a new checkpoint if Q establishes one. Only those processes that have sent messages to Q need to *consider* establishing a new checkpoint. To make use of this, a process Q maintains a set $ckpt\_cohort_Q$ which contains those processes from which Q has received some message since it took its last checkpoint. This represents the set of possible processes that should be asked to checkpoint, if Q establishes a tentative checkpoint. In this set of processes, only those need to establish the checkpoint for which the above condition is satisfied.

Each process has a variable *willing_to_ckpt* to denote its willingness to checkpoint, which is initialized by the process. The initiator Q starts the checkpoint algorithm by taking a tentative checkpoint and sending a request "take a tentative checkpoint and $last\_recd_Q(P)$" to all processes $p \in ckpt\_cohort_Q$. It collects the decision of all these processes, and then disseminates the final decision to other processes. The final decision is: if all $ckpt\_cohorts$ of Q are willing to checkpoint, then establish checkpoint, else undo the tentative checkpoint. The actions of a process P are given in Fig. 5.8.

upon receipt of "take a tentative checkpoint and $last\_recd_Q(P)$" from Q **do**
    if willing_to_ckpt and $last\_recd_Q(P) \geq first\_sent_P(Q)$ **then**
        take a tentative checkpoint
        for all $R \in ckpt\_cohort_P$
            send("take a tentative checkpoint and $last\_recd_P(R)$")
        for all $r \in ckpt\_cohort_P$ **await**($willing\_to\_ckpt$)
        if $\exists r \in ckpt\_cohort_P$, $willing\_to\_ckpt_R =$ "no",
            then $willing\_to\_ckpt_P =$ "no"
    send to Q $willing\_to\_ckpt$
upon receipt of $m =$"make tentative checkpoint permanent" **or**
           $m =$ "undo tentative checkpoint" **do**
    execute command in m
    for all $R \in ckpt\_cohort_P$ **send**(R, m)

Figure 5.8: Checkpoint algorithm for a process P

The algorithm is simple. The initiator process Q sends the request to its $ckpt\_cohorts$, each of which sends it to its own $ckpt\_cohorts$. In this manner, all processes whose messages could have potentially affected the state of Q are sent the checkpoint request message. Each process checks if it needs to establish a new checkpoint and establishes a tentative checkpoint if needed.

To handle failures during the checkpointing, the method can be extended easily. If a process fails and is unable to send its reply (i.e., $willing\_to\_ckpt$), the reply is taken to be a "no" (by assumption, failure can be detected). On recovery, if the failed process was the initiator, it takes a conservative view and undoes its tentative checkpoint, and sends this decision to other processes, which are blocked. Other processes will have to contact the initiator or some other process to find out the final decision.

Rollback Recovery

Once it is decided that the system has to roll back, the rollback recovery needs to be performed. With distributed checkpointing, since the set of checkpoints form a consistent system state, one simple way is to roll back each process to its previous checkpoint. With this algorithm for checkpointing, the simple approach could be to roll back each process to its last permanent checkpoint. Since there is, at most, one permanent checkpoint for each process, and since the permanent checkpoints are established such that together they form a consistent state, this method of rollback will take the system to a consistent state.

However, it may not be the most efficient way of achieving a consistent state. Assume that one particular process initiates recovery (perhaps because the process has temporarily failed). Since this process may not have communicated with all the processes in the system since its last permanent checkpoint, there may not be any need to roll back all processes. In other words, it is possible that the current state of some processes along with the checkpointed state of the remaining processes may together form a consistent state. If this is the case, only those processes whose checkpointed state is taken need to be rolled back. For example, consider the execution of three processes P, Q, and R as shown in Fig. 5.9. In this example, if R initiates rollback (and rolls back to its last checkpoint), then Q must roll back, since R has sent a message to Q after its last checkpoint. However, the process P does not need to roll back, and the current state of P along with the checkpoints of Q and R form a consistent state, as there are no missing or orphan messages in this state.

To minimize the amount of rollback, along with the checkpointing approach, a technique was also proposed for recovery in [KT87]. For any process P and Q, $last\_sent_Q(P)$ is defined as the sequence number of last message that Q sent to P before Q took its last permanent checkpoint. When Q requests P to restart, it sends $last\_sent_Q(P)$ along with the request. The process P rolls back (to its last permanent checkpoint) only if $last\_recd_P(Q) > last\_sent_Q(P)$. That is, P rolls back only if the sequence number of the last message it received from Q after its last checkpoint is greater than the sequence number of the last message sent by Q to P before Q established its checkpoint. In other words, P rolls back if since its checkpoint, P has received messages from Q which were sent by Q after Q established its checkpoint.

The algorithm proposed in [KT87] uses this to minimize the amount of rollback. In addition, it uses a two-phase protocol, similar to the one used for checkpointing, to ensure that either all or none roll back.

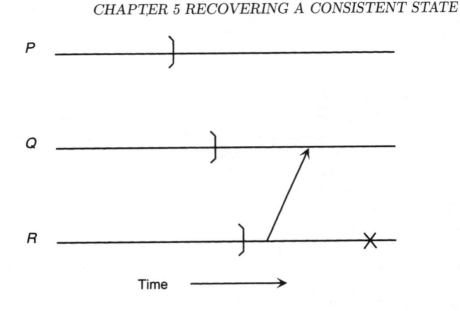

Figure 5.9: Rollback example

5.2.3 Checkpointing using Synchronized Clocks

Now we present a different approach for distributed checkpointing that employs synchronized clocks [CJ91]. Earlier in Chapter 3, we studied the problem of clock synchronization, and discussed protocols for synchronizing the clocks in a distributed system. With synchronized clocks, we can assume that the clocks of the different processes are apart by, at most, β. That is, at any global time, the clock reading of any two different processes in the system is within β of each other.

Let the system consist of processes $P_1, P_2, \ldots$. A process can checkpoint its own local state, and can log the messages it sends or receives. It is assumed that a reliable communication channel exists between processes, and that the message delay is bounded by δ. That is, with a very high probability, a message is delivered to its destination within a time δ of being sent. The initial state of the system $S(0)$ is defined as consisting of the initial states of the different processes $< s_1(0), s_2(0), \ldots >$, and is assumed to be consistent.

The basic approach is that processes checkpoint periodically, each with the same period π. It is assumed that π is much larger than $\delta + \beta$. If the clocks were perfectly synchronized (i.e., we have a global clock), then the set of checkpoints taken at some time $k\pi$ may suffice. Since clocks do not work in perfect synchrony, something more needs to be done to avoid orphan and lost messages. Orphan messages are avoided in this approach by making the checkpointing time a little flexible, such that the set of kth checkpoints of the processes does not contain any message that is sent by a process after establishing its kth checkpoint. This approach also explicitly handles lost messages (rather than leaving it to the communication protocol to handle, as was done in the previous protocol) by using message logging. Times are bounded by using the clock and delay bounds.

Let us now describe the approach in a little more detail. With synchronized clocks and bounds on message delay, we can say that if a message m is sent by a process at local time T, then this message will be received by the receiver process at the latest by its local clock time $T + \delta + \beta$. This is true, since the message will take at most δ time to travel, and the clock of the receiver process is apart from that of the sender by at most δ. It follows that if a message is sent by a process in the time period (according to local clock) $[T - \beta - \delta, T]$, then it will be delivered to the destination by time $T + \delta + \beta$ (according to local clock).

Each process intends to take a checkpoint with a period π. That is, for a process, the kth checkpoint is scheduled at time $k\pi$. Since clocks are not perfectly synchronized, the times when the clocks of different processes will reach $k\pi$ are within a duration β. That is, within a period β, all clocks will reach $k\pi$. Consider the execution of two processes P_1, P_2, shown in Fig. 5.10.

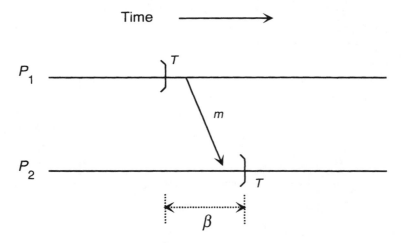

Figure 5.10: Orphan message possibility

In this example, the message m is sent by P_1 to P_2 just after establishing its checkpoint. Since there is no lower bound for message delay, the message can reach P_2 before the clock of P_2 reaches its checkpointing time. This can happen if the message delay is less than β. If this happens, then the set of checkpoints taken by P_1 and P_2 will not be consistent. It will have m as an orphan message. The checkpointed state of P_2 will reflect the receiving of m, but the checkpointed state of P_1 will not reflect the sending of the message. Similarly, missing messages can also occur, where the message is sent by a process before it establishes its checkpoint, but the message arrives at the destination after the destination process has established its checkpoint.

To prevent the occurrence of orphan messages, one method is to prevent a process from sending any messages during the time β after establishing a checkpoint. But this requires restriction on process communication. An alternate method is to establish the checkpoint earlier. In the example in Fig. 5.10, if P_2 establishes its checkpoint before consuming the message m, then the checkpoints of P_1 and P_2 will form a consistent state. This approach does not impose any restriction on process communication.

To avoid missing messages, message logging can be used. One way to do this is to have the senders log the messages they send during the interval $[T - \delta - \beta, T]$ on stable storage. If a rollback is performed, then these messages are retransmitted after rollback. This is like retransmission done by communication protocols for handling message losses. The messages can also be logged at the receiver. A receiver logs any messages it receives in the interval $[T, T + \delta + \beta]$, called the *critical interval*. These messages are added to the queue, if rollback is done.

These approaches can be summarized with the following rules to establish the kth global checkpoint [CJ91]:

> The kth global checkpoint of the system, denoted by $S(k)$, for $k > 0$, is defined as:
>
> 1. $< s_1(k), s_2(k), ... >$, where $s_i(k)$ is the local state of the process P_i at time $T_i^k = min(T, R_i^k)$, where $T = k\pi$, and R_i^k is the time P_i receives the first message sent by some other process P_j after P_j has locally checkpointed its state $s_j(k)$, and,
>
> 2. $< m_{i,j}(k) >, 1 \leq i, j \leq n$, where $m_{i,j}(k)$ is the ordered set of messages with timestamps in $[T - \delta - \beta, T_i^k]$ sent by P_i to P_j and not consumed by P_j until after it checkpoints its local state $s_j(k)$.

These rules for recording the local state ensure that the set of kth checkpoints of each process forms a consistent global state. It should be pointed out that even though the kth checkpoint may be established before its actual scheduled time of $k\pi$, later checkpoints are always scheduled as a multiple of π, and are not relative to the current checkpoint time. A detailed protocol based on these concepts, and a proof of correctness, is given in [CJ91].

5.3   Summary

In this chapter, we focused on the problem of rollback in a distributed system. We have seen that rollback in a distributed system is not straightforward. The goal of rollback is to take the system back to a consistent state. The basic problem is that though we desire a consistent global system state, checkpointing and rollback can only be performed by individual processes. Hence, the problem is to ensure that the checkpointing and rollback by processes is such that after the rollback, the system state is consistent. That is, each process establishes its local checkpoint, and we want the global state after the rollback, represented by a set of process checkpoints, to be consistent.

A state of the system is consistent if it is such that it could be reached by a failure-free execution of the system. Even for a given initial state, the execution of a distributed system can follow different sequences of states, giving rise to many possible consistent states, some of which may not occur during the execution in which rollback is initiated. There are two basic reasons for a set of checkpoints to not form a consistent state: *orphan messages* and *lost messages*. An orphan message represents a situation in which the receipt of a message is reflected in the state of a process, but its sending is not reflected in any other process state. Lost messages represent the converse of this. In checkpointing and rollback, we have to ensure that after rollback, the set of checkpoints is such that there are no lost or orphan messages.

There are two basic approaches to checkpointing and rollback: asynchronous checkpointing and synchronous checkpointing (also called distributed checkpointing). In asynchronous checkpointing, processes establish checkpoints independently, but keep a record of their communication. If a rollback is to be performed, then the communication history is used to roll back the processes such that there are no missing or orphan messages. The major disadvantage of this approach is that there is a possibility of the *domino effect*, in which there is an uncontrolled rollback of processes in an attempt to reach a consistent state. Another disadvantage is that since during rollback, a state that is far back can also be restored, many checkpoints for a process may need to be saved. However, asynchronous checkpointing is simple, and no coordination is needed between the processes. It can only be useful where failures are rare and communication between processes is limited.

Distributed checkpointing takes a different approach. Processes in the system cooperate to establish their local checkpoints, such that the set of checkpoints together is guaranteed to be consistent. That is, the local state recording is done in such a manner that the global state recorded is one which can occur in a normal execution. Cooperation between processes requires interprocess communication for establishing checkpoints. Hence, in this approach, checkpointing becomes more complex, but the recovery is simplified. In addition, only a few checkpoints of a process need to be saved at a given time. For example, one of the schemes discussed in this chapter saves, at most, two checkpoints for a process.

In this chapter we have only discussed the issue of rolling back the system state to a consistent state. We have not discussed the reason for rollback. In some situations, like databases, rollback to a consistent state may be sufficient. There are some other message-logging-based techniques that require further execution by processes after rollback to reach a consistent state. Such methods are more appropriate for supporting process resiliency and are discussed later in the book when we discuss the issue of making processes resilient to failures. There are other checkpointing techniques that are specific to database systems [FGL85, SA89]. For the sake of generality, we have not discussed these techniques. Other techniques have also been proposed that have not been covered in this chapter, and the interested reader is referred to [TKT92, VRL87, YH86].

Problems

1. Consider the interaction of processes given in Fig. 5.11. What are the various

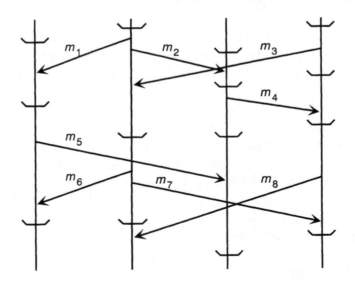

Figure 5.11: Interaction of processes

consistent states in this?

2. If *lost messages* are allowed in a "consistent state," then what are the different consistent states in the interaction shown in Fig. 5.11?

3. What is a domino effect? If "lost messages" are allowed in a consistent state, can a domino effect be avoided during a rollback?

4. The rollback algorithm shown in Fig. 5.4 can also be extended to disallow lost messages. Extend the algorithm for this. What is the execution bound for this modified algorithm?

5. Suppose P_3 fails just before its last checkpoint in the interaction shown in Fig. 5.11. Which consistent states will be reached by the two state restoration protocols discussed in Section 5.1.3?

6. In the example in Fig. 5.11, suppose the process state recovered by a snapshot algorithm is the second checkpoint of each process. What is the state of the channels recorded by the distributed checkpointing algorithm?

7. Assume that a process always has *willing-to-ckpt* as true. Under this condition, can the distributed checkpointing method described in Fig. 5.8 be made more efficient?

8. Can the distributed checkpointing algorithm given in Fig. 5.8 also be extended to disallow lost messages? If it can, extend the algorithm. If it cannot, give your reasons.

9. The two approaches for checkpointing and recovery — asynchronous checkpointing and synchronous checkpointing — have different overheads. Under what conditions will one approach be more suitable (i.e., have lesser overhead) than the other for a given system?

References

[CJ91] F. Cristian, and F. Jahanian. "A Timestamp-Based Checkpointing Protocol for Long-Lived Distributed Computations." *Proceedings of Reliable Distributed Software and Database Systems*, pp. 12–20, 1991.

[CL85] K. M. Chandy, and L. Lamport. "Distributed Snapshots: Determining Global States of Distributed Systems." *ACM Transactions on Computer Systems*, 3(1):63–75, 1985.

[FGL85] M. Fischer, N. Griffeth, and N. Lynch. "Global States of a Distributed System." *IEEE Transactions on Software Engineering*, pp. 198–202, May 1985.

[JV90] T. T. Y. Juang, and S. Venkatesan. "Efficient Algorithm for Crash Recovery in Distributed Systems." *10th Conference on Foundations of Software Technology and Theoretical Computer Science (LNCS)*, pp. 349–361, 1990.

[JV91] T. T. Y. Juang, and S. Venkatesan. "Crash Recovery with Little Overhead." *11th International Conference on Distributed Computing Systems*, pp. 454–461, 1991.

[KT87] R. Koo, and S. Toueg. "Checkpointing and Rollback-Recovery for Distributed Systems." *IEEE Transactions on Software Engineering*, SE-13(1):23–31, January 1987.

[MR78] P. E. Merlin, and B. Randell. "State Restoration in Distributed Systems." *8th International Conference on Fault Tolerant Computing Systems*, pp. 129–134, Toulouse, France, 1978.

[Ran75] B. Randell. "System Structure for Software Fault Tolerance." *IEEE Transactions on Software Engineering*, SE-1:220–232, June 1975.

[Rus80] D. L. Russell. "State Restoration in Systems of Communicating Processes." *IEEE Transactions on Software Engineering*, SE-6(2):183–194, March 1980.

[SA89] S. H. Son, and A. K. Agarwala. "Distributed Checkpointing for Globally Consistent States of Databases." *IEEE Transactions on Software Engineering*, 3(2):1157–1167, October 1989.

[TKT92] Z. Tong, R. Y. Kain, and W. T. Tsai. "Rollback Recovery in Distributed Systems Using Loosely Synchronized Clocks." *IEEE Transactions on Parallel and Distributed Systems*, 3(2):246–251, March 1992.

[VRL87] K. Venkatesh, T. Radhakrishnan, and H. F. Li. "Optimal Checkpointing and Local Recording for Domino-Free Rollback Recovery." *Information Processing Letters*, 25:295–303, July 1987.

[Woo81] W. G. Wood. "A Decentralized Recovery Protocol." *11th International Symposium on Fault Tolerant Computing Systems*, pp. 159–164, Portland, 1981.

[YH86] R. M. Yanney, and J. P. Hayes. "Distributed Recovery in Fault-Tolerant Multiprocessor Networks." *IEEE Transactions on Computers*, C-35(10):871–878, October 1986.

Chapter 6

Atomic Actions

In this chapter, we look at another fault tolerant service: atomic actions. The goal here is to make some identified operation appear as atomic, even if failures occur in the system. That is, the service to be preserved despite failures is the atomicity of operations. In applications which require atomic actions, if atomicity is preserved, the consistency of the system state is automatically guaranteed.

A user-defined action can be considered as a sequence of primitive operations or steps which are executed indivisibly by the hardware. That is, the primitive operations are executed by the hardware in such a manner that either the operation is completed fully (and successfully) or the state of the system remains unchanged and there is no effect of the primitive operation on the system state. However, the user-defined action by itself is not executed atomically by the hardware. The goal of supporting atomic actions is to execute the user-defined action atomically. That is, to execute the action so that either the action completes fully and successfully, or it appears as if the action had never started, and there are no effects of the action on the system state.

In this chapter, we will discuss some methods for supporting atomic actions. We will focus only on systems with non-replicated data, where if some failures occur before the action has been completed, then the only thing that can be done is to make it appear as if the action had never started. We will not discuss the other possibility, where the action can be completed successfully even if some failures occur. This is the topic of the next chapter.

6.1   Atomic Actions and Serializability

An atomic action is a mechanism which permits the user to specify an operation as atomic. An atomic action enjoys the same benefits of atomicity, i.e., indivisibility, non-interference, and strict sequencing, as are enjoyed by the primitive hardware instructions [Lom77]. Our goal is to provide an abstract machine that executes the user-defined operations atomically, in the same manner as the actual hardware of a computer system executes its instructions atomically. The task of building many applications, particularly database applications, will be simplified considerably if such a facility is available.

An atomic action can be viewed in many ways. An action is atomic if during the execution of the action, the process performing it is not aware of the existence of any other activity and cannot observe any state changes that may occur outside the action. Furthermore, no other process is aware of the activity of this process, and its state changes are concealed from outside the action. To view it in another manner, an action is atomic if it can be considered, as far as other processes are concerned, as indivisible and instantaneous. This clearly implies that only the initial state (before the action starts executing) or the final state of the action can be viewed, and no internal state is visible. This is what is called the "all-or-nothing" property of atomic actions, i.e., either an atomic action performs its computation fully or does not perform the computation at all (or is made to appear as if it has not performed at all).

The problem of supporting atomicity is quite straightforward in a uniprocess environment. Before starting the execution of the action to be executed atomically, the state of the system can be checkpointed on the stable storage. If the action completes (i.e., there is no failure before it completes), then the "all" part of the "all-or-nothing" property is automatically satisfied. If there is a failure, then, on recovery, the checkpointed state of the system can be restored, which effectively removes all the effects of the partially executed action, thereby satisfying the "nothing" part of the all-or-nothing property. In a distributed system, since data can be accessed concurrently by different processes, supporting atomic actions becomes more complicated. Concurrent access to shared data can cause the data state to become inconsistent unless the concurrent access is properly coordinated. In this section, we discuss the concept of transactions and serializability on shared data.

6.1.1   Transactions

Though atomic actions form a general primitive for building reliable and fault-tolerant distributed applications, they are of particular interest in the context of databases, and a large amount of work has been done in the area from the database perspective. Much of our discussion will also be in this context.

We consider a database as a set of data items or objects. Two basic operations can be performed on a data item: read and write. We assume that reading or writing one data item is *atomic*, and is performed in an indivisible manner by the hardware. That is, read and write operations on a particular data are always performed in some sequence, and a new operation starts only after the previous operation is finished. We will not discuss how this atomicity of reading and writing is achieved: one method is given in [LS79a], and the reader is referred to this reference.

In a database context, the action to be executed atomically is called a *transaction*. A transaction is a logical user operation that performs a sequence of reads and writes on entities. In many database-type applications, many different data items have to be read or written to perform one logical operation. For example, for performing the logical operation of "transferring some money from account A to account B," data for both accounts A and B have to be read/written.

Transactions are the fundamental logical unit of computation in a database system. If the database is consistent to start with, then a successful isolated execution of any transaction is guaranteed to leave the database in a consistent state. However, concurrently executing transactions may violate consistency if their operations are not coordinated. Consider again the example of transferring money from an account A to another account B. Let's suppose that the account A has $1,000 and account B has $2,000, and $500 has to be transferred. A transaction to perform this logical operation will have the sequence of actions shown in Fig. 6.1. A typical transaction

1. **begin transaction**
2. **read** account A
3. **read** account B
4. add $500 to account B
5. subtract $500 from account A
6. **write** new value of account A
7. **write** new value of account B
8. **end transaction**

Figure 6.1: A transaction

always starts with a begin-of-transaction (BOT), and ends with an end-of-transaction (EOT) command. Actions between these comprise the transaction. An EOT is often preceded by a *commit* command, which ensures that the effects of the transaction have been made permanent on the database. For now, we will not distinguish between the two.

Each of the steps in this sequence is a primitive action that is executed indivisibly by the underlying hardware and operating system. Now suppose two transactions, the first, transferring $500 from account A to account B, and the second, transferring $200 from account A to account B, are started simultaneously (i.e., they are executing concurrently). By the execution model of concurrent processes (described in Chapter 2), the steps of the two transactions can interleave in many different ways. Consider the following execution of the two processes: steps 1 and 2 of the first transaction are executed, then steps 1 through 5 of the second transaction are executed, then the rest of the steps (3 through 6) of the first transaction are executed, and finally the remaining part of the second transaction (step 6) is executed. In this execution, which is possible, the final result will be that account A will have $800, and account B will have $2,500. With these two transactions, the expected final state is that account A has $300 and account B has $2,700. Clearly, the resulting state of the two accounts is not consistent with the expected state.

Now consider the effect of failures. Suppose the process executing the transaction shown in Fig. 6.1 fails after performing step 3. In this case, the account of B will reflect the credit, but there will be no corresponding debit from A's account! Clearly, this state is inconsistent. What is desired is that the "all-or-nothing" property for the transaction is preserved even in the presence of failures. The "all-or-nothing" property can be trivially satisfied by reinitializing the system on each failure, which is clearly not desirable. Hence, another requirement for atomic actions is *durability*. Durability means that if an action has successfully completed (i.e., the action has committed), then its effects are never lost (due to failure or any other reason).

It is clear that both concurrent access and failures can violate atomicity. To support atomic actions, mechanisms have to be provided for handling both. In the databases context, the synchronization methods employed to handle concurrent access are often called *concurrency control protocols*, while the techniques to preserve atomicity in the face of failures are frequently called *recovery protocols*. We will discuss both of these in this chapter, although our stress will be on the recovery aspects.

6.1.2 Atomicity and Serializability

Before we discuss schemes for properly implementing transactions, let us clearly understand the indivisibility requirement for transactions. We define a transaction T as a sequence of n steps. That is, $T = ((T, a_i, e_i))_{i=1}^{n}$, where T is the transaction name, a_i is the operation performed in step i (for purposes of defining transactions, an operation is either R (read) or W (write)), and e_i is the data entity on which the operation is performed.

Consider m concurrent transactions $T_1, T_2, ..., T_m$. Any sequence of operations obtained by collating the operations of the different transactions is called a *schedule*. In a schedule, the order of operations of a transaction is maintained, but operations of different transactions can interleave in any manner. A schedule represents a possible execution of the transactions, in which operations of different processes interleave. A schedule is called a *serial schedule* if all the operations of a transaction occur together (i.e., contiguously) in the schedule. A serial schedule represents a serial execution of the transactions in which the execution of a new transaction is initiated only when the execution of the previous transaction is completed. Clearly a serial schedule will never lead to any inconsistency, as a new transaction starts only after the previous one has completed fully and hence no transaction ever sees the internal state of another transaction. However, it also does not allow any concurrency between different processes executing different transactions.

The problem of consistency occurs when the interleaving of operations of different transactions is allowed, that is, the schedule is non-serial. Non-serial schedules have the potential to lead the collection of data entities to an inconsistent state, but they also permit concurrent access to shared data. Since the transactions are to be executed atomically, the internal state of a transaction should not be visible to any other transaction, and a transaction should appear as a primitive, indivisible action to others. This means that no two transactions should appear to be concurrent and that the net result of executing different transactions should be as if the transactions were executed serially in some order. This is called the *serializability criteria*. Serializability means that the schedule of transactions should be such that it is equivalent to some serial schedule. This is one of the most important properties of atomic actions.

Now we need to clearly define what is meant by the equivalence of schedules [EGLT76]. On a schedule S, we define a *dependency* relation $DEP(S)$ as a ternary relation $T \times E \times T$, where T is the set of transactions and E is the set of entities. A value $(T_1, e, T_2) \in DEP(S)$ if for some $i < j$:

$$S = (..., (T_1, a_i, e), ..., (T_2, a_j, e), ...),$$

and there is no k such that $i < k < j$ and $e_k = e$, and either (or both) a_i or a_j is a write operation. The relation DEP captures the dependency between operations of different transactions. An operation depends on another operation that has occurred before it if the earlier operation is on the same entity as this operation is. For example, if (T_1, e, T_2), then T_1 could be writing a value to e, which is later read by T_2. Since an earlier read of an entity does not affect a later read, it is not included in the definition of DEP.

Two schedules S_1 and S_2 are defined to be *equivalent* if $DEP(S_1) = DEP(S_2)$. A schedule S is serializable, if $DEP(S)$ is the same as DEP of some serial schedule. With transactions, we require that the schedule be such that it is serializable. If the schedule of a set of transactions is serializable, it implies that each transaction sees the same state as it would see in some serial execution of transactions. Since serial execution of transactions is assumed to lead to a consistent state of the system, a serializable schedule will also lead to a consistent state.

Clearly, for a serial schedule S, if $(T_i, e_l, T_j) \in DEP(S)$ for some entity e_l, then it implies that $(T_j, e_m, T_i) \notin DEP(S)$ for any entity e_m. This condition implies that we can define a binary relation $<$ on the set of transactions, such that $T_i < T_j$ if $(T_i, e_l, T_j) \in DEP(S)$ for some entity e_l. This relation is an acyclic relation because of the condition above. Since a serializable schedule is equivalent to a serial schedule, it follows that the condition holds for a serializable schedule also. In fact, this is a sufficient condition for a schedule to be serializable. That is, for a serializable schedule, we can construct an acyclic relation $<$ on the set of transactions as defined above. This condition is frequently used to prove that a given scheme for concurrency control in databases preserves serializability.

If serializability is preserved, then the state of the database after executing a set of transactions is consistent. Serializability essentially restricts the set of possible valid executions to a subset of all executions that are possible in a general concurrent execution. A consistent state here can also be viewed as a subset of consistent or valid states possible in a system with unconstrained concurrency (as discussed in Chapter 2).

A great deal of work has been done in studying and formalizing the concept of serializability. We have presented here just a brief description based on the earliest work on this problem [EGLT76]. Many more models of execution and transactions exist, and the interested reader is referred to [BSW79, BG81, BHG87, Pap79].

6.2 Atomic Actions in a Centralized System

In this section, we will consider the issue of supporting atomic actions in a system where data is centralized, but concurrent operations can access the data. This situation is very common, particularly for database systems. Even with a distributed system, often the database is organized such that the data itself is on one server node, and the other nodes mostly process transactions and then forward them to the node which has the data for actually performing the operation.

We will first consider the issue of concurrency control, i.e., how to control access by concurrent transactions to shared data such that atomicity is not violated because of concurrency. Then we will discuss how atomicity is preserved even in the face of failures. For failures, we will focus only on the failure of nodes. Since there is only one node containing the data, nothing can be done about the data once the node fails, and the state of the database may be inconsistent at the time of the failure. The goal of supporting atomicity in this model is that *after* the failed node recovers, it performs actions (called *recovery activities*) such that the database state is made consistent and the atomicity of transactions is preserved. As we will see, for supporting the recovery activities, special actions have to be performed during normal computation as well.

6.2.1 Concurrency Control

One of our goals is to execute concurrent transactions in such a manner that their final schedule is serializable. Clearly, some restrictions on transactions and their interactions will have to be imposed so that the serializability criterion is satisfied. Protocols that impose such restrictions are called *concurrency control protocols*. A large number of concurrency control protocols have been proposed [BHG87, BG81]. We will discuss only one particular protocol for ensuring serializability.

The problem of concurrent access is also present in operating systems which have shared resources or data structures that are accessed by different processes. In the context of operating systems, this is solved by requiring that *critical, shared data* be accessed by different processes in a mutually exclusive manner. The problem is called the problem of *mutual exclusion*. One of the earliest primitives proposed to solve this problem was the *semaphore*. Other solutions have also been proposed.

The approach of mutually exclusive access to shared resources is suitable in the context of operating systems where the shared data is typically small and accesses are needed to these data infrequently and for a very short duration. In the context of databases, where the shared data may be large, and actions that need to be executed atomically may not be small or infrequent, this approach is too restrictive. We will present here one protocol for concurrency control called *Two-Phase Locking (2PL)*, that allows limited concurrent access to shared data, without violating the serializability requirement. Two-phase locking is the earliest and also the most commonly used protocol. Many commercial databases use two-phase locking for concurrency control.

Two-phase locking protocol [EGLT76] employs the locking of entities for access control. A transaction can *lock* an entity by requesting a lock on the entity (or performing a lock operation), and can release the lock on an entity by an unlock operation. A lock may be granted to a transaction immediately or the transaction may be delayed until the lock is available. Locks can be *read locks* or *write locks*. If a transaction T_i holds a read lock on an entity e_k, then no other transaction can be granted a write lock on the entity e_k. However, other transactions can be granted read locks on E_k. On the other hand, if a T_i holds a write lock on E_k, then no other transaction can be granted read or write locks. In other words, multiple transactions can concurrently hold read locks on an entity, but a write lock is exclusive.

Two-phase locking imposes the following restrictions on each transaction:

1. A transaction T can read/write on an entity e_i if, and only if, T possesses a read/write lock on e_i.

2. A transaction cannot request a lock after releasing any lock.

The first restriction is just to ensure that each transaction is *well formed*. The second restriction is due to the serializability requirement. The second condition, according to which a transaction is not allowed to request any lock once it releases any of the locks it holds, divides a transaction into two phases: a growing phase and a shrinking phase. In the *growing phase*, the transaction requests locks on entities. Once it releases any lock, it enters the *shrinking phase*, since after this, it cannot request any further locks and can only release locks. Due to the existence of the growing and shrinking phases, this protocol is called the two-phase locking protocol.

Let us informally show that the 2PL does indeed satisfy the serializability requirement. Suppose S is a schedule of concurrent transactions, each following the two-phase locking protocol. Since concurrent read operations do not pose any consistency problem, we assume that each lock of a transaction is a mutually exclusive lock. For each transaction T_i, we define a $SHRINK(T_i)$ as the least integer j such that T_i unlocks some entity in the step j of S. Since each transaction follows the 2PL, $SHRINK(T_i)$ is well defined. $SHRINK(T_i)$ specifies the start of the shrinking phase.

We define the relation $<$ on the set of transactions as $(T_i < T_j)$ if $(T_i, e, T_j) \in DEP(S)$ for some entity e. If $(T_i, e, T_j) \in DEP(S)$, it implies that T_i has performed an action on e before T_j. This implies that T_i, which held the lock when it performed the operation on e, released the lock before T_j performed the operation. That is, its shrinking phase must have begun before T_j performed an action on e. Also, T_j must hold the lock when performing the operation on e, which implies that it has not yet released the lock, implying that the shrinking phase has not yet begun. This implies that $SHRINK(T_i) < SHRINK(T_j)$. By defining $T_i < T_j$ if $SHRINK(T_i) < SHRINK(T_j)$, we have a total ordering of transactions, and an acyclic relation $<$ on the set of transactions. This shows that if all transactions follow the 2PL, serializability will be satisfied. Many variations of the 2PL have also been proposed [BHG87].

Deadlocks

Two-phase locking can result in deadlock. Consider a simple example in which a transaction T_i first intends to lock entity x, then lock entity y, and another transaction T_j that intends to lock these two entities in the reverse order. Deadlock is clearly possible in this case; T_i locks x, T_j locks y, and now neither can lock the other entity and both will continue to wait.

There are different ways to handle deadlock caused by the two-phase locking protocol [BHG87]. First is to use *timeout*. If a transaction has been waiting for too long a time, then it is simply aborted. If there was indeed a deadlock, then it will be broken. If there was no deadlock, this will be a case of a simple transaction abort. In both cases there is a performance penalty on the transaction.

Another method is to detect a deadlock precisely. This is done by building a waits-for graph for currently active transactions. If a cycle is found, it implies that there is a deadlock, and then one or more of the transactions in the deadlock are aborted.

6.2.2 Failure Recovery

Now we discuss how failures are handled in this system of centralized data with concurrent transactions. First, let us consider the failures in a database [HR83]. As we have seen above, there are situations where a transaction may need to be aborted. Besides the situations in which the system performs the abort, the user may also abort a transaction. Besides transaction aborts, we can have node failures (called a *system failure* in database context), in which the processing stops and the contents of the volatile memory are lost. In databases, another failure mode of interest is *media failure*. In this, the secondary storage that survives node failures also gets corrupted. Since we assume that stable storage is available, and have seen methods to support stable storage, we will not discuss methods to handle this type of failure. Hence, there are two types of failures that we need to handle:

- *Transaction Failure.* A transaction is aborted. In this failure mode, besides the stable storage contents, the contents of the volatile memory are also available.

- *System Failure.* A hardware failure stops the processing. Contents of the volatile memory are lost, but the contents of the stable storage survive the failure.

The goal of the recovery methods for handling these failures is to ensure that if any of these failures occur, the database is taken to a consistent state by recovery. That is, the state of the database contains the result of all the committed transactions, and does not contain the results of any incomplete transaction. Such a state is often called a *transaction consistent* state. In case of system failure, recovery procedures are executed after the system is repaired. When the failure occurs, the system may be in an inconsistent state. After the system is repaired, before regular transaction processing is resumed, the recovery activities ensure that the database is brought to a consistent state. Clearly, any recovery method that can maintain consistency under system failure can also handle transaction failure. Hence, we will focus mostly on the system failure.

For recovery, only the data in the stable storage is available. Since the goal of the recovery procedure is to make sure that the effects of all successful transactions are actually reflected in the database, and the effects of all incomplete transactions are removed, the recovery procedure has to be able to perform these two operations:

- *UNDO* — The effects on the database of all the transactions that were incomplete at the time of failure have to be "undone." The recovery procedure must be able to identify the set of transactions that have not completed at the time of failure, and be able to undo all the operations performed by any of these transactions.

- *REDO* — Results of some of the complete transactions may not be reflected at the time of the failure in the state of the database that is present in stable storage. Such transactions must be "redone," such that their effects appear in the database.

Some extra information is needed which can be used by the recovery procedure to perform these two activities. This extra information is frequently provided by maintaining a *log* of operations performed by the transactions. Log data is redundant information, collected for the sole purpose of recovery. Since the volatile storage is lost in system failure, the log is kept in stable storage. Each operation of a transaction that modifies any object in the database also writes a log record. To support the UNDO and the REDO of operations, the log record contains the old and new values of the object being modified (the actual representation may be more efficient than keeping both copies, but we will not worry about such issues). The UNDO of an operation restores the old value of the object, while the REDO of an operation restores the new value of the object.

This use of the log requires that there always be an UNDO entry in the log. For example, consider the situation where there is an operation that is performed on the database, but before it could be logged, a system failure occurs. In this case, during recovery there is no record of the operation in the log, and the operation cannot be undone. A similar problem can occur if a transaction commits but there is a failure before it logs the redo values. A REDO cannot be performed. To handle this situation, the *write ahead log (WAL) protocol* is used. The protocol states [Gra78]:

1. Before over-writing an object in the stable storage with uncommitted updates, a transaction should first write its undo log for this update.

2. Before committing an update to an object in the stable storage, the transaction must write the undo and redo log.

With the undo-redo log, which follows the WAL protocol, if a failure occurs, during recovery the incomplete transactions are undone, while the committed transactions are redone. This permits the recovery activities to take the database state to a transaction consistent state. Though it seems that the problem is now solved, there is one practical problem with this approach. This strategy requires redoing of all the committed transactions, even if they were done a long time ago. Clearly, this is not feasible. To bound the amount of REDO that needs to be done during recovery, *checkpoints* are used [HR83].

Checkpoints are a means to have the copy of the database on the stable storage reflect the state of the current database at some time instance. Frequently during processing, parts of the database are brought into the main memory buffers, and the processing is performed on them. Hence the current state of the database, which reflects all the changes performed on it, is defined by the state of the database in the stable storage and of its buffers in the main memory. Checkpointing actually means writing all the buffers that may be present in the volatile memory at a time instance on their respective positions in the stable storage copy of the database. This makes the actual copy of the database in the stable storage equivalent to the current copy of the database.

A checkpoint is established by completing the current operations (the read or write of entities) of various transactions that are currently in progress, then writing all the buffers back onto the database. While the buffers are being written, further processing of actions is stopped. To limit the amount of rollback, a database system periodically establishes a checkpoint. Another method to bound the amount of redo is to require that at commit time, the changes made by a transaction are propagated (in a database often called *forced*) to stable storage. In a sense, this is another way to perform a limited checkpointing at defined times. The overhead of this makes it less attractive in a centralized database, though it is used in distributed databases.

Let us illustrate the use of an undo-redo log by an example [HR83]. Consider the execution of the transactions shown in Fig. 6.2. Assume that the WAL protocol is

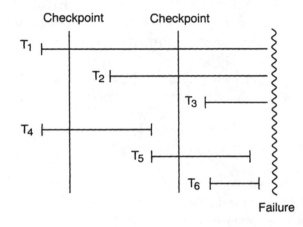

Figure 6.2: A recovery example

being followed for writing the log. In this example, during recovery after the crash, UNDO has to be applied for the entire transactions of T_1, T_2, and T_3. REDO has to be performed for only those actions of T_5 that are performed after the checkpoint. REDO also has to be performed for all actions of T_6. Nothing needs to be done for T_4, as its effects are already reflected in the database (guaranteed by the checkpoint taken after the commit of T_4).

One final note about recovery. Since recovery may force undo of some operations, if there are other operations that depend on the undone operation, then that operation will also have to be undone. We know that this type of dependence can lead to a domino effect during recovery. To prevent this situation from occurring, typically a *strict two-phase locking* protocol is used, where the locks held by a transaction are all released together. That is, the second phase in the 2PL is performed by a single step. This avoids the situation that some uncommitted value may be read by some other transaction, which can occur if an ordinary 2PL is used.

6.2.3   Optimum Checkpoint Interval

As we have seen, checkpoints are periodically established in a database system to support recovery from failures. During recovery, the system first rolls back to the previous checkpoint (i.e., restores the checkpointed state), and then performs the REDO/UNDO of transactions from the log. After recovery, further transactions are performed. This is often referred to as the *rollback and recovery (RR)* model.

The performance of the system employing the RR approach depends critically on the frequency of checkpointing, or the checkpoint interval. As the checkpoint interval increases, the recovery time increases, which decreases the system availability. On the other hand, as the checkpoint interval increases, the checkpointing overhead decreases, which increases the system availability. Consequently, there may exist an optimum checkpoint interval that maximizes the overall system availability. Here we consider the problem of selecting an optimum checkpoint interval such that the database availability is maximized, or the overhead is minimized.

Many different models and solutions have been proposed for this problem [CBDU75, GD78, Gel79, You74]. Most of these consider different assumptions, different input parameters, and different performance metrics. Here, to illustrate the basic concepts, we will discuss the problem of checkpoint interval selection based on a simple model proposed in [CBDU75]. In this model, *availability*, that is, the fraction of time the system is available for performing user transactions, is considered as the metric. The problem is to select the checkpoint interval that maximizes the system availability.

System Model and Assumptions

The system employing the rollback and recovery approach is assumed to establish checkpoints at *fixed intervals*. We consider site failures only. When a failure occurs, first the fault is repaired (perhaps by replacing the failed component), and the database is restored from the most recent checkpoint. Then the transactions in the log are redone. It is assumed that no user operations can be performed after failure until the recovery is complete. The user transactions that arrive during this time are assumed to be queued up. After recovery, the transactions from this queue are the first to be executed. To model this system, the following assumptions are made:

1. The checkpoint interval is fixed, and is represented by T.

2. Failure occurs at random times, and the failure is detected immediately. The lifetime of the system is exponentially distributed with mean $1/\lambda$. That is, the *failure rate* of the system is λ, and the mean time to failure (MTTF) of the system is $1/\lambda$.

3. Transactions arrive at a constant rate of μ transactions per second.

4. No transactions can be performed while a checkpoint is being established.

5. The time required to reprocess the log is proportional to the number of entries in the log.

6. Transactions that arrive between failure and recovery are queued up, and the time required to process this queue is much shorter than the MTTF of the system.

7. No failure occurs during recovery.

The metric considered is availability. Availability can be measured by the number of transactions that are denied access to the database due to checkpoint and recovery activities. In other words, availability can be assessed by the number of transactions arriving during a checkpoint or recovery.

Let F be the expected time to establish a checkpoint, and R be the expected time to restore a copy of the checkpoint. The time R, besides the time for actually restoring the checkpoint, also includes any time needed to repair the system. If the failure is detected at time t after the last checkpoint, then let $h(t)$ be the expected recovery time. This time clearly depends on t (that is why h is a function of t) and increases monotonically with t, since the audit trail increases in size as t increases. By assumption, the time to process the audit trail is proportional to its size. Let k be the proportionality constant. This constant is called the *compression* factor. If the arrival rate of transactions that update the database is a constant μ', then the size of the audit trail is $\mu't$. If the average rate of processing requests from the audit trail is b, the time taken to process the audit trail is $\mu't/b$. We then have the proportionality constant $k = \mu'/b$. Since the fraction of transactions that update the database is typically low, the compression factor k can be expected to be small.

Determining the Optimum Checkpoint Interval

Let $V(T)$ be the total expected time spent in recovery between two successive checkpoints, given that the checkpoint interval is T. $V(T)$ is a monotonically increasing function with T. The total overhead time associated with checkpointing and recovery activities during a checkpoint interval is the cost of checkpointing and the cost of recovery. That is, the total overhead is $F + V(T)$. Let $r(t)$ be the expected overhead in one unit of time. We then have

$$r(T) = \frac{F + V(T)}{T},$$

and the availability $\alpha(T)$ of the system is

$$\alpha(T) = 1 - r(T).$$

The expected recovery time, if failure is detected at time t, is $h(t) = R + kt$. Let $C(x)$ be the expected cost of recovery in the interval $t = x$ to $t = T$, i.e., from x to the next checkpoint. Clearly, $C(T) = 0$ and $C(0) = V(T)$. Let us try to determine the function $C(x)$ first.

Consider the interval $(t - \delta t, t)$. The probability of detecting a failure in this interval is $\lambda \delta t$. If a failure occurs in the interval, the cost is $h(t)$ (the cost of performing recovery) $+ C(t)$. If no failure occurs, the cost is $C(t)$. Therefore we have

$$C(t - \delta t) = \lambda \delta t [h(t) + C(t)] + (1 - \lambda \delta t) C(t).$$

Taking the limit as δt tends to 0, we get

$$\frac{d(C(t))}{dt} = -\lambda h(t) \text{ for } 0 \le t \le T.$$

$C(t)$ can be obtained by solving this differential equation. We know that $h(t) = T + kt$. Integrating and using this value of $h(t)$ we get

$$C(t) = \int_0^t (-\lambda R - \lambda kx) dx$$

$$= -\lambda Rt - \frac{\lambda kt^2}{2} + K,$$

where K is a constant. Taking the boundary value $C(T) = 0$, we get $K = \lambda Rt + \frac{\lambda kt^2}{2}$. Using this value of the constant, we get

$$V(T) = C(0) = \lambda RT + \lambda kT^2/2.$$

Hence,

$$r(T) = \lambda R + \lambda kT^2/2 + F/T.$$

Differentiating r with respect to t and equating to 0 gives

$$T_{opt} = \sqrt{\frac{2F}{\lambda k}}.$$

The corresponding value of the unit overhead is

$$r_{opt} = \lambda R + \sqrt{2\lambda k F}.$$

The expression for T_{opt} gives the optimum value of the checkpoint interval for this system model. The expression for r_{opt} gives the value of $r(t)$ for this optimum checkpoint interval, which will be the minimum value of $r(t)$. In other words, if the checkpoint interval is set to T_{opt}, then the availability $(1 - r(t))$ will be the maximum.

It is worth pointing out that the optimum checkpoint interval is independent of the cost of restoring a checkpoint (R), though the overhead per unit of time does depend on it. It has also been seen that the percentage change in function r caused by a change in the parameters (called the *elasticity* of a function) λ, R, k, and F is small [CBDU75]. This suggests that even if there is some error in estimating these parameters, it will not greatly influence r, and the optimum value of T.

Example: Suppose the MTTF of a system is 16 hours (i.e., $\lambda = 1/16$), the compression factor is 1/8, and the checkpoint establishment and restoring times are 1 hour. For this system we get $T_{opt} = \sqrt{(2 * 1 * 16 * 8)} = 16$ *hours*, and $r_{opt} = 1/16 + \sqrt{2 * (1/16) * (1/8) * 1} \approx .19$. Hence the system availability is approximately 81%. If the checkpoint establishment time is reduced to 1/16 hours (approximately 3.75 mts), say by establishing the checkpoint on a separate disk rather than on the tape, then the checkpoint interval will be reduced to 4 hours. Further reductions in checkpoint establishment time do not reduce the checkpoint interval significantly.

6.3   Commit Protocols

In the previous section, we discussed methods for supporting atomic actions in a system with centralized data. We have seen that a transaction ends its computation by a commit or EOT command. The goal of the commit command is to make sure that all the effects of the transaction are reflected in the database, and that they are never undone in the future. The activity of actually committing a transaction is simple in a centralized database. The "commit protocol" essentially ensures that the redo log of the transaction is written before the commit. This ensures that if the node fails after committing, enough data is available in the log to redo the committed transactions.

In a distributed system, the situation is more complex. The data is distributed over many nodes. Each node manages some data entities, and only that node can access those entities. A process (transaction) that wants to perform an operation on an entity must request the node managing that entity to actually perform that operation. Hence, different operations of a transaction may be performed on different nodes.

Unlike a centralized system, where a failure means complete failure (i.e., no data is available), in a distributed system, a failure of a node does not stop all computation of a transaction. Only those parts of the transaction that are to be performed at the failed node are affected, the other actions remain unaffected. This complicates the activity of committing a transaction. Since a transaction is an "all-or-nothing" operation, if some part of the transaction cannot be done, then all the activities of the transaction must be undone to give the effect that nothing was done by the transaction.

View this situation in another manner. In a distributed system, it is possible that a node may "abort" that part of the transaction that is being performed at that node. This abort may occur because the node fails, or because for some reason the node is unable to perform the requested action for the transaction. If this happens, then even if other nodes are able to perform their parts of the transaction, the entire transaction must be aborted. Only if all the nodes taking part in the transaction are willing to commit, can a transaction commit. For this, a *commit protocol* is required. A commit protocol ensures that either the entire transaction commits, that is, all nodes taking part in the transaction commit, or the entire transaction aborts, that is, all nodes taking part in the transaction abort. This is called the property of *atomic commit.*

Though commit protocols are needed for ensuring the atomicity of transactions in a system where data is distributed, there is considerable work on this topic. Hence, we discuss commit protocols in a separate section. In the next section, we will discuss the issue of supporting atomic actions in an environment where data is distributed, and will see how commit protocols are employed.

6.3.1   Two-Phase Commit Protocol

The goal of a commit protocol is to ensure that either all the nodes taking part in the transaction commit the transaction, or all of them abort. For the purposes of discussion, we will assume that there is a process on each node that takes part in the transaction that performs the activities of the transaction on that node (including executing the activities of the commit protocol).

The simplest and certainly the most popular commit protocol is the *two-phase commit protocol (2PC)* [Gra78]. In this protocol, the node where the transaction is initiated (or the process executing the transaction) is called the *coordinator*. The other nodes (or processes on those nodes) that take part in the transaction are called *participants*. The two-phase protocol is a centralized master-slave protocol, where the coordinator acts as the master and the participants as slaves.

The protocol works in two phases. In the first phase, the coordinator sends a "commit-request" message to all participants. Each participant then sends its vote to the coordinator about its willingness to commit. If for some reason a participant is unable to locally perform its part of the transaction, it sends a NO (i.e., abort) message, otherwise it sends a YES (i.e., commit) message. These reflect the local decision of each node.

In the second phase, the coordinator collects the responses from all the participants. If all of them are YES (and the coordinator's own local decision is YES), the coordinator sends a COMMIT message to all the participants. Otherwise, the coordinator decides to abort and sends an ABORT message to all participants that

voted YES (those that voted NO have already decided to locally abort the transaction).
Each participant waits for the decision of the coordinator. When it receives the
message, it acts accordingly. This protocol, like other commit protocols, can be
modeled by a set of finite state automata (FSA), with one FSA representing one site
[Ske81, SS83]. The FSA for the coordinator and a participant in the 2PC is shown
in Fig. 6.3 [Ske81, SS83].

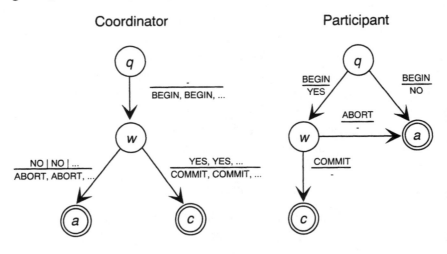

Figure 6.3: The FSAs for the two-phase commit protocol

The state of an FSA represents the state of the protocol at that particular node.
A transition in an FSA consists of receiving one or more messages, (performing
some computation) and sending zero or more messages. These FSAs are usually
non-deterministic, and they have two possible final states (representing the two final
outcomes possible for a commit protocol): the commit state c, and the abort state
a. In the FSAs for the 2PC, each FSA has four states: an *initial* state (q), a *wait*
state (w), an *abort* state (a), and a *commit* state (c). Each transition in the FSA is
marked by the conditions on the messages received (the "numerator") that cause the
transition, and the messages the FSA sends (the "denominator").

Timeout Actions
    If there are no failures during the execution of the commit protocol, it is clear
that the 2PC protocol ensures the atomic commit property. However, the protocol
is very vulnerable to failures. At many stages in the protocol, a process (participant
or the coordinator) is waiting for some messages to arrive. If the messages do not
arrive due to network failure or sender failure, the process will remain blocked. To

avoid this, *timeout actions* are added to the protocol. When waiting for a message, the process moves to another state if a timeout occurs [BHG87]. In the FSAs of the processes, this gets reflected as *timeout transitions* [SS83].

Let us consider the different places where a process is waiting for a message in the 2PC and add failure transitions [BHG87]. The first situation is when a participant is in the initial state q where it is waiting for the "request-commit" message. Since this happens before the participant has given its vote to the coordinator, and since at this state each participant can locally decide to abort or commit, if a timeout occurs, the participant can safely decide to abort. The next situation is when the coordinator is waiting in state w for votes from the participants. Since in this state the coordinator has still not reached a final decision (and has not informed any participant about it), it can safely decide to abort if a timeout occurs.

The last situation is when a participant times out when, after voting YES, it is waiting in state w for the final decision of the coordinator. For now we assume that this happens because the coordinator has failed. It is a consequence of the 2PC that if a process has voted NO, it knows that the final outcome will be to abort, but if it has voted YES, it does not know what the final decision will be. Therefore, unlike the other two cases, in this case the participant must consult other participants to decide what to do.

The activities that must be performed to make the decision are performed by a *termination protocol*. A termination protocol is executed by a site when the continued execution of the commit protocol is not possible due to the failure of some other sites. The goal of a termination protocol is to ensure that all the operational sites reach the same final state (commit or abort). One possible protocol is that when a participant P times out in state w, it asks other participants about what decision they have received. If there is one operational participant Q that has received a commit decision (and has voted YES), or has voted NO (and therefore knows that the final decision will be to abort), it can tell the process P what the final decision about the transaction commit is. However, in the situation where the coordinator failed after being able to send its decision to only a few of the participants, if all those processes that have voted NO or have received the final decision of the coordinator have also failed, there is nothing that P can do but wait till a process, which knows the final decision, recovers. Clearly, the 2PC will be subject to blocking even with timeout transitions, even if only site failures occur.

Recovery

We have seen above how a site failure can be handled by the timeout actions of other operational sites. Now let us consider the second aspect of site failures: a failed site which is recovering. We assume that a site keeps its current state in stable storage, hence upon recovery it can determine the state in which it failed. During the period that the site was unoperational, other sites could have reached a decision regarding commit. The recovering site has to make sure that it makes a decision that is consistent with the decisions of others. It is clearly desirable that the protocol be such that the recovering site can decide the final state, based on its local state. This is called *independent recovery* [SS83, BHG87].

Though desirable, it is not always possible to have a protocol that supports independent recovery. In the 2PC, let us consider the failure of a participant process P. If P fails in state q, since it has not voted YES yet, and since we know that a timeout due to its failure causes the coordinator to decide on aborting, P can safely abort the transaction after recovery. Similarly, if P fails after sending an ABORT message, it can safely abort.

However, if P fails in the wait state w, upon recovery it cannot decide on its own whether to abort or commit, as the final decision could have been either commit or abort. This situation is exactly similar to the case where P gets a timeout in state w. Hence P can reach a decision using the termination protocol discussed above. As mentioned above, with this protocol, P may get blocked if it is unable to communicate with sites that know the final outcome regarding the transaction commit.

How a site remembers the state it was in when it failed, and other related issues for recovery, will be discussed later in the chapter when we discuss the log-based method for supporting atomic actions in distributed systems.

The two-phase commit protocol requires a total of $3n$ messages in the absence of failures, if there are n participants in the system. Some variations have been proposed to reduce this message overhead. First is the *presumed commit* protocol [MLO86]. Since the majority of the transactions commit in a typical database, this protocol exploits this to reduce the number of messages in the absence of failures. Another protocol is the *early prepare* protocol [SC89], in which each participant enters a prepared state before replying to the coordinator. Some other protocols have been proposed to handle failure conditions [CK85, CR83, YJ89].

6.3.2   Nonblocking Protocols and the Three-Phase Protocol

We have already seen that even with timeout transitions, in the 2PC commit protocol a process may get blocked if sites fail. Specifically, if a participant fails in its state w, then blocking can occur. A protocol that never requires an operational site to block even if other sites fail is called a *nonblocking protocol*. In a nonblocking protocol, the sites that are operational can always reach a decision about whether they should commit or not. Two-phase commit is an example of a blocking protocol. It is clearly very desirable for a protocol to be nonblocking. Here we will use the FSA model described above to discuss conditions that a protocol must satisfy in order to be nonblocking [Ske81].

One of the features of nonblocking protocols is that if the communication network can fail (i.e., two processes cannot communicate even though the sites are operational), then there can be no protocol that is nonblocking [BHG87]. The reason for this is motivated by the example of the 2PC. If the network fails when a participant *P* is in the wait state, then since *P* cannot communicate with other processes, it cannot reach a decision until after the communication failure is repaired. Hence, in looking for nonblocking protocols, we assume that the network is reliable and only site failures are considered. It is also assumed that site failures can be reliably detected by the use of timeouts.

We define the *concurrency set* of a state of an FSA as the set of states that may be concurrently occupied by other states, and define a state of an FSA to be *committable* if occupancy of that state by the site means that all sites have voted YES on committing the transaction. Clearly, a site will be able to safely abort only if the concurrency set of the local state in which it failed does not contain a commit state. On the other hand, a site can safely decide to commit, if its local state is committable.

A blocking situation arises whenever the concurrency set for the local state contains both a commit and an abort state, or whenever the site is in a noncommittable state and the concurrency set for that state contains a commit state. In both these situations which are based on the local state, it cannot be deduced whether other FSAs will abort or commit. This leads to the basic condition for a nonblocking protocol (called the fundamental nonblocking theorem in [Ske81]): A protocol is *nonblocking* if, and only if, it satisfies both these conditions for every state in every participating site FSA:

1. There exists no local state such that its concurrency set contains both an abort and a commit state.

2. There exists no noncommittable state whose concurrency set contains a commit state.

This result can be used to check if a protocol is nonblocking or not. The question now is how to make a blocking protocol into a nonblocking protocol. Commit protocols typically work in phases. For each state in the FSA of one site, typically there is a corresponding state in the FSA of other sites. In the 2PC, even though the FSA for the coordinator and the participant are different, they have the same type of states. A protocol is said to be *synchronous within one state transition* if one site never leads another site by more than one state transition during the execution of the protocol [Ske81]. The 2PC is synchronous within one state transition. The concurrency set of a given state of an FSA in such a protocol can contain the similar state in other FSAs or an adjacent state, because an FSA is never ahead of another by more than one transition.

Due to this property of a protocol that is synchronous within one state transition, we get the following property. A protocol that is synchronous within one state transition is *nonblocking* if, and only if:

1. It contains no local state adjacent to both a commit and an abort state.

2. It contains no noncommittable state that is adjacent to a commit state.

From this, we can see that the 2PC is not nonblocking, since the wait state (w) violates both these constraints. These constraints can be satisfied by introducing a *buffer* state between the wait state w and the commit state c. In terms of phases, the introduction of the buffer state adds another phase in the protocol, and the 2PC becomes a *three-phase commit (3PC) protocol*. The buffer state can be treated as a *prepare to commit* state. The FSA for the 3PC is shown in Fig. 6.4 [Ske81].

In the 3PC, after the coordinator gets YES votes from all the participants, instead of committing, it sends a "prepare to commit" message to all participants, and moves to its state p. On receiving this "prepare" message, a participant sends an ack and moves to its own prepare state p. Finally, when the coordinator receives acks from all the participants, it sends a commit message to all participants.

It can be shown that the 3PC protocol has no state which has both c and a in its concurrency set. Once a process has reached its "prepare to commit" state, it knows that it will commit eventually. And before this state, it has the option of unilaterally aborting the transaction. Since once a process reaches state p, it always commits, the state seems redundant. Indeed, it is not of any real use in a failure-free situation. However, if failures occur, the existence of this state makes this protocol nonblocking.

Since this is a nonblocking protocol, we should be able to construct timeout actions for each process so that if a site is waiting for a message, it can reach a final state that is consistent. If a coordinator times out in w or if a participant times out in q, the timeout actions are the same as in the 2PC. Consider the case where a coordinator times out in the state p, where it is waiting for acks from the participants. The coordinator knows that the failed participants must have voted YES,

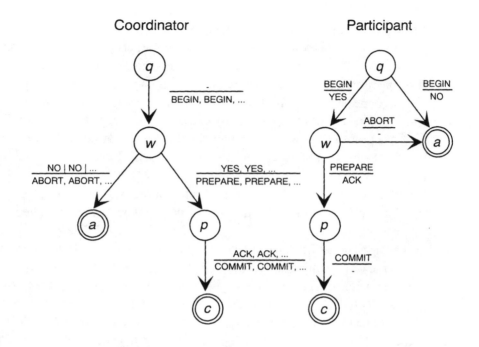

Figure 6.4: FSA of the three-phase commit protocol

and were therefore prepared to commit. Hence, if a timeout occurs, the coordinator simply ignores it and proceeds to commit by sending COMMIT messages to other participants.

The final two situations are when a participant times out in state w or in state p. We will discuss the first case only; the second one can be handled similarly. If a participant times out in w because the coordinator failed, it does not know if the coordinator had decided to send it the "prepare-to-commit" message or the ABORT message. Hence, it must communicate with other processes to reach a consistent decision. This is done, as discussed earlier in the 2PC, by a termination protocol.

The termination protocol works as follows. One of the operational sites is chosen as the *backup coordinator* by an *election protocol* (for election protocols, the reader is referred to [Gar82]). The new coordinator first makes the commit decision, based on its local state only, and then ensures that other sites follow the same decision. The coordinator uses the following rule to make the decision [Ske81].

Decision rule for backup coordinators. If the concurrency set for the current state of the backup contains a commit state, then the transaction is committed. Otherwise, it is aborted.

After making the decision, the backup coordinator issues a message to all sites to make a transition to its local state, and waits for an acknowledgment from each operational site. It then sends the commit or abort message to each site. The first phase of this protocol is needed, since the backup may fail. By bringing all other sites in the same state as itself, it ensures that the next backup will make the same commit decision. If the backup is initially in a commit state, then it can omit the first phase of this protocol. As we can see with the three-phase protocol, in all cases, the failure of sites does not block any other operational site. Hence this is nonblocking protocol.

Now let us consider recovery from failures in the 3PC [BHG87]. Again we assume that a process remembers the state it was in when it failed. The recovery actions of the coordinator are similar to those as in the 2PC. If a participant fails before having sent a YES vote, it can safely decide to abort. The corresponding timeout in the coordinator also causes the decision to abort. If the participant failed in state w or p, it needs help for recovery after it recovers. Upon recovery, it sends a message to all other processes to find out about the final commit decision. Since the 3PC is nonblocking, all operational sites would have taken a consistent decision to commit or abort. Hence, the recovering site can always get the final decision from any one of the sites that have not failed.

6.4   Atomic Actions on Decentralized Data

Now let us consider the problem of supporting an atomic action or transaction when the data on which the transaction is performed is distributed on multiple nodes. The problem is more complex, since there is now no single data manager that is controlling the entire data. Both concurrency control and failure recovery are more difficult. We have already seen that committing an operation in such a system requires the use of commit protocols.

We consider a database system as a set of data entities which are distributed over the set of communicating nodes in the distributed system. Each data entity is stored at exactly one site, and the site at which the data is stored *manages* the data. A transaction is initiated at a particular node by a process called the *initiator* or the *coordinator*. To access data objects at a remote node, a new process is created at the site having the data. This process acts on behalf of the coordinator process and performs the operations on the local data, as may be required by the coordinator. It returns the results of the operations to the coordinator. Hence, in a system with decentralized data there are multiple processes that perform different parts of a transaction. These processes are coordinated by the initiator process.

The goal of atomicity is still the same: to make the transaction appear as if it were atomic. For serializability, this means that not only are the effects of different transactions serializable on each individual node, but the overall effect is also serializable. Similarly, the "all-or-nothing" property means that either the effects of a transaction are reflected at all nodes, or there is no effect of a transaction at any node. Because the requirements of serializability and recoverability are global and span all nodes, the problem of supporting atomic actions becomes more complex.

6.4.1 Concurrency Control

Through concurrency control, we have to ensure that serializability is supported. The problem is not as simple as letting each node perform its own concurrency control protocol, which can support only local serializability. To ensure global serializability, it is also necessary that the equivalent serial order of a schedule is the same at all the nodes. That is, the dependence ordering between transactions is the same at all the nodes.

The two-phase locking protocol can easily be extended for a decentralized case. The coordinator requests read or write locks on an entity x from the node on which x is stored. The lock is granted following standard lock-conflict rules. Since any request for a lock on x will be forwarded to the node on which x is stored, the manager of x will have complete information about all the locks granted/requested on x, and hence can determine whether to grant the lock or not. So, requesting or granting of locks is straightforward.

For global serializability, it is the releasing of locks where care is needed. To enforce this globally, the two-phase property is maintained, and a node can release a lock on x only when it is sure that no lock will be requested on any other entity in the entire system. That is, even though a transaction T may not need to request any further locks from a node i, the node i cannot release the locks held by T unless it is sure that T will not request any further locks from *any* node. This is the key difference in distributed 2PL from the centralized 2PL. One simple way to fulfill this requirement is to follow the *strict 2PL* protocol. In strict 2PL, all the locks are released at the end of the transaction. When a transaction reaches the end (EOT), it issues a commit command. This commit command can be taken to be the signal to release locks.

As in the centralized case, the distributed 2PL can also get into a deadlock. In fact, the delays involved in communication and the lack of a global observer make it more prone to deadlocks. A database system must detect and resolve the deadlock. Timeouts can be used, as in a centralized case, to guess the presence of deadlocks. However, deciding the timeout is harder in a distributed system due to unpredictable communication delays. The second approach is to build the wait-for graph (WFG). It is easy to see that the local WFG at a node may not contain a cycle, while the global WFG may contain a cycle. This implies that local deadlock detection at a node will not suffice to determine if the distributed system has deadlocked. For detecting a deadlock in a distributed system, a *global deadlock detection* protocol has to be performed. Such a protocol will necessarily require communication between nodes to construct a global WFG. Different protocols have been proposed for deadlock detection in a distributed environment. We will not discuss these here. The interested reader is referred to [CMH83].

Another approach to concurrency control, which does not use any form of locking, is *timestamp ordering (TO)* [BHG87]. This approach will work for the centralized case also, but is well suited for a distributed system. In timestamp ordering, a transaction T_i is assigned a unique timestamp $ts(T_i)$. This timestamp is attached to each action requested by the transaction. A node simply orders conflicting actions according to their timestamps. If $a_i[x]$ and $a_j[x]$ are conflicting actions, then the node controlling x processes $a_i[x]$ before $a_j[x]$ if, and only if, $ts(T_i) < ts(T_j)$. Since each action carries the timestamp of the transaction, a node can locally determine the order in which the conflicting operations are to be performed.

The main problem with this approach is what should be done if, after an action has been performed, a request with a lower timestamp arrives. This scenario is clearly possible, since the timestamps will be assigned by different nodes (a method to assign unique timestamps is described below), and there are random delays in the request for an action arriving from different nodes. In this case, a simple rule is followed: a request that arrives too late (i.e., after a conflicting action with a higher timestamp has been performed) is rejected. Clearly, if an action of a transaction is rejected, that transaction has to be aborted (and proper recovery performed). The transaction can then be resubmitted later with a larger timestamp.

In a distributed system, where transactions may arrive at different nodes, one method to assign unique timestamps is as follows. Each node is assumed to have a unique id-number. The timestamp at a given time is taken to be the value of the local clock (which may be a physical or a logical clock) concatenated with the node-id (as least significant bits). So, in case the clock values at different nodes are the same when two different timestamps are being assigned, the tie is broken by the node-id. To minimize the actions getting rejected by the rule above, it is best if the clocks are closely synchronized.

6.4.2 Failure Recovery Using Logs

We have seen earlier how logs are used in the central site case to support atomic actions even in the face of node failure. Now let us discuss how logs are used to support atomicity in the distributed system [BHG87]. Once again, the two failures that are of interest are transaction failures and site failures. We assume that each site keeps a log of actions performed at that site. That is, there is no global log, and the log is also distributed. Due to the lack of a global log, it is hard to REDO transactions. To avoid redoing of transactions, before a transaction commits, all its changes are propagated to the copy of the database on the stable storage.

A transaction can be aborted at any site taking part in the transaction. If it is aborted at one node, we know that the commit protocols will ensure that all other sites taking part in the transaction also abort. Each site aborts the transaction by using the UNDO command using its local log. This ensures that the transaction is undone at all sites.

Recovery from site failures is harder to handle. The failure of a site, regardless of the point during the execution of a transaction where the failure actually occurs, finally gets reflected as timeouts in other sites during the execution of the commit protocol. The commit protocol is really the only place the failure of a site is detected by others, hence the failure-handling activities during commit protocols are the key to proper recovery from failures. We have discussed this briefly while discussing commit protocols, and will discuss other issues here. As the two-phase commit protocol is the most popular protocol, and most frequently used, for the rest of the discussion we will assume that the two-phase commit protocol is used for atomic commitment.

If a site fails and recovers, it has to perform some recovery activities. Like the central site case, during recovery a site needs to UNDO all actions of those transactions that finally aborted. For this, the site has to first determine whether a transaction committed or aborted. This problem did not exist in the single site case, as the failed site could determine from its own log whether the transaction had committed or aborted. We have discussed some of the methods for determining the final outcome of the transaction above while discussing commit protocols.

One of the key assumptions while discussing recovery for two-phase commit protocols was that on recovery, a site "remembers" the state it was in. This is implemented using the logs. To ensure that sufficient information is present in the log (besides for undoing operations) for recovery, the following rules have to be used for writing on the log [BHG87]:

1. When the coordinator initiates the commit protocol, it writes *start-2PC* on the log, along with the participants of the transaction.

2. If a participant votes YES, it writes a yes record in the log *before* sending the YES message to the coordinator. If it votes NO, it writes an abort record either before or after sending the message.

3. *Before* the coordinator sends a COMMIT message to participants, it writes a *commit* record on the log.

4. If the coordinator sends an ABORT message, it writes an *abort* record on the log either before or after sending the message.

5. After receiving a COMMIT (or ABORT) message, a participant writes a *commit* (or *abort*) record in the log.

If these rules are being followed for log writing, a site S can determine upon recovery if it was the coordinator for some transaction by the presence of the *start-2PC* record in the log. If this record is not present, the recovering site can only be a participant.

On recovery, a coordinator for a transaction does the following. If there is a *commit* or an *abort* record on the log, it implies that the coordinator had made a decision before failure, and that it should implement that decision. If neither record is present, then the coordinator can decide to abort by inserting an *abort* record in the log. For this to work it is crucial that the commit record is written before sending the COMMIT messages.

If the recovering site is a participant, it does the following. It the log contains a *commit* or an *abort* record, it implies that the site had reached a decision before failing, and that decision has to be implemented. If the log does not contain even a *yes* record, it means that either the site failed before voting or voted NO. In either case, it can decide to abort by inserting an *abort* record on the log. If there is a *yes* record but no *commit* or *abort* record, then the site cannot unilaterally decide what to do and will have to use a termination protocol. We have discussed one such protocol earlier while discussing the two-phase commit protocol. This method of entering records on the log and using the recovery method described above ensures that a transaction on distributed data is atomic.

6.4.3　Implementing Atomic Actions Using Object Histories

Now we will discuss another method for supporting atomic actions on distributed data that was proposed by Reed [Ree83]. This method does not use logs, but uses object histories instead to support atomicity. Object histories reflect the changes made to objects over time, and are used both for recovery as well as for coordinating access to data by different actions. Updating an object is viewed as creating a new version, while reading an object is viewed as reading the proper version. Recovery is viewed as selecting the proper version during rollback.

Pseudotime

The proposed approach tries to serialize atomic actions based on their real-time ordering. Since no unique real time is available in distributed systems, the approach uses *pseudotime*. Each read/write operation is assigned a particular pseudotime, and these operations are coordinated using this pseudotime in such a way that a read operation always returns the latest (in terms of pseudotime) value. For this approach to work, pseudotime must satisfy some properties. First, if a step a_1 of an atomic action occurs before step a_2 of that atomic action, then the pseudotime of a_1 should be less than the pseudotime of a_2. Second, to ensure that atomic actions are serializable, we require that for two atomic actions A and B, either all steps in A precede (in pseudotime) all steps in B, or all steps of B precede all steps of A. Third, we would like pseudotime to be loosely linked with real time. That is, if two steps occur far apart in real time, then their pseudotime ordering should be the same as their real-time ordering.

Now let us see a possible implementation of pseudotime. Assume that the clocks of the different nodes are synchronized, and run at approximately the same rate as real time. Earlier in Chapter 3, we discussed methods to satisfy this property in a distributed system. When an atomic action is started, it gets a timestamp from the local clock. Like in timestamp ordering, we assume that the timestamp is the value of the clock to which the unique identifier of the node is appended as the least significant bits. Clearly, the timestamp of any two operations will have some ordering on them. Also, the third requirement is satisfied, since clocks are synchronized.

The pseudotime for a step is generated by obtaining a new timestamp and prefixing it (as in higher-order bits) with the timestamp for the atomic action to which this step belongs. This method will satisfy the first two requirements described above if the timestamp for a step is more than the timestamp of the previous steps of the operation. One way to easily satisfy this is by having the coordinator of the atomic operation assign the timestamps.

Recovery

Let us now see how recovery from failures is implemented using object history and pseudotime. Each object is viewed as a sequence of *object versions*. The sequence of object versions is also called *object history*. Each write to an object creates a new version, and appends it to the object history. The timestamp of the write that creates a new version is recorded with the version.

Since the goal of recovery is to ensure atomicity of the operations even in the face of failures, each object version is actually written in two steps. First, a write operation creates a tentative version in the object history. This is a version whose existence is conditional upon the later completion of the atomic operation. The set of tentative versions created by an atomic operation is called a *possibility*. In the second step, all the tentative versions are made visible, if the operation commits. If the operation aborts, the tentative versions are discarded. Before the operation has committed, a tentative version is not allowed to be read by steps of any operation, other than the operation that created it. This prevents the reading of a version that might later be erased, which may cause other operations to abort (if not prevented, these aborts may cause domino effect). The commit of an operation is assumed to be atomic. Any commit protocol can be used for this.

Coordinating Object Reading and Writing

The properties of the timestamps are used for coordinating object reading and writing by the steps of different operations such that serializability is preserved even in the face of concurrent access. The read and write requests carry their timestamps. When a read request with a timestamp t arrives, it is immediately satisfied by reading the "appropriate" object version. The object version with the largest timestamp (recorded during the write that created the version) that is less than t is the one that is read. For reading, tentative versions created by this atomic operation are considered, but the tentative versions of other operations are not. During the read, the read also attaches a "read timestamp" to the object. That is, at any time, an object version also carries the maximum timestamp of the reads that have accessed the object.

Now let us consider the write operations. Since in a distributed system the message delays are unbounded, no assumptions can be made about the order of arrival of requests. Clearly, if a write request arrives with a timestamp that is less than the already executed read request, it cannot be executed, as it would cause the value previously read during the read operation to become incorrect. Consequently, such write requests are rejected. Such a "late arriving" write request is detected by the fact that its timestamp is between the interval formed by the timestamp of creation of the object version, and the maximum read timestamp of that version. Otherwise, a new version is created and entered into the history according to the timestamp of the write command. Though we have assumed that the object history exists in its entirety, an easy method of pruning the history — such that in most cases only the most recent version of the object needs to be stored — is given in [Ree83].

6.4.4 Nested Atomic Actions

So far, we have been treating an atomic action as a monolith, which can be considered as a sequence of steps, where each step is a primitive operation, executed indivisibly by the hardware. This approach is sufficient for a database application, where transactions generally do not have an internal structure. However, frequently an operation is not "flat" and has a structure of its own. In other words, an action is composed of other actions, which may not be primitive operations. These are called *nested atomic actions* [Mos86]. Nested actions naturally occur if we want to make a remote procedure call atomic [LG85]. Since a procedure may invoke other procedures, which may invoke other procedures, and so on, we naturally get a nested atomic action. A similar situation occurs if an object-action model is being used, where it is desired that an operation on an object be atomic [LS82, LS83]. Again, since an operation (or method) on an object may invoke other operations on other objects, we naturally have nested atomic actions.

A nested action is one which consists of subactions. These subactions may execute concurrently or sequentially, and on different sites. Making such an action atomic implies that this structure of the action cannot be visible from the outside, as one of the basic properties of an atomic action is that its internal structure is not visible from outside the action. However, the subactions of an action, though not visible from outside, appear as atomic actions to other subactions of that action. That is, if we treat the atomic action as the "universe," then in this universe, each subaction is an atomic action, and consequently the structure of a subaction is not visible to another subaction. This method of structuring provides a safe method to support concurrency within an action.

Nesting of actions allows only strict containment of a subaction in an action. This implies that a nested action will form a hierarchy, and the relationship of the actions and subactions can be represented using a tree [Mos86] in which nodes represent actions. The root of the tree is called the *top-level* action. The subactions of an action are represented as children of the node for that action.

Nesting of actions impacts the concurrency control, or preserving atomicity despite concurrency. Here we will present an approach for locking in nested actions based on [Mos86]. We assume that only the *leaf* actions directly perform the read and write operations on data. These actions can be easily satisfied by creating subactions for any action in a higher-level action that is a primitive operation. The following rules apply for locking in nested atomic actions:

1. For an action to perform an operation, the action must hold an appropriate lock.

2. If an action requests locks, the request can be granted only if all holders of the lock (if any) are ancestors of the requesting action.

3. When an action commits, its locks are given to its parent, if any, or released if it is a top-level action.

4. When an action aborts, its locks are released.

The second rule ensures that the action is *within* all actions that hold a lock on the data object. Since only leaf actions are assumed to access data directly, this ensures that no other action that wants to access data directly has the lock. When a subaction commits and releases the locks, they are inherited by the parent, thereby allowing other subactions of this parent to acquire these locks. These two rules ensure that each subaction is atomic with respect to other subactions, and that atomicity at each level is preserved.

Nesting of actions also impacts the commitment and recovery process. As subactions are atomic actions in their own right, they abort or commit independently. A subaction can abort without forcing its parent to abort. However, the committing of a subaction has a different meaning than the committing of a top-level action. A commit of a subaction is conditional; if a subaction commits but its parent action aborts, then the effects of this subaction also have to be undone to preserve the atomicity of the top-level action. That is, successfully completing and committing a subaction does not guarantee the permanence of the effects of the subaction. Its effects are made permanent only when the top-level action commits. And if an action aborts, not only its effects have to be undone, but the effects of its subactions (even if the subactions have committed earlier) have to be undone as well.

One method of supporting recovery using the shadow technique is described here briefly [Mos86]. In the shadow recovery technique in a database, when a transaction acquires a lock on some data, a copy of the data is made, and all work is performed on that copy. This copy is known as the *shadow*. When the transaction commits, its shadows are installed in place of the original versions. If the transaction aborts, its shadows are discarded. Shadow recovery techniques are similar to the log-based techniques discussed earlier in the chapter, in that all keep two copies of the data object. In shadow recovery methods, the operation is performed on the shadow, while in log-based methods, the operation is performed on the original data, while the old copy is kept on the log. This requires that the installation of the shadows be made to appear atomic. One method for this has been described in [LS79a].

For performing shadow recovery for nested actions, the following rules apply [Mos86]:

1. When a transaction acquires a lock on some data, a copy of the data is made (the shadow), and all operations are performed on the shadow.

2. When a transaction commits, its shadows are inherited by its parent, in favor of any versions the parent may hold for the same data. When a top-level action commits, its shadows are installed in the database as permanent copies.

3. When a transaction aborts, its shadows are discarded.

These rules imply that multiple copies of a data item may be in existence at a given time; up to one copy for each level of nesting. (Whereas in non-nested actions, only two copies exist at a given time.) The reason for the inheritance of shadows has been given above; the commit of a nested action is provisional. Its effects are not made permanent until the top-level action commits. By this, the versions are propagated up the tree, and will reach the root. Then when the root commits, the effects will finally be made permanent. Other models for nested actions have also been proposed [Svo84].

6.5 Summary

In this chapter, we have discussed the problem of making a user-defined action an atomic one. Atomic actions are primitive operations in databases, and form a basic primitive for building reliable distributed applications. An atomic action is an operation that appears as primitive and indivisible to all other operations in the system. One property of an atomic action is that either it completes fully, or it appears as if the action has not performed any action at all. Another fundamental property of atomic actions is that no two atomic actions should appear to overlap or execute concurrently. This implies that the final effect of executing the atomic actions should be as if they were executed serially in some order. This is called the *serializability criteria*. Both concurrency and failures can violate the atomicity of an operation. To guard against concurrent access violating atomicity, concurrency control protocols are used. Recovery methods are used to ensure that failures do not violate atomicity.

We first considered a database system in which the data is centralized. A concurrency protocol in this environment is the *two-phase locking* protocol. In this protocol, an action requests a read or a write lock on entities as it needs them, but once it releases any lock, it is disallowed from requesting any further lock. This protocol is one of the most commonly used protocols and ensures serializability.

The goal of failure recovery in this environment is to perform some recovery actions after the node becomes operational again, such that the atomicity of actions is preserved. One method of supporting recovery is to use logs. The log is kept on the stable storage and for each action that changes a data item, it records the old and new value of a data item. Rules for updating the log were also discussed. Besides this, the state of the shared data is checkpointed periodically. Recovery from failure is performed using this log. For recovery, starting from the checkpoint, all committed transactions are redone, and all incomplete transactions are undone.

In this approach, the cost of recovery clearly depends on the frequency of checkpointing (i.e., the time period between checkpoints). The longer the time between checkpoints, the longer the expected time is for recovery. However, if checkpoints are established more frequently, the cost of checkpointing increases. We also discussed the issue of the optimal checkpointing interval, and discussed a model that can be used to analytically determine the interval that will give the best availability.

The general case of atomic actions is when the action spans multiple sites. That is, the data is distributed over many sites and a transaction has to get parts of its work done on different sites. In this context also, two-phase locking can be used for concurrency control. However, a system has to make sure that the two-phase nature of lock request and release is maintained globally. Two-phase locking can get into deadlock, which will require global cycle-detection algorithms in this system. Another technique is to timestamp transactions, and then serialize the transactions in the timestamp order. The problem in this approach is that due to unpredictable delays in the network, a request may arrive after a higher timestamp request has been serviced.

Central to preserving the all-or-nothing property in the face of failures in such an environment are commit protocols. Since the execution of a transaction is distributed over many sites, we must be sure that if a transaction commits, its effects are made permanent on all the sites that take part in the transaction, and if it aborts, its effects are undone on all such sites. This requires a commit protocol. The most commonly used protocol is the *two-phase commit protocol*. In this protocol, the parent node that initiated the transaction (called the coordinator) at commit time first asks other sites (called participants) whether they want to commit or not. A participant can unilaterally decide to locally commit or abort. All the participants send their local decisions to the coordinator. If all the participants are ready to commit, the coordinator decides to commit and sends a request to all participants to commit. If any participant decides to abort, the coordinator decides to abort and sends an abort request to each participant.

The atomicity of the transaction depends on the atomicity of the commit protocol. If a site fails during the protocol, it performs recovery actions after it becomes operational again. To perform the recovery activities, a site needs to know its state at the time it failed. This is done by recording the state and related data on a log kept on the stable storage. During recovery, a site has to first make a decision regarding committing (aborting) a transaction that is consistent with the decision of other participants and the coordinator of that transaction, and then perform the actual undo/redo activities. If a site can decide based on its local data only (that is available from the log) whether to commit or abort, it is called an *independent recovery*. Otherwise, the site has to communicate with other sites to make its decision.

Besides the failed site, in the situation where the transaction is being executed on many sites, other sites that are operational have to decide what to do (i.e. commit or abort) if some sites fail. This is done by adding *timeout actions* in the protocol. At any place where a site is waiting for a message, if a timeout occurs, then the site assumes that the expected message will not arrive. There are situations where the operational sites have to remain blocked until the failed sites recover. Those protocols where the operational sites never block due to failure of some sites are called *nonblocking protocols*. The two phase commit protocol is blocking in that there are some scenarios in which the operational sites cannot take a decision which will be consistent with the decision of others, though in most situations operational sites can decide whether to abort or commit. To make the protocol a nonblocking protocol, another phase is added and the protocol is converted into a *three phase nonblocking protocol*. In this protocol, in all conditions, if some sites fail, then the remaining sites can make their decision regarding commitment without waiting for the failed sites to recover.

Finally, we also discussed the issue of nested actions. A nested action consists of subactions that are nested within an action. In this structure, the structure of the top-level action is not visible to other actions. A subaction is a subaction with respect to other subactions of the same action. A commit has a different meaning for a subaction and a top-level action. If a subaction commits, its commitment is conditional. If a top-level action aborts, then the effects of all the subactions, even if they have committed, have to be undone.

Problems

1. Consider the following schedule:
$R_1(x)R_3(z)R_1(y)R_3(y)W_3(z)R_2(y)R_1(z)R_2(z)W_2(z)W_1(y)W_2(z)W_1(z)$. Is this schedule serializable?

2. A schedule can be modeled as a graph as follows. Nodes are the transactions and an arc is drawn from T_1 to T_2 if (i) T_1 writes an entity which is later read by T_2, (ii) T_1 writes an entity that is later written by T_2, and (iii) T_2 reads an

entity that is later written by T_1. Show that this graph is acyclic only if the schedule is serializable.

3. Show that the 2PL produces a graph that is acyclic.

4. What is the need for UNDO and REDO entries in the log? Why is write ahead log protocol important?

5. Consider the execution of the transactions given in Fig. 6.5. What will be done

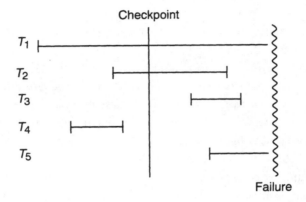

Figure 6.5: An example execution of transactions

during recovery for each of the transactions?

6. Why is a commit protocol needed for implementing atomic actions in a distributed system?

7. What is the need for converting the two-phase commit protocol to the three-phase protocol? What are the situations under which the 2PC will not support atomicity but the 3PC will?

8. Using logs for recovery, will the 3PC guarantee atomicity under all situations? If not, construct a scenario in which it will not provide atomicity.

9. Give justification for the rules of locking for nested transactions.

10. What is the relationship between the set of consistent states of a system as defined in Chapter 2, and the set of consistent states with atomic actions?

References

[BG81] P.A. Bernstein, and N. Goodman. "Concurrency Control in Distributed Database Systems." *ACM Computing Surveys*, 13(2):185–221, June 1981.

[BHG87] P. A. Bernstein, V. Hadzilacos, and N. Goodman. *Concurrency Control and Recovery in Database Systems*. Addison-Wesley, 1987.

[BSW79] P.A. Bernstein, D.W. Shipman, and W.S. Wong. "Formal Aspects of Serializabiity in Database Concurrency Control." *IEEE Transactions on Software Engineering*, SE-5(3):203–216, May 1979.

[CBDU75] K. M. Chandy, J. C. Browne, C. W. Dissly, and W. R. Uhrig. "Analytic Models for Rollback and Recovery Strategies in Databases." *IEEE Transactions on Software Engineering*, 1(1):100–110, March 1975.

[CK85] D. Cheung, and T. Kameda. "Site-optimal Termination Protocols for a Distributed Database under Networking Partitioning." *4th ACM SIGACT-SIGOPS Symposium on Principles of Distributed Computing*, pp. 111–121, 1985.

[CMH83] K.M. Chandy, J. Misra, and L.M. Haas. "Distributed Deadlock Detection." *ACM Transactions on Computer Systems*, 1(2):144–156, May 1983.

[CR83] F. Chin, and K.V.S. Ramaro. "Optimal Termination Protocols for Network Partitioning." *2nd ACM-SIGACT-SIGMOD Symposium on Principles of Database Systems*, pp. 25–35, Atlanta, March 1983.

[EGLT76] K. P. Eswaran, J. N. Gray, R. A. Lorie, and I. L. Traiger. "The Notions of Consistency and Predicate Locks in a Database System." *Communications of the ACM*, 19(11):624–633, November 1976.

[Gar82] H. Garcia-Molina. "Elections in a Distributed Computing System." *IEEE Transactions on Computers*, C-31(1):48–59, January 1982.

[GD78] E. Gelenbe, and D. Derochette. "Performance of Rollback Recovery Systems Under Intermittent Failures." *Communications of the ACM*, 21(6):493–499, June 1978.

[Gel79] E. Gelenbe. "On the Optimum Checkpoint Interval." *Journal of the ACM*, 26(2):259–270, April 1979.

[Gra78]   J. N. Gray. "Notes on Database Operating Systems." In *Operating Systems: An Advanced Course*, Springer-Verlag, 1978.

[HR83]   T. Haerder, and A. Reuter. "Principles of Transaction-Oriented Database Recovery." *ACM Computing Surveys*, 15(4):287–317, December 1983.

[LG85]   K.-J. Lin, and J. D. Gannon. "Atomic Remote Procedure Call." *IEEE Transactions on Software Engineering*, SE-11(10):1126–1135, October 1985.

[Lom77]   D. B. Lomet. "Process Structuring, Synchronization, and Recovery Using Atomic Actions." *ACM Conference Language Design for Reliable Software, SIGPLAN Notices 12, 3*, pp. 128–137, March 1977.

[LS79a]   B. Lampson, and H. Sturgis. *Crash Recovery in a Distributed Database System*. Technical Report, Palo Alto, California: Computer Science Laboratory, Xerox Park, 1979.

[LS82]   B. Liskov, and R. Scheifler. "Guardians and Actions: Linguistic Support for Robust, Distributed Programs." *Proceedings of the Ninth Annual Symposium on Principles of Programming Languages And Systems*, pp. 7–19, 1982.

[LS83]   B. Liskov, and R. Scheifler. "Guardians and Actions: Linguistic Support for Robust, Distributed Programs." *ACM Transactions on Programming Languages And Systems*, 5(7):7–19, 1983.

[MLO86]   C. Mohan, B. Lindsay, and R. Obermarck. "Transaction Management in the R^* Distributed Database Management System." *ACM Transactions on Database Systems*, 11(4):378–396, December 1986.

[Mos86]   J. E. B. Moss. *An Introduction to Nested Transactions*. Technical Report 86-41, Amherst, Massachusetts: University of Amherst Massachusetts, COINS, September 1986.

[Pap79]   C.H. Papadimitriou. "The Serializability of Concurrent Database Updates." *Journal of the ACM*, 26(4):631–653, October 1979.

[Ree83]   D. P. Reed. "Implementing Atomic Actions on Decentralized Data." *ACM Transactions on Computer Systems*, 1(1):3–23, February 1983.

[SC89]   J. W. Stamos, and F. Cristian. "A low-cost Atomic Protocol." Research Report RJ 7185 (67664) 12/5/89, IBM Research Division, IBM Research Division Yorktown Heights, New York, December 1989.

[Ske81] D. Skeen. "Nonblocking Commit Protocols." *ACM SIGMOD*, pp. 133–142. ACM SIGMOD, ACM, 1981.

[SS83] D. Skeen, and M. Stonebraker. "A Formal Model of Crash Recovery in a Distributed System." *IEEE Transactions on Software Engineering*, SE-9(3):219–228, May 1983.

[Svo84] L. Svobodova. "Resilient Distributed Computing." *IEEE Transactions on Software Engineering*, 10(3):257–268, May 1984.

[YJ89] S.-M. Yuan, and P. Jalote. "Fault Tolerant Commit Protocols." *Proceedings of Fifth International Conference on DATA ENGINEERING*, pp. 280 – 286, February 1989.

[You74] J. W. Young. "A First Order Approximation to the Optimum Checkpoint Interval." *Communications of the ACM*, 17:530–531, September 1974.

Chapter 7

Data Replication
and Resiliency

In the last chapter, we discussed the problem of making a user-level action into an atomic one. A user-level action is a logical operation that accesses or modifies many data objects. The goal of an atomic action is to ensure that either the action completes successfully, or it appears as if the action had not executed at all. That is, the state of partially executed actions should never be visible, even if failures occur. We saw that if a node fails, making even some of the data objects required by the action unavailable, there was nothing else to do but to "abort" the action and make it appear as if nothing had happened.

In this chapter, we will discuss a different approach where the action can be completed successfully even if some failures occur in the system. That is, we want the action to be *resilient* to failures. The goal is still to execute the actions atomically, with the difference that we are interested in successful completion, rather than rollback, if failures occur. Due to this, the techniques employed are quite different from the techniques for supporting atomic actions discussed in the previous chapter.

Clearly, if a data object resides at a single node, then nothing can be done to successfully complete an action which needs that data item, if that node fails. Hence to be able to finish an operation despite failures of nodes, data items need to be replicated on many nodes, such that failures of a few nodes do not make some data item inaccessible to user operations.

Data replication, though it provides resiliency against failures, introduces new problems of consistency and replica management. Since the purpose of replication is to provide tolerance against failures, the replication should not be visible at the user or action level. For performing actions, it should appear as if there is a single copy of each data item. An action will perform operations on the logical data items, and the underlying system will map it to operations on the multiple copies of the data items. To be correct, the mapping must ensure that the concurrent execution of actions on replicated data is equivalent to a correct execution on non-replicated data. That is, the execution should be equivalent to a serial execution of actions on non-replicated data. This correctness property is called the *one-copy serializability* criterion. The methods to manage replicated data such that the one-copy serializability criterion is satisfied are called *replica control algorithms*. One-copy serializability requires that the different copies of a data object must be in a *mutually consistent* state so that the user actions get the same view of the data object. Due to this consistency requirement, replica control algorithms are also called *consistency control algorithms*.

In a system with replication, different data items are replicated on different nodes. Each node manages some copies of some data items. For simplicity of exposition, we will assume that all the data objects are replicated on all the nodes in the system under consideration.

There are two types of failures that need to be handled by a replica control algorithm: node failures and communication failures. Node failures cause copies of the data on that node to become inaccessible. The rest of the network is connected and the remaining copies of the data objects are available. The replica control algorithms have to ensure that even if some sites fail, making some copies of a data item unavailable, the operations on the logical data can be performed, and the one-copy serializability criterion is satisfied.

The second failure, which is a lot more disruptive, is a communication failure leading to network partitioning. In this, nodes and links fail in a manner such that the remaining nodes are partitioned into *groups*. Nodes in each group or *partition* can communicate with each other, but cannot communicate with nodes of the other group. Ideally, a replica control protocol should also maintain one-copy serializability under network partitioning. Clearly, if no restriction is placed on processing in different partitions, then the mutual consistency of the different copies cannot be preserved when the network reconnects, and a user operation may get a different view of the data object depending on which copies of the data object it accesses, thereby violating the one-copy serializability criterion. A replica control protocol that can handle partitions must place restrictions on processing in different partitions so that mutual consistency is not violated. That the protocol has to do this without any communication between different partitions is one of the major challenges.

In this chapter, we will describe some replica control methods to mask the failures in a system with replication. Replica control methods can be *optimistic* or *pessimistic* [DGS85]. In optimistic strategies, if network partitioning occurs, no restriction is placed on processing in any partition in the hope that operations being executed in different partitions will not conflict. The pessimistic strategies, on the other hand, prevent inconsistencies from occurring by limiting access to data. During partitioning, each partition makes the worst-case assumptions about what is happening in other partitions, and operates under these pessimistic assumptions. There are three common pessimistic approaches for replica control: primary site, active replication, and voting. We will discuss all three approaches during the course of the chapter.

The focus of the chapter is how to make data resilient to node failures (by replicating the data). We do not discuss the effect of failure on the process which performs the actions, and which wants to access the data. For now, we assume that the processes executing the actions remain alive; failures only make some copies of the data unavailable. How to make the processes themselves resilient to failures is the topic of the next chapter.

7.1 Optimistic Approaches

As mentioned above, optimistic strategies do not place any restriction on processing, if a network partitioning occurs, in the optimistic hope that operations being executed in different partitions will not conflict. Under this optimistic assumption, the serializability in each group can be preserved, but overall processing may not satisfy the one-copy serializability criterion, and global inconsistencies may arise (i.e., copies from different partitions may not be mutually consistent). If global inconsistencies arise, then optimistic strategies try to resolve them after different partitions join and are able to communicate with each other. The different optimistic strategies differ from each other in how they resolve the inconsistencies, since there is really not much that needs to be done by these strategies during the processing. In this section, we will briefly discuss some optimistic approaches. The pessimistic approaches will be discussed in later sections, and will form the bulk of this chapter.

During a network partitioning, if operations are performed in each partition independently, the copies of data in different partitions may be inconsistent. When the partitions rejoin, such inconsistencies have to be detected, and resolved, if possible. One approach that can be used to detect inconsistencies that occur due to write operations in different partitions is *version vectors*. This technique was employed in the LOCUS operating system [S[+]83].

In this approach, files are treated as the basic data objects, and are the unit of replication. A file f can have many copies, all on different nodes. An update is said to originate from a node i if the request from the user arrived at node i. Whenever an update is to be performed on f, all copies of f that are accessible from the node from where the update request originated are updated. Each copy of a file has associated with it a *version vector*, whose size is n, where n is the number of sites at which the file is stored. The version vector V of a copy of the file f represents the number of updates originating at different nodes that were performed on this copy. That is, at a node j, the ith vector entry v_i keeps count of the number of updates originating from site i that were performed on the copy of f at the node j.

Clearly, if the network is fully connected, then each update will be performed on each copy of the file, and the version vector of each copy will be the same. However, if a partitioning occurs, then the version vectors of the different copies in different partitions may diverge, depending on the nature of operations performed in different partitions.

A vector V of a copy of a file is said to *dominate* another vector V' of another copy of the same file, if $v_i \geq v'_i$ for all $i = 1, ..., n$. If a vector V dominates V', it indicates that for every node j, more updates made from j were performed on the copy with V, as compared to the copy with V'. In other words, updates seen by the copy with V' are a subset of updates seen by the copy with the version vector V. Two vectors are said to *conflict* if neither dominates. This represents the case where the copies have seen different updates.

When two groups join and are able to communicate with each other, vectors are compared. If a vector of one group dominates the other, then though this situation also represents an inconsistency (the states of the two copies are not the same), this inconsistency can be resolved easily by copying the file with version V onto the copy with version V', since the copy with V is a more recent copy of the file than the copy with V'. If the vectors of the groups that are joining conflict, then there is no straightforward way to resolve the inconsistency, and the version vector approach leaves it to the manager of the system to manually do whatever is necessary.

In other words, in this optimistic approach, if after partitioning the operations performed in the different operations are non-conflicting, then the version vector method provides an approach for combining the different versions in different partitions into a single consistent version after the partitions rejoin. But if the operations performed in the different groups conflict, then no mechanism is provided to ensure that this is resolved and mutual consistency is violated.

Consider the example of a three node network whose partition graph is shown in Fig. 7.1 [DGS85]. The nodes A, B, and C have initially the same vector, each entry being 0 (we consider a single file case). The system partitions into two groups, one containing nodes A and B, and the other containing the node C. Now suppose the node A makes two updates on the file. Since A and B are connected, the version vectors of nodes A and B will be $< 2, 0, 0 >$, while the version vector of node C is $< 0, 0, 0 >$. Now suppose node B splits off with node A and joins node C. Since

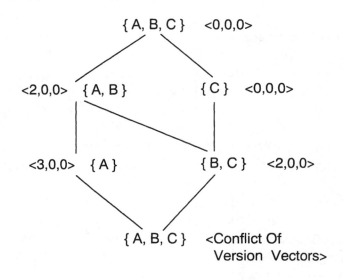

Figure 7.1: Example with version vectors

the version vector of node B dominates the version vector of node C, the conflict is resolved by copying the file from node B to node C (along with the version vector). Now during this grouping, suppose node A and node C both make update requests. The request of node A will make the version vector of node A $< 3, 0, 0 >$, as the update by C will have no effect on the version vector at node A. Similarly, the version vector at node B or C will be $< 2, 0, 1 >$. Now if these two groups join, the version vectors conflict, since no vector dominates the other. This has to be resolved manually.

Version vectors can detect only inconsistencies arising due to updates on a single file. They cannot detect read-write conflict, as the reads on a file are not recorded. If an action or a transaction accesses multiple files, as is common in databases, then besides the write-write conflict, the read-write conflict also has to be detected in order to detect the violations of transaction serializability. Consequently, for such applications, the version vectors approach is not suitable.

An extension of this approach was proposed in which both reads and writes of transactions are logged [Dav84, DGS85]. When the different groups rejoin, then a precedence graph is formed to detect inconsistencies. In order to be able to construct a precedence graph, each partition maintains a log of all reads and writes on data items. It is assumed that a transaction always reads a data item before writing it, and each partition follows some concurrency control protocol such that transactions in the partition are serializable. For a partition i, let the serialization order (i.e., the serial order to which the execution of the transactions is equivalent) of the transactions be $T_i 1, T_i 2, ..., T_i n$.

When the partitions rejoin, a precedence graph is constructed as follows. Transactions are nodes in this graph, and edges represent dependencies between transactions. For two transactions $T_i j$ and $T_i k$ in the same partition i, an edge is added from $T_i j$ to $T_i k$ if (a) $T_i k$ has read a value produced by $T_i j$, or (b) $T_i j$ read a value that was later modified by $T_i k$. The concurrency control protocol of the partition will always ensure that the precedence graph of transactions in a partition is always acyclic. To complete the precedence graph, conflicts between transactions of different partitions must also be represented. An edge is added from node $T_i j$ (representing a transaction in partition i) to $T_l k, i \neq j$, if $T_i j$ has read an item written by $T_l k$. This edge represents a read-write conflict between the two transactions operating in two separate partitions. A write-write conflict will be reflected as two read-write conflict edges.

If there is no conflict between transactions of different partitions, the precedence graph will be acyclic. If the graph is not acyclic, it means that there are conflicts. Conflicts are resolved by aborting some transactions till the precedence graph is acyclic. There are many different ways to select the transactions to be aborted [Dav84]. Once the graph is acyclic, all inconsistencies have been resolved and the databases of the different partitions can be merged. Note that aborting transactions in order to resolve inconsistencies arising due to the optimistic strategy may require that committed transactions also be aborted. That is, with partitioning, a transaction commit is not final, as it may need to be aborted later when the partitions rejoin.

7.2   Primary Site Approach

In this section, we describe the *primary site approach*, which is a pessimistic strategy for managing replication to support resiliency [AD76]. This approach has been used in a variety of contexts, not just for supporting data resiliency. In a distributed system, this approach works well if only nodes can fail, or if both nodes and communication links can fail but node failures can be distinguished from network partitions. We will first describe the general strategy, and then one particular implementation of resilient data objects using this approach.

7.2.1   Basic Approach

The goal of the primary site approach is to continue providing access to the data (in general, any resource) even if some nodes or links in the system fail. For now, we assume that only node failures occur in the system, and the operational nodes stay connected. The goal now is to ensure that operations on the data can be performed even if up to k nodes in the system fail. That is, the goal is to support *k-resilient* data objects.

For supporting *k-resilient* data, the data is replicated on at least $k + 1$ nodes in the system. One of the nodes having the data is designated as *primary*, and the rest are designated as *backups*. The nodes are logically organized in a linear fashion, with the primary as the first node. All requests for operations on the data are sent to the primary site. If a request is sent to a backup site, the backup forwards the request to the primary.

If the operation requested is a read, then the primary site simply performs the operation and returns the results to the requesting process. If the operation is an update, then *before* performing the update, the primary site sends the update request to at least k of its backups. When all these backups have received the request, then the primary performs the operation, and returns the results, if any. All the backups perform the update operations they receive from the primary site. Since all requests arrive first at the primary site which forwards the update requests to other backups, all backups also get the requests in the same order as the primary site (since the communication channels are assumed to be reliable and order-preserving). Hence, on performing these requests, the data at the backups will be in the same state as the data on the primary. An alternative method to reduce the computation to be performed by the backups is for the primary to periodically checkpoint the state of the data object on the backups. In this case, the backups only need to perform the operations that were performed by the primary after the checkpoint. These are typically performed only when a backup becomes the primary.

Now consider what happens if some sites fail. If more than k sites fail nearly simultaneously, then nothing can be done, as the degree of replication is only $k + 1$. If the total number of failures is less than k, then this scheme can mask the failures. Suppose that the failed sites are backup nodes. In this case, the user service is not disrupted, as the user gets its responses from the primary site.

If the primary site fails, then a new primary has to be elected. There are various ways for electing a primary (the reader is referred to [Gar82] for a discussion on election algorithms). We describe one simple approach. Since the nodes are ordered in a linear chain, the highest node in this chain that is alive becomes the new primary. The new primary is now responsible for performing the user operations. If the primary site records each operation on the backups, then the new primary site can start performing user requests after it has processed all the operations forwarded to it by the previous primary. If checkpoints are used, the backup starts executing from the last checkpoint and first performs all the operations performed by the previous primary since the last checkpoint was established.

The one-copy serializability criterion is clearly satisfied when there are no failures, since all requests go to the single site — the primary site. Since all backups also get the update requests in the same order as the primary site, they are in the same state as the failed primary after performing the requests. Hence, when a backup takes over as primary, again the overall one-copy serializability criterion is preserved.

Now let us discuss failures that cause network partitioning. In this case, clearly only the partition that has the primary site can function, the other partitions cannot. That is, requests originating in the partition having the primary site can be serviced by the primary site. Requests originating in the other partitions cannot be forwarded to the primary site, and hence cannot be serviced. Hence, two different approaches are used for masking these two types of failures. In case of node failures which do not cause partitioning, the failure of a primary site is handled by one of the backups taking over the role of the primary. In the case of partitioning, no such action is done and the partition that has the primary site continues to function.

Since the primary site method employs two different approaches to handle node failures and network partitions, it can only work if network partitions can be distinguished from node failures. That is, the approach can work only if a node that is unable to communicate with the primary site can determine if this is due to site failures or network partitions. In the first case, where it knows that the primary site has failed, election is held to select a new primary. In the second case, the node simply waits until the partitions merge and it is able to communicate again with the primary.

7.2.2   Resilient Objects Using the Primary Site Approach

Now we describe an implementation of the primary site approach for supporting resilient objects [BJRA85]. Objects here are not simple data objects that are read or written, but are treated as an instance of abstract data types, as described earlier in Chapter 2. These types of objects give rise to nested actions, and the implementation has to handle that correctly. This method aims to support *k-resilient* objects. It also handles only node failures, and uses checkpointing to transfer state information from the primary site to the backups.

The objects are deterministic and if an operation is invoked on different copies of an object that are in the same state, then each object will execute the same sequence of steps and will reach the same state after the operation is completed. An operation on an object may be a *top-level operation* or a *nested operation*. A top-level operation is one that is requested by a user process. An operation on an object may invoke operations on other objects, giving rise to nested operations.

Each operation on an object is a sequence of steps $A = \{a_1, a_2, ..., a_n\}$, where each step a_i is a primitive operation, which could act on the data object or be a call to an operation on another object. If a step is a call to another operation, this gives rise to nested actions, and the step is called an *external step*. The *index* of an external step a_i is i.

Since an operation on the object is not a primitive operation, but consists of a sequence of primitive steps, nodes may fail during the execution of operations. Besides ensuring that the data object is accessible even if up to k sites fail, we also want the data to be resilient so that the ongoing operations are not disrupted by failures. Hence, another goal of supporting resilient objects is *forward progress*, which means that even if up to k nodes fail, the executing operations will be successfully completed.

Each object is replicated on at least $k + 1$ sites, one of which is the primary site, to which operations on the object are sent. The primary site periodically *checkpoints* the state of the object on the backups. During checkpoints, enough information is transmitted by the primary site to its backup so that any backup is capable of completing the ongoing operation from the checkpoint.

Checkpointing is not sufficient for ensuring forward progress. If the last checkpoint was established after the step a_i of an operation A by the primary site before it failed, then the backup which becomes the primary will start executing A from that state. A problem arises if the primary site had performed an external step since its last checkpoint. The new primary site does not know about this (since the checkpoint does not reflect the external call), and hence will invoke the external operation again. That is, for an operation A, the call to the external operation is made twice due to failure, while in normal processing, only one such call is made. This can clearly lead to an inconsistent state. Hence, the new primary site should not execute such external calls again. At the same time, the new primary site has to get the results of the external call in order to complete the processing starting from the checkpoint.

This is achieved as follows. Each operation A is assigned a unique operation-id (a timestamp-based scheme can generate unique-ids). A primary site makes this operation-id known to the backups before it starts executing A. Each step is assigned a unique step-id which is the operation-id concatenated with the index of the step. If there is an external call during the operation A, then the step-id of the step responsible for the call becomes the operation-id for that operation. The same method is followed in further nested calls, if any. At the end of the external call, the primary site transmits the results of the step to all the backups *before* it returns the result to the caller of the operation. Each backup keeps the results of these calls indexed with the step-id of the call. These are called *retained results*: when an external call is made, then its results are retained by the backups. This is a form of limited checkpointing by the primary site.

Retained results can solve the problem described above. When an execution of an operation needs to make an external call, the node (the current primary site) executing the operation first checks to see if there are any retained results for this step-id. If so, it simply returns the result of the operation and does not make the external call. Note that since each operation is deterministic, starting execution from a checkpoint, a new primary site will assign the same step-id to the external call, since the index of the step will be the same as in the original primary site. This scheme makes sure that an external call is executed exactly once on the object, and no results are lost due to failures. The retained results can be deleted once the parent operation responsible for the nested call terminates.

To ensure one-copy serializability, proper concurrency control is also needed. With the primary site approach, since all requests are routed to the primary site, any centralized concurrency control protocol can be used. In the method described above, two-phase locking was used. However, this is not sufficient to handle failures. For masking a failure completely, the new primary site must also have all the information about the locks, otherwise it may resolve concurrent requests in a manner that may never occur with a centralized database. This can be done simply by the primary site distributing the information about locks to its backups. This can be done at each lock operation, or by piggybacking the information on other message exchanges to reduce the communication cost.

7.3   Resiliency with Active Replicas

In the primary site approach for supporting resiliency, only the primary site is really active and services user requests. The backups are largely passive replicas which record operations forwarded to them by the primary. By keeping only one copy active, supporting the one-copy serializability property is simplified. In this section, we will discuss another approach for supporting resiliency where all the replicas are simultaneously active. Since all replicas are active, other conditions have to be satisfied to ensure that the one-copy serializability property is satisfied and the different copies remain mutually consistent. As we will see, one way to satisfy the condition is by atomic broadcast. Though we are discussing this approach for supporting data resiliency, like the primary site approach, the method of active replication is very general and has also been used in other contexts to support resiliency. This approach is the most suitable for supporting resiliency against node failures only. Hence, we assume for this section that only node failures occur, and the communication network stays connected.

7.3.1 State Machine Approach

The method of using active replicas is also called the *state machine approach* [Sch90]. This approach views the system as consisting of servers and clients. In the case of data replication, the nodes having the copy of the data will be servers, while the nodes requesting operations on the data will be clients. We assume that the clients and servers are separate nodes. The state machine approach is a general approach for supporting fault tolerance by replication. It can handle Byzantine failures as well as fail stop failures. Our discussion is limited to fail stop failures only and is based on [Sch90].

In the state machine approach, resiliency against failures is supported by replicating the servers on different nodes. For *k-resiliency* (i.e., a system that can mask up to k node failures), the data is replicated on at least $k + 1$ nodes. Instead of sending a request to a designated node, a request is sent to all replicas. All replicas are equivalent and perform the request, and any can send the reply for the operation. Since any replica is allowed to service any request, to preserve one-copy serializability, it is essential that all replicas service a request in the same state so that all will provide the same result.

If each replica is initially in the same state, and gets the same set of requests in the same order, then each will produce the same output for an operation (as objects are deterministic). Hence, the key for supporting resiliency is to ensure that all replicas get the same sequence of requests. This, in turn, requires *agreement* and *order* properties be satisfied [Sch90]. Agreement states that all nonfaulty replicas receive every request, and order states that every nonfaulty replica process the requests in the same order.

For fail stop processors, the agreement requirement can be relaxed. [Sch90]. The requirement of order can be relaxed. If a request r is such that its processing does not modify the state of the state machine, then that request needs to be sent to only one nonfaulty state machine. This is so because the response from a nonfaulty state machine is guaranteed to be correct and the same as the response from other nonfaulty state machines. (Note that this does not hold if Byzantine failures are possible, since in that case, the response of a state machine cannot be trusted.)

The order requirement can be relaxed for requests that commute [Sch90]. Two requests r and r' commute for a state machine if the outputs produced by the state machine and the final state of the state machine by processing r before r' are the same as would result from processing r' before r. Clearly, if the result of executing two requests is the same, regardless of the order in which they are executed, then the order in which they are received at different state machines is not important. We will consider the general case only where we do not make any assumptions about the commutativity of operations.

Agreement can be satisfied by a Byzantine agreement protocol, if the failures are Byzantine, or by a reliable broadcast protocol, if nodes are fail stop. Since we assume that the nodes are fail stop, agreement can be satisfied by reliably broadcasting each request to all the replicas. We have seen protocols for reliable broadcast earlier in Chapter 4.

The order requirement can be satisfied by assigning unique identifiers to requests and having state machine replicas process the requests according to the total order relation on the identifiers of the requests. This means that at any given time, a state machine should process a request that not only has the smallest identifier, but should not accept a future request that may have a smaller identifier. A request at a state machine replica is considered to be *stable* if no request can come later to the state machine from any client which has a smaller identifier [Sch90]. This means that the order requirement can be satisfied if each state machine replica processes the stable request with the smallest identifier. Since each request is reliably broadcast to each replica, if each replica follows this rule for servicing a request, then all replicas will service the requests in the same order. This reduces the problem of satisfying the order requirement to determining the stability of a request.

Stability can be determined if requests are assigned unique identifiers using the logical clocks discussed earlier in Chapter 2 and by using the following approach [Sch90]. If these clocks are used for assigning identifiers to requests, then we know that the identifiers will be consistent with the "causal" relationship. With logical clocks, a request r is stable at a state machine if the state machine has received a request with a *larger identifier* than r from *every* nonfaulty client in the system. Since the replica has received requests with a larger identifier from all clients, the property of logical clocks ensures that no request can be received later from a client with a request with a smaller identifier than what has already been received by the state machine. This implies that the state machine will never receive a request from any node which will have a smaller identifier than that of r. Hence, the request r is stable at the state machine.

There are various other ways to determine stability for satisfying the property [Sch90]. One approach to satisfy both the agreement and order is to use atomic broadcast. This approach will be used in the example discussed later in the section.

7.3.2   Resilient Objects Using Atomic Broadcasts

We now consider the object-action model for supporting resiliency which uses the state machine approach discussed above. With objects, we can have nested operations, since an operation on an object may invoke other operations. We have already seen, while discussing the implementation of resilient objects using the primary site approach, that this introduces new problems. Here we will discuss one method that supports resilient objects by using active replicas [Jal89]. As with the state machine approach, we assume that the sites can fail, but that the network does not get partitioned.

Each data object is replicated on all the nodes in the system. Any process can request operations on the replicated objects. A node employs messages to request operations (on behalf of processes or operations on processes) and to return the results of an operation. A request for an operation is sent to all the nodes, and the operation is performed on all the replicas of the object. The requests for operations are broadcast to all the nodes by using an atomic broadcast protocol. We have discussed various methods to atomically broadcast a message earlier in Chapter 4. The use of atomic broadcast protocol ensures that each operational node gets every request, and that the different requests are delivered at different nodes in the same order. This ensures the mutual consistency of different replicas.

If an operation is requested on an object O_1 and that operation performs an operation on another object O_2, then all the nodes performing the operation on O_1 will request the operation on O_2. These are *images* of the same independent request. For consistency of data objects, only one of these requests should be serviced. For this, a numbering scheme is used. Each operation on an object is assigned an id-number. The id-numbers should be such that each independent request has a unique id-number, and all images of an independent request have the same id-number. If these conditions are satisfied, the images of a request can be identified by comparing id-numbers. A top-level request is always an independent request, with only one image.

Assume that each node is assigned a unique node number and has a counter that is incremented whenever the node receives or broadcasts a message. For a top-level operation request at a node, the id-number of the request is the node number of that node followed by the value of the counter. For a nested operation, the id-number of the request is the id-number of the parent request followed by a sequence number, where the sequence number is one more than the number of nested operations requested by the parent operation before requesting this nested operation.

A message to request an operation on an object carries the id-number of the request. Each node maintains two queues. For a node i, the queue req_i is the queue where requests are kept, and res_i is the queue which stores the results of the operations. A request (result) is broadcast by a node only if a copy of that request (result) does not exist in the respective queue, that is, if there is no request (result) in req_i (req_i) with the same id-number as the incoming request (result). Due to this checking, a request cannot be deleted from the queue immediately after it has been serviced. It has to be kept until no other copy of the request can arrive. For this, when a request is serviced or a result is returned to the caller, it is not deleted from the queue, but is merely *marked*. A request or a result can be deleted only after a "sufficient" time has elapsed (which depends on the communication delays and the relative processing speeds of nodes). The actions to be performed by a node i are shown in Fig. 7.2.

$*[$

request (r) $\rightarrow$
if $r \notin req_i$ then broadcast(r)

$\square$ receive (m) $\rightarrow$
if m is a request for an operation then
if $m \notin req_i$ then add (req_i, m)
if m is a result then
if $m \notin res_i$ then add (res_i, m)

$\square$ not empty $(req_i) \rightarrow$
r = first unmarked request from req_i
a = result of performing the operation r
mark (req_i, r)
if (i is a requester for the operation r) then return (a)
if $a \notin res_i$ then
add(res_i, a)
broadcast(a)

]

Figure 7.2: Actions of a node i for supporting resilient objects

When a request is generated at a node, it is broadcast only if the same request does not already exist in its request queue. If it exists in the queue, it means that this is a nested operation request and some other node has already broadcast it. When a request is received, it is added to the request queue if the same request does not already exist in the queue. Similar action is taken when a result is received.

If there are requests in the queue, the first unserviced (i.e., unmarked) request is considered. The operation is performed and the request is marked. Marking a request in the request queue implies that the operation has been performed on the local replica. If the node is also a requester for this operation, the result is returned (to the requesting process). For a nested operation, all nodes are requesters; for a top-level operation, only one node is the requester. If a result with the same id-number already exists in the result queue, the result is marked; otherwise the result is added to the queue, marked, and broadcast.

It might appear that only one message for each request or result will be broadcast. However, in some cases, more than one message may be transmitted for a request (result). This happens because of the delay in delivering a broadcast message. Another node may broadcast the request (result) before it gets the message from some other node. Hence, the scheme for supporting resiliency has to handle duplicate requests.

It is clear that as long as at least one node is alive, operations can be performed on the data objects. The use of atomic broadcast for requests ensures that all active copies perform the same sequence of operations and are always mutually consistent and up-to-date. Any object is capable of servicing a request, and an ongoing operation is successfully completed even if nodes fail during its execution.

So far, we have focused on an operation on an object. However, a transaction or a user action may consist of many operations on different objects and proper concurrency control measures have to be applied to ensure one-copy serializability. With active replicas, any of the concurrency control methods can be used. The basic requirement is that all replicas (or state machines) use the same method for concurrency control that resolves conflicting requests in the same manner. If this is ensured, since the same requests arrive at each replica in the same order, each replica will face the same conflicts and will resolve it in the same manner, thereby preserving mutual consistency.

One method is to use the two-phase locking protocol. For each object, two more operations are defined: *lock* and *unlock*. When a user action makes a request for an operation on an object, it first performs a lock operation on that object. If the result of the lock operation is the granting of the proper lock, the request for the operation is made. When no more requests need to be made, all the objects locked during the operation are unlocked by the unlock operation.

Another issue with active replicas is *reintegration of failed nodes*. We have so far implicitly assumed that when a node fails, it remains failed, and we have shown that the remaining nodes in the system can satisfy any request. However, in reality, when a node fails, it recovers after it is repaired. Clearly, a repaired node cannot be reintegrated into the system directly, since its state is now out of date (i.e., the failed and recovered state machine has an old state). First, the recovered node will have to update its state before servicing any request. For proper reintegration, the repaired node will have to update its request based on the state of other nodes in the system.

One way to support reintegration is to define an operation called *state (O)* for an object O, which returns the state of the object O. Suppose a node n becomes alive after having failed. Then n first requests the operation *state (O)* for each object O that resides on the node to update its copy of the object. It starts servicing requests only after it receives the result of the state (O) operation. Suppose the node n' services this state (O) request of n. It is possible that n may miss requests that arrive in the system after n' prime sends the result of state (O) but before n actually starts receiving requests. To avoid this after sending state (O), for some time the node n' also forwards to n the requests for operations that it gets.

7.4   Voting

In this section, we will discuss another pessimistic approach for replica control that employs voting. By *voting* we mean that performing an operation on replicated data is decided collectively by replicas through voting. A voting algorithm ensures that conflicting operations are not performed concurrently. A major advantage of many of the voting algorithms is that they can mask both node and communication failures, and do not require that a node distinguish between the two types of failures.

Voting-based methods have become extremely popular, and in recent times a large number of voting algorithms have been proposed. Voting schemes can be broadly considered as belonging to two categories: *static methods* and *dynamic methods*. In static approaches, the vote assignment and quorum requirements do not change, while in dynamic methods, vote assignment, total number of copies, or other information about the system may change with time in an attempt to adapt to the changing system state (in terms of failures or recoveries). We will discuss protocols of both of these in this section.

7.4.1   Static Voting Methods

Weighted Voting

The first voting approach was proposed by Thomas in [Tho79], which proposed a restricted form of voting. The concept was later generalized to *weighted voting* [Gif79]. Here we discuss the general weighted voting method.

In weighted voting, each replica of the node is assigned some number of votes. Any node that wants to perform a read operation on the data must first acquire at least r votes from the nodes in the system before it can actually read the data. Similarly, a node must first acquire at least w votes before it can write the data. The r and the w are called the *read quorum* and the *write quorum*, respectively. Let the total votes (i.e., the sum of votes of each of the replicas) be v. The quorums must satisfy two conditions:

1. $r + w > v$

2. $w > v/2$

The first condition guarantees that every read and write quorum intersect. This not only ensures that a read and a write operation cannot be performed concurrently, it also ensures that every read quorum has a replica that contains the latest copy of the data in which the latest update is reflected. The second condition ensures that two write quorums intersect, which prevents write-write conflicts, and if the system is partitioned into two groups, it allows a write to be performed in, at most, one group. Note that two read quorums need not intersect, as there is no read-read conflict.

The read and write operations work as follows. Each replica of the data has a *version number* associated with it, which is initialized to 0. When a transaction performs a read or a write operation on the replicated data, it first broadcasts a request for votes to all the nodes. All nodes that receive this request reply to the sender with the version number of their replica and the number of votes they possess. The requester node collects these votes until it has received replies from a group of nodes whose votes are equal to or more than required for the quorum. After acquiring the quorum, the node can perform the operation.

For a read operation, the node checks the version number of all the replicas in the read quorum that it has collected. Since each read and write quorum intersect, at least one of these replicas will be the latest, and will have the highest version number. Hence, the requester node reads the data from one of the nodes in the quorum that has the highest version number.

For the read to work, it is essential that after a write operation, all nodes in the write quorum have the latest copy of the data. In a write operation, the requester node makes sure that all the nodes in the quorum are written using the latest value. This may require reading values from some quorum members and writing them onto others before performing the operation. After the write operation, all the replicas in the write quorum will have the latest copy of the data.

The weighted voting approach can handle both site and communication failures, without requiring a node to distinguish between them. If a requesting node is unable to collect the quorum, then it cannot perform the operation, regardless of whether it was unable to get the quorum due to node failures or due to network partitioning. Under only site failures, read and write operations can be performed if the set of nodes that are alive (and connected) have a total of votes that is greater than w. If the number of votes is less than w, but more than r, then only read operations can be performed. If they are less than r, then even read operations cannot be done.

Suppose the system partitions into two groups of nodes. Since $w > v/2$, at most, one group can have the write quorum. Hence, updates can be performed in, at most, one partition, thereby disallowing situations where inconsistencies can result. In the partition that has w votes, read operations can also be performed (as $r < w$). However, the other partition will not even have a read quorum, since $r + w > v$. This makes sure that only those read operations are allowed that can access the latest copy of the data. In general, if the system partitions into multiple groups, the following scenarios are possible:

1. One group has a read and a write quorum, and all other groups have neither read nor write quorums. In this case, all activity is allowed in one group, while no operations can be performed in others.

2. Some groups have a read quorum, but no group has a write quorum. In this situation, read operations can be performed in many groups, but updates are performed in none.

3. No group has even a read quorum. In this, no operation can be performed in any group. This may happen if the groups are very small.

It is clear that weighted voting preserves consistency by disallowing situations where inconsistencies can occur. The performance of voting clearly depends on factors like vote assignment, read and write quorums, ratio of read and write operations, etc. We will discuss some of these issues later in the chapter.

In a homogeneous system, frequently it is assumed that each node has one vote. There are two extremes for quorum selection in this case. The first is *read one and write all*, in which r is 1, and so w equals v (to satisfy $r + w > v$). In this case, for reading, any node can be read, but an update must be made on all the nodes in the system. If even one node has failed, update operations cannot be performed. If an update is allowed, then when the failed node recovers, it may perform a read operation (as $r = 1$), thereby giving outdated data to the requester. The second is *majority voting*, where both r and w equal the majority of total votes (i.e., $\lceil v/2 \rceil$). In this case, for both read and write operations, a majority of the nodes must take part. If a network partitions, the majority group functions (if one exists), while the others do not.

Example. Consider a system with six nodes A, B, C, D, E, and F, each with one vote. Let w be 4 and r be 3; these satisfy the constraints on vote assignment. If the node B fails but the rest of the nodes remain connected, then operations will be performed in the rest of the nodes, as each node will be able to get a quorum of 4. If, due to communication failure, the network partitions into two groups $\{A, B, C, D\}$ and $\{E, F\}$, then in the first group, both read and update operations can be performed, while in the second group, no operation is allowed. If the communication failure partitions the set of nodes into the groups $\{A, B, C\}$ and $\{D, E, F\}$, then the read operation will be permitted in both, but no update operation will be permitted in either partition. If nodes C and D fail and partition the remaining nodes into groups $\{A, B\}$ and $\{E, F\}$, then no operation of any kind will be permitted in either group.

Hierarchical Voting

A major problem with majority voting is that the number of nodes required in a quorum for performing an operation increases linearly with the number of replicas. Many schemes have been proposed recently which arrange the nodes in a logical structure and define the quorum based on that in order to reduce the communication cost [AA89, Kum91a, LG90, CAA90a]. We will now discuss one such scheme, called *hierarchical voting* [Kum91a]. The hierarchical method reduces the number of nodes that must be in a quorum by introducing a multiple-level algorithm that involves multiple rounds of voting.

In the hierarchical approach, the set of nodes is logically organized as a multiple-level tree. The root level is level 0, and the leaves exist at level m, where m is the depth of the tree. The physical copies of the object are stored only at the leaves of the tree, or at level m. The higher-level nodes of the tree correspond to logical groups. We assume that all nodes at a level have the same number of children. The number of nodes (each representing a logical group) at level 1 is represented by l_1. The number of subgroups of a node at level i is represented by l_{i+1}. Note that l_{i+1} is not the number of nodes at level $i + 1$, but the number of children of a node at level i. The total number of nodes at level $i + 1$ will be $l_1 * l_2 * ... * l_i * l_{i+1}$.

A quorum is associated with each level. A read (write) quorum at a level i is defined as the number of subgroups of a node in the level $i - 1$ quorum that must be included in the quorum to obtain a read (write) access to the group. That is how many of the l_i nodes must be included in the quorum for each level $i - 1$ node that is included in the level $i - 1$ quorum. The read (write) quorum at level i is denoted by r_i (w_i). Note that the definition is recursive, and hence the process of acquiring a quorum at a level will be recursive. A quorum at level 1 implies quorum collection at all levels right down to level m. Hence a quorum consensus algorithm just needs to specify the quorum requirements at level 1.

Suppose that a quorum consensus algorithm requires a read quorum of r_1 at level 1, and a write quorum of w_1 at level 1. It has been shown that this quorum consensus algorithm is correct (i.e., it will provide write-write and read-write mutual exclusion) if for all levels $i = 1, 2, ..., m$,

1. $r_i + w_i > l_i$, and

2. $2w_i > l_i$

The reason for the correctness is as follows. At level 1, the conditions ensure that any read and write quorums will have at least one node in common at level 1. At level 2, when a quorum is collected in the subgroups of this common node, again the conditions will ensure that there is at least one node in common. This will continue all the way down to level m, and at least one physical copy (i.e., leaf node) will be common to the two quorums. Hence, once the quorums at each level are fixed (satisfying the conditions given above), then a read operation must collect a quorum of $r_1(w_1)$ of level 1 nodes. The recursive definition of a quorum, then, ensures the consistency. An algorithm for collecting the quorum is given in [Kum91a].

It is clear that with this approach, for a read operation, for each node in the quorum at level 1, r_2 nodes will be needed in the quorum, and for each node at level 2, r_3 nodes will be needed in the quorum, and so on. Hence, the total number of physical copies in a read quorum is $r_1 * r_2 * \ldots * r_m$, and the total number of physical copies in a write quorum is $w_1 * w_2 * \ldots * w_m$.

If each l_i is kept as 3 (an algorithm is given in [Kum91a] to organize a given set of nodes into a multiple-level tree with l_i as 3), then the depth of the tree is $log_3(n)$, where n is the total number of replicas of an object. The total number of physical copies that are finally read are $2^{log_3(n)}$, which is equivalent to $n^{0.63}$. That is, for an operation with a hierarchical voting method, only $n^{0.63}$ replicas need to be read, whereas in majority voting, $\lceil (n + 1)/2 \rceil$ number of replicas will be read. Clearly, for higher values of n, there will be a reduction in the number of copies to be read. However, the cost for this is that the quorum collection process requires $log_3(n)$ rounds, whereas it requires only one round in majority voting.

Example.   Consider a collection of 27 replicas organized in a three-level hierarchy, as shown in Fig. 7.3 [Kum91a]; in this, l_1, l_2 and l_3 are 3 each. There are various read and write quorums possible that will satisfy the constraint at each level that $r_i + w_i > 3$. For different quorums, a different number of leaf nodes are eventually read. Some of the different possible combinations of quorums and the number of copies that are read or written are shown in Table 7.1 [Kum91a] (in

No.	r_1	w_1	r_2	w_2	r_3	w_3	R	W
1.	1	3	1	3	1	3	1	27
2.	1	3	1	3	2	2	2	18
3.	1	3	2	2	2	2	4	12
4.	2	2	2	2	2	2	8	8

Table 7.1: Possible quorums

the table, the last two columns, R and W, represent the total number of copies read

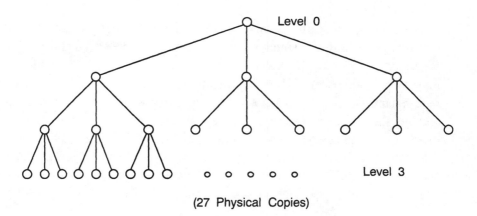

Figure 7.3: Hierarchical voting example

or written). Note that if the read and write quorums are set at 2 each, then a write quorum can be collected with as few as 8 copies. With the weighted voting technique, the write quorum is at least 14. Also, note that R and W are often less than 27.

Besides hierarchical voting, other variations of voting have been proposed. The approach proposed in [AJ92] aims to reduce the communication overhead of voting. The proposed method divides the set of nodes into logical groups of intersecting nodes. The cardinality of each group is $\sqrt{2N}$ (for a N node system). For collecting a quorum, a node first needs to communicate only with the members of its own group. If some of these nodes have failed, the node may need to communicate with other nodes. Hence, the cost of communication, when no failures occur, is reduced from $O(N)$ to $O(\sqrt{N})$.

The technique presented in [JA92] aims to reduce the storage overhead that is incurred in replicating the data on all the nodes. In this approach, a file of the size $|F|$, which is to be replicated, is encoded and then broken into n parts, each of the size $|F|/m$. The n parts are then stored on different nodes. The coding scheme is such that any of the m parts of the file are sufficient to reconstruct the entire file. The read and write quorums have to be redefined when a file is coded and split in this manner. The quorum requirement is not straightforward and the minimum sufficient quorum and maximum necessary quorums, as well as the read and the update algorithms with these, are specified in [JA92].

The *multi-dimensional voting* (MD voting) approach is a generalization of weighted voting which offers more flexibility [CAA90b]. In MD voting, the vote assignment to each node is a k-dimensional vector of non-negative integers. The read and write quorum requirements are also k-dimensional vectors. Each dimension of the vote and quorum assignment is similar to regular voting and can be combined in many ways, making MD voting more powerful and flexible. In addition, a number p is defined $1 \leq p \leq k$, which specifies the number of dimensions for which a quorum must be satisfied. Hence MD voting requires that in a dimension, the number of votes required must be greater than or equal to the quorum requirement for that dimension, and this should be satisfied for p different dimensions. A MD voting algorithm can therefore be characterized by the number of dimensions it has and the number of dimensions in which a quorum is needed, and is represented by $MD(p, k)$. A key issue in MD voting is how to select the quorum values (it is not always the majority) and the value of p. Methods for selecting these are discussed in [CAA90b].

7.4.2   Dynamically Adaptive Methods

By nature, the static voting methods do not adapt to changes in the system due to failures. For example, with weighted voting, if due to repeated partitioning, the system breaks into small groups, no group will be allowed to perform (update) operations. The reason for this is that weighted voting always requires that the number of sites necessary for performing an operation is the majority (if majority voting is being used) of the total number of sites in the system. So, if a system partitions with one group as the majority group, and if this group further partitions, then no group may have the majority. In this section, we will study some approaches that generalize the weighted voting strategy to avoid this problem of repeated partitioning. These approaches adapt the voting strategy to changes in the system by changing the voting parameters.

Dynamic Voting

Dynamic voting is different than the majority voting scheme in that for an update it requires a majority of the copies that are accessible at the time of the update. By this, it solves the problem caused by repeated partitioning. There are two slightly different approaches that have been proposed for dynamic voting [JM87, Dav89]. The discussion here is based on the method proposed in [JM87], which considers a system in which each node is assigned one vote.

For each copy of the data d_i at node i there is a *version number* VN_i (initialized to zero), which counts the number of successful updates to d_i. The *current version number* of the data d is the maximum taken over the version number of all replicas of d. A replica d_i is said to be *current* if its version number is the same as the current version number of d. A group is said to be a *majority partition* if it contains a majority of the current copies of d.

With each copy d_i is also associated another integer called the *update sites cardinality*, SC_i, which reflects the number of sites that participated in the most recent update to d_i. Initially, SC_i is set to the total number of sites in the system. Whenever a copy d_i is updated, then SC_i is set to equal the total number of copies of d which were updated during this update.

With dynamic voting, a site can perform an update if it belongs to a majority partition. Therefore, a site has to first determine if it belongs to a majority partition. Consider the case where site 1 wants to perform an update operation. It requests all the nodes it can communicate with to send their version numbers and update sites cardinality. Let the nodes which respond to the request of node 1 be node 2, ..., m. The node determines the maximum version number from all the responses it gets (and its own version number). This version number may be the current version number. It also determines the maximum update sites cardinality from all the responses. If the number of nodes which have the maximum version number is less than half of the maximum update sites cardinality, this set does not form a majority and the operation is rejected. Otherwise, the set of nodes having the maximum version number form a majority and the update is performed on all of them. The version number and the update sites cardinality of the nodes is also updated. The actions performed for an update are shown in Fig. 7.4.

$$M = max\{VN_i : 1 \le i \le m\} \text{ (an integer)}$$
$$I = \{i : VN_i = M, 1 \le i \le m\} \text{ (a set)}$$
$$N = max\{SC_i : i \in I\} \text{ (an integer)}$$

if $|I| \le N/2$ **then** reject the operation
else

for all sites in I **do**
        perform the update
        $VN_i = M + 1$
        $SC_i = |I|$

Figure 7.4: Performing an update with dynamic voting

Clearly, dynamic voting will permit operations to be performed in groups that do not form a majority of the total nodes. Once it allows operations in such groups, to preserve consistency, it has to also ensure that no further group can perform any operation without including any node from this group. That is, if there are groups that do not currently form a majority group and no operation is being performed in them, rejoining of these groups may form a group which may even have a majority of the total nodes in the system. Even in this case, this group cannot be allowed to perform operations (or it cannot be allowed to form the majority group) until it reconnects with the group that has the current copies.

Suppose after the joining of groups, a site i realizes that it has a copy that is not current. First, it has to "catch up" and update its state. A node is allowed to update its state if, and only if, it belongs to a majority group. Suppose that node 1 can communicate with sites $2, \ldots, m$. The copy of the node 1 is not current if its version number is less than the version number of some site in the group $\{2, \ldots, m\}$, or if it has the highest version number and the set of nodes that have the highest version number do not form a majority partition. If node 1 realizes that its version number is not current, in order to "catch up" it has to perform some actions. First, it determines that the group it belongs to forms a majority group, since only in that situation it can update. If it is a part of a majority partition, it updates by requesting the missing updates. The actions for updating the state are shown in Fig. 7.5.

$$M = max\{VN_i : 1 \leq i \leq m\}$$
$$I = \{A_j : VN_j = M, 1 \leq j \leq m\},$$
$$N = max\{SC_k : k \in I\}$$
if $|I| \leq N/2$ **then** the node i cannot update its state
else

> Get state from a node with a current copy
> Set VN_i to M
> Set SC_i to $N + 1$

Figure 7.5: Updating state dynamic voting

Example. Let us illustrate this approach by an example [JM87]. Suppose there are five nodes A, B, C, D, and E which have copies of a data d and which initially form one partition. After nine update operations on d, each of the five copies will have a version number of 9 (reflecting nine update operations), and an update sites cardinality of 5 (since there are five nodes in this partition). Now suppose that the communication network fails and partitions this group of nodes into two groups $\{A, B, C\}$, and $\{D, E\}$. If A gets another update operation, it will be able to communicate only with B and C. Since these three nodes form a majority partition, an update is performed on all three. After this operation, the state of the different copies is [JM87]:

	A	B	C	D	E
VN:	10	10	10	9	9
SC:	3	3	3	5	5

Since *A* can communicate only with *B* and *C*, after the operation, the version number of the majority group becomes 10, and the group's update sites cardinality becomes 3 (as only three nodes perform the update). The state of the other two nodes stay the same. Suppose that the majority partition further partitions, forming two groups {*A, C*} and {*B*}, and *A* gets an update operation. With weighted voting, *A* cannot perform this operation, since {*A, C*} together do not form a majority of the total number of nodes in the system. However, they do form a majority of the current copies (as there are three current copies). Hence, operations are allowed in this partition. After this operation, the state of the system will be [JM87]:

	A	C	B	D	E
VN:	11	11	10	9	9
SC:	2	2	3	5	5

Let us now consider the joining of groups. Suppose that the groups {*B*} and {*D, E*} join, forming a new group {*B, D, E*}. No operation should be allowed in this group, as no node in this group has the latest copy of the data, and allowing an operation will violate consistency (a read operation will be able to "see" old data). Let us see how dynamic voting handles this. Suppose that *D* wants to update a copy of the data by using dynamic voting. It will find *M* is 10, and the set *I* contains only *B*, and *N* is 5. Since the |*I*| is not *N*/2, *D* is not allowed to update its state with others. If it were allowed, then after the update, *B, D, E* will have a version number of 10, and an update sites cardinality of 5, which will give {*B, D, E*} a majority, thereby leading to an inconsistency. So, even though group {*B*} has joined with {*D, E*}, each node is in the same state as it was before joining. Hence, for the purposes of performing operations, they are still treated as separate groups. If a request for an operation comes, say, at *B*, it cannot perform that operation, since the set *I* which it will form will contain only *B*, and *N* will be 3. So, the set *I* does not form a majority group and hence the operation cannot be performed. This preserves the mutual consistency of the data. It should be clear that if a group is formed by joining a group with the group that currently forms the majority group, the new group will also have a majority.

Dynamic Reassignment of Votes

Now let us discuss another dynamic technique by which the availability loss due to partitioning can be reduced. The approach of dynamic voting is to make the majority partition the set of total nodes in the system, so that it can handle further partitions. A somewhat different approach is to change the votes of the node in the majority partition such that the loss of nodes is properly compensated and further partitioning can be handled. This is the approach of *dynamically reassigning votes* [BGS86].

The first approach for reassigning votes is the *overthrow technique*. In this technique, after a partition or a failure, for each node x outside the majority group, there will be one node in the majority group that supplants x, such that loss of x is not felt. Consider a system in which only one node x has been partitioned from the rest, and the votes of x are $v(x)$. Suppose that it is decided that the node a in the majority group is to supplant x. This decision can be made by simply ordering the nodes and selecting the highest node in the majority partition. The new votes of a have to be such that they cover the voting power of a before failure, plus the voting power of x, plus the increase in the majority caused by the increase in the total number of votes. If a increases its votes by $2v(x)$, the total number of votes will also increase by this amount, and the majority will increase by $v(x)$. Since the new votes of a provide the votes for x, as well as this increase in the majority, it can be shown that all the majority groups that used x can be formed by using a instead. The side effect of supplanting x is that node a becomes "more powerful," as it has more votes now and will be needed more often in forming majority groups.

The second method for dynamically reassigning votes is the *alliance technique*. In this, instead of supplanting a node x by one node, a group of nodes in the majority partition are used. If there are N nodes in the majority partition, a node x can be supplanted by assigning $\lceil (2v(x)/N) \rceil$ extra votes to each node. Since we can assign surplus votes, another way is to assign each node $2v(x)$ extra votes, or we can assign each node $v(x)$ votes, if the total number of nodes is more than two. Other distribution methods are also possible.

Now consider what happens when the node x rejoins the majority group. Clearly, something needs to be done, otherwise x will get "marginalized" and its votes will be reduced relative to the votes of other nodes. One way to avoid this is to have each node relinquish the extra votes it acquired because of x, after x rejoins. To implement this would require that each node keep track of how many votes it acquired when some node was excluded. Another method is to increase the vote of x when it rejoins. This method will continue to increase the vote assignment, and finally all nodes have to revert back to their original assignment to avoid making the size of the vote unmanageable.

Example. Consider a system with four nodes and initial vote assignment as $v(a) = 6$, $v(b) = v(c) = v(d) = 5$ [BGS86]. That is, the total votes are 21, and the majority is 11. Assume that node a gets disconnected from the rest, leaving $\{b, c, d\}$

as the majority group with 15 votes. Using the overthrow technique, assuming b is to get the extra votes, the new vote assignment will be:

$$v(a) = 6, v(b) = 17, v(c) = v(d) = 5.$$

The total votes are now 33, and the majority is 17. With the alliance technique, where each node gets $v(x)$ extra votes, the final vote assignment is:

$$v(a) = 6, v(b) = v(c) = v(d) = 11.$$

The total votes with this reassignment are also 39, and the majority is 20.

Suppose now that node c separates from the group $\{b, c, d\}$. If no vote reassignment was done, then the group $\{b, d\}$ will have a total of 10 votes, which is not a majority. However, with reassignment by the overthrow technique, this group will have a total of 17+5=22 votes, which forms the majority. In the reassignment by alliance technique, the votes of this group are 11+11=22, which also forms the majority. As we can see, in this situation, without reassignment, no group will have a majority, but with reassignment, one group does have a majority.

Besides dynamic voting and dynamically reassigning votes, many other methods have been proposed that try to adapt the voting system to changes in the system caused by failures. The *missing writes* approach tries to improve the read performance of weighted voting [ES83]. In weighted voting, if r is 1 (and w is equal to the number of nodes), read performance is good, but then updates are stopped as soon as one node fails. If r (and w) are a majority, then the read performance is poor. In this approach, the system works in two modes. In the normal mode for a read operation, only one copy is read (i.e., r is 1), and for a write operation, all copies are updated. If some copy cannot be accessed in a write operation, then the system runs in the failure mode. In the failure mode, the missing-writes approach works like majority voting; both read and write operations require a majority. By doing this, the performance of read operations is improved when the system has no failures. Again, this method works only if nodes fail or if node and communication failures can be distinguished.

The method of *voting with ghosts* tries to improve the write availability of weighted voting [RT88]. In this approach, if a node fails, a *ghost* is started within the same group as the failed node, and is assigned the same number of votes as the failed node. A ghost is a process without storage. Therefore it cannot reply to a read request, and so does not participate in a read quorum. Ghosts are allowed to participate in a write quorum. The write operation has an additional restriction in that it must contain at least one non-ghost copy. Since a ghost is not allowed to take part in a read quorum, the intersection of a read quorum with a write quorum (recall that with weighted voting, a read quorum must intersect with every write quorum) can only contain non-ghost copies. This ensures that the read operation will get the latest data. When a node comes back up, it replaces the ghost only after it has obtained the latest data. This can be done by the ghost of the node acquiring a read quorum and then reading the latest copy and installing it on the recovered node.

Another technique is to use the *regeneration of objects* [PNP88]. In this method *configuration data* about the replicated data is kept in a directory, which is itself replicated. If a node fails, its effect is not felt in a read operation. However, if in a write operation the required quorum is not obtained, then new copies of the data are created on different nodes and the configuration data is updated. In this manner, the degree of replication is maintained and the change in location of replicas is reflected by properly maintaining the configuration data. The method of *available copies* [BG84], and *voting with witnesses* [Par86] are similar.

7.4.3   Vote Assignment

In a voting method, an update is performed on a group of nodes. The groups of nodes that can be formed for an operation are such that they always intersect with each other. This ensures that if an update is to be performed in a group, then no other group is performing updates. This also ensures that there is a write-write mutual exclusion. The strength of a voting algorithm lies in the fact that it is able to support mutual exclusion without communication between nodes. A majority voting strategy defines a set of groups of nodes, such that each group has a majority of votes.

The performance of a voting system, particularly when network partitioning occurs, will clearly depend on the assignment of votes to different nodes. Consider the example of a system consisting of four nodes: a, b, c, and d. If we assign one vote to each node, then the possible groups for performing an update are:

$$\{\{a, b, c\}, \{a, b, d\}, \{a, c, d\}, \{b, c, d\}\}.$$

That is, these are the groups whose votes add up to a majority of votes (i.e., at least three out of four nodes). Now consider an assignment that gives a two votes and the rest one vote each. The majority is still three votes, so the groups that have a majority are:

$$\{\{a, b\}, \{a, c\}, \{a, d\}, \{b, c, d\}\}.$$

This set of groups is clearly preferable to the previous grouping, as the system can continue to perform updates (at least in one group) in all the groups of the previous grouping, as well as some more. For example, if after a partition, the groups are $\{a, b\}$ and $\{c\}$, then the latter set of groups will allow updates to be performed in one group while the former will not allow any updates.

This example clearly shows that the reliability of a voting-based system depends critically on the vote assignment. If partitions occur, vote assignments will determine whether updates are allowed or not. We say that a voting system has *halted* if no operation can be performed on any node, that is, there is no group that has a majority of votes. A system is *up* otherwise. The goal of vote assignment is to maximize the steady-state probability that the system is up. Here we will discuss some approaches to assigning votes in a majority voting system.

Using Coteries

Here we discuss an approach to vote assignment by enumerating the possible groups that can be formed by majority voting [GB85]. By a vote assignment we get a set of groups (where each group is a set of nodes), such that each group has a majority of votes. In addition, the intersection of any two groups is non-null. Such a set of groups is called a *coterie* [GB85]. Formally, if U is the set of nodes that compose the system, then a set of groups S is a *coterie* if:

1. $G \in S$ implies that G is not empty and is a subset of U.

2. If $G, H \in S$, then G and H must have at least one node in common.

3. There are no $G, H \in S$ such that $G \subset H$.

The second condition is called the *intersection property*, and the last condition ensures *minimality*. For example, if $\{a, b\}$ is a group, then clearly $\{a, b, c\}$ will also form a group and is not included in the coterie.

A coterie R is said to *dominate* another coterie S, if for each group in S, there is a group in R that is its subset. If there is no coterie that dominates a coterie S, then S is *nondominated (ND)*. If R dominates S, then clearly R is preferable over S, and consequently we want to avoid considering it while deciding the vote assignment. In the example given above, the second coterie dominated the first one (which is why it was superior). Hence, for vote assignment purposes, we only need to consider ND coteries. For the remainder of the discussion, a coterie will mean ND coteries.

Now let us discuss vote assignments. Let U be the set of nodes in the system. A *vote assignment* is a function $v : U \rightarrow N$ (N is nonnegative integers) and $v(a)$ is the number of votes assigned to a node a. For a vote assignment v, the total votes $TOT(v)$ is the sum of votes for all the nodes in the system, and the majority $MAJ(v)$ is defined as $\frac{TOT(v)}{2} + 1$, if $TOT(v)$ is even, and as $\frac{TOT(v)+1}{2}$ if $TOT(v)$ is odd. The set of *majority groups* (i.e., groups, each having a majority of votes) of a vote assignment v is Z, where:

$$Z = \{G | G \subseteq U \text{ and } \sum_{a \in G} v(a) \geq MAJ(v)\}.$$

The minimal elements of Z (i.e., those groups having no subset in Z) form a coterie, and are called a *coterie corresponding to v*.

Now we can define what similar vote assignments are. Two vote assignments are *similar* if, and only if, their corresponding coteries are the same. Hence, in a system with an odd number of nodes, a vote assignment that gives 1 vote to each node is similar to another vote assignment that gives 3 votes to each node.

It has been shown that if the number of nodes in the system is five or less, then for all possible coteries there is a vote assignment. That is, for any coterie S, there is a vote assignment v whose corresponding coterie is S. Hence, one possible method for selecting the best vote assignment (for a system with five or fewer nodes) is to first enumerate all possible coteries. An algorithm for enumerating coteries for a system is given in [GB85]. Once the coteries are enumerated, select the coterie that yields the best reliability for the given system, that is, select the one in which the probability of the system being operational is the highest. Finally determine the vote assignment that corresponds to this coterie.

To determine the vote assignment that corresponds to a given coterie, the coterie can be converted into a set of linear equations. Since each group in the coterie must have a majority of votes, for each group G we get, $\sum_{a \in G} v(a) \geq MAJ(v)$. If a solution exists, then it can be determined by solving these inequalities. If no vote assignment exists that corresponds to a coterie, then the inequalities will lead to a contradiction.

If the number of nodes is more than five, then there exist coteries with no vote assignment corresponding to them (though there exists an MD voting that corresponds to it [CAA90b]). Hence, selecting a vote assignment by selecting a corresponding coterie will not be straightforward. Furthermore, the number of different possible vote assignments in a system with n nodes is 2^{n^2} [GB85], and the number of coteries generated is more than this according to the enumeration algorithm. Hence, for large systems, the approach of enumerating all the coteries for evaluation is of limited use for selecting vote assignments.

Heuristics for Vote Assignment

Another approach to selecting the vote assignments is not to try for the very best, but to use some heuristics that may suggest the best vote assignment or a vote assignment that is close to the best. Here we describe some heuristics that have been proposed [BG87]. A vote assignment is *uniform* if each node gets the same number of votes, and if the number of nodes is odd. This means that each node is assigned one vote. If the number of nodes is even, then one node has two votes, while the rest have one vote each. A *singleton assignment* is one in which all the votes are assigned to a single node, that is, one node has one node and the remaining nodes have zero votes. A singleton assignment makes the system similar to a primary site system.

Heuristic I. For each node i, multiply its reliability by the sum of reliabilities of the links incident upon i. Round the number obtained, and this number represents the votes assigned to the node i. If the total number of votes is even, then the node with most votes gets one extra.

Heuristic II. For each incident link to node i, multiply its reliability by the reliability of its other end-point node. These products are summed and finally multiplied by the reliability of i to get the votes assigned to i. Rounding and making the total number of votes odd is done in the same manner as in Heuristic I.

Heuristic III. This heuristic attempts to find a cluster of nodes that is most likely to exist, and assign votes only to it. A link is considered *weak* if the product of its reliability and the reliability of one of its end points is less than 0.5. Weak links are first removed, which may partition the network. From this reduced graph, the biconnected components are determined. A biconnected component of a graph is a subgraph in which there are at least two paths from any node to any other node, that is, removal of one node cannot cause the subgraph to become disconnected. The biconnected components are assigned votes separately using Heuristic II. Out of these, the assignment that maximizes the probability that the system is up is taken as the vote assignment.

Example. Let us illustrate these heuristics by an example [BG87]. Consider the graph shown in Fig. 7.6(a), which also shows the reliabilities of the nodes and links. For this graph, Heuristic I will result in the assignment:

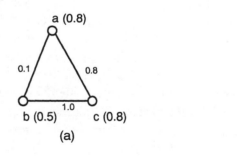
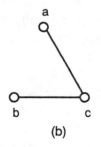

Figure 7.6: An example

$$v(a) = \text{round}(0.8(0.1+0.8)) = 1$$
$$v(b) = \text{round}(0.8(0.8+1.0)) = 1$$
$$v(c) = \text{round}(0.5(0.1+1.0)) = 1$$

Heuristic II will give:

$$v(a) = \text{round}(0.8(0.5*0.1+0.8*0.8)) = 0$$
$$v(b) = \text{round}(0.8(0.8*0.8+1.0*0.5)) = 1$$
$$v(c) = \text{round}(0.5(0.1*0.8+1.0*0.8)) = 0$$

Heuristic III will first produce the transformed graph, which is shown in Fig. 7.6(b). This graph has three biconnected components, each with a single node. The three assignments for these three biconnected components are therefore $< 1, 0, 0 >$, $< 0, 1, 0 >$, and $< 0, 0, 1 >$. The second and the third assignments will result in a system reliability of 0.8, and so any of these can be chosen.

As enumerating all possible vote assignments is difficult for a system consisting of six or more nodes, it is hard to evaluate the effectiveness of these heuristics for such systems. For a system with five or fewer nodes, best vote assignment can be determined by enumerating the coteries, and then determining the reliability of this assignment. In experiments, it has been found that for such systems, one of the heuristics provides the best possible reliability [BG87]. Also, for larger systems, in many cases the heuristics give a vote assignment which offers a reliability close to the best-known (through simulation) reliability.

The example above seems to suggest that singleton or uniform assignments may frequently offer the best reliability. It has been shown that for homogeneous systems where the reliability of nodes is the same and is greater than 0.5, if the links are perfectly reliable (i.e., have a reliability of 1.0), then uniform assignment is better than any nonuniform assignment [BG87]. It has also been shown that if the system has two nodes, and the links are perfect, then both uniform and singleton assignments yield the same reliability. And for a larger system with perfect links and a node reliability greater than 0.5 (but less than 1.0), in general, uniform assignment is better than singleton assignment. Another heuristic has been proposed in [Kum91b], which uses a randomized algorithm for vote assignment.

An Integer Programming Approach

Another approach for assigning votes is based on integer programming. For a network, first the top k groups are determined (perhaps using simulation), where k is a parameter and is chosen so that most of the likely groups are included. These groups represent the most likely partitions in case of failures. With these k groups, the vote assignment problem is formulated as an integer programming problem, with the objective of minimizing the average number of operations that cannot be satisfied due to partitioning.

The criteria used for selecting the top k groups is the average number of operations that are performed by the system per unit of time in a group. For a group, the rate of arrival of requests is the sum of arrival rates at the nodes in the group. The average number of operations performed in a group per unit of time is the product of the rate of arrival of requests and the fraction of time (in the life of the system or a long period of time) for which this group exists. For integer programming, we have to select k groups that have the highest number of operations performed per unit of time. The simplest way of determining these groups is through simulation, using the steady-state probabilities for nodes/links to be up, as is done in [Ven92].

With the top k groups known, the goal is to assign votes in such a manner that these groups have a majority of votes. It is easy to observe that it may not always be possible to assign a majority of votes to all the groups. Hence, the aim is to assign votes in such a way that the groups getting a majority of votes have the maximum average operations performed in them. This can be formulated as an integer programming problem. Three different formulations have been proposed in [Ven92]. We will describe one formulation here. Let n be the number of nodes in the system, and T_i be the average number of operations performed per unit of time in a group G_i.

The problem formulation is such that we get a vote assignment which assigns a majority of votes to a subset of k groups for which the sum of T_i is the maximum. Let X_i be a binary variable which is zero if group G_i has a majority of votes, and is one otherwise. By defining X_i in this manner, we can formulate this as a minimization problem. The integer programming model is:

Minimize:

$$\sum_{i=1}^{k} (T_i * X_i)$$

subject to:

$$\frac{1}{2}(\sum_{j=1}^{N} v(j) + 1) - \sum_{k \in G_i} v(k) \le d * X_i (i = 1, \dots, k)$$

$$X_i = 0 \text{ or } 1 \ (i = 1, \dots, k).$$

Since $X_i = 0$ represents the ith group getting the majority of votes, $T_i * X_i$ will represent the average number of operations lost due to the ith group not getting a majority of votes. The objective function is trying to minimize the sum of the average number of operations lost due to the groups not getting a majority of votes.

The first term in constraint (for a group G_i) is $1/2(\sum_{j=1}^{N} v(j+1)$ which represents the majority of votes. The second term $\sum_{k \in G_i} v(k)$ represents the votes assigned to group G_i.

Case 1. When X_i is zero, the constraint will become

$$\frac{1}{2}(\sum_{j=1}^{N} v(j) + 1) - \sum_{k \in G_i} v(k) \leq 0$$

which makes sure that the ith group will have votes greater than or equal to the majority of votes.

Case 2. When X_i is one, the constraint becomes

$$\frac{1}{2}(\sum_{j=1}^{N} V_j + 1) - \sum_{k \in G_i} V_k \leq d.$$

The value of d should be such that when X_i is one, whatever the votes assigned to group G_i are, the constraint is still satisfied. As the value on the left-hand side will be, at the most, the majority of votes (since votes are positive), the value of d is chosen so that it is greater than the possible majority of votes needed to satisfy the constraint. This also means that the constraint allows a majority of votes to be assigned to group G_i when X_i is one. We have to make sure that whenever X_i is one, the ith group will not have the majority of votes. Since the objective function is trying to minimize $T_i * X_i$, integer programming will always try to assign all X_i's as zero. According to Case 1, $X_i = 0$ means that G_i gets the majority of votes. If it is not possible to assign the majority of votes to all the groups, then some X_i's will have to take the value one. The objective function will select a subset out of the k groups so that the sum of T_i for these groups is the maximum, and it will assign the corresponding X_i as zero. The constraint will force these groups to get a majority of votes. All the other groups which have corresponding X_i as one will not get a majority of votes, since the objective function would have assigned X_i as zero if it could have gotten the majority of votes. To ensure that the constraint is satisfied even when G_i does not have a majority (and votes assigned to group G_i can even be zero), d must be greater than or equal to the majority of votes.

Example. Let us consider a three-node fully connected network, with each component having a reliability of 0.9. Let the arrival rates of requests at all the nodes be 200 per unit of time and let $k = 3$. The top 3 partitions are {1,2,3}, {1,2}, and {2,3} (the group {1,3} is equally likely to {1,2} or {2,3}). The fraction of total simulation time for which these groups are present is (found through simulation) approximately

0.7, 0.08, 0.08, respectively. The average number of operations performed in each of the groups per unit of time is therefore 420, 32, and 32, respectively. The above formulation will result in (choosing d to be 500):

Minimize:

$$420X_1 + 32X_2 + 32X_3$$

subject to:

$$-V_1 - V_2 - V_3 - 1000X_1 \leq -1$$

$$-V_1 - V_2 + V_3 - 1000X_2 \leq -1$$

$$V_1 - V_2 - V_3 - 1000X_3 \leq -1$$

$$X_1, X_2, X_3 = 0 \text{ or } 1$$

Solving this will result in a vote assignment of (0,1,0). This vote assignment gives a majority of votes to all the three groups ({1,2,3},{1,2},{2,3}). Since node 2 is present in all the groups, it has given all the votes (1 vote in this case) to node 2, which will give a majority of votes to all the above groups.

7.5   Degree of Replication

We have discussed various techniques to manage replicated data. So far, we have focused only on the correctness of approaches, that is, the replica management algorithm should ensure a single-copy view. However, the goal of replication is to increase reliability and availability by keeping the data accessible even when failures occur in the system. It is clear that the reliability of a system will generally increase as the number of replicas, or the *degree of replication*, increases, since more replicas will be able to mask more failures. However, it is not clear how the degree of replication will affect system availability.

Since the algorithms for replica management involve overhead which usually increases as the number of replicas increases, it is unlikely that the system availability will continue to increase as the degree of replication increases. There are two opposing forces for the degree of replication: the increase in reliability as the degree of replication increase tends to increase availability, whereas the increase in overhead tends to decrease availability. In this section, we will study the effect of the degree of replication on the system availability, and the optimum degree of replication that maximizes the system availability. We will study the two most popular techniques: the primary site approach and majority voting.

7.5.1   Primary Site Approach

We first discuss the effect of the degree of replication on the availability of the primary site approach. The discussion is based on the models proposed in [HJ89b, HJ89a]. Consider a network of N homogeneous nodes, each with a lifetime that is exponentially distributed with the mean $\frac{1}{f}$. The sites are linearly ordered. At the start, the first site is chosen as the primary site; all the other sites are specified as the backups. The state of the primary site is periodically checkpointed on all the backups with the rate c, and the time required for a checkpoint is $\frac{1}{h}$. The service time for an operation on the data is exponentially distributed with the mean $\frac{1}{\mu}$, and the inter arrival time of requests for operations in the system is exponentially distributed with the mean $1/\lambda$. If the primary site fails, all operations after the last checkpoint are first redone by the new primary site in order to reach a consistent state. Let $\frac{1}{r}$ be the time required for recovery. $1/r$ is assumed to be much smaller than $1/f$. A failed site is repaired and it rejoins the system after it is repaired. The repair service is exponentially distributed with the rate δ.

It is assumed that the checkpointing cost is exponentially distributed, and the primary site also checkpoints the state on itself. Let b be the expected cost of checkpointing by the primary on a backup. The primary site checkpoints its status on its backups, one at a time. Assuming that the cost of establishing a checkpoint is the same at each node, we get the total cost of checkpointing as $\frac{1}{h} = b \times N$.

The availability of this system, α, is defined as the fraction of time that the system is available for serving user requests. The system can be in one of the two states: the normal state or the idle state.

- Normal state: the state in which at least one site is working. In this state, the system performs three kinds of activities: operations, recovery, and checkpoints.

  - Operations: the primary site is available for serving user requests. Let T_N be the random variable representing the total time that the system is operating.

  - Recovery: the system is recovering from the primary node failure. Let T_R be the random variable representing the total recovery time of the system.

  - Checkpoints: the primary site is checkpointing its status on the backups. Let T_C be the random variable representing the total checkpointing time.

- Idle state: the state in which all sites have failed. In this state, all sites are waiting to be repaired and no services can be provided. Let T_I be the random variable representing the total idle time.

The availability α is the fraction of time that the system is available for user requests. If O is the expected overhead, then $\alpha = 1 - \frac{O}{L}$. The overhead occurs because checkpointing, recovering, and repairing are needed to make the system operational. The expected overhead within the period L is given by $O = E(T_I) + E(T_R) + E(T_C)$, where $E()$ represents the expected value of a random variable. To compute the overhead within a large period L, we need to compute the expected idle time, checkpointing time, and recovery time.

$E(T_I)$. The system is idle when all sites have failed. Let p_0 be the probability that no site is alive. Since we assume that both the lifetime and the repair time of a site are exponentially distributed, we can represent the system by a Markovian model, where the state of the system is the number of working sites. For this model, we have $p_0 = 1/\sum_{k=0}^{N} (\frac{\delta}{f})^k \frac{1}{k!}$. Therefore,

$$E(T_I) = \frac{L}{\sum_{k=0}^{N} (\frac{\delta}{f})^k \frac{1}{k!}}.$$

It should be noted that the larger the N, the smaller is the p_0.

$E(T_R)$. To compute the total recovery time, we first determine the number of failures during the period L. Since the system is in the normal state for $(1 - p_0)L$ seconds and the mean time between failures is $\frac{1}{f}$, the total number of failures during the period L is given by $L(1 - p_0)f$. Hence, the expected total time spent for recovery is:

$$E(T_R) = \frac{L(1 - p_0)f}{r}.$$

$E(T_C)$. The primary site checkpoints its state at a rate of $1/c$, and no checkpointing occurs during recovery. Hence, the expected number of checkpoints during L is: $c.((1 - p_0)L - \frac{L(1-p_0)f}{r})$. Therefore, the total time that the system is in the checkpointing state is:

$$E(T_C) = \left(\frac{(1 - p_0)L - \frac{L(1-p_0)f}{r}}{1/c} \right) \times \frac{1}{h}.$$

From the above equations, the overhead can be computed as follows:

$$O = p_0 L + \frac{L(1 - p_0)f}{r} + \left((1 - p_0)L - \frac{L(1 - p_0)f}{r} \right) \cdot \frac{c}{h}.$$

The availability of the system is given by:

$$\alpha = (1 - p_0)(1 - \frac{f}{r})(1 - \frac{c}{h}).$$

The three terms in the expression for availability reflect the contribution of the three overhead-generating activities on the system. If the idle time of the system (reflected by p_0) or the checkpointing cost $(1/h)$ or the recovery cost $(1/r)$ increases, the availability decreases.

If a failure occurs, all the operations performed since the last checkpoint have to be redone. As the number of operations performed between the two checkpoints is λ/c, on an average $\lambda/2c$ operations need to be redone. Hence, it takes an average of $\frac{\lambda}{2\mu c}$ time to redo the requests since the last checkpoint. The recovery cost, $\frac{1}{r}$, is equal to $\frac{\lambda}{2\mu c}$. If the number of sites is fixed, the optimal checkpoint rate is determined by differentiating this expression with respect to c and setting the result to zero. From this we get:

$$\frac{\lambda}{2\mu c^2} - \frac{1}{fh} = 0.$$

Solving this equation, we get the optimal checkpoint rate as $c^* = \kappa\sqrt{h}$, where κ is given by $\kappa = \sqrt{\lambda f/2\mu}$. Using this value of the checkpoint interval in the expression for availability, we get the best availability with respect to checkpoint interval. Using this, we can study the effect of degree of replication and find the optimal value of N such that α is maximized. The availability of the system with c^* can be written as:

$$\alpha = (1 - p_0)\left(1 - f(\frac{\lambda\sqrt{Nb}}{2\mu\kappa})\right)(1 - \kappa\sqrt{Nb}).$$

As N increases, p_0 decreases, thereby increasing availability. On the other hand, increasing N increases the overhead of checkpointing, which reduces the availability. Hence, there is some value of N which maximizes α.

It is difficult to get the optimum degree of replication which maximizes α by differentiating the above equations and solving for N. A numerical computation is needed to search the optimum value of N. We illustrate it by an example [HJ89a].

Example. A fault tolerant system has N identical nodes, each with a mean lifetime of 600,000 seconds (approximately 1 week). The mean service rate of the system is 5 transactions per second ($\mu = 5$), the total arrival rate is 3 transactions per second ($\lambda = 3$), and the mean repair time is 50,000 seconds ($1/\delta = 50,000$). When the primary server is performing a checkpoint, it takes 500 milliseconds to copy its status to a backup server (b=0.5). The availabilities are shown in Table 7.2. From the table, we

No. of Nodes	Availability
1	0.92215
2	0.98684
3	0.99559
4	0.99719
5	0.99746
6	0.99742
7	0.99729
8	0.99713
9	0.99698
10	0.99682

Table 7.2: An example

can see that this optimal N is 5. Increasing N beyond 5 will decrease the availability. However, the availabilities with $N = 2$ and $N = 3$ are only 1% less than the optimal availability. Hence, $N = 2$ and $N = 3$ also provide near optimal availability, and may be chosen due to practical considerations.

7.5.2 Majority Voting

Now we consider the issue of degree of replication and its effect on the availability of a majority voting system, based on the model proposed in [HJ93]. Consider a system consisting of N identical nodes, each having a replica of the data and with a mean lifetime of $1/f$. The average time to perform an operation on replicated data is exponentially distributed with the mean $\frac{1}{\mu}$. It is assumed that the node failures do not cause the network to partition. When a node fails, it is immediately sent to a repair server. After repair, the node rejoins the system as a working node. Assume that there is only one on-line repair server which uses the first-come-first-serve (FCFS) service discipline to repair failed nodes, and whose repair time is exponentially distributed with the mean $\frac{1}{\delta}$.

The system can perform operations as long as there are a sufficient number of working nodes in the system. Let M be the minimum number of nodes which must be working in order for the system to provide services. The threshold of M depends on the voting algorithm used in the controller and the type of operation (read or update). If the system uses a majority voting algorithm, M is equal to $\lceil \frac{N}{2} \rceil$. If the number of working nodes is less than M, the system cannot provide services and a total failure occurs. When a total failure occurs, all activities are suspended and the system has to be repaired before any service can be resumed. The system has the following two states:

Normal state: In this state, there are a sufficient number of working nodes to provide normal services. Let T_N be the random variable representing the time the system is in the normal state. T_N can also be interpreted as the life of the system. Let $E(T_N)$ represent the expected value of T_N.

Failure state: In this state, the system encounters a total failure. All services are suspended. Assume that negligible requests arrive when the system is in this state. Let T_F be the random variable that represents the time the system is in the idle state.

To compute the $E(T_N)$ and the $E(T_F)$ of the system, define the system state as the number of working nodes. The system is in state i when there are i nodes working at that moment. With this, the state $M - 1$ represents a total failure of the system; in this state, all activities are suspended except for repairing the failed nodes. Define $t(i, j)$ as the expected time for the system starting at state i and first visiting state j.

There are two components in $t(i, i - 1)$. First, the system has to stay in state i for s_i time units. Then, a transition occurs. It may go to state $i + 1$ or to state i. If it goes to state $i - 1$, it reaches the goal. On the other hand, if it goes to state $i + 1$, it has to take $t(i + 1, i)$ time for the system to go back to state i again and then it takes another $t(i, i - 1)$ time for the system to reach state $i - 1$. The probability of going to state $i + 1$ from state i is $\frac{\delta}{i \cdot f + \delta}$. This can finally be written as a recurrence equation (the details are given in [HJ93] and are omitted here):

$$t(N, N - 1) = \frac{1}{Nf},$$
$$t(i, i - 1) = \frac{1}{if} + \frac{\delta}{if} \cdot t(i + 1, i) \text{ for } i = N - 1, \cdots, M.$$

The mean time to failure (MTTF) of the system is the duration between the time that the system starts services and the time that the system fails. And the mean time to repair of the system is the duration between the time that the system fails and the time that the system is working again. From the definitions, the MTTF of the system is equal to $E(T_N)$, and $E(T_N)$ is the expected time for the system to travel from state M to state $M - 1$. Hence, we have $E(T_N) = t(M, M - 1)$, or:

$$\text{MTTF} = E(T_N) = t(M, M - 1).$$

Using the above recurrence equation, $t(M, M - 1)$ can be determined. It is hard to obtain a closed-form solution from the recurrence equation. The recurrence equation can easily be solved numerically to determine $E(T_N)$. The mean time to repair (MTTR) is $E(T_F) = \frac{1}{\delta}$.

The availability of the system, α, is defined as the probability that the system is available to processing requests at any time. As described in the previous section, the system is cyclic, having a normal state and a failure state. Therefore, the probability that the system is available to processing requests is the portion of time that the system is in the normal state. In other words, the availability can be represented as:

$$\alpha = \frac{E(T_N)}{E(T_N) + E(T_F)} = \frac{t(M, M-1)}{t(M, M-1) + \frac{1}{\delta}}.$$

The computation of $t(M, M-1)$ is specified in the recurrence equation above.

From the definition of system availability, it is clear that system availability is optimized when the MTTF is maximized. The MTTF is a function of the degree of replication, N. For a majority-consensus voting system, the total number of non-failure states is $\frac{N+1}{2}$. Therefore, when N increases, the total number of non-failure states increases. That is, there are more failures that can be tolerated (degree of fault tolerance). In this case, increasing N tends to increase the MTTF. But, on the other hand, the failure transition rates between states also increase as N increases. For example, the transition rate from state N to state $N-1$ is Nf. Hence, increasing N increases the failure transition rate from state N to state $N-1$. Similarly, increasing N increases the transition rates from state $N-1$ to state $N-2$, from state $N-2$ to state $N-3$, etc. In this case, increasing N tends to decrease the MTTF. In other words, increasing N increases the degree of fault tolerance but also increases the failure transition rates. Therefore, there is an optimal N such that the availability of the system is maximized.

The value of the optimal N depends on the ratio of the life of a node and the repair time of the repair server. If the ratio is very large and if N is small, the degree of fault tolerance becomes a dominant factor. In this case, increasing N increases the degree of fault tolerance and, hence, improves the system availability. The system availability increases as N increases until N becomes too large and the failure transition rates become dominant. At that point, any further increase of N results in the decrease of system availability. This threshold point (the optimal degree of replication) usually occurs at a large N when the repair time is small (compared to the life of a node). On the other hand, if the ratio is small and N is small, the failure transition rates become the dominant factor. Consequently, increasing N degrades the system availability. Therefore, the optimal degree of replication in this case is a small number.

Example. Consider a majority-voting system with each node having a mean life of 30 days. The optimal degrees of replication of the system for different repair times are numerically computed. Table 7.3 gives the optimal degrees of replication for various repair times. From the table, we find that the optimal N for system availability

Repair time (day)	Optimal N	Optimal MTTF	Optimal α
1	15	4794	0.999791
2	9	213	0.990735
3	5	85	0.965909
4	5	57	0.93429
5	3	45	0.9
10	3	30	0.75
15	3	25	0.625

Table 7.3: Effect of degree of replication in majority voting

is 15 when the repair time is 1 day. As expected, the optimal N decreases as the repair time increases. If the mean repair time is greater than 5 days, the optimal N is always 3 (since we are considering a majority-voting system, the minimum degree of replication is 3).

Note that when the repair server takes 15 days to repair a failed node, the MTTF of the system is shorter than that of a node (25 days $vs.$ 30 days) and the availability of the system is smaller than that of a node (0.625 $vs.$ 0.667). In other words, when the repair time is 15 days, using the voting approach for fault tolerance does not improve the MTTF and availability of the system.

7.6 Summary

In this chapter, we have discussed the problem of making data resilient to failures in the system. That is, masking node and communication failures in the distributed system to users in order to perform operations on data. Resiliency is supported by replicating the data on multiple nodes. Since the goal is to mask failure, and replication is a technique to support this, replication should be "hidden" to the users of the data. That is, even with replication, it should appear that there is a single copy of the data in the system, and one-copy serializability is maintained. There are two basic approaches for managing replication. First is the *optimistic approach*, where no restriction is placed on access to data. Consequently, if partition occurs, the copies of the data object in different groups may become divergent. The second approach is called the *pessimistic approach*, in which access to replicated data is controlled such that inconsistency never results, and single-copy serializability is preserved.

The goal of an optimistic approach is to resolve any inconsistencies that may arise due to unrestricted processing during partitioning. This attempt to resolve the inconsistencies is made after the groups rejoin, and is not always successful.

We have discussed one particular method based on *version vectors* for resolving this inconsistency. With each copy of a file, a version vector is associated, which represents the number of updates, originating at different nodes, which are performed on the copy. If a version vector of a group dominates the version vector of another, it means that one group has seen a subset of updates of another group and the inconsistency is resolved easily. If no version vector dominates, it represents a conflict situation. Conflict resolution is left to the user.

We have discussed three pessimistic approaches for replica control: the primary site approach, the state machine approach, and voting. In the *primary site approach*, one of the sites having the data is designated as primary, while the others are designated as backups. All requests for the operations on the data are sent to the primary site. The primary periodically checkpoints the state of the data on the backups. If the primary fails, one of the backups becomes the primary and starts performing the operations. The single-copy serializability is preserved, since all the requests for operations on the data are performed at a given time by only one node. If communication failures cause the network to get partitioned, then the partition that has the primary site is able to perform the operations on the data, while the others cannot access the data. This requires that the nodes which are alive must be able to distinguish between node failures and network partitions.

The second approach we discussed utilized *active replicas*. This is also called the *state machine approach*. In this approach, all replicas of the data are kept simultaneously active. A request for an operation is sent to all the replicas, and any replica can service the request. To ensure that the replicas are mutually consistent and that one-copy serializability is maintained, all the requests for operations must be sent to all the replicas, and the different requests must be processed by the different nodes in the same order. This ensures mutual consistency. One way to support the properties of mutual consistency and one-copy serializability is to use *atomic broadcast*. A request for an operation is atomically broadcast to all nodes having the copy of the data. Atomic broadcast ensures that the different requests are processed by different nodes in the same order. This approach works only for node failures.

The third approach we discussed was *voting*. In voting, for performing a read or an update operation on the data, the requesting node has to first get a "quorum" of votes from the nodes. The group of nodes that give the requester the quorum is such that a group performing the read operation always has a node with the latest update, and the read-write and write-write mutual exclusion property is supported. That is, when a group is performing a read or an update operation, no other group can perform an update operation. This property provides the single-copy view of the replicated data. Since voting treats all failures uniformly, it can handle both site failures and network partitioning and preserve data consistency. Voting algorithms can be static or dynamic. In static voting, all parameters for voting are fixed, while in dynamic approaches, some parameters may be changed as failures and recoveries take place in the system.

We have discussed some static voting algorithms. The first one is weighted voting. In this, each copy of the object is assigned certain votes. A node wishing to perform a read or a write operation must collect a read quorum of r votes or a write quorum of w votes, respectively. The quorums are such that w is greater than half of the total number of votes and $r + w$ is greater than the total number of votes. These restrictions ensure that any two write quorums intersect and any read and write quorums intersect. One of the nice features of this approach is that it treats node failures and communication failures uniformly; the weighted voting strategy works even if the network partitions. A generalization of this approach that can reduce communication overhead is *hierarchical voting*. In this, nodes are logically organized in a hierarchy and quorums are collected at each level for an operation.

We discussed two different dynamic methods for voting. In *dynamic voting*, an operation is allowed if it has a quorum of a majority of the previous majority partition. In other words, if a partition occurs, the majority partition is taken to be the "system." If a further partition occurs, a majority of the nodes of this system are needed for an operation. On rejoining of groups, a node may update itself if it can communicate with some member of the last majority group. The second approach that we discussed is *dynamic reassignment of votes*. In this approach, if nodes fail, the votes to the nodes are reassigned such that the effect of failed nodes is compensated. One method of reassignment is to assign twice the votes of nodes that are not in the majority partition to nodes in the majority partition. This way, the effect of nodes that are in the minority partition is compensated.

The performance and reliability of voting systems depend considerably on the votes assigned to a node. We have discussed the problem of vote assignment, and have discussed three approaches to it. The first one is based on *coteries*, in which all possible groups that can be formed by vote assignment are assigned. This approach is only useful for small systems. The second approach is the use of heuristics, and we discussed a few different heuristics for vote assignment. The third approach we discussed considers the most likely partitions and then formulates the vote assignment problem as an integer programming problem.

These three replica-control approaches mask replication and failures by different techniques. The primary site approach masks replication by routing all requests to one site. The active-replicas approach manages replicas by ensuring that all sites get the requests in the same order, and hence all replicas are always equivalent, and capable of servicing any request on the data. The voting approach masks replication by ensuring mutual exclusion between groups performing the operations. The first two approaches work well when only sites can fail, but no partitioning occurs. The primary site approach can also be used under network partitioning, if partitioning can be distinguished from site failures. Voting is a general approach which supports mutual exclusion of operations without communication between nodes of different groups. Hence, it treats both node failures and network partitioning uniformly, and can handle both.

Finally, we discussed the issue of degree of replication. Clearly, in no system can we continue to benefit by increasing replication. Though the reliability may increase, so will the cost of managing the replicas. Hence, it is likely that there may be some optimum degree of replication. We have discussed analytic models for determining the optimal degree of replication for the primary site approach and weighted voting.

We have assumed throughout the chapter that some nodes are always alive. That is, we focused on masking the failure of nodes and communication failures entirely by the use of replication. Hence, the issue of recovery was not discussed. However, there can always be situations where all the nodes in the network may fail. Such a situation is called *total failure*. In such situations, some recovery activities will be needed after the nodes recover from failure. However, before any recovery can be performed, the most recent replica has to be obtained. The node that failed last will have the most recent replica, and hence, this requires that we determine the last node to fail. We will discuss this problem of determining the last process to fail in the next chapter. Most of the recovery activities from a total failure will clearly be performed by the last node to fail, after it recovers. We will not discuss the methods for recovering from total failure.

Problems

1. What additional problems does data replication introduce?

2. Suppose there are four nodes — A, B, C, and D — in a system, each with a replica of a file f. Suppose node B fails at time T_1, separating A from {C, D}. At time T_2, B comes back up and reconnects the network. If version vectors are being used, under what conditions will there be no conflicts, and under what conditions there will be conflicts?

3. One method for supporting the primary site approach is to have only the primary site perform the operations, but periodically checkpoint information on stable storage, which is accessible to backups. Suppose the primary site uses two-phase locking for concurrency control. What information should be checkpointed on the stable storage and when?

4. In the state machine approach, devise another method to check for the stability of a request using synchronized clocks.

5. How can the state machine approach be used to handle Byzantine failures?

6. The two extremes of voting are where $r = 1$ and where $r = N/2$. What are the differences in performance for these two?

7. Consider a system with 21 nodes. Organize them in a 2-level hierarchy and completely specify the hierarchical voting parameters for it.

8. For the above, compare the performance of weighted voting with hierarchical voting. Under what conditions will weighted voting perform better?

9. In practice, network partitions are rare for many small networks. If a node is expected to partition once into multiple parts and then rejoin soon without further partitioning taking place, under what situations, if any, will dynamic voting be preferable?

10. Compare the two dynamic vote reassignment strategies discussed. Develop another "catch up" strategy for a node when it rejoins.

11. Given the network shown in Fig. 7.7, each link has a reliability of 1.0. What

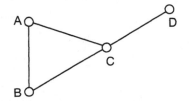

Figure 7.7: Network

would the vote assignment be in this if different heuristics were used? In what way will the vote assignment change if the reliability of C is made 0.9?

12. What are the coteries corresponding to the vote assignment in the above example?

13. Construct an ND coterie to which there is no corresponding vote assignment.

14. Why does the availability not increase continuously with the degree of replication in voting and primary site systems?

15. Consider response time as the performance measure of interest. In a primary site system, what will be the critical factors that will decide if a primary site approach improves response time?

16. Define the capacity of a voting system as the number of operations the system can perform, on an average, per unit of time. Use the capacity as a measure to compare majority voting with a single-node system. Make suitable assumptions.

References

[AA89] D. Agrawal, and A. E. Abbadi. "An Efficient and Fault Tolerant Solution to the Mutual Exclusion Problem." *ACM Transactions on Computer Systems*, 9(1):1–20, February 1989.

[AD76] P. A. Alsberg, and J. D. Day. "A Principle for Resilient Sharing of Distributed Databases." *2nd International Conference on Software Engineering*, pp. 562–570, 1976.

[AJ92] G. Agarwal, and P. Jalote. "An Efficient Protocol for Voting in Distributed Systems." *12th International Conference on Distributed Computing Systems*, pp. 640–647, Yokohoma, Japan, May 1992.

[BG84] P. A. Bernstein, and N. Goodman. "An Algorithm for Concurrency Control and Recovery in Replicated Distributed Databases." *ACM Transactions on Database Systems*, 9(4):596–614, December 1984.

[BG87] D. Barbara, and H. Garcia-Molina. "The Reliability of Voting Mechanisms." *IEEE Transactions on Computers*, C-36(10):1197–1207, October 1987.

[BGS86] D. Barbara, H. Garcia-Molina, and A. Spauster. "Policies for Dynamic Vote Reassignment." *6th International Conference on Distributed Computing*, pp. 195–206, May 1986.

[BJRA85] K. P. Birman, T. A. Joseph, T. Raeuchle, and A. E. Abbadi. "Implementing Fault-Tolerant Distributed Objects." *IEEE Transactions on Software Engineering*, 11(6):502–508, June 1985.

[CAA90a] S. Y. Cheung, M. Ahamad, and M. H. Ammar. "The Grid Protocol: A High Performance Scheme For Maintaining Replicated Data." *6th International Conference on Data Engineering*, pp. 438–445, January 1990.

[CAA90b] S. Y. Cheung, M. Ahamad, and M. H. Ammar. "Multi-dimensional Voting: A General Method for Implementing Synchronization in Distributed Systems." *10th International Conference on Distributed Computing Systems*, pp. 362–369, 1990.

[Dav84] S. B. Davidson. "Optimism and Consistency in Partitioned Distributed Database Systems." *ACM Transactions on Database Systems*, 9(3):456–481, September 1984.

[Dav89] D. Davcev. "A Dynamic Voting Scheme in Distributed Systems." *IEEE Transactions on Software Engineering*, 15(1):93–97, January 1989.

[DGS85] S. B. Davidson, H. Garcia-Molina, and D. Skeen. "Consistency in Partitioned Networks." *ACM Computing Surveys*, 17(3):341–370, September 1985.

[ES83] D. L. Eager, and K. C. Sevcik. "Achieving Robustness in Distributed Database Systems." *ACM Transactions on Database Systems*, 8(3):354–381, September 1983.

[Gar82] H. Garcia-Molina. "Elections in a Distributed Computing System." *IEEE Transactions on Computers*, C-31(1):48–59, January 1982.

[GB85] H. Garcia-Molina, and D. Barbara. "How to Assign Votes in a Distributed System." *Journal of the ACM*, 32(4):841–860, October 1985.

[Gif79] D. K. Gifford. "Weighted Voting for Replicated Data." *7th ACM Symposium on Operating Systems*, pp. 150–162, December 1979.

[HJ89a] Y. Huang, and P. Jalote. "Analytic Models for the Primary Site Approach for Fault Tolerance." *Acta Informatica*, 26:543–557, 1989.

[HJ89b] Y. Huang, and P. Jalote. "Availability Analysis of the Primary Site Approach for Fault Tolerance." *8th Symposium on Reliable Distributed Systems*, pp. 130–136, IEEE Computer Society, 1989.

[HJ93] Y. Huang, and P. Jalote. *Degree of Replication in Voting Systems.* Technical Report TR 93-161, Murray Hill, NJ: AT&T Bell Labs, 1993.

[JA92] P. Jalote, and G. Agarwal. "Using Coding to Support Data Resiliency in Distributed Systems." *8th International Conference on Data Engineering*, pp. 192–199, Tempe, Arizona, February 1992.

[Jal89] P. Jalote. "Resilient Objects in Broadcast Networks." *IEEE Transactions on Software Engineering*, 15(1):68–72, January 1989.

[JM87] S. Jajodia, and D. Mutchler. "Dynamic Voting." *ACM SIGMOD International Conference on Management of Data*, pp. 227–238, San Francisco, 1987.

[Kum91a] A. Kumar. "Hierarchical Quorum Consensus: A New Algorithm For Managing Replicated Data." *IEEE Transactions on Computers*, 40(9):996–1004, September 1991.

[Kum91b] A. Kumar. "A Randomized Voting Algorithm." *11th International Conference on Distributed Computing Systems*, pp. 412–419, 1991.

[LG90] T. V. Lakshman, and D. Ghoshal. *A new $\sqrt{N}$ Multiple Copy Update Algorithm and its Performance Evaluation.* Technical Report CS-TR-2502, College Park, Maryland: Department of Computer Science, University of Maryland, July 1990.

[Par86] J.F. Paris. "Voting with a Variable Number of Copies." *6th International Conference on Distributed Computing Systems*, pp. 50–55, 1986.

[PNP88] C. A. Pu, D. D. Noe, and A. Proudfoot. "Regeneration of Replicated Objects: A Technique and its Eden Implementation." *IEEE Transactions on Software Engineering*, 14(7):936–945, July 1988.

[RT88] R. V. Renesse, and A. S. Tanenbaum. "Voting with Ghosts." *8th International Conference on Distributed Computing Systems*, pp. 456–461, 1988.

[S$^+$83] D. Stott Parker, Jr. et al. "Detection of Mutual Inconsistency in Distributed Systems." *IEEE Transactions on Software Engineering*, 9(3):240–247, May 1983.

[Sch90] F. B. Schneider. "Implementing Fault-Tolerant Services Using the State Machine Approach: A Tutorial." *ACM Computing Surveys*, 22(4):299–319, December 1990.

[Tho79] R. H. Thomas. "A Majority Consensus Approach to Concurrency Control for Multiple Copy Databases." *ACM Transactions on Database Systems*, 4(2):180–209, June 1979.

[Ven92] D. Venkaiah. "An Integer Programming Approach for Assigning Votes in a Distributed System." Master's Thesis, Indian Institute of Technology Kanpur, Department of Computer Science and Engineering, Kanpur, India, March 1992.

Chapter 8

Process Resiliency

In the previous chapter, we considered the issue of making data objects resilient to node and communication network failures. In a distributed application, where multiple processes are cooperating to perform a task, if a node fails, the processes executing on that node stop. This may cause the entire distributed computation to fail even if all data is accessible, as other processes may depend on the failed process for information to complete their processing. In this chapter, we consider the problem of making processes resilient to failures.

The goal of process resiliency is to ensure that a distributed computation proceeds despite the failure of some of its constituent processes. Process resiliency is clearly important in critical applications where the processing cannot be stopped. Without process resiliency, even if data is available, the system may have to be reinitialized and restarted, which may not be acceptable in critical applications. We focus on process failures caused by node failures, and assume that nodes are fail stop. Unless stated otherwise, we assume that processes are deterministic in the sense that from the same state, if given the same inputs, the process executes the same sequence of instructions.

One checkpointing-based scheme for supporting process resiliency could be to establish consistent checkpoints of the distributed system on stable storage, using one of the algorithms discussed earlier in Chapter 5. In this, if some nodes fail, the *entire* system rolls back to some previous globally consistent checkpointed state. This approach requires global checkpoints, which are quite expensive, and consequently of limited practical use for supporting process resiliency. In this chapter, we will consider schemes that support process resiliency without requiring a globally consistent checkpoint to be available and without requiring all processes to roll back.

If the system consists of processes that do not communicate with each other, the problem is conceptually simple. Each process checkpoints its state periodically, and if the process fails, it is restarted on some backup node from its last checkpoint. Only the failed process needs to roll back. Though conceptually straightforward, there are a number of design issues that come up if such a scheme is to be actually implemented. Some of these are discussed in [JS91], which also describes an implementation for process resiliency for stand-alone processes in a network of workstations.

This simple approach for supporting process resiliency is clearly insufficient in systems where processes communicate. More needs to be done besides rolling back the failed process. In this chapter, we will discuss many schemes to support resilient processes in a system of communicating processes. The requirements for recovery and the schemes to implement them differ, depending on the method of interprocess communication. First, we discuss the schemes that support resiliency where remote procedure calls are used for communication. Then we describe the schemes for asynchronous communication, followed by a scheme for supporting process resiliency in CSP, which employs synchronous communication, and supports non-determinism within a process. Finally, we discuss the situation of total failure where all processes fail.

8.1   Resilient Remote Procedure Call

In this section, we discuss techniques to make a remote procedure call resilient to node failures. As described earlier in Chapter 2, a remote procedure call (RPC) is an extension of the procedure-call concept into distributed systems. A process executing on a node may invoke a procedure that executes on a different node. That is, a procedure is allowed to make a call to a procedure whose code is on a different node (and is hence not available for linking). When a procedure A calls a procedure B, A is called a *direct caller* of B. Typically, the process executing A is suspended until the call to B returns.

Since two processes, or more in case of nested remote procedure calls, are involved in the computation, it brings in the possibility of part of the computation failing due to the failure of one of the nodes (unlike in single process systems where the failure will cause the entire computation to fail). Specifically, it is possible that the node executing the remote procedure may fail, which will keep the caller program suspended forever (unless something is done about it). Similarly, the caller program may fail, leading to the situation where the remote procedure has no caller left to which it should return the results. The goal of the schemes presented here is to make computation based on remote procedures resilient to node failures.

In the schemes described here, a procedure is assumed to be *deterministic*. That is, from a given initial state, it will always perform the same sequence of instructions if the same inputs are given.

Note that remote procedure calls also bring in the possibility of concurrent calls to a procedure, a situation that does not exist in ordinary procedure calls. For example, two procedures *A* and *B* executing independently may make calls to a remote procedure *C* concurrently. In other words, there can be multiple concurrent calls to a remote procedure. This requires some concurrency control mechanisms, like locking, to be employed. We will not discuss in detail the problems involved with concurrent calls.

8.1.1   Using the Primary Site Approach

Here we describe an approach to make processes using RPC as the means for communication resilient to node failures by employing the primary site approach. The method described here is a part of a more general fault tolerant system, which masks failure of any single component, including bus failures, power failure, transient failure, I/O channel failure, memory failures, etc. [Bar81]. We will discuss here only the aspects dealing with making processes resilient. It is assumed that processes use messages to communicate, but the messages are structured in a manner similar to an RPC, and the sender of a message requesting some operation waits for the reply message.

The approach uses *process pairs* for supporting resiliency. One of the processes is the *primary* and the other is the *backup*. When a service is requested, the message is first sent to the primary process. If the process does not exist, or is no longer the primary process, the message fails, and the request is sent to the second process. Requests for operations are sent to the current primary process, which handles the request. When the primary receives a request for an operation, it checkpoints the request on the backup process by sending it a message (if the backup exists). This message ensures that the backup has all the information and if the primary process fails, the backup can satisfy the service request. If the primary fails to satisfy the service, the backup becomes the primary and performs the request.

This method may result in the operations requested by the service being performed twice — once by the primary and once by the backup. Though acceptable in some situations, there are other situations where this is not acceptable. To avoid this, the requests performed by a process are assigned sequence numbers, and if the server performs a non-retryable operation, it records the results of the operation. This is done by the primary process checkpointing the complete status of such operations on the backup. If the primary fails during the operation and the backup becomes the primary, then the new primary uses the checkpointed information to obtain the results.

8.1.2 Replicated Call

Another way to make a remote procedure call resilient to node failures is to replicate the remote procedure on many nodes, and when the remote procedure is called, all the replicas are simultaneously executed. As long as one of the replicated calls stays alive, the caller will get the results of the remote call. Here we describe such an approach called a *circus* [Coo84, Coo85].

In a circus, a module is replicated on many nodes. The set of replicas of a module is called a *troupe*. Whenever a call is made to a module, all members of the troupe execute the call. In a circus, the replication of modules is performed in a user-transparent manner by using a stub compiler. From the user's point of view, replication is hidden, and the only difference the user sees is a higher reliability of remote operations.

The troupe of the module that makes a call to a remote procedure is called the *client troupe*, and the troupe of the module to which a call is made is called the *server troupe*. Since all members of a troupe execute concurrently, any procedure call made by a module is replicated. When a module makes a call to a remote module, each member of the client troupe makes a *one-to-many call* to the server troupe. The same call is sent by a module in the caller troupe to each module in the server troupe. Hence, each member in the server troupe gets multiple copies of the call request — one from each of the members in the caller troupe — resulting in a *many-to-one call* from the client troupe. Overall, there is a *many-to-many* call from the caller troupe to the server troupe, as shown in Fig. 8.1 [Coo85].

In a many-to-many connection, the desired semantics are that each member of the server troupe performs the request procedure exactly once, and each member of the client troupe receives all the results. These semantics are called *exactly-once execution of all troupe members*. In one-to-many calls, the client sends the same CALL message, with the same sequence numbers, to each member of the server troupe. This happens because the modules are deterministic, and hence if given the same inputs, perform the same sequence of instructions. This ensures that each member of the troupe will execute the call instruction, and also that it will bear the same sequence number (if all replicas have the same sequence number initially).

In the implementation of a circus, a client troupe member which has made the one-to-many connection normally waits for all the calls to *return* before proceeding. Of course, if the member is informed about the failure of a node of a member of the server troupe, it does not wait for a return message from that troupe member. Of

Client Troupe   Server Troupe

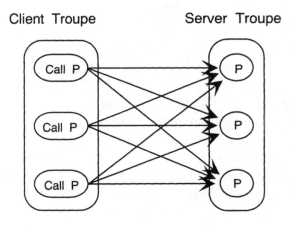

Figure 8.1: Replicated procedure call

all the "copies" of the return message received, all but one are discarded. Note that there is no voting on the result, as fail stop processors are assumed. However, the approach can be generalized to handle different types of failures, which may require voting on the result.

In a many-to-one call, each server replica receives a CALL message from each client troupe member. However, these are all replicas of the same call, and the module is supposed to perform the requested operation only once. If it performs the operation more than once, it may take the system to an invalid state. Hence, when a CALL message comes, a server troupe member has to identify if the different calls are actually copies of the same call, or are distinct. Sequence numbers for CALL messages, along with unique ID for each troupe, can be used for this purpose. In the implementation of a circus, a server troupe normally waits until all the CALL messages have been received, or until it has received the intimation that the node of a client troupe member has failed, before executing the call.

In the approach described above, a client troupe waits for all the return messages. This gives the client members an *error detection* and *error correction* capability, since each can vote on the results. However, this implies that the replicated call will be as slow as the slowest member of the server troupe. If error detection and correction capabilities are not desired, then a *first-come* approach can be followed, in which a client member can proceed as soon as the first return message arrives. This requires the use of unique sequence numbers for calls so that messages for a particular call can be distinguished from the return messages from a previous call (which may be delayed due to a slow server).

In a many-to-one call, more needs to be done to support the first-come approach. If the server proceeds with the call on the first CALL message, when the call from another client member comes, it cannot execute the procedure again, as it will violate the semantics of the RPC. Hence, it has to *retain results* of the call, and whenever a CALL message arrives from another member, the retained result is sent in the return message. Sequence numbers have to be used to distinguish between different calls.

It is clear that this method of replication will mask node failures, so long as all the members of a troupe do not fail. This method is also quite expensive in terms of the number of messages. If a client troupe contains m members and the server troupe contains n members, then the total number of messages required is $O(m * n)$. However, if multicasting is supported by the network, in which by one transmission the message can be sent to multiple destinations, then $O(m + n)$ messages will be needed.

As mentioned above, concurrent requests to an RPC are possible. This requires synchronization so that the calls are *serializable*. However, a stricter synchronization is required with a replicated RPC; not only should the concurrent calls be serializable, but the calls on the different modules in a server troupe should serialize in the *same order*. A commit protocol has been proposed in [Coo85] to ensure this. The protocol is *optimistic* in that it considers conflicts unlikely and does not impose any restrictions. If it detects that different troupe members are serializing in a different manner, it converts such a situation into a deadlock situation, which leads to an abort and retry of one or more of the calls.

In the proposed commit protocol, a server troupe member calls the function *ready-to-end* when it is ready to commit or abort. A *call-back protocol* is followed in which this call is translated into a call to the client troupe, thereby reversing the client-server roles. The client troupe waits for each of the members in the server troupe to make the *ready-to-end* call before responding to any of the calls. It returns true if it gets a call from each server troupe. If the function returns true, the server troupe member commits, otherwise it aborts.

Let us see by means of an example how this protocol works. Suppose S_1 and S_2 are two members of the server troupe S, and C and C' are two client troupes. Suppose C performs an operation O at S, and C' performs an operation O' concurrently at S. If both server troupe members commit O and O' in the same order, say O followed by O', then both S_1 and S_2 will first make the ready-to-end call to C and then to C'. Both the clients will get the calls from both S_1 and S_2 and hence will reply true to their requests.

Now suppose that S_1 tries to commit O first, but S_2 tries to commit O' first. Then S_1 will make a ready-to-end call to C, and S_2 will make the call to C'. Both will wait for replies from client troupes to make the call to the other client troupe while the client troupes are waiting for the second troupe member to make the ready-to-end request. Hence, there is a deadlock. The deadlock can then be broken by aborting some operation. Hence, the commit protocol ensures that all concurrent requests are serialized in the same order at all server troupe members, or a deadlock is caused.

8.1.3 A Combined Approach

Now we describe a scheme that employs a combination of the replicated-call and the primary-standby approach, in an effort to exploit the advantages of both the approaches [YJT88]. In the proposed scheme, fault tolerance is provided by having copies of a procedure reside on multiple nodes (copies of a procedure together are called a *cluster*). Each copy is known as an incarnation. The incarnations are organized in a linear chain. For the ith incarnation, the $(i + 1)$st incarnation forms its backup. A service request is made to the primary incarnation, which is the first copy in the chain that has not failed. The primary callee then propagates the call to its backup, which in turn sends the call to its own backup. In this manner, all the incarnations are invoked. The result of the call is returned to the client by the primary callee. If the primary callee fails, its backup incarnation assumes the role of the primary and replies to the client.

In a nested RPC call, a service invokes a call to another remote procedure. The service acts as a client when making the nested call. Only the primary incarnation will actually make the call; other caller incarnations just wait for the result. The result received by the primary caller is propagated to all other caller incarnations in the cluster. If the primary caller fails to acknowledge the result, another copy of the result will be sent to its backup incarnation.

There are 4 types of messages in the proposed scheme. A *call* message invokes an RPC call. A *result* message contains the return values of an RPC call. A *done* message is sent to inform a secondary callee that the call is completed. These 3 types of messages require their recipients to acknowledge (with an *ack* message). If no acknowledgement is received within a defined time period, the sender will check the status of its receiver. If it has failed, the same message will be sent to the receiver's immediate subordinate. This simple discipline helps to ensure that every active incarnation in the cluster will receive the same message in the event of failures.

Execution without Failures

In this scheme, the secondary incarnations play an active role. All the incarnations in the callee cluster execute a call, and every incarnation in a caller cluster receives a copy of the result. However, if the primary callee does not fail during a call, the caller makes a single call and only one copy of the result is sent to the caller cluster. All communications between the clusters are carried out by their respective primary incarnations. A secondary incarnation will only interact with external processes if all its superior incarnations have failed and it has assumed the role of the primary.

Fig. 8.2 shows the sequence of messages that are transmitted in an RPC call from a 2-caller cluster to a 3-callee cluster [YJT88]. On receiving a call, the primary

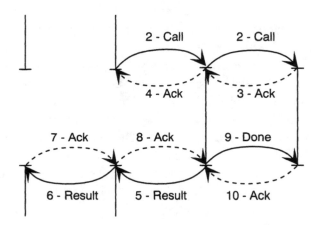

Figure 8.2: Messages sent during an RPC call

callee sends the same call to its immediate subordinate. The incarnation, in turn, sends the call to its immediate subordinate. On receiving an acknowledgment to the call it has sent, a callee incarnation performs the requested service. A secondary callee, on completing a call, waits for a go-ahead message from its immediate superior. The primary callee will send its result to the primary caller and wait for an acknowledgment. On receiving the acknowledgment, the primary sends a done message to inform its immediate subordinate that the call is completed. This message is propagated to all other secondary callees.

In the caller cluster, the primary, after sending an RPC call, waits for the result. The secondary callers will also wait for the result. However, they are not required to send any call messages. Each secondary caller receives the result from the incarnation before it.

Execution with Failures

After sending an RPC call to the primary callee, the caller waits for an acknowledgment. If, before the acknowledgment is received, the caller detects that the primary callee has failed, the same message is sent to the primary callee's backup. If the backup callee has already received a similar call from the old primary, it acknowledges the message but takes no other actions. If the primary crashes after sending the acknowledgment, the caller takes no action. The immediate subordinate of the crashed primary will take over its role and send the result to the caller.

If the primary callee fails after it has sent its result but before it has sent the done message to its secondary, the caller may receive more than one copy of the same result. The new primary is not aware that the failed primary has already sent the result and will send another copy. The primary caller acknowledges the duplicate result but takes no other actions.

If a secondary callee incarnation fails before it acknowledges a call message, on detecting the failure, its immediate superior will send the same call to the failed incarnation's immediate subordinate. Between sending the call message and the done message, an incarnation need not be aware of its immediate subordinate's status. If a callee incarnation fails to acknowledge the done message, the message will be sent to its immediate subordinate.

If a primary caller fails before it has received and propagated the result of a call, its immediate subordinate will assume its role and send the same call message. The callee cluster may receive duplicates of the same message. The duplicate requests are discarded, though the result of the call is now sent to the new caller. A caller incarnation is not aware of the status of its subordinates before propagating the result of a call. If a caller incarnation fails to acknowledge the receipt of the RPC result, the same message is sent to its immediate subordinate.

8.2 Resiliency with Asynchronous Message Passing

In this section, we consider the problem of making a system of processes communicating by asynchronous message passing resilient to process failures. One method for recovery is to roll back the entire system to an earlier consistent state. We have discussed in an earlier chapter how to checkpoint a consistent state of a distributed system. This approach requires that many processes other than the failed process, perhaps all the remaining processes, to also roll back.

Another method, which requires only the failed process to roll back, is to use message logging to recover lost messages. In this approach, when a process fails, it is restarted on a different node from a previously saved checkpoint. Just after the rollback of the failed process, the system state is not likely to be consistent, as there may be missed messages (messages which processes have sent, but the state of the failed process does not reflect as having received them) or orphan messages (those messages that have been received by others but the state of the failed process does not reflect as having sent them). To ensure that the system reaches a consistent state, these messages have to be recovered and retransmitted. For this, *message logging* is used, in which some messages are logged on stable storage during normal computation and are available during recovery. During recovery, the messages that are lost due to failure and rollback are recovered "properly" using the message logs.

In this section, we first present a model for message-logging-based schemes and develop conditions for proper message recovery in asynchronous systems. Then we discuss some of the approaches that have been proposed for supporting process resiliency using message logging.

8.2.1   Conditions for Message Recovery

We first discuss the conditions for message recovery, as described in [Jal89]. Consider a distributed system with a fixed set of processes that may execute on different nodes. Each process is assumed to be deterministic, so that given the same inputs, the process will execute the same sequence of instructions. Processes communicate exclusively through asynchronous message passing. A process sends a message to another process P_i by executing *send* (P_i , msg), and receives a message by executing *receive(msg)*.

We assume that a reliable logical channel exists between every pair of processes. When a process P_j executes *send* (P_i , msg), it sends msg using the appropriate channel. On arrival, a message for P_i is appended to the queue $msgQ_i$. We assume that infinite memory is available for $msgQ_i$. When P_i executes a receive, it receives the first message in $msgQ_i$. If there is no message in $msgQ_i$, then the execution of receive is delayed until a message arrives. The behavior of a process can be sensitive to the order in which it receives the messages.

As defined in Chapter 2 and Chapter 3, we assume that messages sent by a process to another arrive in the order they were sent, but messages sent by different processes to a process may arrive in any order. This means that a receive command of a process may return different messages in different executions of the system, depending on the order of arrival of the messages. As defined earlier in Chapter 2, the execution of the distributed system is considered a sequence of system states, with state transitions occurring due to some event performed by a process. A system state S is *valid* (or *consistent*) if S occurs in some failure-free execution (i.e., an execution of the system in which no process fails).

In a message passing system, messages sent from different processes can arrive at a process in different sequences. Let M be a sequence of messages. Each message in M is of the form (m, j), where m is the message content, and j is the identity of the sender process. A sequence of messages M' is defined as a *partial order preserving permutation* of the sequence M (represented as $M' \in popp(M)$), if M' contains the same messages as M, and for all j and for all $(m_1, \ j)$, $(m_2, \ j) \in M$, $(m_1, \ j)$ precedes $(m_2, \ j)$ in M' if, and only if, (m_1, j) precedes (m_2, j) in M.

Replacing $msg\,Q_i = M$ with $msg\,Q_i = M'$, where $M' \in popp(M)$, in a valid state produces a valid state. That is, if a failure-free execution can produce a state in which M is the sequence of messages waiting in the queue to be received by P_i, then there is another failure-free execution of the system where these messages get added to the queue in some order which is in $popp(M)$.

If a process fails, the system state is not valid. The goal of recovery for process resiliency is to take the system to a valid state after a failure occurs. When a process P_i fails, $msg\,Q_i$ is lost. Only checkpointed information survives the failure. As a result of a process failure, in addition to losing messages in the message queue and channels, messages the process received since its last checkpoint are also effectively lost. These lost messages must be recovered. In a recovery from the failure of a process P_i, the messages of interest are messages P_i has received since its last checkpoint, the messages in $msg\,Q_i$ at the time of the failure, and the messages in the channels at the time of failure for P_i.

Let P_i be the only process that fails. Suppose it fails at time F, and restarts (on another node) from a previously saved checkpoint taken at time C. On restart, $msg\,Q_i$ is initially empty. Let MA_i be the concatenation of the following: (1) sequence of messages that P_i has received between times C and F, (2) the value of $msg\,Q_i$ at time F, and (3) the value of $chmsg_i$ at time F. Assume that when P_i is restarted, a sequence of messages MA'_i is added to $msg\,Q_i$. Then the system is in a valid state, if P_i sent no messages between C and F, and $MA'_i \in popp(MA_i)$ [Jal89].

Since P_i has sent no messages between times C and F, no other process has any knowledge of the state of P_i. Hence, the situation after rollback is equivalent to P_i not having executed the receives between C and F, but having all the messages in $msg\,Q_i$ in the order $MA'_i \in popp(MA_i)$, which is also a valid state. Therefore, the system state obtained in the manner described above is a valid state.

Let us now consider the case where P_i sends messages between times C and F. This situation is different from the case where it sends no messages between C and F, as some other processes have "seen" the internal states of P_i between C and F. Since the other processes that have seen the state of P_i are not rolling back, on restart, P_i must execute the same sequence of instructions as it did before failure and produce the same messages with the same sequence numbers. Since the messages generated during the reexecution of the instructions between C and F are duplicates of the previous ones, these messages may either not be transmitted (if the sender somehow knows that the receiver has an earlier copy) or if they are transmitted, they must be discarded by the receiver. This can be done, since on reexecution, P_1 is following the same sequence of instructions and will assign the same sequence numbers, as in the execution before failure, to the retransmitted messages. We assume that all messages are transmitted, and duplicates, if any, are discarded by the receiver.

Let MB_i be the messages received by P_i after time C but before executing its last send command prior to failure at time F. Assume that $msgQ_i$ and the channels are empty at the time of failure. Further assume that the last communication command P_i executes between C and F is a send. If on restart of P_i, some sequence of messages MB_i' is added to $msgQ_i$, then the system reaches a valid state if $MB_i' = MB_i$ [Jal89].

The reason for this is as follows. The state after rollback of P_i may not be valid, since some other processes have received a message sent by P_i, but P_i is at C where it has not executed the corresponding send command. If $MB_i' = MB_i$, then after restart, P_i will execute the same sequence of instructions and send commands between C and F as before and will produce the same messages. As these messages are discarded, after P_i reaches F, the system is in a state where all the send commands of P_i for which corresponding messages exist in the message queues of other processes have been executed and there are no extraneous messages in the system. This is a valid state. If $MB_i' \neq MB_i$, then on restart, P_i may execute a different sequence of instructions and the messages sent after restart can, in general, be different from the messages sent originally by P_i. If this happens, the resulting system state may not be valid.

Now we can see that the requirements for message recovery are different, depending on whether or not the failed process sent a message between C and F. That is, the requirements for message recovery before and after the last message sent between C and F are different. The last message sent by P_i between C and F forms a dividing line. Let the sequence of messages received by P_i between C and F be $M_i = MB_i ; MA_i$ (the ";" is the concatenation operator), where MB_i (for *before* messages) is the sequence of messages received by P_i before the last message sent by it between C and F, and MA_i (for *after* messages) is the concatenation of the sequence of messages received by P_i after that, $msgQ_i$ at time F, and messages in the channels at time F. Either MB_i or MA_i or both may be null. Together, MB_i and MA_i include all messages that must be recovered. Let M_i' be a sequence of messages added to $msgQ_i$ on restart. Then the *message recovery condition* is that the system will reach a valid state if $M_i' = MB_i' ; MA_i'$ such that $(i).MB_i' = MB_i$, $(ii).MA_i' \in popp(MA_i)$. If multiple processes fail, then these conditions must be satisfied for each failed process.

As an example, consider execution of a system consisting of three processes P_1, P_2, P_3, as shown in Fig. 8.3 (assume that the message queues are empty and there are no messages in the channels). P_2 is the process that establishes a checkpoint at C, fails at F, and restarts from C. In this example, message m_4, sent by P_2 forms the

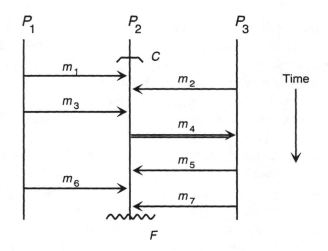

Figure 8.3: An example

dividing line. By the message recovery condition, m_1, m_2, and m_3 must be received by P_2 on restart in the same order as received by P_2 in the original execution, i.e., in the order m_1; m_2; m_3. Otherwise, the message contents of the send command, if and when executed by P_2 on restart, may be different from m_4, and the system may not reach a valid state. However, messages m_5, m_6 and m_7 can be received in any order that is an element of $popp(m_5;m_6;m_7)$. Hence, besides the order $m_5;m_6;m_7$, the orders $m_5;m_7;m_6$ and $m_6;m_5;m_7$ are also acceptable for reaching a valid state.

Clearly, the message recovery condition is satisfied if $M_i' = M_i$. This, however, is stricter than necessary and can be difficult to satisfy. For example, the ordering of old messages already sent can be established by checkpoints, but recovering the last message sent by checkpointing can be particularly difficult, due to the possibility of failure between establishing a checkpoint and sending a message. If retransmission is used, then a fixed ordering cannot be achieved by simple retransmissions, and some other method is needed for message ordering, like a centralized controller or atomic broadcast, as used by some of the schemes. The partial order of the second part of the message recovery condition allows some flexibility during message recovery.

8.2.2   An Approach Based on Atomic Broadcast

Here we describe an approach [BBG83, B$^+$89] for message logging and recovery that was implemented in the Aurogen/Targon system. It requires that *all* the messages be recovered in the same order. Since this cannot be achieved by simple retransmission, it uses atomic broadcast to ensure the proper ordering of messages. As we have seen earlier, atomic broadcast protocols for general networks can be quite expensive. However, the proposed system uses specialized bus hardware and low-level driver software to support atomic broadcast [BBG83, B+89].

To support process resiliency, any process whose failure is to be tolerated is also replicated on a different node. Hence, we have process pairs with a *primary process* and a *backup process*. The backup is kept as an inactive process. The primary and the backup processes execute on separate nodes. The goal of the backup process is to take over the role of the primary process, in case the primary fails.

In order to avoid complete recomputation by the backup, a primary process and its backup are periodically synchronized so that the backup can recover from a more recent state. A primary executes a *sync* operation periodically. In the sync operation, a message is constructed that consists of: (i) all the pages in the address space of the primary that were modified since the last sync was sent to the message server, (ii) all machine-independent information about the process's state, like the address of the next instruction to be executed, accounting information, etc., (iii) channel information for every open channel, including the number of messages read since the last sync operation.

The sync message is sent to the host node of the backup process. Once the sync message has been placed on the outgoing message queue, the primary can continue its execution; it need not wait for the message to be delivered. If the primary fails before the message can be delivered, the backup will then use the information from the old sync operation. When the sync message arrives at the backup's node, the state of the backup process, the state of the channels, and other state information is updated.

Just providing the backup with the state information is not enough; message recovery also has to be performed. The goal of this scheme is to deliver the messages to the backup in the same order as the primary. This is achieved by an atomic three-way message delivery. Whenever a process P needs to send a message to another process Q, it actually sends three messages: one to Q, one to the backup of Q, and one to its own backup, as shown in Fig. 8.4. In order to make sure that the backups of P and Q are capable of taking over the role of primary, this scheme requires that these three messages be atomically broadcast. That is, either all three processes get a message or none of them does, and the arrival of messages to the three destinations is never interleaved with any other message, and different messages arrive at the processes in the same order.

In the scheme, atomic broadcast was implemented by a specialized bus and a bus protocol. In the protocol, a machine wishing to send a three-way message first gains control of the bus and then transmits the three destination addresses on the

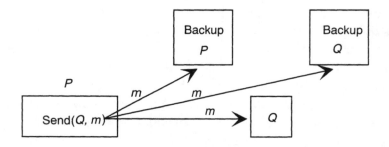

Figure 8.4: Messages in Aurogen

bus. On seeing its address on the bus, a destination node prepares to receive the message. If it cannot, it sends a nack message to the sender. If the sender receives no nack within a specified period of time, it sends the message on the bus. The bus protocol ensures that the message is transmitted without errors. All the destination nodes then receive the message from the bus. Hence, by using a single, reliable hardware bus the three-way atomic broadcast is easily ensured. This also implies that the scheme cannot be easily implemented in a distributed system without the specialized hardware. For supporting this method in a general distributed system, atomic broadcast protocols will have to be used. As we have seen earlier in Chapter 4, such protocols are frequently quite expensive.

If a process fails, its backup process starts execution from the previous checkpoint. Since the backup has the messages in its queue in the same order as the primary received them, and since the processes are deterministic, the backup will perform the same sequence of instructions as the primary and will soon reach the state of the primary, from where it can continue as the primary would have continued. During recovery, a backup process also ensures that all messages sent by the primary between its last checkpoint and failure are not retransmitted. Since the primary also sends a copy of any message it sends to its backup, the backup can easily determine which messages the primary had already sent. Hence, no duplicate messages are generated. This scheme can also tolerate multiple failures, and was implemented in a commercial system called Aurogen.

8.2.3 A Centralized Approach

Ensuring that the messages are recovered in the same order as before failure can also be done by using a centralized message exchange through which all messages are routed. In this approach, the centralized exchange is essentially a global observer of the distributed system which has the entire knowledge of the message passing that has occurred in the system. For such an approach to work, the message exchange is required to be very reliable. Here we describe a centralized approach called *publishing* [PP83] for process resiliency, that uses a *recorder process* to log messages, and a *recovery process* to coordinate the recovery activities.

Publishing assumes that the messages are broadcast over a network like Ethernet. There is a recording process on the network that records any message sent by one process to another. This process executes on a dedicated node that performs recording and recovery. To guard against the possibility of the recorder process missing a message (which is received by the destination), it employs an acknowledgment protocol. With this, a receiver discards a message if it does not receive the acknowledgment from the recorder. This ensures that the recorder has a "copy" of every message that has been exchanged between any two processes. Furthermore, the messages for a receiver are recorded in the same order as the order in which the receiver receives them. The recorder is also responsible for keeping checkpoints of processes. The architecture of publishing is shown in Fig. 8.5.

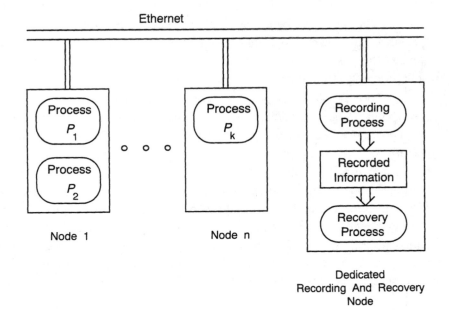

Figure 8.5: Architecture of publishing

If a process fails, the recovery process initiates the recovery. The recovery process also executes on the dedicated recording and recovery node. It first finds another node on which the failed process will execute, and initiates a new process. The new process is given the last checkpoint of the failed process and the operating system of the new node is given the sequence number of the last message sent by the failed process. With this number, the operating system ensures that those messages that were sent by the process before failing are not sent again during recovery. The messages needed by the new process are sent to it by the recorder process in the same order as the process had received them before failure. Hence, the new process starts from a checkpoint state of the failed process, and gets the same messages as the failed process. Since processes are deterministic, the new process reaches the state of the failed process, from where it can continue the task of the failed process.

8.2.4   Sender-Based Message Logging

Sender-based message logging is an approach that has been proposed for recovering from a single process failure [JZ87]. Processes are considered as senders and receivers. Though a process may send and receive messages, it is its receiver actions that are important for recovery; if a process fails, the messages it has received need to be recovered. In this scheme, the failure of one receiver process can be masked. The messages are logged locally by the processes which send messages to the failed process. If a receiver fails, by the single failure assumption, all the senders are assumed to be alive, and take part in recovery. Though not stated explicitly, the method does exploit the partial order property of the message recovery condition.

In sender-based logging, if the failure of a process P is to be tolerated, a message sent by a process to P is logged by the sender of the message itself. Whenever P receives a message from another process, it returns a *receive sequence number (RSN)* to the sender of the message. The sender adds this RSN of the message to the log of the message. The RSN of a message indicates the order in which the message was received relative to other messages sent by different senders. Therefore, the RSNs of the different messages in the log of the different senders specify a total order on those messages, which is the same as the order in which P received the messages.

On the failure of P, P is restarted on another node from its last checkpoint. On recovery, P broadcasts requests for retransmission of logged messages. The senders of the messages resend the logged messages in the ascending RSN order. Since RSNs of the messages form a total order, which is the same as the order in which P received the messages before failure, on recovery, P obtains these messages in the same order as it did before failure.

Let us now consider the scheme in a bit more detail. Each process in the system maintains the following information:

- A *send sequence number (SSN)*, which represents the number of messages sent by the process. This is used for detecting and discarding duplicate messages that can be sent during recovery. It can also be used by a process to suppress the sending of duplicate messages.

- A *receive sequence number (RSN)*, which represents the number of messages received by a process (from any source). The RSN is incremented each time the process receives a message.

- A *message log* of messages sent by the process. The message log contains the data of the message, its SSN, and the RSN assigned to it by the receiver. This log need not necessarily be kept in stable storage, and is initially kept in the volatile memory. The log is moved to stable storage when the process state is checkpointed.

- A table of the highest SSN value received from various processes. This is used for duplicate message detection.

The process state is periodically checkpointed. During checkpointing, besides the process state, the value of its SSN, RSN, message log, and the table of SSNs is also saved on the stable storage. If the process fails, it restarts on a different node from the last saved checkpoint.

Whenever a process sends a message, it logs the message in its local log. However, immediately after sending a message, a process knows the SSN it assigned to the message, but does not know the RSN assigned to it by the receiver message. The RSN of the message is recorded when it becomes available. Hence, the messages in the log may be *fully logged* or *partially logged*. Fully logged messages are those for which the RSN value is also stored in the log, and partially logged messages are those for which there is no RSN value. As the receiver node may fail before sending the RSN, the recovery method has to work with logs that can contain partially logged messages.

Fig. 8.6 shows an example of a distributed log for this scheme. The example shows two processes Q and R that send messages to the target process P. Suppose the process P has the RSN counter value of 5, before Q and R start sending messages. Suppose Q sends four messages, and R sends three messages. The network first delivers the first message of Q, then the first message of R, then the remaining two messages of Q, and finally the remaining messages of R. If the SSN of both Q and R start with 1, then the figure shows the SSN and RSN for the log of the processes

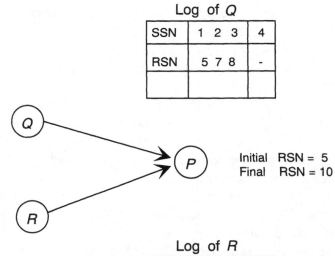

Figure 8.6: An example log for sender-based logging

Q and R. Fig. 8.6 shows the log of the processes at a time when P has sent RSNs to all messages but the last message. Note that the log of Q has one partially logged message. As time progresses, and if P does not fail, this partially logged message will also become fully logged.

Suppose that a process Q wants to send a message m to a process P. The steps in the message logging protocol are as follows:

- Process Q sends m to P and inserts m (along with its SSN) in the local log.

- Process P sends to P an acknowledgment containing the RSN value assigned to m.

- Process Q adds RSN for this message in the log and sends an acknowledgment for the RSN back to Q.

Except for the last message, the other messages are there in a regular message exchange, except that they carry some extra information due to the logging protocol.

The last message is the only additional message needed for recovery. In addition to these messages, there is a restriction on the receiver process. After sending the RSN back to the sender, the receiver process P can continue execution, but cannot send any message to any process until it has received the acknowledgment for the RSN from the sender. We will see why this restriction is needed for ensuring the correctness of recovery.

Recovery is performed when a receiver process P fails. P restarts on a different node from the last checkpoint and broadcasts a request to other nodes for resending the messages. On receiving this request, all processes send all the fully logged messages they had sent to P. These messages are sent in the order of their RSNs. In its request for retransmission, P can also send the value of the SSNs for different sender processes, as it recovered from the checkpoint. This value can be used by the senders to only send those messages that have a higher SSN. Messages with lower SSNs will be discarded as duplicates by P.

The messages received by P from the senders are consumed by P in the order of their RSNs. As the messages that were assigned an RSN by P form a total order, P gets the same sequence of messages as it did before the failure, and therefore executes the same sequence of instructions as it did before failure. Due to this, it produces the same messages as it did earlier, and will assign them the same SSNs. Any messages resent by P during rollback and reexecution are discarded as duplicates by other processes by using the SSNs.

However, there are still the partially logged messages that were sent by senders and received by P, but P failed before sending their RSNs to the senders. The protocol states that the senders should send the partially logged messages after sending the messages with RSNs.

Since there is no RSN attached to the partially logged messages, there is no total ordering imposed on them by P. Hence, they will be received and consumed by P in the order in which they are delivered by the communication network, which could be different than the order in which P received them before failure. However, as the partially logged messages are sent after the fully logged messages, they will be consumed after the fully logged messages. Furthermore, since P was constrained from communicating with any process if acknowledgment of the RSN for any message it received was pending, it is clear that P would not have sent any message to any process after receiving any of the partially acknowledged messages. Hence, receiving these messages in a different order cannot affect any other process. That is, no process other than the receiver process can be affected by the partially logged messages. Hence, the order of receiving these messages is a purely internal matter for P, and hence any order in which the messages can be delivered is acceptable.

As we can see, the partially logged messages can be received during recovery by P in any order that has the same partial order as the one before failure, which is satisfied by retransmission. The sender-based logging therefore exploits the second property of the message recovery condition though it does not state it explicitly. By having the senders of messages log the messages, the logging overhead is distributed. However, this also means that none of the senders can fail, and hence this scheme can handle only one process failure at a time. The scheme does not require any specialized hardware for implementation.

8.2.5 Optimistic Recovery

Here we present an approach called *optimistic recovery* [SY84, SY85] in which the dependency between processes is tracked. This allows checkpointing and message logging to take place asynchronously (i.e., they can be done at any time and not at defined points). On failure, if it is determined by the dependency information that some messages are lost, then those processes that depend on these messages also have to roll back. Hence, unlike most other schemes, in this approach, processes other than the failed process may also have to roll back. As in other schemes, processes are assumed to be deterministic. Hence, the behavior of a process (including what messages it sends) can be defined entirely by its initial state and the sequence of messages it receives.

A process P_i is considered as a sequence of *state intervals*. A process P_i enters the state interval $I_i(n)$ when it is ready to process its nth message $m_i(n)$ (recall that in asynchronous communication the messages for a process are queued). During a state interval $I_i(n)$, a process may send any number of messages, but whenever it receives the next message, it enters the next state interval. Due to determinism, the state obtained by restoring a previous state of P_i in its previous state intervals $I_i(n-d)$ and by replaying the messages $m_i(n-d)$ to $m_i(n)$ (in order) back to P_i will be a valid state.

As a result of failures and rollback, messages may be lost and retransmitted during reexecution. To uniquely identify a message, an *incarnation count* is maintained by each process. This count is incremented each time the process rolls back. The incarnation count is sent with each message, along with the sequence number of the message and the message content. Incarnation counts are also needed during recovery.

State intervals of processes are partially ordered by a causality relation. A state interval $I_i(n)$ (of process P_i) *immediately causes* another interval $I_j(m)$ (of process P_j) if a message sent from $I_i(n)$ is dequeued by P_j to start its mth state interval. This relation is like the relation "occurred before" as defined by Lamport [Lam78] and discussed earlier in Chapter 2, and induces a partial ordering over a set of state intervals called *causal precedence*. A state interval $I_i(d_i)$ is said to *depend* on intervals $I_1(d_1)$, $I_2(d_2)$, ..., $I_n(d_n)$, if for each $j \neq i$, $I_j(d_j)$ causally precedes $I_i(d_i)$ (i.e., $I_i(d_i)$ occurs before $I_j(d_j)$ in the partial ordering). In this, $< d_1, d_2, ..., d_n >$ is called the *dependency vector*, DV_i, of the process P_i. The dependency vector determines if a rollback of a process P_i is feasible. If $DV_i = < d_1, d_2, ..., d_n >$, then the current state of the process P_i depends on state intervals $1, 2, ..., d_k$ of a process P_k, but not on intervals after it. Hence, recreating the current state by rollback and replay will be successful only if for all processes P_k, $k = 1, 2, ..., n$ messages sent by P_k up to (and including) the state interval $I_k(d_k)$ can be recovered and resent to P_i.

Each process keeps track of its current dependencies on other processes (more precisely, their state intervals). To help in keeping the dependency vector current at all processes, each process appends its dependency vector to each message it sends. The dependency vector of a message m is represented by $m.DV$. Upon receiving a message m, a process P_i updates its dependency vector as follows:

$$DV_i(j) = \begin{cases} DV_i(j) + 1 & \text{for } i = j \\ max(DV_i(j), m.DV(i)) & \text{for } i \neq j. \end{cases}$$

Transmitting the dependency vector in each interaction between processes and updating the dependency vector in this manner ensures that a process always has the exact knowledge of the state intervals on which it depends. That is, if a process enters the state interval $I_i(n)$ (by dequeuing the nth message), then if it depends, directly or indirectly, on any message sent by P_k in state interval $I_k(p)$, then the kth element of DV_i will have a value p. Hence, at any time, the dependency vector of P_i represents the state intervals of other processes (or the messages received by other processes) on which $I_i(n)$ causally depends. Hence, if any one of the messages corresponding to the state intervals in the DV cannot be recovered after a failure, then $I_i(n)$ can also not be recovered.

Periodically, the complete state of the process is checkpointed on the stable storage. In addition, the messages for each process in the queue are also logged on stable storage. This is called the *input message log*. The input message log contains the contents of the message, as well as the order of messages in the message queue. The logging can be done at any time, and there is no synchronization between logging the input messages and the other events of the process. Due to asynchronous logging, the input message log may fall behind the process. Note that in this scheme, the message logging is being done by the receiver of the processes, in contrast to the scheme we discussed earlier where the logging was done by the sender.

If a process P_i fails, then the messages that have been sent to P_i before failure but were not logged by P_i are considered as *lost messages*. State intervals that depend upon lost messages are *orphan state intervals*. Messages which are either lost, or which are generated from orphan state intervals, are called *orphan messages*. State intervals that can never become orphans are called *committable*. Let $< d_1, d_2, ..., d_n >$ be the dependency vector of a state interval $I_i(m)$. Then if for each j, $j = 1, ..., n$ all messages sent to P_j up to the messages d_j have been logged, $I_i(m)$ is committable.

This clearly means that if messages are logged more frequently by processes, the more quickly computations will become committable. Also, it requires that a process P_i know which messages have been logged. This information is kept by a process in a *log vector (LV)* which contains the current knowledge of the process about how far each process has logged. Clearly, in a state interval, if a component of the log vector is greater than or equal to the corresponding component of the dependency vector for that state interval, then the state interval is committable.

Maintenance of log vectors requires that each process inform others about how far it has logged, or its own version of LV. This can be done by adding the LV onto each message sent by a process, or by periodically broadcasting the LV. A process, on receiving an LV from another process, updates each component of its current LV to the maximum of its previous value and the value received.

Since logging is done asynchronously by the receiver processes, a message may be lost forever if both the sender and the receiver fail. Hence, each sender of a message also saves the message until it is informed by the receiver that it has been logged. That is, until its log vector indicates that the message has been logged. These saved messages are used for message recovery.

During normal operation, the checkpoints of a process are accumulated (unlike in some other schemes where only the latest checkpoint is saved). However, a process P_i may discard a checkpoint C; if another checkpoint C' has been established after C, the process will never be required to recover any state interval between C and C', either to undo the effects of orphan messages, or to resend messages lost by some other process. If the state C' is committable, then no rollback prior to C' will be required for undoing effects of orphan messages. If all messages sent by P_i between C and C' are logged by the receivers, then no interval between C and C' will be required for message recovery. If no state interval between C and C' is needed for recovery, then the checkpoint C is discarded.

If a process fails, it recovers by restoring its earliest checkpoint. If the failure is due to the failure of the host node of the process, the process will be restarted on a different node during recovery. After rolling back, the process "replays" the log (i.e., the messages that were logged) and "reexecutes" the lost computation. After the log has been replayed, the process increments its incarnation count, and continues with normal processing.

Besides this rollback and recovery of the failed process, actions have to be taken to handle the following situations correctly: (1) the failed process looses the messages it had received but not logged, (2) during reexecution with replay of messages the process may resend some messages, and (3) other processes may have received messages that have now become orphans.

The first case is handled by the senders resending the messages. The process detects that messages are being missed when it receives a message from another process with a higher sequence number than expected. It then requests the missed messages. Since a sender buffers a message till it is logged, there is no problem in resending the message.

Duplicate messages are detected by the use of sequence numbers and an incarnation count. A message is a duplicate of a previously received message if their sequence numbers *and* their incarnation counts are the same. Hence, if a process receives a message from another process P_i, it looks at its log (both in volatile memory and in stable storage) to check the sequence number and the incarnation count. If the incarnation count for the new message is the same as the incarnation count of the messages received from P_i earlier, and its sequence number is less than the sequence number of the last received message from P_i, then the message is a duplicate. The duplicate messages are discarded.

It is the third case that causes problems for tracking a dependency. This situation occurs if a process receives a message whose sequence number is smaller than expected (that is, messages with higher sequence numbers were received earlier), but whose incarnation count is higher than previously. That is, the message which was sent by the old incarnation has been sent by the new incarnation of the process. This situation occurs when a process P_i rolls back due to failure and loses some messages. On rollback, P_i first processes the messages it has logged. The messages that it has received but not logged are now lost, and hence all its state intervals after the logged message are now orphans, and all messages sent earlier by P_i after consuming its last logged message are now orphan messages. These orphans, together with any state intervals that causally depend on them, have to be destroyed. The recovery action for this depends on how far another process P_j has progressed in processing an orphan message. There are the following cases:

1. If the orphan has not yet been logged, it is deleted from the queue, or not put on the queue if it has not already been put there.

2. If the orphan has been logged but not processed, it is removed from the queue and the log is modified.

3. If the orphan has been processed, it represents the worst case. In this case, P_j

is rolled back to a state before all the orphans were processed.

Let us consider an example the execution of two processes P_i and P_j. The execution of the processes and their checkpointing and message logging is shown in Fig. 8.7. The execution of the instructions and the checkpointing and message

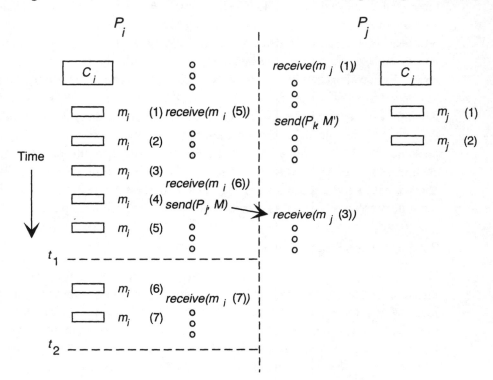

Figure 8.7: Optimistic recovery example

logging is shown separately, as logging is done asynchronously, and has no temporal connection with the execution of instructions. Suppose the process P_i fails at time t_1, when it is in the state interval $I_i(6)$ (of the 0th incarnation), and has logged messages up to $m_i(5)$ (i.e., message $m_i(6)$ has not been logged yet, though it has been received). On recovery, P_i will roll back to C_i, and replay messages $m_i(1)$ through $m_i(5)$. Then it will increment its incarnation count to 1, and start executing. When it executes the $send(P_j, M)$, it will send M to P_j with the same sequence number as before, but with a higher incarnation number, which will tell P_j that the earlier M is now an orphan. Hence, P_j will roll back to C_j to undo the effect of the orphan message.

However, if P_i fails at t_2, the recovery is easier. At t_2, it has logged messages up to $m_i(7)$. Hence, when it replays the message, it will execute the $send(P_j, M)$

command and will send M with the same sequence number and same incarnation count. M will then be discarded as a duplicate by P_j. No rollback of P_j is needed in this case.

The basic idea behind this approach is to log messages to ensure that they are recovered in the same order. However, if some messages have not been logged, then all computation depending on those messages have to be undone, which means that processes other than the failed process also roll back. However, no domino effect occurs, since every process logs messages, and the rollback of a process forces other processes to roll back only if some messages have been lost. That is why the scheme has been termed as *optimistic* — it assumes that the failures will occur rarely, and when they do there will be few lost messages, and consequently, limited rollback.

Other optimistic recovery schemes have also been proposed. The scheme presented in [JZ90] requires only a small amount of extra information be sent in each message (as opposed to the entire dependency vector in the scheme discussed above), but then the processing is centralized. In the scheme described in [SW89], separate messages are used to distribute the dependency information.

8.2.6 A Distributed Scheme

Here we describe the scheme proposed in [Jal89] which does not try to recover all the messages in the same order, and fully exploits the flexibility offered in the message recovery condition discussed earlier. In this scheme, logging is done by the sender as well as the receiver. Logging by the receiver is used to ensure total ordering, while logging by the sender is used to ensure partial ordering. The scheme is distributed and can handle the simultaneous failure of multiple processes.

The basic approach employed to support fault tolerance is to restart a failed process on a backup host by using a previously checkpointed state. We refer to the two host nodes of a process P_i as $primary(P_i)$ and $backup(P_i)$. We assume that for a process P_i, $primary(P_i)$ and $backup(P_i)$ do not both fail. We also assume that the process can be restarted from a checkpoint on the backup host.

Each message is assigned a unique, monotonically increasing sequence number. An incoming message is a duplicate of a previous message if its sequence number is less than the highest sequence number already received from that process. Duplicates are discarded by a receiver. Due to rollback, if a send was executed before the failure occurred, then the message sent by the backup will have the same sequence number, and can be discarded as a duplicate. The following additional information is maintained by each node:

receivemsg Q_i: A queue that contains the messages (in order) received by a process P_i since its last send command. Each time a receive command is executed by

P_i, the message received by P_i is appended to $receivemsgQ_i$. Then $receivemsgQ_i$ is set to null after P_i sends a message. This queue is used to establish message checkpoints, which are later used to recover messages in MB_i, if P_i fails.

$sendmsgQ_i$: This is a set of queues for a process P_i. It contains one queue for each process P_j. In it, messages sent to P_j by P_i are saved in the order they are sent. When P_i sends a message to P_j, a copy of the message is appended to $sendmsgQ_i[P_j]$. This is used for retransmitting messages of MA_j, if P_j fails. Reducing the size of these queues is discussed later.

Two kinds of checkpoints are needed to support recovery. The first is the *state checkpoint* from which the process restarts after failure. A state checkpoint for a process P_i is periodically established on $backup(P_i)$ and includes the state of the process, the highest sequence numbers of messages it has received and sent to different processes so far, and $sendmsgQ_i$. The backup node discards previous state checkpoints for P_i when a new checkpoint is established.

To ensure the first clause of the message recovery condition, *message checkpoints* are employed. A message checkpoint is established for a process P_i by sending $receivemsgQ_i$ to the backup and resetting $receivemsgQ$ to empty before executing any send command by P_i. Note that sending a message checkpoint and the message is *not* assumed to be atomic, and a failure between these actions does not cause any problems.

To ensure proper message recovery, many nodes have to take part in recovery. Specifically, the nodes that are the backup hosts for the failed processes and the nodes whose processes have communicated with the failed processes take part in recovery. When a node i detects that a process P_k has failed, it executes the procedure *perform-recovery$_i$*. The *resident_set* of a node is the set of processes executing on that node. The procedure, shown in Fig. 8.8, is executed by a node every time the failure of some process is detected [Jal89]. The Boolean array FAILURE is used to locally record the failure of a process. This information is used to handle concurrent failures.

In Part I of the recovery procedure, the host of the failed process is changed to its backup host so that messages to be sent to P_k are properly routed, as messages sent to $primary(P_k)$ are discarded and do not reach P_k. The fact that process P_k has failed is also recorded. This is needed to handle concurrent failures and is utilized by Part II. Then the messages in the $sendmsgQ$ of different processes on this node are sent again (in order) to P_k. This may result in sending some messages that P_k had received before the checkpoint. Such messages will be discarded as duplicates.

Part II contains actions to be performed by the node if it is the backup host of P_k. The node first retrieves the state checkpoint of P_k and the message checkpoints are added to the front of $msgQ_k$. As we are making no assumptions about the order in

procedure perform-recovery$_i$ (P_k)
begin

(∗ *PART I* ∗)

change host node of P_k to $backup(P_k)$
FAILURE [P_k] := True
for each $P_l \in$ *resident_set* of node i **do**
      for each m $\in$ *sendmsg* $Q_l[P_k]$ **do**
           send(P_k , m)
end

(∗ *PART II* ∗)

if n_i is $backup(P_k)$ **then begin**
      retrieve state checkpoint
      add message checkpoints to the front of $msg\,Q_k$
      delete any duplicates in $msg\,Q_k$
      for each process P_l, $P_l! = P_k$ **do**
           if FAILURE [P_l] **then**
               for each $m \in$ *sendmsg* $Q_k[P_l]$ **do**
                  send(P_l , m)
      start executing P_k
endif
end

Figure 8.8: Recovery procedure for node i, on failure of P_k

which a failure is detected, some nodes may perform recovery before $backup(P_k)$ does, in which case there may be some messages in $msg\,Q_k$ when the recovery is initiated. Some of these messages may be duplicates of messages included in the message checkpoints and are therefore deleted. Duplicate detection is done easily by using sequence numbers.

If there is another failed process P_l for which the recovery procedure had been executed earlier by the node, then messages sent by P_k to P_l will have to be resent. This action would be performed by $primary(P_k)$ in Part I on the failure of P_l. If $primary(P_k)$ fails before the recovery for P_l is complete, then these messages are retransmitted by the backup host in Part II (information in FAILURE is needed for this). This also raises the possibility of the messages needed for recovery being sent twice, once by $primary(P_k)$ and once by $backup(P_k)$. However, duplicate messages will be discarded at the receiving end.

It can be seen easily that if there is only one process failure, the message recovery condition is satisfied. Suppose the failed process is P_k. Recall that the message condition states that the messages to be recovered are $M_k = MB_k; MA_k$, where MB_k are the messages received by P_k before it sent the last message before failing, and MA_k are the messages it received after sending the last message. Let M'_k be the order in which the recovery messages (messages in message checkpoints and messages sent during the execution of the recovery procedure by different nodes) are added to $msg Q_k$. Let MB'_k be the sequence of messages in the message checkpoints. During recovery, these messages are added to the front of the $msg Q_k$. Since the order of messages is maintained in message checkpoints and a message checkpoint is established before each send, $MB'_k = MB_k$. Since all messages sent by other processes to P_k are retransmitted during recovery and the duplicates are discarded, the messages recovered after MB'_k contain only the messages in MA_k. Let these messages be MA'_k. Because the order of messages sent by a process to P_k is maintained during retransmission, we will get $MA'_k \in popp(MA_k)$. Hence, both parts of the message recovery condition are satisfied.

In the multiple failure case, a process failing after the recovery of another failed process has completed poses no problems. Even in the case of simultaneous failures, the first part of the message-recovery condition is satisfied by the message checkpoint of each process. For satisfying the second part of the condition, if there are two failed processes P_l and P_k, then it has to be shown that despite failure, the process P_k (P_l) retransmits all the messages to P_l (P_k).

If $backup(P_l)$ performs recovery for P_k before the recovery of P_l, then the messages in $sendmsg Q_l[P_k]$ at C are retransmitted in Part II during recovery for P_l (because FAILURE[P_k] is true). Messages sent by P_l after C are sent on reexecution of P_l, as $MB'_l = MB_l$. If $backup(P_l)$ performs recovery for P_l before the recovery of P_k, then messages in $sendmsg Q_l[P_k]$ at time C and any messages P_l sent after restart are retransmitted in Part I during recovery for P_k. Remaining messages are sent on reexecution of P_l. Hence, multiple failure can also be handled. As can be seen, the information in FAILURE is needed for correct operation in those conditions where the primary host of a process fails before completing recovery for the failure of another process. In other situations, it causes duplicate messages to be sent.

The overhead during recovery of this method has two parts. The first part is the overhead of reexecuting the nullified computation, which may involve sending of duplicate messages (due to reexecution of send commands). Taking state checkpoints frequently will reduce this, but will also increase the overhead during normal computation. The second part of the recovery overhead occurs in sending messages in $sendmsg\,Q_l[P_k]$, for each process P_l. This overhead can be reduced considerably by sending the $sendmsg\,Q$s of all the processes in the *resident_set* of a node together in one message.

The size of $sendmsg\,Q$s can also be pruned. Clearly, the messages sent by P_l before the last message checkpoint for P_k was established need not be retransmitted and are actually discarded as duplicates by the backup. These messages need not be saved in $sendmsg\,Q_l[P_k]$. However, the other processes have to be informed about the sequence numbers of the last messages logged, so that they can prune their $sendmsg\,Q$. This can be done by transmitting the sequence number information to others at recovery or at each checkpoint.

8.3   Resiliency with Synchronous Message Passing

The schemes discussed above consider asynchronous message passing, and require each process to be deterministic, i.e., given the same inputs, the process performs the same actions. Both these assumptions do not hold, for example, in languages like CSP [Hoa78] and Ada which allow non-determinism within a process, and employ synchronous message passing. In this section, we discuss a scheme for making a CSP program resilient to the failure of one of its constituent processes [Jal92]. CSP was discussed earlier in Chapter 2.

For a process P_j, assume that the code is of the form:

$$P_j :: \text{Initialize}; *[G_1 \rightarrow C_1 \square G_2 \rightarrow C_2 \ldots \square G_n \rightarrow C_n].$$

It is assumed that each $G_i \rightarrow C_i$ contains at least one I/O command, and that each C_i is just a sequence of commands. Due to synchronous message passing in CSP, the sender and the receiver processes synchronize at each communication. This is implemented by some handshake protocol, which must necessarily include an ack or a signal from the receiver to the sender (to unblock the sender). Assume that a receiver can send some information to the sender in this ack or signal. Also assume that each process is executing on a separate node, and a node fails by stopping. We restrict our attention to a single node failure, causing a single process to fail. Assume that each node detects the failure of a node (and its process) within a finite time, and that the failure of the process is signaled by the node to the process executing on it. Whenever a process P_i tries to communicate with a failed process, a failure is signaled to P_i. This signal is used for exception handling. The process whose failure is to be handled is assumed to be specified at design time.

The basic goal of supporting process resiliency is to ensure that the state of P reaches a valid state in a finite time after the failure of the specified process. Without loss of generality, assume that P_0 is the process whose failure is to be handled. Let the recovery process be P_r that executes on a separate node. The basic approach is to periodically checkpoint the state of P_0 with P_r. If P_0 fails, the process P_r starts on the backup node to take over the role of P_0. P_r will contain some recovery code, followed by the code for P_0. That is, on failure of P_0, P_r first performs some recovery actions, and then executes the code of P_0.

The approach is to take the system to a valid state by recovery. After that, the network of processes will behave like the original network. The goal of the recovery activities is to ensure that P_r reaches the state in which P_0 was just after its last communication command before failure. From this state, it can execute the normal code of P_0. This is different from the approach of static reconfiguration proposed in [Sha85]. In [Sha85], a failed process is merged with another process. However, the computation during which the failure occurs has to be aborted entirely, and the system has to be reinitialized and restarted with the new configuration.

One way to ensure that P_r reaches the proper state is to make sure that during recovery P_r goes through the same sequence of states as P_0 did. Note that in CSP this *cannot* be achieved merely by providing to P_r the messages that P_0 received between its last checkpoint and failure in the order in which P_0 received them. That is, unlike the schemes with deterministic processes, merely by starting P_r from the last checkpoint of P_0 and providing it the messages in the same order as P_0 received them before failure will not ensure that P_r performs the same sequence of actions as P_0 did before failure. In addition to recovering the messages in the original order, it has to be ensured that wherever there is a non-deterministic choice, some "decision" is taken during recovery by P_r as was done by P_0 before failure.

To support recovery for P_r, other processes also have to perform some recovery activities. On detecting the failure of P_0, P_i performs some recovery activities and then continues with its normal computation. These recovery activities consist of sending to P_r information about those messages that were sent to P_0 and whose effects may be lost due to failure.

8.3.1 Recovery of Failed Process

To recover the messages, the communication commands of P_0 that sent a message or an ack to other processes need to be identified. The command that performed the last send/receive before failure also needs to be identified. To aid this, a simple static numbering scheme that is based on the code of the process is used. Each I/O command is assigned a *command number*, based on its syntactic location, which uniquely identifies the I/O command.

The numbering scheme is as follows. If an I/O command occurs in the guard G_i (remember, at most, one input command can occur in a guard), it is assigned the number i. An I/O command in a command list C_i is assigned a number that is formed by concatenating i and the sequence number of the I/O command in C_i. For example, an I/O command in $G_5 \rightarrow C_5$, which is syntactically the third I/O command in C_5, is assigned the number 5.3.

During normal computation, the process P_0 periodically checkpoints its state with P_r. This checkpoint is timestamped by P_0's clock. If P_0 sends a message to another process P_i, it timestamps the message (by its own clock) and also sends the command number of this output command. For an input command with P_i, P_0 sends the command number in the ack or the signal it sends to P_i, and also timestamps it. Hence, with any I/O command, the receiver or the sender process knows when P_0 sent or received the message and knows the command number of the I/O command that output or input the message. Note that at any time one of the P_i's knows the command number of the last I/O command successfully executed by P_0 (this does not hold for asynchronous communication systems, due to buffering by the system).

Each process P_i maintains a list called $io - list_i$. After executing each communication command with P_0, P_i appends an entry in the $io - list_i$. An entry in the $io - list_i$ is of the form: $< ts, cmd, msg >$, where ts is the timestamp of the message or the ack/signal sent by P_0, cmd is the command number in P_0 of the corresponding I/O command which was sent by P_0 to P_i, and msg is the message sent by P_i to P_0 (for an input command this is null). How to reduce the size of these lists is discussed later. When the failure of P_0 is signaled to P_i, it sends its $io - list_i$ to the process P_r. P_r later uses this information for its own recovery activities.

If P_0 fails, a process P's host node will signal the failure of P_0. We assume that this failure is treated by P_i as an exception condition. When a failure is signaled to P_i, then the handler associated with the exception is executed.

Once P_0 fails, its role is taken over by P_r. Note that due to static declaration of processes, P_r is not created on failure. During normal computation, P_r repeatedly receives the CP from P_0 and saves it. On being signaled the failure of P_0, P_r exits this loop. This is shown below with the local exception handler. (The statements in [ ] after the I/O command form the exception handler. This notation is similar to the one proposed in [Cri82].) We call this CODE-1:

$$*[P_0 ? CP \rightarrow \text{save CP}] \ [\text{failure}(P_0) \rightarrow \text{skip}].$$

P_r also has a handler for the failure of P_0, which performs part of the recovery activities of P_r. In this handler, P_r first receives all the io-lists from all the P_is. These are merged into a large list, which is sorted by the ts field of the entries in the list. We call this list IO-LST. From this list, all the elements whose ts is less than the timestamp of the last checkpoint received by P_r are discarded. The IO-LST now contains information about all the I/O commands executed by P_0 after its last checkpoint. Moreover, the entries in the IO-LST are in increasing timestamp order, and the timestamp in each entry is according to P_0's clock. Therefore, these entries are in the order in which P_0 executed the I/O commands. Hence, due to the synchronous message passing, we have a total order among the entries for I/O commands that P_0 executed with different processes, and this order is the same as the order in which P_0 executed these I/O commands. This handler of P_r is shown in Fig. 8.9 [Jal92] (n[ ] means that the body is repeated n times).

$$
\begin{aligned}
&\text{failure}(P_0) \rightarrow \\
&\quad \text{n[} P_1 \ ? \ io - list_1 \rightarrow \text{skip} \\
&\qquad \Box P_2 \ ? \ io - list_2 \rightarrow \text{skip} \\
&\qquad\qquad \vdots \\
&\qquad \Box P_n \ ? \ io - list_n \rightarrow \text{skip} \\
&\quad] \\
&\quad \text{IO-LST} = \text{merge}(io - list_1 \ldots io - list_n) \\
&\quad \text{sort-by-ts(IO-LST)} \\
&\quad \text{discard(IO-LST , ts-of-last-cp)} \\
&\quad \text{exit}
\end{aligned}
$$

Figure 8.9: Handler of P_r

In CSP, due to the internal non-determinism of processes, besides recovering the messages, we have to ensure that the same sequence of guarded commands is actually executed by P_r as was executed by P_0. It is for this that the I/O commands were numbered.

The command number of each entry contains the guard number. Since we assume that there is at least one I/O command in each guarded command, the list of command numbers in the IO-LST can tell us the list of guarded commands that were executed. As an example, suppose that the list of command numbers in the IO-LST is 3, 3.1, 3.2, 5.1, 5.2, 5.3, 1.1, 8, ... This means that first $G_3 \rightarrow C_3$ was executed, then $G_5 \rightarrow C_5$ was executed, then $G_1 \rightarrow C_1$, and then $G_8 \rightarrow C_8$. Note that the I/O commands in a guarded command $G_i \rightarrow C_i$ will occur together in this list. Using this list, the exact sequence in which guards were executed by P_0 can be determined. In addition, the command number of the last I/O command that was successfully executed by P_0 can also be determined. Due to the syntactic numbering scheme, this tells us the location of the statement that P_0 would have executed after this I/O command. We will refer to this statement by the label L.

This information is used by P_r for completing the recovery. P_r first retrieves the last CP of P_0 and then executes from the CP the guarded commands in the code of P_0 in the order specified in the IO-LST. This requires a deterministic order in execution and so the code of process P_0 cannot be used without modification. Also, during this execution, P_r must not send any message that was already sent by P_0, and for any input command, it should actually get the message from the IO-LST. Furthermore, the last guarded command specified in the guard list may not have been executed fully by P_0 before it failed. Hence, this guarded command must not be executed fully by P_r. P_r should execute it only to the last communication command executed by P_0 before failure.

After all this is done, the state of P_r is the same as the state of P_0 at the statement just after the last communication command executed by P_0. Recovery is complete once this state is reached. After this, the control should be transferred to the statement following the statement corresponding to this communication command in the regular code of P_0. We assume that control can be transferred by a *goto* statement. From then on, P_r will execute the code of P_0 and behave like P_0. To specify this part of recovery, we define the following functions on IO-LST:

- next-guard: returns guard number of the first entry.

- next-msg: returns the msg of the first entry.

- delete: deletes the first entry.

- end-of-list: returns true if the list is empty.

We have seen part of the recovery scheme above (CODE-1), where the *io-lists* were collected and IO-LST was formed. For completing recovery, from a guarded command $G_i \rightarrow C_i$ of the process P_0, we form an augmented command list CA_i as described in Fig. 8.10 [Jal92]. The label L refers to the statement in the code of P_0 following the last communication command in the IO-LST.

With the augmented command list CA_i, the remaining recovery of P_r can be specified. The code for remainder of the recovery of P_r is given in Fig. 8.11 [Jal92] (this code is referred to as CODE-2).

The scheme shown above ensures that: (1) the guarded commands executed by P_0 between its last CP and failure are executed in the same order by P_r as P_0 did before failure, (2) no output command executed by P_0 is executed again by P_r, (3) all input commands executed before by P_0 receive data locally, and (4) after the last I/O command in the IO-LST has been executed, the control is transferred to the control

0. Initialize CA_i to be C_i.
1. If G_i has an input command,
    add it as the first statement in CA_i.
2. After each I/O command in CA_i, add:
        delete (IO-LST)
        if end-of-list(IO-LST) then goto L
3. Replace each input command $P_i?m$ by:
        m := next-msg(IO-LST)
    Each output command $P_i!exp$ is deleted
    (or replaced by execution of exp,
    if exp has any local side effects.)
4. At the end of CA_i add the statement
        guard := next-guard(IO-LST)

Figure 8.10: Constructing the augmented command

```
CODE-2: restore CP
        guard := next-guard(IO-LST)
        *[ guard=1 → CA₁
           □ guard=2 → CA₂
           □ guard=3 → CA₃
              ⋮
        ]
```

Figure 8.11: Remaining recovery of P_r

point after that command in the regular code of P_0 (by the *goto* statement in the rule 2 above). After this, P_r will be in the same state as P_0 was at this control point, and the regular code of P_0 is executed.

It is clear that from the information collected from other processes about the I/O commands executed by P_0 before it failed, the actions of P_0 after the CP were repeated by P_r from the CP in the same sequence. This "tracing" of actions is till the last I/O command successfully executed by P_0. After this, the regular code of P_0 is executed. The case where P_0 fails during an I/O command is discussed later.

8.3.2   Reconfiguring the Processes

After P_r completes recovery, the computation of P_0 is performed by P_r. However, the I/O commands of a process P_i explicitly specify P_0 as the source/destination. These processes have to be properly modified such that before P_0 fails they perform the I/O commands with P_0, but after P_0 fails these I/O commands are instead performed with P_r. Since CSP does not allow dynamic binding of names to I/O commands, this property has to be incorporated in the code for each P_i.

For this, we extend the code of each P_i by local exception-handling commands. We only have to concern ourselves with the I/O commands in P_i which have P_0 specified as the source/destination. There are two cases for this: (1) an I/O command with P_0 occurs in the guard of a command $G_k \rightarrow C_k$ of P_i, and (2) the I/O command occurs in the command list C_k.

If the I/O command is in the command list, we use exception handling. Consider a command P_0 ?/! m in P_i. If P_0 fails, P_i will be blocked at this command till the failure exception is signaled. We assume that the underlying system signals the failure whenever P_i tries to communicate with a failed P_0. If a failure is signaled, the handler associated with the I/O command is executed. After the execution of the handler, the control is transferred to the statement immediately following the I/O command. To handle the failure of P_0, each I/O command in P_i with the source/destination as P_0 is augmented with an exception handler as follows:

$$P_0 \ !/? \ m[\text{failure}(P_0) \rightarrow P_r \ !/? \ m].$$

If P_0 has failed, a failure will be signaled to P_i and the I/O command is executed with P_r. However, as long as P_0 is alive, the exception handler will not be invoked and the I/O command with P_0 will be executed successfully. Now consider the case where the I/O command is in the guard. A guard containing an input command fails if the source process has failed. For each guarded command $G_k \rightarrow C_k$ in P_i which has an input command with P_0 in the guard, we add another guarded command $G'_k \rightarrow C'_k$ in P_i. This guarded command is obtained by replacing in $G_k \rightarrow C_k$ all I/O commands with the source/destination as P_0 with similar I/O commands but with the source/destination as P_r. So, we get:

$G_k \rightarrow C_k$ /*I/O cmds with P_0 */
$\square G'_k \rightarrow C'_k$ /* I/O cmds with P_r */.

If P_0 fails the guard G_k will fail. However, the corresponding guard G'_k, with input from P_r, will be activated and the guarded command $G'_k \rightarrow C'_k$ will be executed (if it is selected).

The overhead for this scheme during normal computation occurs due to maintenance of *io-lists* and due to the checkpointing of the state of P_0 with P_r. Since information about any communication command executed after the last checkpoint of P_0 is actually discarded, the size of *io-lists* can be bound. A simple method is to have P_0 send the timestamp of the last checkpoint to other processes, along with other information sent by P_0. With this, each process can discard the old entries from its *io-list*.

8.4   Total Failure and Last Process to Fail

In the schemes discussed above, the failure of a few processes is masked so that the overall computation can continue. However, all fault tolerant schemes have limitations on how many failures they can mask. The number of failures that can be handled typically depend on the amount of redundancy employed. For example, in a replicated procedure call, if a procedure is replicated on k nodes, then up to $k - 1$ failures can be tolerated by the system. In this section we consider the issue of what happens if a total failure occurs.

A *total failure* occurs whenever all processes cooperating to perform a distributed task fail [Ske85]. The schemes discussed above cannot handle total failures, since whenever a total failure occurs, by definition, the failures cannot be masked. However, some recovery can be performed when the failed processes restart. Often, to satisfactorily recover from total failure requires reconstructing the state just before the total failure. This requires determining the last process to fail, since the last failed process will have the latest state of the system.

For example, in a replicated procedure call, if all the replicas fail, we have a total failure. To recover from this total failure, we must determine the last replica to fail, as it has the latest state of the procedure, and the system operation can begin only when the state of this last failed replica is available. A similar situation exists when data is replicated to increase availability. If a total failure occurs and all the data-manager processes fail, then the system can start operation again only after the last data-manager process to fail becomes operational, since it has the latest version of the data. Hence, in these situations, recovery from total failure requires that the last process (or in general, the last processes) to fail be determined. In this section, we discuss the problem of the last process to fail and a proposed solution to this problem. The discussion and the solution are based on the work of Skeen [Ske85].

A *process group* is a finite set of communicating processes. What constitutes a process group depends on the application (e.g., in a replicated procedure call, the processes executing the replicated call may form the process group). We only consider the case of *static* groups, where the membership of the process group is fixed over time and is known to all members of the group. We are interested in the total failure of the process group. We assume that a process fails by halting, and that the failure of a process can be detected by other processes. This detection typically will involve some delay (since frequently timeout-based schemes are used). In other words, there is a time gap between the failure of a process and its detection by another process. We can represent this failure detection by assuming that a failing process i sends a *failed(i)* message to other nodes, which arrive at the destinations after some delay. Since processes can also fail concurrently, the general problem here is one of determining the set of processes which fail last. We denote this set by LAST.

8.4.1   Preliminaries

We have seen earlier in Chapter 2 that it is not straightforward to specify in a distributed system if an event happened before another. A partial ordering that specifies the "happened-before" relation can be defined on a set of events in a distributed system [Lam78]. This relation, represented by $\rightarrow$, is also discussed in Chapter 2. For convenience we define it again here.

On a set of events is a relation that satisfies: (1) If a and b are events in the same process, and a is performed by the process before b, then $a \rightarrow b$. (2) If event a is the sending of a message and event b is the receiving of the same message, then $a \rightarrow b$. (3) If $a \rightarrow b$ and $b \rightarrow c$ then $a \rightarrow c$. Two events a and b are said to be concurrent if neither $a \rightarrow b$ nor $b \rightarrow a$. That event $a \rightarrow b$ implies that a can affect the event b. Concurrent events cannot affect each other.

This happened-before relation will be used to specify LAST. As we have modeled a failing process i as sending a *failed(i)* message to others, the ordering of the failure event and its detection can easily be modeled with $\rightarrow$. To focus on failures and their detection, define a *failed before* relation, denoted by FB, on processes in the group, as follows [Ske85].

Definition. Let i and j be two processes; i *FB* j if, and only if, there exists some event a in j such that (i's failure event) $\rightarrow a$.

The relation FB says that a process i is considered to have failed before another process j only if i's failure could affect some event in j. Two processes i and j fail *concurrently* if neither i *FB* j nor j *FB* i. Clearly, FB is a partial ordering. With FB, we can define LAST as the set of processes whose failures could not have affected events in other processes. That is, a process i is in LAST only if *no* process receives the message *failed(i)* [Ske85].

Definition. LAST $= \{j | \neg \exists i (j \; FB \; i)\}$.

In order to determine LAST after a total failure, each process in the process group has to maintain some information. Let P represent the process group. Each process i in P has to maintain the following information on stable storage such that the value just before failure is available to the recovery process:

1. P_i — i's *cohort set* — a subset of P known to i.

2. f_i — i's *mourned set* — a subset of P_i composed of processes that have failed and whose failures are known to i.

A process's mourned set is *complete* if it contains all the processes that have failed before it. We assume that the cohort set of i contains i and f_i, and that f_i contains all processes from which the failure message was received directly. Since a process $i \in LAST$ only if no other process has received its failure message, we have:

$$LAST = \bigcup_{i \in P} P_i - \bigcup_{i \in P} f_i.$$

After a total failure, data from only a few processes may be available — typically those processes that have recovered from the failure. Let R be the set of processes whose data is accessible. Initially, R is empty. As processes recover, they join R. At any given time, only the cohort set and the mourned set of the processes in R are available for determining LAST.

For determining LAST, with information available from only a subset of the total processes in the process group, we first determine a set of candidates for LAST. We have:

$$CAND_R = P - \bigcup_{i \in S} f_i, \text{ where } R \subseteq P.$$

Clearly $CAND_R$ is the set of processes that have failed before no other, according to the mourned set of the processes in R. We clearly have $LAST \subseteq CAND_R$ for any R, and $LAST = CAND_P$ (i.e., when R is the complete process group). We are now ready to discuss the actual issue of determining LAST.

8.4.2 Determining LAST Using Complete Information

First we consider the problem where the mourned set of each node is complete. It has been shown that with complete mourned sets, $CAND_{LAST} = LAST$ [Ske85]. This says that with complete mourned sets, LAST can be determined from the mourned set of the members of LAST itself. However, to use this for determining LAST, we need some way to determine if R (the set of processes whose mourned set is available) is equal to $LAST$.

It has also been shown that for an arbitrary subset R of P, with complete mourned sets, if $CAND_R \subseteq R$, then $CAND_R = LAST$ [Ske85]. Since $LAST \subseteq CAND_R$, this is true if $CAND_R \subseteq R$ implies $CAND_R \subseteq LAST$ (or equivalently, $CAND_R \subseteq CAND_{LAST}$). Assume that $CAND_R \subseteq R$. If $CAND_R \subseteq CAND_{LAST}$, then by replacing $CAND$ with its definition, we get $P - \bigcup_{i \in R} f_i \subseteq P - \bigcup_{i \in LAST} f_i$. Simplifying this we get $\bigcup_{i \in LAST} f_i \subseteq \bigcup_{i \in R} f_i$. This is true, since $LAST \subseteq R$ (because $LAST \subseteq CAND_R$).

This result establishes the sufficient condition for determining LAST. It can also be shown that $R = LAST$ is also a necessary condition [Ske85]. Based on this theorem, LAST can be determined. The algorithm for determining LAST is given in Fig. 8.12 [Ske85]. This is a distributed algorithm that is executed by each process

function *DetermineLast*(i, P, f_i) : set-of-processes

local   j: process;
         $CAND_R$, f': set-of-processes;

begin
        R := { i }
        $CAND_R$:= P - f_i
        broadcast message (i, f_i) **to** P
        while ($CAND_R \not\subseteq R$) **do begin**
            receive($< j, f' >$);
            R := R $\cup$ { j }
            $CAND_R$:= $CAND_R - f'$
      end
      return $CAND_R$
   end

Figure 8.12: Distributed algorithm for determining LAST

when it recovers after a total failure.

On recovery, a process first broadcasts its mourned set to every member of the process group. Also, it repeatedly receives this message from other processes that may recover and send this message. On receiving the mourned set, it checks if the condition of the theorem is met. When the condition is met, $LAST$ is determined.

8.4.3 Determining LAST Using Incomplete Information

The algorithm given above works if the mourned set of each process is complete. It has been shown that determining that f_i is complete for a process i is difficult, and that completeness has to be ensured through system architecture and design. Clearly, the problem of finding LAST with an incomplete mourned set is more difficult than finding LAST when mourned sets are known to be complete. Here we consider the problem of finding LAST when the mourned set of a process may not be complete [Ske85].

Definition. Let $R \subseteq P$. FB_R is the smallest relation on P satisfying (1) if $j \in R$ and $i \in f_j$, then $i \; FB_R \; j$, and (2) if $i \; FB_R \; j$ and $j \; FB_R \; k$, then $i \; FB_R \; k$.

FB_R defines a set of possible candidate relations for the FB relation. The *closure of a mourned set f_i with respect to R*, denoted by f_i^R, is defined as the set $\{j | j \; FB_R \; i\}$. f_i^R is the set of process failures before i that can be inferred from the available data (by using transitivity). If $i \in R$ and mourned sets are complete, then $f_i^R = f_i$. We assume that the closure can be computed by a function called *closure* (i, R). Given the data in R, $P - f_i^R$ describes the set of processes not failing before i. In other words, processes in $P - f_i^R$ fail concurrently with or after i. From this it can be determined if a process is in LAST, using the result that for an arbitrary process i, if $i \in CAND_R$ and $(P - f_i^R) \subseteq R$, then $i \in LAST$ [Ske85].

A distributed algorithm based on this theorem for determining if a process is in LAST is given in Fig. 8.13 [Ske85]. This algorithm works much like the one described in Fig. 8.12. However, it is testing for membership of a process in LAST, while the previous algorithm was determining LAST itself. In case of incomplete mourned sets, to determine complete LAST, all processes have to recover, as each recovered process can only determine if it is a member of LAST, and this information has to be compiled.

It can be shown [Ske85] that this algorithm is not merely a generalization of the algorithm for complete mourned sets. If the mourned sets are complete, even then, this algorithm may require more information than is needed by the earlier algorithm. This means that we cannot use this algorithm as a general algorithm which reduces to the earlier one if the mourned sets are complete. To use the earlier algorithm, we have to know a priori that the mourned sets are complete, which itself is a difficult exercise and has to be inferred from architectural and design constraints.

function $Membership\ Test(i,\ P,\ f_i) : Boolean$

local   j: process;

$\qquad$ $CAND_R$: set-of-processes;

$\qquad$ f: array 1 .. P of set-of-processes;

begin

$\qquad$ R := { i }

$\qquad$ $CAND_R$:= P - f_i

$\qquad$ **broadcast message** (i, f_i) **to** P

$\qquad$ **while** ($i \in CAND_R \wedge (P - closure(i,\ R)) \not\subseteq R$) **do begin**

$\qquad\qquad$ **receive**($j,\ f[j] >)$;

$\qquad\qquad$ $R := R \cup \{\,j\,\}$

$\qquad\qquad$ $CAND_R := CAND_R - f[j]$

$\qquad$ **end**

$\qquad$ **if** ($i \in CAND_R$ **then return** (true)

$\qquad\qquad\qquad\qquad$ **else return** (false)

end

Figure 8.13: Distributed algorithm for determining LAST with incomplete mourned sets

8.5   Summary

In this chapter, we considered the problem of making processes resilient to node failures. Under this topic, we considered the following areas: making remote procedure calls resilient, making processes communicating with asynchronous message passing resilient, and making a CSP program using synchronous communication resilient. Lastly, we discussed the issue of total failure and how to determine the last processes to fail.

Three different techniques were discussed for remote procedure calls. The first uses process pairs with the primary-site approach. In this approach, the state of the primary is periodically checkpointed on the backup. If the primary fails, the backup takes over as the primary. In replicated procedure calls, the remote procedure is replicated on multiple nodes. The set of replicas is called a troupe. The replication results in a many-to-many call from the callee troupe to the caller troupe. The discussed scheme ensures that as long as one member of the troupe is alive, the remote procedure is completed successfully, and all the caller members get the results. The last technique is a combination of the two approaches: it uses multiple concurrently active copies of the procedure, but the caller makes a call only to the primary, which then passes the necessary information to the backups.

For systems that use asynchronous message passing for communication, the approach taken by most schemes for making a process resilient is to roll back the failed process to a previously checkpointed state and use the logged messages to reach a valid system state. We first discussed the requirement of message recovery and the conditions that must be satisfied by recovered messages. It was shown that requiring all messages to be recovered in the same order as before the failure is stricter than necessary. Messages received before the last message was sent by the failed process need to be recovered in the same order, but for the messages received after the last message was sent during message recovery, only partial order needs to be preserved during recovery.

We then discussed some schemes to support process resiliency. The first approach we discussed was employed in a system called Aurogen. This approach uses process pairs with each process having a backup. The state of the process is periodically transmitted to the backup. When a process sends a message to another process, the message is atomically broadcast to three processes: the destination process, the backup of the sender, and the backup of the destination. Atomic broadcast ensures that the backup of a process receives the same message sequence as the process. It also ensures that the backup knows precisely which messages were actually transmitted by the process before failing. If a process fails, its backup starts executing from the last checkpoint. As it has all the messages received by the process before failing and in the order in which the process received them, it simply uses these messages to reach the state the process was in before failing. The messages sent by the process between the last checkpoint and failure are suppressed by the backup.

In the second approach, a centralized message exchange is used. All messages are sent to this exchange which then sends them to the destination process. The exchange also logs the messages. If a process fails and is restarted on another node, the message exchange replays all the lost messages in the order in which it has sent them earlier to the failed process. It also suppresses the duplicate messages that may be generated on rollback and reexecution.

The sender-based logging approach is designed to handle a single failure only, and if a process fails, all the processes that sent it messages are assumed to be alive. A process logs the messages it sends to other processes. The receiver process sends a receive sequence number (RSN) to the sender which represents the order in which the message was received relative to other messages from other processes. The sender processes also record the RSN with the logged messages. If a process fails, it restarts from a previously saved checkpoint, and broadcasts a request for retransmission. All sender nodes send the messages from their logs in the order of their RSNs. Since RSNs form a total order, on recovery, the logged messages will be received in the same order as they were received earlier. Those messages for which no RSNs were assigned due to failure are sent in the end and are recovered in any order in which the network delivers them.

In optimistic recovery, messages are logged by the receiver and dependencies caused by messages are tracked by sending dependency information with all messages. Logging of messages is asynchronous and the information about which messages have been logged is also transmitted with each message. On failure, if a process has in its log all such messages that could affect other messages it has sent, then it only needs to roll back. The messages received earlier but not logged are retransmitted by senders. If the messages that were lost because they were not logged include messages on which some messages sent to other processes depend, then other processes have to roll back. The dependence information is used to determine which process should roll back. This is the only scheme that we discussed in which processes other than the failed process may have to roll back to ensure proper recovery.

Finally, a distributed scheme was discussed that directly implements the conditions for proper message recovery. It uses message logging at the receiver to ensure the same order of recovered messages. Whenever a process sends a message to another process, it logs all the messages it received since the last message checkpoint. On recovery, the message checkpoints are used to recover the messages in the same order as before. Messages that are not logged are retransmitted by the senders. Hence, for these messages, only the partial order is preserved. The scheme can also handle multiple failures.

Then we discussed the issue of process resiliency in a system using synchronous message passing. We described a scheme that supports resiliency in CSP programs. In this, besides recovering the messages in the same order, due to non-determinism, it has to be ensured that during the reexecution, the backup executes the guards in the same order as they were executed before the failure. A numbering scheme is used to determine the order in which guards were executed before failure. Exception handling is employed to perform recovery and reconfigure the system after a failure has occurred, and a backup process replaces a process. The scheme can handle only a single process failure.

Finally, we discussed the issue of total failure. A total failure occurs when all the processes in a process group fail. Frequently in recovery from a total failure, the identity of the set of last processes to fail, LAST, is needed, since these processes have the latest information. Conditions for determining LAST were discussed, and two algorithms were given. The first works when the failure information of each process is complete. The second is to be used when the failure information may not be complete.

Problems

1. With a replicated remote procedure call, what types of failures can be handled? Can it be extended to mask Byzantine failures of processors?

2. In a 3-replicated system, if a top-level call has 2 further levels of nested calls, what is the minimum number of messages in a replicated remote procedure call?

3. What is the number of messages in the above example if a concurrency control protocol is also being used?

4. With asynchronous message passing, if the communication network is such that it guarantees delivery from A to B but does not guarantee the order of delivery of messages, what will be the condition for message recovery? In the example in Fig. 8.3, what orders are then acceptable?

5. What is the purpose of two sequence numbers (SSN and RSN) in sender-based message logging? Can one suffice?

6. How will optimistic message recovery work if sender-based logging is used instead of logging by the receiver?

7. Combine sender-based message logging with receiver-based logging to efficiently satisfy the message recovery conditions.

8. In the distributed scheme of Section 8.2.6, received messages are logged by a process before it sends a message. In order to bound the number of messages to be logged, one method is to log the received messages in case no message is sent in a time period T. How will this work and how can the queues saving the received messages be pruned using this?

9. In the scheme for CSP, static numbering of guards is used during recovery. How will this numbering work if the nesting of guards is allowed?

10. What is a total failure? What is the goal of recovery if total failure occurs?

11. Assume that failures occur far apart. That is, when a node fails, all others know about the failure before any other node fails. Devise a method to determine LAST for such a system.

12. Under what situations will a system have complete information for determining LAST?

13. Combine a data resiliency approach with a process resiliency method to design a system that can mask up to 2 node failures. What is the minimum number of nodes needed for this?

References

[B⁺89] A. Borg et al. "Fault Tolerance Under Unix." *ACM Transactions on Computer Systems*, 7(1):1–24, February 1989.

[Bar81] J. F. Bartlett. "A Nonstop Kernel." *7th ACM Symposium on Operating Systems*, pp. 22–29, 1981.

[BBG83] A. Borg, J. Baumback, and S. Galzer. "A Message System Supporting Fault Tolerance." *9th ACM Symposium on Operating Systems, 17:5*, pp. 90–99, 1983.

[Coo84] E. C. Cooper. "Replicated Procedure Call." *3rd ACM Conference on Principles of Distributed Computing*, pp. 44–55, 1984.

[Coo85] E. C. Cooper. "Replicated Distributed Programs." *10th ACM Symposium on Operating Systems*, pp. 63–78, 1985.

[Cri82] F. Cristian. "Exception Handling and Software Fault Tolerance." *IEEE Transactions on Computers*, C-31(6):531–540, June 1982.

[Hoa78] C. A. R. Hoare. "Communicating Sequential Processes." *Communications of the ACM*, 21(8):666–677, August 1978.

[Jal89] P. Jalote. "Fault Tolerant Processes." *Distributed Computing*, 3:187–195, 1989.

[Jal92] P. Jalote. "Dynamic Reconfiguration of CSP Programs for Fault Tolerance." *22nd International Symposium on Fault Tolerant Computing Systems*, pp. 50–56, Boston, 1992.

[JS91] P. Jalote, and R. Sriram. *Fault Tolerant Processes in a Network of Workstations.* Technical Report, IIT Kanpur, Department of Computer Science, 1991.

[JZ87] D. B. Johnson, and W. Zwaenepoel. "Sender-Based Message Logging." *17th International Symposium on Fault Tolerant Computing Systems,* pp. 14–19, 1987.

[JZ90] D. B. Johnson, and W. Zwaenepoel. "Recovery in Distributed Systems Using Optimistic Message Logging and Checkpointing." *Journal of Algorithms,* 11:462–491, 1990.

[Lam78] L. Lamport. "Time, Clocks, and Ordering of Events." *Communications of the ACM,* 21(7):558–565, July 1978.

[PP83] M. L. Powell, and D. L. Presotto. "Publishing: A Reliable Broadcast Communication Mechanism." *9th ACM Symposium on Operating Systems, Operating Sys. Rev: 17,* pp. 100–109, 1983.

[Sha85] S. Shatz. "Post Failure Reconfiguration of CSP Programs." *IEEE Transactions on Software Engineering,* 11(10):1193–1202, October 1985.

[Ske85] D. Skeen. "Determining the Last Process to Fail." *ACM Transactions on Computer Systems,* 3(1):15–30, February 1985.

[SW89] A. P. Sistla, and J. L. Welch. "Efficient Distributed Recovery Using Message Logging." *8th ACM Symposium on Principles of Distributed Computing,* August 1989.

[SY84] R. E. Strom, and S. Yemini. "Optimistic Recovery: An Asynchronous Approach to Fault Tolerance in Distributed Systems." *14th International Symposium of Fault Tolerant Computing Systems,* pp. 374–379, 1984.

[SY85] R. E. Strom, and S. Yemini. "Optimistic Recovery in Distributed Systems." *ACM Transactions on Computer Systems,* 3(3):204–226, August 1985.

[YJT88] K. S. Yap, P. Jalote, and S. K. Tripathi. "Fault Tolerant Remote Procedure Call." *8th International Conference on Distributed Computing Systems,* pp. 48–54, June 1988.

Chapter 9

Software Design Faults

So far, we have focused on masking the failure of nodes and the communication network in the system. We have seen how consistency or atomicity can be maintained and how resiliency can be supported in spite of failures. In this chapter, we consider the problem of making software fault-tolerant to faults in software. The current state of the art is such that the hardware is very reliable, and its reliability continues to improve with time. Software, on the other hand, is not so reliable, even though the role of software in computer systems is increasing. Clearly, making a system fault-tolerant to faults in software is a desirable goal.

The root cause of failure of hardware components like nodes and links is frequently some physical failure. Software, in contrast, has no physical properties; it is a totally conceptual entity. Hence, physical faults cannot exist in software. Software faults are always *design faults*. That is, a fault in the software is due to incorrect design or the presence of "bugs," which are usually caused by human errors (in contrast to physical failures, which are caused by natural laws). To build software that can handle faults in its components, we need techniques that can cope with design faults. We will call such software *fault tolerant software*.

It should be pointed out that fault tolerant software is different from *software fault tolerance*, which encompasses all techniques for fault tolerance supported in software, including the ones designed to handle failures of hardware components. In other words, fault tolerant software is a subarea of software fault tolerance. However, the two terms have been frequently used interchangeably in literature, are not standardized, and are typically used loosely.

We will first look at a special case of a distributed system: a uniprocess system. In this, we consider the case where there is a single process executing the software which has design faults. Later, we will consider the case of distributed systems with

355

multiple processes that are communicating with each other through message passing.

9.1   Approaches for Uniprocess Software

In this section, we consider the situation in which the software is executed by a single process. A program consists of various components, each of which is a module or a subprogram (which may have nested subprograms). Some of the components may be faulty, i.e., may have design faults in them. The goal of fault tolerant software is to ensure that the software system does not fail despite the presence of faulty components. In other words, the failure of some of the software components is masked and the failure of the software system is averted.

It is clear that replicating the same component will not help in coping with design faults. In hardware, component replication is used effectively because the design of the hardware is assumed to be correct, and the goal is to handle only failures that occur due to physical reasons. If, however, a component has a design fault, then all the replicas of the component will also have the same design fault, and hence the fault cannot be masked. Therefore, to cope with design faults, *design diversity* may be needed. That is, we need to have different components which have different designs in order to cope with design faults.

There are two main methods for organizing diverse designs to build fault tolerant software: *the recovery block approach* and *N-version programming*. We will describe each of them in this section, and then discuss some other techniques. But first, we will describe the framework of exception handling, which is general enough to allow both forward and backward error recovery for supporting fault tolerant software.

9.1.1   Exception Handling Framework

We have seen earlier in Chapter 1 that there are many different phases in supporting fault tolerance, and that redundancy is employed for most of these phases. If fault tolerance is being implemented in software, it is desirable to have language constructs or some structuring framework within which the different phases can be implemented and the redundancy organized. Exception handling is one such framework which provides language primitives to organize redundancy and perform activities to support fault tolerance. Exception-handling primitives for languages have been proposed [Goo75, LS79, LP80]. Here, we do not focus on the language issues relating to exception handling, but on the fault tolerance aspects of exception handling [Cri82, Cri84]. We consider a software system as a hierarchy of modules, each module implementing some specifications. This hierarchy can be represented as an acyclic graph, in which modules are represented by nodes, and an arrow from a node M to a node N means that M is a user of the module N, and successful completion of M depends on successful completion of N.

The response of each module can be partitioned into two categories: normal or abnormal. Normal responses are the ones the module produces if everything works correctly (including the modules below it which this module uses) and the abnormal responses signify that something is wrong. The abnormal responses from a module are referred to as *exceptions* and signify some exceptional condition in the module or the modules below it. The exception-handling framework provides mechanisms for signaling exceptions. It also provides mechanisms for handling exceptional conditions so that the exception can be masked at higher levels. By using the exception-handling primitives, software fault tolerance can be programmed. Note that exception handling provides a framework which supports the design of fault tolerant software, it is not a technique for fault tolerance. Fault tolerance has to be programmed using the primitives provided by exception handling. That is why this approach is also called *programmed exception handling*.

Consider the situation where a module (or underlying operating system or hardware) is performing a task on behalf of some other module and is unable to perform the task satisfactorily. In that case, it *signals* an exception to the caller module. Examples of this are *divide by zero*, *overflow*, etc. which are signaled by the hardware to the calling module. The caller module then gets an exception, which indicates to it that something out of the ordinary has occurred and something extra has to be done to cope with it.

In the exception handling framework, measures provided within the module or the program for dealing with the exceptions are called *exception handlers*. A handler for an exception is invoked if that exception is signaled. And this handler contains the extra actions that the programmer has programmed to cope with this exceptional situation. Note that the handler may contain a rollback to a previous state (backward recovery) or perform actions to correct the state by some other means (forward recovery). Hence, the exception handling framework can support both forward and backward error recovery.

Here we discuss the exception handling model as proposed by Cristian [Cri82]. A procedure P is considered to provide some service, called the *intended service*. This intended service can be specified by the *standard post condition* of P. Whether an execution of P satisfies the standard post condition depends on the input state in which P was executed. The set of all possible input states for P is called the *input domain* of P. The set of states in the input domain of the module P for which P provides the intended service are called the *standard domain*, *SD*, of P. If the execution of P starts outside SD, then the standard post condition cannot be ensured.

Hence, an *exception occurs* when the module P is invoked in a state that is outside its standard domain. Consequently, the set of states in the input domain that do not fall in the SD are called the *exception domain, ED*.

The designer of P may anticipate the possibility of P being invoked in its exceptional domain, and may want to take measures to handle these situations. However, a designer may not be able to anticipate all possible exceptions. Based on this, the exceptional domain itself can be partitioned further, based on the nature of the exceptions. The *anticipated exceptional domain, AED*, is the subset of ED that represents exceptional situations for which exception handling has been used. That is, the designer anticipated these exceptions and provided the necessary actions to be taken if the exception occurs. The remainder part of the ED is called the *unanticipated exceptional domain, UED*. If the procedure P is started in UED, its behavior is unpredictable. A *failure* of a module occurs if it is invoked outside its standard domain or its anticipated exceptional domain, that is, P is invoked from its UED. The different parts of the input domain of a module are shown in Fig. 9.1.

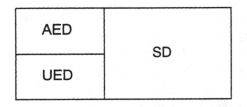

Figure 9.1: Standard and exceptional domains

An *exception mechanism* is a set of language constructs which allow a software designer to express that the standard continuation of a module is to be replaced by an exceptional continuation when an exception is detected. A procedure P may signal an exception E to its caller by the *signal E* primitive. This exception will be signaled to the invoker of P at the point of invocation. The designer can specify an exceptional continuation by specifying a *handler H* for the exception in the following manner:

$$P[\textbf{excep } E \rightarrow H].$$

Hence, an exception is detected by a module when it gets a signal from a lower-level module. At the lowest level, an exception may be signaled by the hardware operation, which may then be propagated. In addition to exceptions that are detected by the hardware, a module itself may detect an exception by using some assertion on the state of the system. In this case, it specifies the handler as follows:

$$[B \rightarrow H].$$

Here, if the condition *B* is true, it signifies that an exceptional situation has occurred, and the handler *H* is executed.

When an exception is detected, it signifies that the system state is erroneous. Hence, the goal of the handler is to perform error recovery. The highest possible goal of a handler *H* is to mask the exception at higher levels. That is, provide recovery so that the occurrence of the exception is masked, and the procedure satisfies the standard post condition. However, in many situations, the handler may not be able to mask the exception entirely, and has to signal an exception to its invoker (who may then try to mask the exception). In such situations, for a procedure *P* which can signal an exception *E*, an *exceptional post condition* is specified. The goal of the exception handler for *E* in *P* is to perform recovery actions so that this exceptional post condition is satisfied before it signals exception *E*. Since the handler is designed by the designer, it may use any form of recovery. Hence, both forward and backward error-recovery techniques may be employed within a handler.

Since handlers are provided for anticipated exceptions only, to avoid a module failure caused by the module being invoked from its UED, it is desirable to provide *default handlers*. A default handler is provided by the system, and is invoked whenever there is no exception handler provided by the designer. Design faults often lead to unspecified exceptions. In order to provide a proper framework for supporting fault tolerant software, default exception handling is important. A default handler has to be fairly general, since the nature of the exception is not known. An approach based on backward recovery is best suited for default handlers.

9.1.2 Recovery Block Approach

A recovery block was proposed by Horning et al. [H+74] to provide an approach for organizing diverse designs in order to support fault tolerant software. Though it is designed to handle design faults in software components, it can also cope with erroneous situations in software which are caused by hardware faults. The goal of a recovery block is to mask the failure of some module. Our discussion here is based on the description of recovery blocks given in [Ran75].

A module in software is written to implement some specifications (which approximates an authoritative reference manual, as discussed in Chapter 1). We call this module the *primary module*. It is assumed that the primary module may have some design faults. If the design fault in the module causes the failure of the module, it implies that the state of the module is erroneous. Error detection in a recovery block is done by an *acceptance test*. An acceptance test is an assertion on the state of the module. If the assertion fails, it signifies the presence of an error in the state. Otherwise, the module state is assumed to be error-free. As discussed in

Chapter 1, an acceptance check is not an ideal check, but only an approximation.

If an error is detected by the acceptance test, it is assumed that the module has a design fault and the failure of the module produced the error. For recovery, the recovery block approach employs backward recovery. Before executing the primary, a *recovery point* is established, which saves the state of the process at that point. If an error is detected by the acceptance test, the process is rolled back to the recovery point. By this backward recovery, all the effects of the primary module are "undone," and the system is in a state where it appears as if the primary module were never executed. If the primary module was the cause of the error, this rollback will ensure that the system reaches an error-free state.

For continued service, the recovery block employs an *alternate module*. This alternate module is another implementation of the specifications. That is, it performs the same task as the primary module, but has a different design than the primary module. In case the primary module fails, this alternate module is utilized to perform the required task, namely to implement the given specifications. It is important to realize that the alternate module must have an independent design, so that when the primary fails, the alternate does not fail also.

This method of checking the state after executing the module by an acceptance test and then rolling back and executing an alternate module is repeated. In other words, the recovery block may have multiple alternate modules, which are tried in succession. If all modules fail, then an *error* is signaled, implying that the user of the modules has been informed that the state of the module is in error. This approach of the recovery block can be supported by a language construct of the type shown in Fig. 9.2.

ensure   < *acceptance test* >
by   < *primary module* >
else by   < *alternate module* 1 >
else by   < *alternate module* 2 >

　　　　　．

　　　　　．

　　　　　．

else by   < *alternate module n* >
else error

Figure 9.2: The recovery block construct

The *ensure* clause specifies the acceptance test, the *by* clause specifies the primary module, and the *else by* clauses specify the different alternate modules to be used. An alternate module i is executed only if the primary module and all the alternate modules before i have failed (i.e., the acceptance test has failed for all of them). If all the alternates have been tried, and still the acceptance test is not satisfied, then an error is signaled. It is clear that the specifications of the module will be implemented, if for the given inputs any one of the modules (the primary or the n alternate modules) implement the specifications correctly.

One way to organize the different modules is to have the primary module as the most desirable, with the alternates being less so. For example, the primary module may be the "fastest" way to implement the specifications; but the increased speed brings with it increased complexity and the possibility of design faults. The alternate modules can be less efficient, but simpler, implementations of the specifications. This will ensure that most of the time, the best performance module will execute.

Recovery blocks can be nested. In a nested recovery block, the inner recovery block will occur in one of the modules (primary or alternate) of the outer recovery block. The signaling of an error by the inner block signifies that this recovery block has failed, and the recovery should be tried in the enclosing recovery block. The failure of the inner block means that the module in which this block occurs has failed and is unable to satisfy its specifications, hence the next alternate (in the enclosing block) should be tried. An example of nested recovery blocks is shown in Fig. 9.3.

As we can see in Fig. 9.3, for nesting, the primary or the secondary in a recovery block is treated as an independent module, which can contain a recovery block of its own. In the example shown in Fig. 9.3, the primary module of the enclosing recovery block (with acceptance test $AT1$) contains another recovery block with acceptance test $AT2$ and with p alternate modules. Though having a nested recovery block within the primary makes more sense, there is no such restriction and an alternate module can also have recovery blocks, regardless of whether the primary module has any nested recovery blocks or not.

Through nested recovery blocks, the situation where the acceptance test of a recovery block fails because of a propagated error is also handled. In a recovery block, damage confinement is assumed to be limited to the state affected by the modules in the block. In other words, rollback to the recovery point assumes that the state in the recovery point is error-free. If this assumption is not true, then the acceptance test of a recovery block may fail, not because the primary and secondary modules are faulty, but because of propagated errors. This situation implies that the error started at some time before the recovery point. Clearly, in such a situation, a rollback to the recovery point of the inner block will not suffice, as this error is due to the failure of activities outside this block. Nested blocks allow recovery from such situations by allowing a rollback to occur in the outer block.

ensure $AT1$
by

       begin   (* primary module *)

       ...

       ...

       ensure $AT2$

           by M_1
           else by M_2
           else by M_3

              :

else by M_p
else error

       ...

end   (* of primary *)
else by   *alternate module* 1
else by   *alternate module* 2

   .

   .

else by   *alternate module n*
else error

Figure 9.3: Nesting of recovery blocks

The recovery block approach is a method of structuring redundancy for supporting fault tolerant software. A few implementations of the recovery block have been described in literature [AK76, Shr78, LGH80, PJ91]. As we can see, it can easily be supported as a language construct, though some support from the underlying operating system is needed. An implementation of the recovery block scheme requires support for backward recovery, which requires support from the operating system to access the state of the process. It may also require a *recovery cache* to support efficient rollback. The flow of control between modules, and the execution of the acceptance test, can easily be supported by the compiler itself.

The recovery block approach can also be supported easily within the exception handling framework described earlier. As mentioned above, the input domain of each program can be partitioned in a standard domain, an anticipated exception domain, and an unanticipated exception domain (UED). For a standard domain, the program works correctly, and for an anticipated exception domain, the program has exception handlers to take care of the situation. If the program starts executing from the UED, then it will fail. Such an invocation of a program is called a *failure* occurrence [Cri82]. Any behavior is possible in a failure occurrence. As mentioned above, default exception handling can be used to program fault tolerance for such situations.

The default exception handler has a difficult task. The exception handler is invoked when the exception has not been identified. And it is supposed to perform recovery and then mask the failure, if possible, without knowing the nature of the problem. The recovery block scheme has these properties and can be used for default exception handling. For simplicity, we assume that there are only two modules in the recovery block M_0, the primary module, and M_1, the alternate module. The acceptance test is AT. The recovery block can be programmed as follows [Cri82]:

$$\text{RB} \equiv M'_0 [\rightarrow \textbf{reset}; M'_1 [\rightarrow \textbf{reset}; \textbf{signal} \textit{failure}]]$$

where,

$$M'_i \equiv \textbf{begin } M_i; [\neg AT \rightarrow \textbf{signal} \textit{failure}] \textbf{ end}, i = 0, 1.$$

This implementation assumes that there is a *reset* command which restores the last recovery point of the program. If no name (or Boolean condition) is given before $\rightarrow$, it is assumed to be a default handler. As we can see, in this implementation, the failure exception is detected using the acceptance test assertion AT, and nested default exception handlers are employed to support the use of the alternate module as the default exception handler.

Though conceptually straightforward, and not too hard to implement either, recovery blocks have some difficulties in their being used as a means for developing fault tolerant software. The main drawback of this approach which limits its applicability is its reliance on acceptance tests for detecting errors and initiating recovery. Acceptance tests are assertions on the state of the module, which, if they fail, signify that the state is erroneous. Writing such assertions is a difficult problem. There are no general rules to design acceptance tests, and they have to be developed on a case-by-case basis. Also, since an acceptance test is not a complete error-detection test, its "coverage" may be limited and may allow errors to slip by.

However, the fact that an acceptance test is not a complete test can also be used to support a *gracefully degrading system*, in which the different modules provide different levels of service (with service of the primary being the most desirable), each satisfying some minimal service, which is ensured by the acceptance test [AL81]. There are also situations where multiple correct outputs are possible (e.g., finding a root of an equation, or a topological sorting of a graph). Acceptance tests can also be used for such applications where multiple correct outputs are possible.

One advantage of the recovery block scheme is that it naturally lends itself to supporting fault tolerance for only some defined critical modules, rather than for the entire system. In other words, it is likely that replicating an entire system may be prohibitively expensive and it may be desirable to have fault tolerance for some key modules. This can easily be supported using the recovery block approach.

The performance of the recovery block, in cases where the primary module satisfies the acceptance test, is the same as that of the primary module, plus the overhead of setting the recovery point and executing the acceptance test. The performance degrades only in cases where the primary module fails. However, if some modules fail, then the execution time of the recovery block is the total of the execution times of all the versions that have to be executed before the acceptance test is satisfied. That is, though the expected execution time of the recovery block may be closer to that of the primary module (assuming that the primary succeeds in most cases), the worst-case execution time is the sum of the execution times of all the modules. Hence, the variation in the execution time of a recovery block is large, which might make it unsuitable for real-time applications.

9.1.3   N-Version Programming

The use of multiple computations is a fundamental method for supporting fault tolerance. Multiple computations are implemented by N-fold replication, with $N \geq 2$. Such systems achieve fault tolerance by the execution of multiple computations, each programmed to deliver output from the same initial conditions and inputs. An approach using multiple computations requires the consistency of initial conditions and inputs for all N computations, and a reliable decision algorithm that determines a single decision result from the multiple results that are produced [Avi85]. A method to handle design faults is to have N computations with different designs.

N-version programming is one such approach, which was proposed by Chen and Avizienis [CA78]. A more recent article describing the approach was written by Avizienis [Avi85]. This approach is modeled after the NMR approach which has been successful in hardware. As mentioned in Chapter 1, in the NMR approach, the module is replicated N times, and voting is used to determine the majority, which is taken to be the correct result.

Since NMR is designed to cope with the physical failures of components, the same component is replicated N times. In N-version programming, since the goal is to mask software design faults, the N versions have different designs. That is, the different versions of a module in N-version programming are independently designed to satisfy the common specifications of the module. The same input is given to the different versions, which compute their respective outputs. The results of the different versions are given to a *voter* which determines the *majority* and gives it as the output of the module. With this arrangement, the simultaneous failure of up to $N/2 - 1$ versions can be tolerated, since the remaining versions that are working correctly form a majority. The arrangement for three versions of P_1, P_2, and P_3 is shown in Fig. 9.4.

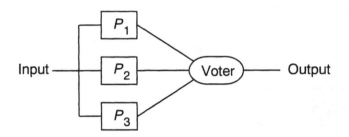

Figure 9.4: N-version programming approach

In contrast to acceptance tests, the voting check used in N-version programming seems to be a more general method of error detection, whose coverage can be kept as large as desired. However, the voting check in software is not as general as the voting check of NMR systems in hardware, on which the N-version programming is modeled. In NMR, bit-wise voting can be done regardless of the nature of the module. However, in software, problems occur when the output to be voted upon is a floating number. Then "inexact voting" has to be employed, and the decision algorithm may need to determine the final value from a set of similar, but not identical, outputs. Similar results are those that are within some range of each other. In such situations, the "tolerance" of the decision algorithm has to be specified, and the method of determining the final value also has to be specified (it might be the mean or median of the similar values, if they form a majority). This tolerance is likely to be application-specific, which will make the voter somewhat application-dependent.

Another limitation of voting is that it cannot be employed in situations where multiple correct outputs are possible. There are frequently situations in computation where multiple solutions are possible, and all of them are correct and acceptable. An example of this is finding a root of an nth order equation. This problem has n different correct answers, and in fact, the different known algorithms for finding the root frequently converge to different roots. Even the same root-finding algorithm may reach a different root, if it starts its search from a different point. Clearly, in such situations, the lack of majority does not indicate the presence of errors. Hence, voting cannot be used.

There is another fundamental problem with voting called the *consistent comparison problem* that limits the generality of the voting approach for error detection [BKL89]. It is known that the numerical outputs of programs may differ slightly due to the finite precision arithmetic that is employed in digital computers. On the face of it, it appears that this can lead to the problem of similar results, as discussed above. However, it can also lead to the same phenomenon as multiple correct outputs, for which voting is not suitable.

We illustrate this phenomenon by the use of an example [BKL89]. Consider a system employing three versions. Suppose that at some point within the computation, an intermediate result is compared with an application which is dependent on constant C_1. As a result of finite precision arithmetic, it is possible that the three versions may have slightly different values of the intermediate result. As there is a comparison with C_1 within the program, it is expected that the intermediate value may be less than or more than C_1, and in the two cases, since different paths are executed, different final results may be output. However, both these outputs are correct. So, if there are three versions and the intermediate result is close to C_1, it is possible that the actual value of two of them may be less than C_1, and the actual value of the third may be more than C_1. In this case, two versions will take one path and the third will take another path. Both these paths will result in different, but correct, outputs.

Similarly, at a later stage, there may be a comparison of another intermediate value with another constant C_2. If the two versions which took the same path compute the value to be very close to C_2, it is possible that in one case the comparison may succeed and in the other it may fail. In this case, the two versions will take different paths. Hence, we now have a situation where all three versions take different paths and reach three different results. And all these three results are correct.

Thus, due to finite precision arithmetic, the different versions may arrive at different final states because they take different paths during their computation. A solution to the consistent comparison problem requires that all correct versions make the same decisions when performing comparisons. This is not possible as long as there is finite precision arithmetic, which results in similar, but not exact, values. It has been proved that there is no general solution to the consistent comparison problem [BKL89]. It has also been shown that techniques such as approximate comparison, random selection, using means, etc. do not solve this problem.

The implication of the consistent comparison problem is that unlike the situation in hardware, voting cannot be used as a general method for detecting errors when design diversity is being used. Voting has to be used carefully and the effect of application on voting has to be understood properly.

The implementation support for N-version programming is likely to be more complex than that of the recovery block approach. It is frequently implemented with the help of a *driver program*. The driver program is responsible for invoking different versions and giving them the same inputs. It also waits for all the versions to complete their executions, and then compares their results to determine the final result. Multiple processes are needed for the N-version programming approach, which requires more resources. If the *N*-versions are executed as concurrent processes, starting the different processes and waiting for their completion requires synchronization between the driver program and the different versions. Since the driver has to wait for all the versions to finish, with N-version programming we will *always* get a performance that is the same as that of the worst module. The advantage of this property is that the execution time of an N-version programming system is quite predictable. N-version programming also does not naturally lend itself to supporting fault tolerance only for some specified critical modules of a software system.

The two approaches described above — the recovery block approach and N-version programming — both employ design diversity in an effort to increase the reliability of software. Models for estimating the reliability of software employing these techniques are given in [AKL88, GAA80, SGM87]. It should be clear that for these approaches to be most effective, it is important that the failures of the different versions be independent and not co-related. The best case for both these approaches is that the different versions fail on different inputs. For this, it is necessary that the designs of the different modules be totally independent.

If the different versions have to be programmed, then this independence requirement may necessitate the use of "separate programmer teams." The reason for this is that a programmer (or a team) having programmed one version, is unlikely to think very differently while designing the second version, and is likely to make the same mistakes, particularly if the mistakes occur due to a misunderstanding of the specifications. Having different programmer teams, working totally independently of each other, may lead to modules failing independently. However, there are many subtle reasons that may bring in dependence, despite the use of separate programmer teams. Some of the causes that can potentially cause dependence are: having programmers with similar educational backgrounds, using the same type of programming language, using common specifications, etc.

Recently, some experiments have been conducted to test the independence hypothesis [KL86]. In the experiments, many programmers from different universities were used to develop different versions. The experiments found that many times, the different versions failed on the same inputs, leading to the conclusion that the failures of the different versions might have been co-related. Various reasons have been proposed for this co-relation [KL86]. These experiments indicate that the independence assumption of design diversity approaches may not hold.

If the failures of the different versions are co-related, then the design diversity approaches will not offer as great an increase in reliability as is anticipated. The actual benefit to reliability will depend on how closely the failures of versions are co-related. Some models which model the effect of co-related failures are given in [EL85, NG90].

Even if the versions are independent, the major drawback in design diversity is the cost. In software, it is known that the cost of development is the main cost. Hence, replicating the design effort multiple times by different programmers certainly drives up the cost. Furthermore, project management, configuration control, versioning, and installation of changes are some of the software engineering issues that are very hard to handle if multiple versions are being developed and maintained.

9.1.4   Other Approaches

The recovery block scheme and N-version programming are the two main approaches for masking software design faults. Though both have serious limitations, no general technique has evolved so far that is truly practical and feasible. The main reason behind this fact seems to be the nature of design faults. Most other fault tolerant measures mask the failure of components by some sort of replication of the component itself, and assume that the component has no design faults. Even in hardware, which can have design faults, most techniques do not address the issue of masking design faults, but focus on other failures, assuming the design to be correct. It is a safe conjecture that the fault-tolerant software problem is hard because masking design faults is hard. Though the recovery block approach and N-version programming are the best-known general approaches for fault tolerant software, some other techniques have evolved over time that may suit some special situations. Here we briefly describe some of these approaches.

Deadline Mechanism

The *deadline mechanism* is based on recovery blocks and attempts to avoid timing failures in real-time systems [CHB79]. In a real-time system, frequently there are deadlines for some tasks which are difficult to meet. A *response period* is the maximum allowable period within which the desired service is performed. With the response period, each time a request for a service occurs, we can determine the *deadline* for the service to complete. A *timing failure* occurs when the real-time system violates one of the timing constraints in its specifications. That is, it is unable to perform some service before its deadline. A real-time system that always responds to requests before the deadline is considered as *timely*. A fault tolerant system for real-time systems has to ensure that the system is timely. The deadline mechanism attempts to ensure that no timing failure occurs in a system by using redundancy and error recovery.

Two algorithms — primary and an alternate — are provided for each service that has to be made fault tolerant. These are organized in a recovery-block-type structure so that the desired service is performed within the deadline either by the primary or the alternate. The upper bound on the execution time for the alternate algorithm is assumed to be known. This time depends not only on the instructions in the algorithm, but also on the execution speed of the processor, and the scheduling policies. For a given system, the deadline mechanism requires that this time be known for the alternate algorithm. However, no such assumption is made about the primary algorithm. So, the primary algorithm is in some sense desirable, but has unpredictable execution time, and may even have errors. The service provided by the alternate algorithm is not as desirable (it may be a degraded service), but is guaranteed to execute within some known time. The goal is to organize the primary and alternates such that, as much as possible, the service is provided by the primary, but not at the cost of having a timing failure. Timing failure has to be avoided, even if that means getting the service from the alternate module. The overall structure can be represented as follows:

> **service** service-name
> **within** response-period
> **by**
> > Primary algorithm
> **else by**
> > Alternate algorithm
> **end**

The *within* clause contains the response period, determined by the specifications of the system, within which the service has to be provided, either by the primary module or the alternate module.

Slack time is defined in this system as the difference between the response period and the maximum execution time of the alternate module. As both these are known, the slack time can be computed. Slack time is what is available to the primary algorithm to provide the service. The deadline mechanism works as follows. When a service is requested, first the primary module is scheduled for execution. If the primary module completes successfully within the slack time, the service has been successfully performed. If the primary is unable to perform the service within the slack time, it is aborted, and the alternate algorithm is scheduled. As the primary may have changed the state, and the state change may not yet be complete, before scheduling the alternate module, backward error recovery may be performed in the same manner as in the recovery block construct.

This scheduling approach is optimistic, as it expects that the primary module, which is possibly faulty, will perform the service most of the time. Only if the primary fails is the alternate attempted. For this scheme to be of any practical use, the primary algorithm should be such that in most of the cases, it can perform the service within the slack time. That is, the expected execution time of the primary is less than the slack time. If this is not the case, then the primary will never be able to complete (or complete very rarely) and the system will mostly get the less desirable service from the alternate. So, though the maximum execution time of the primary need not be known for implementing the mechanism, it is desirable that the expected execution time be known. Other scheduling approaches are also possible and are described in [CHB79].

Distributed Recovery Block

A software system can reach an erroneous state due to design faults in the software, but can also reach an erroneous state due to faults in the hardware. For example, if there is some transient fault during which the hardware does not behave according to its specifications, an erroneous state may result. The failure of an acceptance test in a recovery block does not indicate the cause of the error; it assumes that it is due to some fault in the module that was being executed.

One way to determine if the error was due to a transient hardware problem or a software design fault is to retry the same task a few times. If the output is erroneous every time, then there is a good probability that the task itself is faulty. If no error is detected after one of these retries, then it could be concluded that there was some transient hardware failure in the earlier executions. Though this approach can distinguish between software design faults and transient hardware failures, it is expensive to implement. It is desirable that there be an efficient unified treatment of both types of faults.

Here we describe the *distributed recovery blocks (DRB)* approach for providing a uniform treatment [Kim84, Kim88a]. It combines the recovery block approach with distributed processing to achieve the desired result. To explain the ideas of the scheme, we assume that the recovery block, which will be executed in a distributed manner, has only two modules: a primary and an alternate.

One approach to implement DRB is as follows [Kim83, Kim84]. The primary module is executed on the primary node and the alternate module is executed on a backup node which is different from the primary node. The logic of the acceptance test is duplicated on both the primary and backup nodes. Both nodes receive the input data simultaneously from the previous computation, and compute their modules concurrently. The backup node also turns on a *watchdog timer*. The result of each module is checked on that node which itself uses the acceptance test. If the primary node fails, it sends a notice to the backup node. The backup node then forwards its own output as the final output, assuming that its results pass the acceptance test. If the primary produces results which pass the acceptance test, it forwards them as the result, and sends a notice to the backup node. The backup node does not forward its results. If the watchdog of the backup node times out, it also is taken to represent the failure of the primary module (or the failure of the primary node), and the backup node acts accordingly.

There are other ways to organize the distributed execution of the primary module, alternate module, and the acceptance test. For example, the acceptance-test checking can be done at one node only, or both nodes can have complete replication. Some such methods are described in [Kim84].

Data Diversity

Both the recovery block approach and N-version programming employ design diversity to tolerate residual design faults in the software. The basic idea is that since design faults are to be tolerated, design diversity should be employed. However, if fault intolerance techniques are properly employed for developing software (in Chapter 1 we discussed that fault avoidance and tolerance are complementary), then software is likely to fail infrequently. The faults that remain, the residual design faults, are the cause of unreliability of the software. Most of these residual faults typically cause software failures at some "special inputs," and if the inputs are changed slightly, the same software may not display erroneous behavior. Hence, *data diversity*, in which data is modified, may offer an alternative to design diversity, which is very expensive. Here we describe one such approach [AK87].

In data diversity, the same software is executed for a set of related data points. A decision algorithm then determines the final system output, depending on the output obtained from executing the software with these different data points. For this approach to work, it is essential that data re-expression be possible.

Data re-expression is the generation of logically equivalent data sets. A data re-expression algorithm reassigns values to variables, based on the system specifications. A simple data re-expression scheme for a real variable might be to alter the value of the variable by a small amount. Data re-expression is not limited to changing values of real numbers and values obtained from sensors. Any mapping of a program's data that preserves the information content of those data items is a valid re-expression. For example, the coordinates of an airplane can be translated easily by changing the coordinate system to a new origin.

In general, data re-expression will depend on the application, and will require careful analysis of the specifications to determine valid transformations. Clearly, it is not feasible in all situations. But there are many applications such as control systems dealing with sensor values, or software employing data in statistical computation, or software dealing primarily with real numbers, where re-expression is clearly feasible.

If data re-expression is possible, data diversity can be employed to provide tolerance against residual design faults. Two structures were proposed for employing data diversity [AK87]. The first is the *retry block*, which is modeled after the recovery block. The semantics of the retry block are the same as the recovery block, except that rather than using multiple alternates, the retry block uses only one algorithm. Furthermore, if the acceptance test fails, after restoring the recovery point, the algorithm is reexecuted only after data re-expression. The system repeats this process until it violates some predetermined deadline. (Some maximum limit on the number of executions of the algorithm is needed to determine the equivalent of the "else error" condition in recovery blocks.) The retry block is shown in Fig. 9.5.

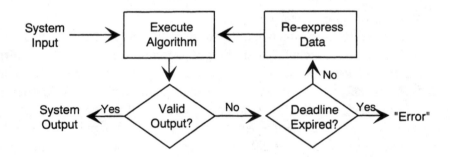

Figure 9.5: Retry block

An *N-copy* system is another structure that is modeled after the N-version programming approach and employs data diversity. In an N-copy system, N different copies of the program are executed in parallel. However, unlike N-version programming, where the different versions are given the same inputs, in an N-copy system, the different copies are given different data, each a re-expression of the original inputs. Voting is done on the outputs of the different copies, as in N-version programming. However, the voting in an N-copy system is more complicated than in N-version programming, since the outputs may differ. An N-copy system is shown in Fig. 9.6.

The main advantage of the data diversity approach is its cost; only one version of the program needs to be written, whereas multiple versions are needed for design diversity. However, the use of data diversity requires a careful understanding of

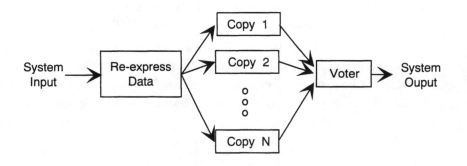

Figure 9.6: N-copy programming

the data dependencies, such that proper data re-expression methods can be devised. Also, the approach is not as general as the design diversity approach; it cannot be used in all circumstances. There are application domains where the possibility of data re-expression does not exist. Some experimental results have been reported that indicate that data diversity may be a feasible alternative to design diversity in some application domains [AK87].

Certification Trails

Another proposed approach is to use *certification trails* [SM90]. This approach has three phases. In the first phase, the primary module executes. During the execution it leaves behind a certification trail, which is a trail of data at intermediate points in the computation. During the second phase, a secondary module is executed. However, the secondary has access to the certification trail left behind by the primary. Because of the access of this trail, the secondary can potentially be made more efficient. In the final phase, the results of the primary and secondary are compared. If they agree, the results are accepted; otherwise an error is indicated.

This method is really like 2-version programming, and is somewhat like the duplex systems in hardware in its capability. It can only detect the presence of errors, but cannot mask the failure. The only advantage over a 2-version possibly is that the secondary module may be less complex. However, the design of certification trails, and designing a secondary that will use those certification trails, can also add more complexity.

9.2   Backward Recovery in Concurrent Systems

In this section, we discuss the use of backward recovery in distributed systems for handling software design faults. It should be pointed out that when considering design faults, there is no conceptual difference between distributed systems and concurrent systems. That is, a system with concurrent processes which may have only one node, is conceptually no different than a system with multiple nodes, since node failure is not an issue.

In a concurrent system, sometimes the software failure is "transient," unlike in uniprocess systems. That is, the failure caused by the software fault occurs only in some situations, but if the software is reexecuted, it does not cause the failure. In other situations, this is not the case, and a fault in the software causes a "permanent" failure. This is called the Bohrbug/Heisenbug hypothesis [Gra85], where the "Heisenbug" is the bug in software that causes transient failures, and "Bohrbug" is the software bug that causes permanent failure.

The concept of Heisenbugs is somewhat counter-intuitive. Software is believed to have only design faults, and a design fault does not "go away" with time. The reason behind this phenomenon of transient software failures is as follows. Most commercial software typically undergoes a series of phases designed to minimize the presence of design faults. Typically, many levels of testing are performed to detect and eliminate bugs before finally using the software commercially. These ensure that the software has a high reliability and that it "usually works." Software typically fails for some special inputs or special environmental conditions, which were not properly handled in the programs. If the input or the environment changes slightly, the software that failed may not fail again.

In a uniprocess software system, this observation can be exploited by explicitly changing the data, as is done in the data diversity approach. In a distributed system, due to concurrency in the system, even if a process does not change its input data, the environment, which frequently forms part of the input for a process, gets changed by the other concurrent events in the system. Hence, if a process with a software fault is reset to some previous consistent state and reexecuted, it may not fail, if it had failed in the first execution. This is a simple method of providing fault tolerance against design faults in a concurrent system. Only error detection capabilities are required.

The above discussion focuses on Heisenbugs. The approach of rolling back a process and restarting will not work for a Bohrbug. For such situations, design diversity may be needed. The key issue, then, for supporting a backward-recovery-based scheme is how to extend the recovery block concept in a system of communicating processes.

9.2.1 Domino Effect, Conversations, and FT-Actions

Rollback is employed in recovery blocks for error recovery. In a communicating system, suppose that the acceptance test of a process rolls back to a previous state. Due to communications between processes, this rollback may require other processes to roll back, such that a consistent system state is obtained. For example, if a process *P* rolls back, and this rollback "undoes" some commands sending messages to a process *Q*, then *Q* must also roll back to a state before the corresponding receives for these messages. This forced rollback may cause uncontrolled rollback, called the *domino effect*. We have discussed the domino effect in more detail earlier in Chapter 5.

Proposed extensions of the recovery block scheme to an environment involving communicating concurrent processes must solve the problem that any exchange of information may propagate an error from one process to another. The reason for the domino effect is that the setting of recovery points in different processes is not coordinated with communication commands. A language construct called a *conversation* [Ran75] has been proposed as an extension to a recovery block scheme to provide a static, backward error-recovery scheme for concurrent processes, thereby preventing the domino effect.

Each process that joins a conversation has a recovery point, an acceptance test, and alternate algorithms. While a process is in a conversation, it may only communicate with other processes in the same conversation. If *any* process fails an acceptance test or otherwise detects an exception, every process in the conversation performs a rollback to its recovery point, established on entry to the conversation, and uses an alternate algorithm. This restriction on communication limits the propagation of errors and eliminates the possibility of the domino effect. With conversations, the recovery line is the collection of recovery points of the processes taking part in the process. Recovery points of different processes have to be established in a coordinated manner. Fig. 9.7 shows the concept of conversations.

This concept of conversations implies that the set of processes taking part in the conversation are fixed. If in one try, the conversation does not succeed (that is, one of the acceptance tests detects an error), it is assumed that the same set of processes will make another attempt, and finally reach the same acceptance tests. This is somewhat restrictive in concurrent systems, where if a group of processes in a conversation fails in an attempt, a different group of processes may attempt an alternate strategy for achieving the desired goal, and then check for success using different acceptance tests.

The concept of *dialog* has been proposed as a generalization of the conversation concept to take care of this restriction [GK85]. In a dialog, processes establish their

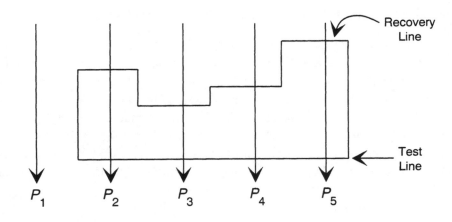

Figure 9.7: Conversations in concurrent systems

independent recovery points, and communicate only with processes taking part in the dialog. A dialog succeeds if the acceptance test of all participating processes succeeds. In this case, each process discards its recovery point and proceeds. A dialog fails if any of the acceptance tests fail. In this case, the processes restore their recovery points and then proceed. Nothing is said about what should happen after success or failure; in both cases the dialog is complete. In particular, there is no obligation for the process to enter into another dialog with the same set of processes. A language construct called *colloqy* has been proposed which is a collection of dialogs [GK85]. Each dialog determines its constituent processes dynamically. If a dialog fails, processes are allowed to get into another dialog, the constituent processes of which may be different from the earlier dialogs.

Though a dialog is more general than a conversation, we will limit our attention to the conversation construct, as it is somewhat easier to handle. Conversations are a form of atomic actions, which have been found to be useful in supporting recovery and fault tolerance. Before we discuss the details of recovery schemes using conversations, let us discuss the role of atomic actions in fault tolerance in a system with communicating processes.

Most of the techniques for structuring systems deal with the organization and subdivision of the static (or spatial) structure of the system. However, the pattern of interaction between the components of a system is also of interest, particularly for providing fault tolerance. Interactions between components reflect the dynamic (or temporal) structure of the system. The concept of atomic actions can be used to structure the temporal activity of the system.

An atomic action is an activity, possibly consisting of many steps performed by many different processors, that appears primitive and indivisible to any activity outside the atomic action. To other activities, an atomic action is like a primitive operation which transforms the state of the system without having any intermediate states. An operation that is executed as an atomic action is often said to have the following properties with respect to other operations: non-interference, non-overlapping, and strict sequencing.

Atomic actions may be *planned atomic actions*, which means that the atomic actions were planned during the design of the system and are supported by some run-time mechanism. This is in contrast to *dynamically identified atomic actions*, in which the history of execution is used to determine which activities occurred atomically [BR81]. For programmed fault tolerance, dynamically identified atomic actions are of limited use. We will limit our attention to planned atomic actions.

There are two different views of planned atomic actions. We refer to these as *recoverable atomic actions* and *basic atomic actions* [JC85]. Recoverable atomic actions uphold the "all-or-nothing" view, which requires that either all the objects modified by the action change to their final state, or all of the objects remain in their initial state. Recoverable atomic actions specify that both *indivisibility* and *recoverability* are fundamental requirements for atomicity. This view of atomic actions is particularly useful in database contexts. In our earlier discussion on atomic actions in Chapter 6, this is the model that we used.

However, the model of recoverable atomic actions is not suitable for fault tolerant software. It imposes backward error recovery, which results in inflexibility in cases where different recovery techniques, for example, techniques based on exception handling, may be desired. In basic atomic actions [AL81, Lom77], indivisibility is the only requirement of atomicity, and recoverability is not considered a necessary part. Where recovery is desired, it is constructed by using basic atomic actions. This approach allows the flexibility of using different recovery techniques, which is useful for handling design faults.

Many techniques for supporting fault tolerance have used the property of atomicity. The conversation construct has the restriction that there may be no interaction across the boundaries of the conversation. This restriction guarantees the atomicity of the computation performed inside the conversation. Similarly, the recovery block in sequential systems forms an atomic action with recovery primitives. The dynamic techniques for backward recovery [Kim80, MR78, Woo81] aim to identify that part of the computation which has no interaction with the rest of the computation, thereby employing dynamically identified atomic actions. We will focus on the use of basic atomic actions for supporting recovery. The planned basic atomic action within which recovery and fault tolerance is provided is called an

FT-Action.

The FT-Action should be designed so that the atomicity of the FT-Action is guaranteed. The atomicity guarantee permits the programming of recovery for the construct. The FT-Action should also be able to support both the programming of backward error recovery and forward-error recovery. We will discuss forward recovery later. For supporting a conversationlike structure, the FT-Action needs to have the following properties [JC85]:

Atomicity. The communications of processes in the control structure must be isolated from other processes to guarantee atomicity and prevent *information smuggling*. Hence, in an FT-Action, no communication may take place across the boundaries of the FT-Action.

A recovery line for backward error recovery. In the event of an error, all the processes in the FT-Action have to be rolled back to their respective recovery points. These recovery points form a recovery line. The FT-Action must provide a recovery line in which the recovery points of different processes are properly coordinated.

A test line for the processes. The test line is a set of diagnostic tests, one for each process, which is used to determine whether any errors have occurred. The FT-Action must provide a test line.

Recovery measures. The FT-Action should have primitives for performing recovery. If any process detects errors inside the FT-Action, it is an error for the entire FT-Action and *all* the processes taking part in the FT-Action must cooperatively invoke appropriate recovery measures. FT-Actions should be capable of allowing both forward and backward recovery.

Nesting of FT-Actions. The FT-Actions may be nested. Nesting is needed to program nested recovery techniques, and if recovery is unsuccessful in an FT-Action, it may be attempted in the enclosing FT-Action. Only strict nesting should be permitted.

As we can see, the conversation construct is really a restricted form of atomic action. Many implementations of the conversation construct have been proposed [CAR83, RT79, Shr79]. Here we will discuss two such proposals.

9.2.2 Conversations Using Monitors

Here we briefly describe a proposal to implement conversations in the context of monitors [Kim83]. A monitor is a construct that was proposed as a structured method of providing mutually exclusive access to shared data by concurrent processes. A monitor, like an abstract data type, encloses the shared data and provides some defined operations on the shared data. A process may perform any of the defined operations on the monitor. One of the main differences between monitors and abstract data types is that the implementation of the monitor ensures that there is, at most, one process inside the monitor at any given time. This ensures that processes have mutually exclusive access to shared data.

In addition to mutual exclusion, monitors provide primitives for synchronization between processes. Synchronization is achieved by the *wait* and *signal* operations. In a monitor, some variables can be defined by the type of their *condition*. These are special variables on which only the wait and signal operations can be performed. The condition variables represent conditions about the shared data that require processes to synchronize with each other. When the *wait* operation is performed on a condition variable by an operation defined on the monitor, the process that has initiated the operation is suspended until another process performs the *signal* operation on that condition variable. When a signal is executed, one suspended process is awakened, which enters the monitor again to perform further computation.

Four different strategies have been proposed in [Kim83] to implement conversations, many of them using monitors. Here we briefly describe two of these schemes. The first scheme that we describe uses the *conversation monitor* or *c-monitor* construct [Kim83]. The c-monitor encloses all the communication between processes, thereby supporting the atomicity of the conversation. In a conversation, each process has a recovery-block-like construct. These constructs together form the conversation block. In this approach, each process that is taking part in the conversation uses the c-monitor when it enters its recovery block. This is achieved by declaring the c-monitor it will use by the *using* command just after the ensure statement of the recovery block.

For this approach to work, there are certain rules that must be followed. First, each conversation construct must have its own unique c-monitor. When a process enters its recovery block that belongs to a conversation, it loses any access rights it may have to any other monitor, and gains the access rights to the c-monitor for this conversation. This rule ensures that for the processes taking part in the conversation, for the duration of the conversation, the c-monitor is the only means of communication. On exit, the process regains its other access rights and loses the access rights to the c-monitor. This holds even for the nesting of conversations. If a conversation block is nested within another, on entering the nested conversation, the processes lose their access rights to the c-monitor for the outer conversation and regain them only after exiting the c-monitor for the inner conversation.

Though this approach ensures that processes only communicate with other processes taking part in the conversation, there are some other problems that this scheme cannot handle. The main drawback of the scheme is that it cannot ensure that the nesting is proper. As described, a process not taking part in the outer conversation may be allowed to take part in the inner conversation. It is also not possible to check if a process entering a conversation actually has plans for exiting. If a process enters but does not perform a corresponding exit statement, all other processes may remain blocked at the test line. For these types of situations, this scheme relies on the designer to design the system so that these situations do not occur.

The main reason why the c-monitor scheme cannot handle issues like proper nesting is that the recovery blocks belonging to a conversation are scattered over different processes. One possible method to solve this is to enclose the entire conversation within a monitor. This is the approach taken in the *concurrent recovery block (CRB)* [Kim83]. In this scheme, the process interactions are enclosed within a monitor. The monitors for the different "interaction sessions" are all enclosed within the CRB. The monitor mechanisms ensure that only interaction through the appropriate monitor takes place. The overall construct of the CRB is shown in Fig. 9.8.

As we can see, the CRB has one acceptance test called the conversation acceptance test (CAT). All the primary blocks (or alternate blocks) of different processes together form a try block. The try blocks collectively define an *interacting session*, since only blocks within the same try block may interact with each other. As we can see, each try block has a monitor associated with it. This monitor defines the communication between the processes, and is called a conversation monitor (or c-monitor). When a process enters a c-monitor, it gives up all monitor access rights it possessed, and gains the access rights of the c-monitor. The access rights are restored once it leaves the c-monitor. This ensures that the c-monitor is the only mechanism available to a process for communication with other processes as long as the process is taking part in this conversation.

The CRB works as follows. A try block of the CRB is entered by one process. This process initializes the monitor for that try block, and also initializes the children processes, which will carry out an interacting session. The parent process waits until the interaction session is over and all the processes have terminated. After that, it wakes up and executes the CAT. The rollback and retry semantics of the CRB are similar to the semantics of the recovery block. A c-monitor is discarded once all the processes in it terminate. The CRB implements a restrictive form of conversation.

```
        ensure CAT
        by begin
                init MONITOR.1
                init process₁.1(parameters)
                                :
                init processₙ.1(parameters)
                end
        else by begin
                init MONITOR.2
                init process₁.2(parameters)
                                :
                init processₙ.2(parameters)
                end

        ........
        else error
```

Figure 9.8: The structure of the CRB

This approach of the CRB is somewhat more restrictive than the general definition of the conversation construct. It essentially has a synchronous entry in the conversation block, while the definition allows asynchronous entry. However, the CRB approach can be extended by incorporating a look-ahead execution rule. For details of this, the reader may refer to [Kim83].

The use of conversations necessarily requires restrictions on the process interactions and synchronization between processes for conversation entry and exit. The benefit of this extra effort is that the amount of rollback is bounded and there is no domino effect. However, the same effect can also be achieved by placing some restrictions on the scope of recovery and having the system establish recovery points at some "critical" points, over and above the recovery points established by a process when it enters its recovery block. Here we briefly discuss the scheme called *programmer transparent coordination (PTC)* which uses monitors to implement this approach [Kim88b]. The main advantage of a scheme like PTC is that the designer can structure error detection and recovery of a process independently of the recovery organizations of other processes, something which cannot be done with conversations.

In the PTC scheme, it is assumed that all processes interact only through monitors. A process can perform an operation on the monitor that modifies the state of the monitor variables (called a *monitor update operation*), or it can perform an operation that only reads the monitor variables (called a *monitor reference operation*). The monitor update operation is like sending a message to the monitor, and the monitor reference operation is like receiving a message from the monitor. Consider a simple interaction of two processes, P and Q, through a monitor M, as shown in Fig. 9.9.

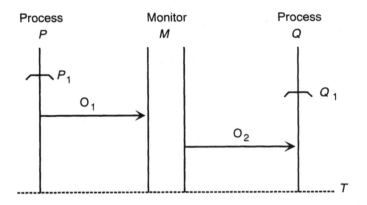

Figure 9.9: Interaction through a monitor

Suppose the process P detects an error (by an acceptance test) at time T and rolls back to its recovery point P_1. In this rollback, besides restoring the state of P, the state of the monitor must also be restored to what it was at the time P_1 was established. This clearly nullifies the reference operation o_2 performed by Q, and hence the process Q will also have to roll back to its recovery point Q_1. That is, Q rolls back due to the revocation of information sent by P. This type of rollback propagation is called *R-propagation*. On the other hand, if Q rolls back because its acceptance test at T fails, one can argue that the error is due to the information Q obtained by operation o_2. Hence, P may actually be faulty, and a rollback of Q must force P to roll back too. This type of rollback propagation is called *S-propagation*.

If S-propagations are permitted, the domino effect can occur. However, if it is assumed that all error detection of a process is done by the process itself, then S-propagation need not be done, since a process is not responsible for detecting errors that occurred in the process which sent it the information. In our example, the failure of the acceptance test of Q does not imply that information sent by P was erroneous. If this is so, then P will detect the error by its acceptance test. Hence, by this assumption, S-propagations are not needed. If S-propagations are disallowed, then by having the system establish some extra recovery points, the domino effect can be avoided. For this, the system will have to save the state of the processes before performing some of the monitor operations. These extra recovery points, called the *branch-RPs*, can be established by the system without the knowledge of the designer, and hence are called programmer-transparent.

The idea behind PTC can best be illustrated by an example. Consider the process interaction shown in Fig. 9.10 [Kim88b]. The recovery points P_1 and P_2

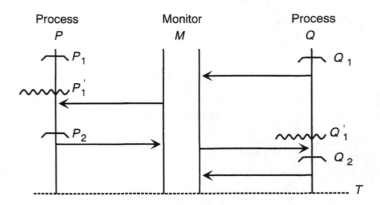

Figure 9.10: An example

are established by the process as they enter their recovery blocks. In addition, the system establishes the branch-RPs P'_1 before the monitor reference operation of P. Similarly, before the monitor reference operation of Q, the branch-RP Q'_1 is established by the system. Besides this, the process Q has the self-defined recovery points Q_1 and Q_2. Now if the process P fails at time T, it will roll back to P_2. Q performs a *minimum distance rollback* by rolling back to the branch-RP Q'_1. If the branch-RPs P'_1 and Q'_1 were not established, this failure of P would have forced P and Q to roll back to P_1 and Q_1, respectively.

Hence, the idea behind the PTC approach is to prohibit S-propagations and to establish branch-RPs to minimize the amount of rollback. We will not discuss further details of this scheme. The rules for rollback and establishing branch-RPs are given in [Kim88b].

9.2.3 Using Distributed FT-Action

Now we discuss a scheme to support a conversationlike structure in CSP based on the framework of FT-Actions [JC86]. The proposed scheme defines an FT-Action in the context of CSP, describes the primitives needed for the FT-Action, and specifies how an FT-Action can be used for backward recovery.

Each process taking part in an FT-Action must declare an FT-Action entry statement. The entry statement is identified by a name and includes a list of all the other processes which will also participate in the FT-Action. The name and lists supplied by each of the processes taking part in the FT-Action are compared at run-time to ensure consistency. The syntax in a process for an FT-Action is shown in Fig. 9.11.

FT-Action A **with** $(P_1, P_2, ..., P_n)$
    code
    exit unless $< e >$
    code
    exit unless $< e >$
    ...
end

Figure 9.11: FT-Action structure

The FT-Action synchronizes recovery schemes involving the processes P_1, P_2, ..., P_n. Each process taking part in the FT-Action should have a similar entry statement. The body of the FT-Action includes *exit* statements, each of which corresponds to a test point within a test line. When a process reaches an exit, it waits for the other processes in the FT-Action to reach their corresponding exits. The exception e of the exit statement is evaluated by an interprocess voting scheme. This scheme combines the exception detected by the processes in the FT-Action, and distributes the resulting exception value to each process. Thus, the test line returns the same exception to each process. In the case that no process detects an exception, the scheme produces a null value. If the exception is null, then the FT-Action is successful and the exit statement terminates the structure. If the exception e is not null, the processes continue in the FT-Action and execute the statements following the exit statement. In general, the implementation of recovery schemes will require the use of several exit statements.

To ensure the atomicity of the FT-Actions, for the duration of the FT-Action, a process P_i only communicates with the processes mentioned in its entry statement of the FT-Action. That is, within the body of the FT-Action, an input or output command in P_1 may only have a process P_2, P_3, ..., P_n as the source or destination process, respectively.

For backward-error-recovery-based fault tolerance, the FT-Action supports a conversationlike scheme involving the processes $P_1, P_2, \ldots, P_n$. Each process executes its primary and may communicate with other processes executing their primaries in the FT-Action. The process then evaluates its acceptance test. An exception is raised if the acceptance test fails or a run-time error is detected. If no exception is raised, the FT-Action terminates. If an exception is raised by any of the processes, then every process invokes backward error recovery. The FT-Action requires the processes to have the same number of alternates. The FT-Action synchronizes the execution of the alternates so that each process keeps in step. The processes may communicate with one another during the execution of an alternate. The specification can be transformed into the FT-Action primitives shown in Fig. 9.12.

FT-Action A **with** $(P_1, P_2, ..., P_n)$
    save state
    primary; acceptance test
    exit unless e
    restore state
    alternate; acceptance test
    ...
    exit unless e
    restore state
    signal error
end

Figure 9.12: FT-Action backward recovery

The state (values of the variables) of each process is saved after it enters the FT-Action. The saved states of all the processes together form the recovery line. Before the first test line (first set of exit statements), each process evaluates its acceptance test to detect exceptions. If one or more processes detect exceptions, the exception e returned by the test line will not be null and the exit statements will not terminate the construct. Instead, the processes restore the saved state and execute the next alternate. After reevaluating their acceptance tests, the processes reach another test line. This sequence is repeated until either the exception returned by a test line is null or the last alternates are attempted. The last alternates are used to *signal* an exception to indicate that the FT-Action has failed.

The FT-Action primitives can be implemented using CSP primitives for communication and synchronization between processes. The details are given in [JC86]. Here we discuss the implementation aspects briefly. A combination of compile-time and run-time checking is used to prevent information smuggling. At compile time, it can easily be checked whether a process only mentions one of the processes listed in its entry statement as the source/destination for its input/output commands. However, this does not check whether the FT-Action boundaries are not violated by the processes mentioned in the entry statement (e.g., by P_1 receiving a message within the FT-Action that was sent by P_2 before P_2 entered the FT-Action). For this, run-time checks have to be performed. A further run-time check must be used to ensure that the processes involved in a particular FT-Action have the same *C-Sets*, where the C-Set of a process for an FT-Action is the set containing the name of the conversation, the name of the process, and the name of the processes specified in the FT-Action statement.

The correct nesting of FT-Actions can be checked at compile time by examining each process. Each process identifier that occurs in the statement of a nested FT-Action must also occur in the statement of any enclosing FT-Action. The entry and exit primitives of an FT-Action can be transformed into CSP primitives. For the purposes of implementation, the processes within an FT-Action are statically ordered, for example, based on their identifiers.

At the entry of a process into an FT-Action, the process is synchronized with others and a C-Set consistency check is performed. The consistency check uses a voting technique based on the two-phase commit protocol, which works as follows. The processes whose identifiers are included in the C-Set of an FT-Action are organized into a chain by using their static ordering. During voting, starting from the head of the chain, each process passes the C-Set information to its successor. If the C-Set of any process does not agree with the information that the process receives, a C-Set exception is passed on. This ensures that the tail process will receive a C-Set exception if the C-Sets are not consistent. Next, the tail process returns the result of the vote back down the chain to the head. In this way, every process receives an exception if the C-Sets are inconsistent. If the C-Sets are inconsistent, the FT-Action is aborted by each process.

The exit primitive is used to terminate an FT-Action, if it is successful. The implementation of the exit primitive also uses a chain-based voting scheme to decide whether an exception has been detected by any of the processes in the FT-Action. If an exception is detected, all the processes in the FT-Action must participate in recovery. Each process resolves any exception it may have received from a predecessor process with any exception it has raised, and sends the result to its successor process. The final result is sent to each process in the FT-Action by transmitting it back down the chain. The *value* of an exception is taken to be null if no exception occurred.

9.3 Forward Recovery in Concurrent Systems

In the previous section, we discussed how a backward-recovery-based scheme can be supported for fault tolerant software in concurrent systems. Here we discuss a proposed framework for supporting forward recovery in concurrent systems [CR86]. Exception handling framework is employed for supporting forward recovery, and FT-Actions are used as the basic structure for supporting exception handling.

A concurrent system consists of multiple processes that execute independently but communicate with each other. In such systems, errors generated by a process may propagate to others by interprocess communication. Furthermore, faults may manifest themselves at different places simultaneously, that is, different processes may experience failure together. For any fault tolerance measure to be effective in such systems, coordination and synchronization of normal activities with activities that support fault tolerance will clearly be needed. Coordination between the fault tolerance measures of different processes will also be needed, otherwise a process may detect and perform recovery on its own, only to find that the overall system state is still not error-free. The interprocess communication will also have to be restricted in order to facilitate recovery.

FT-Actions have been proposed as the basic unit for supporting exception handling in concurrent systems in the framework presented in [CR86]. As defined above, an FT-Action is a planned basic atomic action. That is, there is no interaction between the activities within the FT-Actions and those outside it. With this framework, a system can be considered as consisting of various components, each component being an FT-Action. As in the exception handling framework, if a component detects an exception, it raises the exception locally. The raising of the exception changes its control flow, and it enters the exceptional control flow, which is associated with the exception handlers of the component. If a component fails because it cannot tolerate a fault that has been detected or because its fault tolerant measures are inadequate, it may signal a *failure exception*. A component may also explicitly signal an exception to the user of the component. If an exception is signaled, it is raised within the component to which the signal is sent, and the recovery may then be attempted in that component.

In this framework of FT-Actions as components, these components are somewhat different than components in sequential systems. A component may contain many separate flows of control, with each flow of control representing the activity of a sequential process taking part in the FT-Action. However, the structure of FT-Actions limits the error propagation to within the FT-Action. The two basic principles for structuring fault tolerance in this framework are [CR86]: (1) the operations provided by a fault-tolerant concurrent system should be implemented as FT-Actions, and (2) each fault tolerant measure should be associated with a particular FT-Action and should involve all the processes taking part in the action.

Now let us discuss the rules for exception handling. If a component of an FT-Action detects an exception, it indicates the presence of an error in the FT-Action. If the failure occurred within the FT-Action, then the planned FT-Action structure ensures that the damage is confined to the "walls" of the FT-Action. If the failure had occurred prior to the FT-Action, then the damage may have spread beyond the FT-Action, and the recovery activities of this action may not be sufficient. Nested FT-Actions are well suited for such situations. An FT-Action may consist of many FT-Actions within it. If an internal FT-Action is unable to perform its activity and signals a failure exception, then the enclosing FT-Action performs recovery activities to handle this exception.

Whether one or several components of the FT-Action raise an exception, the fault tolerant measures must necessarily involve all of the processes on that FT-Action. Since an error has been detected within an FT-Action, regardless of which process detected the error, the error may have spread to any of the processes taking part in the FT-Action through interprocess communication. Hence, all processes must take part in the recovery activities.

Every component of the FT-Action responds to the raised exception by changing to an abnormal activity. In other words, the control flow of each process within the FT-Action changes from normal control flow to exceptional control flow, which executes the handler for that exception. The handler may return the component to normal activity, or signal an exception.

Each component of an FT-Action should return the same exception. This rule is more for convenience. Signaling of the same exception ensures that the components agree on the abnormal result that should be returned. Also, since the FT-Action is treated as a single unit, it is appropriate that the unit signal one exception. The fact that it has multiple elements within it should be hidden from the outside.

Finally, if any of the components of an FT-Action do not have a handler for a raised exception, then all of the components should signal an FT-Action failure. Since we are working with planned exception handling, it is important that all components of an FT-Action have exception handlers for a particular exception. That handler may not perform any recovery activity if the process does not need any such activity to be performed. This rule requires the presence of a handler to indicate that the designer has planned for this exception.

These rules will ensure that the handling for the exception is proper. Whether a particular recovery scheme succeeds, depends on the exception and the recovery method. The proposed framework for exception handling in concurrent systems does not specify language mechanisms for exception handling; for this, we will first have to provide language constructs for FT-Actions. The proposed method does imply that exception handling will be done on a per-process basis, just like it is done in uniprocess systems. However, the different exception handlers are not independent. They are all contained in the body of the FT-Action, and may coordinate recovery activities.

9.3.1 Exception Resolution

One of the rules given above for exception handling in the framework of an FT-Action states that there is a single exception for an FT-Action. However, an FT-Action may contain many components, and different components may detect different exceptions. This is possible, as different processes may be monitoring different parts of the system, which may result in different exceptions being signaled. For example, consider a system consisting of two processes P and Q. Suppose that these processes detect and raise two exceptions e_1 and e_2. Two different measures can be provided to deal with these exceptions independently. However, these exceptions may be a manifestation in the processes P and Q of a system-wide exception. That is, the two exceptions, in conjunction, constitute a third exception e which represents that both e_1 and e_2 have occurred. In such a case, a proper fault tolerant scheme will try to handle the exception e. Hence, for exception handling in FT-Actions, some exception resolution is needed that will "combine" the different exceptions detected within an FT-Action into a single exception.

One simple method for resolving exceptions is to prioritize exceptions. If multiple exceptions are detected, then the "highest priority" exception is treated as the exception of the FT-Action. This type of scheme is used, for example, in hardware systems using interrupts, where different components may generate different interrupts simultaneously. The disadvantage of this scheme is that it does not allow representation of situations where the concurrently raised exceptions are merely manifestations of a different, more complicated, exception.

To provide a general method, an *exception tree* can be utilized [CR86]. If several exceptions are raised concurrently, then the multiple exceptions are resolved into the exception that is the root of the smallest subtree containing all the raised exceptions. Exception handling is then performed for this exception. Each FT-Action will have its own tree of exceptions. The root of each exception tree is called the *universal exception*. The universal exception cannot be explicitly raised or signaled; it can only be raised or signaled after exception resolution.

With this form of exception resolution, in general, the damage assessment for an exception will become less accurate and will depend on the damage assessments for the exceptions in its subtree. That is, for such exceptions, only weaker assertions can be made about the state of the system. The exception handlers for exceptions should therefore have weak enough preconditions to provide fault tolerance for specific exceptions. The damage assessment for the universal exception must assume that the entire state of the system has been corrupted.

As an example of exception resolution, consider the nested FT-Actions shown in Fig. 9.13 [CR86]. In this, the atomic actions and the exceptions they can raise

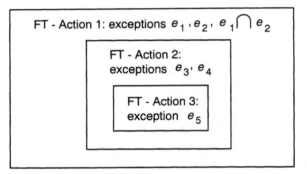

Figure 9.13: Three nested FT-Actions

are given. The exception resolution trees for each of the atomic actions is shown in Fig. 9.14 [CR86]. The "combined exception" for the two exceptions e_1 and e_2 has been represented as $e_1 \cap e_2$.

9.3.2 Exception Handling with FT-Action

Let us consider how the methods described above may be employed. For this, we first need constructs that specify FT-Actions in concurrent systems. We use here the FT-Action construct, whose syntax was shown in Fig. 9.11, to illustrate the use of exception handling [JC86]. How to support exception handling with the FT-Action primitives is shown in Fig. 9.15.

The FT-Action coordinates forward-error recovery for the processes P_1, P_2, ..., P_n. It terminates if no exceptions are raised during the execution of the algorithms. If an exception is raised by any process, then *all* the processes are notified of the exception. Each process will then execute its exception handler *handler (e)* for that exception. Forward-error recovery completes when every process either *signals* an exception or successfully completes its handler. If an exception is *signaled* in an FT-Action, the FT-Action terminates abnormally with an exception and, if it is nested within another FT-Action, the exception is raised in the containing FT-Action.

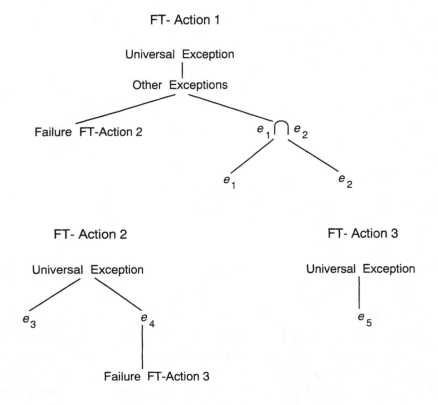

Figure 9.14: The three exception trees

The first test line of the FT-Action is used to resolve any exceptions that may have been signaled in the FT-Action. It employs the exception resolution scheme described in Fig. 9.13 and Fig. 9.14 to return the same exception to each process. If the exception e returned by the test line is null, the exit statement terminates the FT-Action. Otherwise, each process attempts recovery by executing the handler for e. If the final exception e, returned by the voting at the first exit statement, is not the same as the exception raised by the process, it means that others have also raised some exception and all the exceptions have been resolved into the final exception e. In this case, the process invokes the handler for e. If the exception is the same as what the process has raised, the process signals this exception, since it is not capable of handling it (otherwise it would have handled it when it was raised). Since the handlers may also raise or signal exceptions, the second exit statement is needed. In this exit statement, the exceptions raised by the handlers are resolved. If all handlers succeed,

FT-Action *A* **with** $(P_1, P_2, ..., P_n)$

    algorithm

    exit unless *e*

    [

        $e = \text{my-signal} \rightarrow$ **signal**(e)

        $e \neq \text{my-signal} \rightarrow$ handler(e)

    ]

    exit unless *e*

    [

        $e = \text{my-signal} \rightarrow$ **signal**(e)

        $e \neq \text{my-signal} \rightarrow$ **signal error**

    ]

end

Figure 9.15: Forward recovery with FT-Action

then the final exception will be null and the FT-Action will terminate, otherwise it either signals the exception or signals an error (signifying that the exception cannot be handled within this FT-Action).

Let us now briefly consider how the exception mechanisms described here can be implemented. We have seen how planned error detection, where errors are detected at specified points, and as employed in the conversation construct, is implemented in an FT-Action. For backward recovery, the error detection was done in the end at the test line. With exception handling, a process may raise an exception at a point other than at the end of some computation. In this situation, the processes in the FT-Action should not continue with the normal computation. Instead, all the processes should execute the exit statement and start the process of exception resolution.

Because of the synchronous message-passing scheme of CSP, it is not possible simply to discontinue the normal computation of the process which detects the error. Other processes which communicate in a normal manner with this process will wait indefinitely, since the corresponding input or output command will not be executed by the process. A mechanism is required by which all the processes are notified of the occurrence of the exception. On being notified of the exception, a process should then start exception resolution. The mechanism should also be capable of handling the occurrence of multiple exceptions.

The scheme proposed in [JC86] uses a centralized process called the *broadcaster process* for each FT-Action. A process that detects an exception communicates with the broadcaster process. The broadcaster process informs other processes taking part in the FT-Action that an exception has occurred. The broadcaster process works in two phases. In the first phase, it waits for input from any of the processes in the FT-Action. Any process which detects an exception outputs an appropriate message to the broadcaster process. In the second phase, the broadcaster process informs the processes taking part in the FT-Action that an exception has been detected. The broadcaster process only informs the processes that an exception has occurred. The exception resolution and the identity of the final exception is communicated to the processes by the voting scheme used at the test line of the FT-Action.

9.4 Summary

In this chapter, we considered the problem of handling software design faults. As software has no physical properties, the only faults it can have are design faults. Hence, masking software failures requires methods to handle software design faults. With design faults, there is no conceptual distinction between a distributed system and a concurrent system, as the other components are assumed to be working correctly. For handling design faults, a distributed system, or a concurrent system, is considered as a set of processes communicating through message passing. One or more of the processes may fail because of the presence of design faults. The goal of fault tolerance here is to provide the system with service despite the presence of these faults. As software is generally not as reliable as hardware, fault tolerant software is an important area.

First, we considered a special case of concurrent systems: a uniprocess system. In this, there is a given program, and the goal is to structure the program so that it can mask the failure of some of its component modules. There has been considerable interest in this area, though only two general techniques have been proposed to mask design faults. The two techniques are the recovery block approach and N-version programming. The recovery block approach is based upon the primary-standby approach, while N-version programming is modeled after the NMR systems. Both of these approaches utilize design diversity to support fault tolerance. For both of these approaches, multiple versions of the module whose failure is to be masked are needed. These modules are assumed to have independent failures, that is, their designs are so different that they have different faults and fail on different inputs.

In the recovery block approach, the different modules are structured within a language construct. Before the execution of the primary module is initiated, a recovery point is established, in which the state of the program is saved. When the primary module completes, its results are checked by an acceptance test, which is an assertion on the state of the system. The module is unable to perform the desired service. In that case, the saved state is restored, and an alternate module is tried. Again, the acceptance test is applied after the module completes. This rollback and retry by a different module continues until either the acceptance test succeeds or we run out of alternates. In the latter case, an error is signaled, signifying the inability of the fault tolerant strategy to mask the failure.

In N-version programming, the different versions are given the same input and are started in the same initial state. The final output of the different versions is collected and voted upon by the voter. The majority is taken as the final output. The main difference between the recovery block approach and N-version programming is how errors are detected; in the former by acceptance test, and in the latter by voting.

The error detection mechanisms of the two schemes are also their limiting factors. The main limitation in the recovery block approach is the acceptance tests, as writing good acceptance tests is difficult and there are no general methods for developing good acceptance tests. The voting check seems to be a general method, but cannot handle the situation where multiple correct answers are possible. In addition, some anomalies can result due to inexact arithmetic that is used in digital computers.

Besides these two approaches, we also discussed some approaches which may be useful in some specific situations. The deadline mechanism is based on the recovery block approach and is aimed at avoiding timing failures in a real-time system. The distributed recovery block executes the primary and the alternates concurrently in a distributed environment in an attempt to uniformly treat both software design faults and transient hardware faults.

The data diversity approach, as the name suggests, employs data diversity rather than design diversity. It has been observed that programs typically fail on some special inputs. In such situations, if the inputs are modified a little, or if the input data is expressed in some other manner, the failure may not occur. This approach exploits the fact that the accuracy of the input is not very strict in many situations, and data re-expression is possible in some applications. In this approach, if a program fails, the same program is executed again but with slightly different, or re-expressed data, if the program fails with original data. This reexecution and error detection can be organized as it is in the recovery block approach or in N-version programming.

Then we considered the problem of handling design faults in a concurrent system. First, we considered backward recovery in such systems. With backward recovery, the domino effect is possible. A language construct called a conversation, which is an extension of the recovery block structure, has been proposed which restricts the process interactions such that the domino effect is avoided, and if a process fails, the recovery line to which the system should roll back is defined a priori. In a conversation, the processes enter asynchronously. Inside the conversation, the processes communicate with each other such that all interactions between processes are limited within the conversation. Processes execute their acceptance tests independently, but proceed only if all acceptance tests pass. If any of the acceptance tests fail, all processes roll back to their recovery points and attempt alternates. Different realizations of the conversation construct were discussed. Two different techniques were described for supporting conversations in systems using monitors for communication.

Finally, we discussed the problem of supporting forward recovery in concurrent systems. A model based on planned basic atomic actions was discussed. The model proposes that these actions be used as the basic unit to support exception handling. An exception hierarchy is used to resolve exceptions into a single exception, if multiple exceptions are detected within an atomic action.

Problems

1. How is a software fault different than a hardware fault?

2. The failure of *any* program can be viewed as being caused by the input. Justify this statement.

3. If failures of different software versions are co-related, but there is perfect voting and the acceptance test is complete, which of the two — recovery block or N-version programming — will be preferable?

4. Data diversity is one method to change the input of a process. In a distributed system, where a process receives and sends messages, what types of re-expression can be done without violating the semantics of the system?

5. Can you explain why data diversity works using the SD/ED model?

6. If we view input in a broader sense and include events and the environment state as part of it, then other forms of re-expression may be possible. Suggest some.

7. Propose other methods for exception resolution in a concurrent system.

8. Suppose you want to test whether the different versions are independent. Design an experiment for this.

9. If N-version programming is to be used, suggest ways to improve the independence between versions.

10. Suppose N-version programming is to be used for only one module of a large uniprocess software system. Suggest ways to support this without having diversity for the entire software system.

References

[AK76] T. Anderson, and R. Kerr. "Recovery Blocks in Action: A System Supporting High Reliability." *2nd International Conference on Software Engineering*, pp. 447–457, October 1976.

[AK87] P. E. Ammann, and J. C. Knight. "Data Diversity: An Approach to Software Fault Tolerance." *17th International Symposium on Fault Tolerant Computing Systems*, pp. 122–126, Pittsburgh, 1987.

[AKL88] J. Arlat, K. Kanoun, and J.-C. Laprie. "Dependability Evaluation of Software Fault Tolerance." *18th International Symposium on Fault Tolerant Computing Systems*, pp. 142–147, Tokyo, Japan, 1988.

[AL81] T. Anderson, and P. A. Lee. *Fault Tolerance Principles and Practice*. Englewood Cliffs, NJ: Prentice Hall, 1981.

[Avi85] A. Avizienis. "The N-Version Approach to Fault Tolerant Software." *IEEE Transactions on Software Engineering*, SE-11(12):1491–1501, December 1985.

[BKL89] S. Brilliant, J. C. Knight, and N. G. Leveson. "The Consistent Comparison Problem in N-Version Software." *IEEE Transactions on Software Engineering*, 15(11):1481–1485, November 1989.

[BR81] E. Best, and B. Randell. "A Formal Model of Atomicity in Asynchronous Systems." *Acta Informatica*, 16:93–124, 1981.

[CA78] L. Chen, and A. Avizienis. "N-Version Programming: A Fault Tolerance Approach to Reliability of Software Operation." *8th International Symposium on Fault Tolerant Computing Systems*, 1978.

[CAR83] R. H. Campbell, T. Anderson, and B. Randell. "Practical Fault Tolerant Software for Asynchronous Systems." *Proceedings of SAFECOM'83*, 1983.

[CHB79] R. H. Campbell, K. H. Horton, and G. G. Belford. "Simulations of a Fault Tolerant Deadline Mechanism." *9th International Symposium on Fault Tolerant Computing Systems*, pp. 95–101, Madison, Wisconsin, June 1979.

[CR86] R. H. Campbell, and B. Randell. "Error Recovery in Asynchronous Systems." *IEEE Transactions on Software Engineering*, SE-12(8):811–826, August 1986.

[Cri82] F. Cristian. "Exception Handling and Software Fault Tolerance." *IEEE Transactions on Computers*, C-31(6):531–540, June 1982.

[Cri84] F. Cristian. "Correct and Robust Programs." *IEEE Transactions on Software Engineering*, SE-10(2):163–174, March 1984.

[EL85] D. E. Eckhardt, and L. D. Lee. "A Theoretical Basis for the Analysis of Multiversion Software Subject to Coincidental Errors." *IEEE Transactions on Software Engineering*, SE-11(12):1511–1517, December 1985.

[GAA80] A. Grnarov, J. Arlat, and A. Avizienis. "On the Performance of Software Fault Tolerant Strategies." *10th International Symposium on Fault Tolerant Computing Systems*, pp. 251–253, 1980.

[GK85] S. T. Gregory, and J. C. Knight. "A New Linguistic Approach to Backward Error Recovery." *15th International Symposium on Fault Tolerant Computing Systems*, pp. 404–409, 1985.

[Goo75] J. B. Goodenough. "Exception Handling: Issues and a Proposed Notation." *Communications of the ACM*, 18(12):683–696, December 1975.

[Gra85] J. Gray. *Why Do Computers Stop and What Can Be Done About It?* Technical Report 85.7, Cupertino, CA: Tandem Computers, June 1985.

[H+74] J. J. Horning et al. "A Program Structure for Error Detection and Recovery." In E. Gelenbe and C. Kaiser, editors, *Lecture Notes in Computer Science, 16*, pp. 171–187. Springer Verlag, 1974.

[JC85] P. Jalote, and R. H. Campbell. "Atomic Actions in Concurrent Systems." *5th International Conference on Distributed Computing Systems*, pp. 184–191, Denver, 1985.

[JC86] P. Jalote, and R. H. Campbell. "Atomic Actions for Fault-Tolerance Using CSP." *IEEE Transactions on Software Engineering*, SE-12(1):59–68, January 1986.

[Kim80] K. H. Kim. "An Implementation of a Programmer Transparent Scheme for Coordinating Concurrent Processes in Recovery." *Proceedings of COMSAC80*, pp. 615–621, 1980.

[Kim83] K. H. Kim. "Approaches to Mechanization of the Conversation Scheme Based on Monitors." *IEEE Transactions on Software Engineering*, SE-8:189–197, May 1983.

[Kim84] K. H. Kim. "Distributed Execution of Recovery Blocks: An Approach to Uniform Treatment of Hardware and Software Faults." *4th International Conference on Distributed Computing Systems*, pp. 526–532, San Francisco, CA, May 1984.

[Kim88a] K. H. Kim. "Approaches to Implementation of Repairable Distributed Recovery Block Scheme." *18th International Symposium on Fault Tolerant Computing Systems*, pp. 50–55, Tokyo, Japan, June 1988.

[Kim88b] K. H. Kim. "Programmer-Transparent Coordination of Recovering Concurrent Processes: Philosophy and Rules for Efficient Implementation." *IEEE Transactions on Software Engineering*, 14(6):810–821, June 1988.

[KL86] J. C. Knight, and N. G. Leveson. "An Experimental Evaluation of the Assumption of Independence in Multiversion Programming." *IEEE Transactions on Software Engineering*, SE-12(1):96–109, January 1986.

[LGH80] P. A. Lee, N. Gehani, and K. Heron. "A Recovery Cache for the PDP-11." *IEEE Transactions on Computers*, C-29(6):546–549, June 1980.

[Lom77] D. B. Lomet. "Process Structuring, Synchronization, and Recovery Using Atomic Actions." *Proceedings of ACM Conference on Language Design for Reliable Software, SIGPLAN Notices 12, 3*, pp. 128–137, March 1977.

[LP80] D. C. Luckham, and W. Polak. "Ada Exception Handling: An Axiomatic Approach." *ACM Transactions on Programming Languages and Systems*, 2(2):225–233, April 1980.

[LS79] B. H. Liskov, and A. Snyder. "Exception Handling in CLU." *IEEE Transactions on Software Engineering*, SE-5(6):546–558, November 1979.

[MR78] P. E. Merlin, and B. Randell. "State Restoration in Distributed Systems." *8th International Symposium on Fault Tolerant Computing Systems*, pp. 129–134, Toulouse, France, 1978.

[NG90] V. F. Nicola, and A. Goyal. "Modeling of Correlated Failures and Community Error Recovery in Multiversion Software." *IEEE Transactions on Software Engineering*, 16(3):350–359, March 1990.

[PJ91] J. Purtilo, and P. Jalote. "An Environment for Developing Fault Tolerant Software." *IEEE Transactions on Software Engineering*, 17(2):153–159, February 1991.

[Ran75] B. Randell. "System Structure for Software Fault Tolerance." *IEEE Transactions on Software Engineering*, SE-1:220–232, June 1975.

[RT79] D. L. Russell, and M. J. Tiedeman. "Multiprocess Recovery Using Conversations." *9th International Symposium on Fault Tolerant Computing Systems*, Madison, Wisconsin, 1979.

[SGM87] R. K. Scott, J. W. Gault, and D. F. McAllistor. "Fault Tolerant Software Reliability Modeling." *IEEE Transactions on Software Engineering*, 13(5):582–592, May 1987.

[Shr78] S. K. Shrivastava. "Sequential Pascal with Recovery Blocks." *Software Practice and Experience*, 8(2):177–185, 1978.

[Shr79] S. K. Shrivastava. "Concurrent Pascal with Backward Error Recovery: Implementation." *Software Practice and Experience*, 9:1021–1033, 1979.

[SM90] G. F. Sullivan, and G. M. Masson. "Using Certification Trails to Achieve Software Fault Tolerance." *20th International Symposium on Fault Tolerant Computing Systems*, pp. 423–431, 1990.

[Woo81] W. G. Wood. "A Decentralized Recovery Protocol." *11th International Symposium on Fault Tolerant Computing Systems*, pp. 159–164, Portland, 1981.

Bibliography

[AA86]   J. A. Abraham, and V. K. Agarwal. "Test Generation for Digital Systems." In D. K. Pradhan, editor, *Fault-Tolerant Computing Theory and Techniques*. Englewood Cliffs, NJ: Prentice Hall, 1986, pp. 1–94.

[AA89]   D. Agrawal, and A. E. Abbadi. "An Efficient and Fault Tolerant Solution to the Mutual Exclusion Problem." *ACM Transactions on Computer Systems*, 9(1):1–20, February 1989.

[ABF90]   M. Abramorice, M. A. Breuer, and A. D. Friedman. *Digital Systems Testing and Testable Design*. New York: Computer Science Press, 1990, p. 1.

[AD76]   P. A. Alsberg, and J. D. Day. "A Principle for Resilient Sharing of Distributed Databases." *2nd International Conference on Software Engineering*, pp. 562–570, 1976.

[AF86]   J. A. Abraham, and W. K. Fuchs. "Fault and Error Models for VLSI." *Proceedings of the IEEE*, 74(5):639–654, May 1986.

[Agr88]   P. Agrawal. "Fault-Tolerance in Multiprocessor Systems Without Dedicated Redundancy." *IEEE Transactions on Computers*, 37:358–362, March 1988.

[AJ92]   G. Agarwal, and P. Jalote. "An Efficient Protocol for Voting in Distributed Systems." *12th International Conference on Distributed Computing Systems*, pp. 640–647, Yokohoma, Japan, May 1992.

[AK76]   T. Anderson, and R. Kerr. "Recovery Blocks in Action: A System Supporting High Reliability." *2nd International Conference on Software Engineering*, pp. 447–457, October 1976.

401

[AK87]   P. E. Ammann, and J. C. Knight. "Data Diversity: An Approach to Software Fault Tolerance." *17th International Symposium on Fault Tolerant Computing Systems*, pp. 122–126, Pittsburgh, 1987.

[AKL88]   J. Arlat, K. Kanoun, and J.-C. Laprie. "Dependability Evaluation of Software Fault Tolerance." *18th International Symposium on Fault Tolerant Computing Systems*, pp. 142–147, Tokyo, Japan, 1988.

[AL81]   T. Anderson, and P. A. Lee. *Fault Tolerance Principles and Practice.* Englewood Cliffs, NJ: Prentice Hall, 1981.

[AM73]   D. A. Anderson, and G. Metze. "Design of Totally Self-checking Circuits for M-Out-Of-N Codes." *IEEE Transactions on Computers*, C-22:263–269, March 1973.

[And83]   G. R. Andrews. "Concepts and Notations for Concurrent Programming." *ACM Computing Surveys*, pp. 3–44, March 1983.

[Avi76]   A. Avizienis. "Fault-Tolerant Systems." *IEEE Transactions on Computers*, C-25(12):1304–1312, December 1976.

[Avi85]   A. Avizienis. "The N-Version Approach to Fault Tolerant Software." *IEEE Transactions on Software Engineering*, SE-11(12):1491–1501, December 1985.

[B⁺89]   A. Borg et al. "Fault Tolerance Under Unix." *ACM Transactions on Computer Systems*, 7(1):1–24, February 1989.

[B⁺90]   P. Banerjee et al. "Algorithm-based Fault-Tolerance on a Hypercube Multiprocessor." *IEEE Transactions on Computers*, 39:1132–1142, September 1990.

[Bar81]   J. F. Bartlett. "A Nonstop Kernel." *7th ACM Symposium on Operating Systems Principles*, pp. 22–29, 1981.

[BB91]   R. Bianchini Jr., and R. Buskens. "An Adaptive Distributed System-Level Diagnosis Algorithm and its Implementation." *21st International Symposium on Fault-Tolerant Computing Systems*, pp. 222–229, June 1991.

[BB92]   R. P. Bianchini Jr., and R. W. Buskens. "Implementation of on-Line Distributed System-Level Diagnosis Theory." *IEEE Transactions on Computers*, 41(5):616–626, May 1992.

[BBG83]   A. Borg, J. Baumback, and S. Galzer. "A Message System Supporting Fault Tolerance." *9th ACM Symposium on Operating Systems, 17:5*, pp. 90–99, 1983.

[Ben83]   M. Ben-Or. "Another Advantage of Free Choice: Completely Asynchronous Agreement Protocols." *2nd ACM Symposium on Principles of Distributed Computing*, pp. 27–30, Montreal, Quebec, August 1983.

[BG81]   P.A. Bernstein, and N. Goodman. "Concurrency Control in Distributed Database Systems." *ACM Computing Surveys*, 13(2):185–221, June 1981.

[BG84]   P. A. Bernstein, and N. Goodman. "An Algorithm for Concurrency Control and Recovery in Replicated Distributed Databases." *ACM Transactions on Database Systems*, 9(4):596–614, December 1984.

[BG87]   D. Barbara, and H. Garcia-Molina. "The Reliability of Voting Mechanisms." *IEEE Transactions on Computers*, C-36(10):1197–1207, October 1987.

[BG88]   D. Bitton, and J. Gray. "Disk Shadowing." *Proceedings of the 14th VLDB Conference*, pp. 331–338, 1988.

[BGN90]   R. Bianchini Jr., K. Goodwin, and D.S. Nydick. "Practical Application and Implementation of Distributed System-Level Diagnosis Theory." *20th International Symposium on Fault-Tolerant Computing Systems*, pp. 332–339. IEEE, June 1990.

[BGS86]   D. Barbara, H. Garcia-Molina, and A. Spauster. "Policies for Dynamic Vote Reassignment." *6th International Conference on Distributed Computing*, pp. 195–206, May 1986.

[BHG87]   P. A. Bernstein, V. Hadzilacos, and N. Goodman. *Concurrency Control and Recovery in Database Systems*. Addison-Wesley, 1987.

[BJ87]   K. P. Birman, and T. A. Joseph. "Reliable Communication in the Presence of Failures." *ACM Transactions on Computer Systems*, 5(1):47–76, February 1987.

[BJRA85] K. P. Birman, T. A. Joseph, T. Raeuchle, and A. E. Abbadi. "Implementing Fault-Tolerant Distributed Objects." *IEEE Transactions on Software Engineering*, 11(6):502–508, June 1985.

[BKL89]   S. Brilliant, J. C. Knight, and N. G. Leveson.   "The Consistent
           Comparison Problem in N-Version Software." *IEEE Transactions on
           Software Engineering*, 15(11):1481–1485, November 1989.

[BN84]   A. D. Birrell, and B. J. Nelson. "Implementing Remote Procedure Calls."
           ACM Transactions on Computer Systems, 2(1):39–59, February 1984.

[BR81]   E. Best, and B. Randell. "A Formal Model of Atomicity in Asynchronous
           Systems." *Acta Informatica*, 16:93–124, 1981.

[Bra87]   G. Bracha. "Asynchronous Byzantine Agreement Protocols." *Informa-
           tion and Computation*, 75(2), 130–143, 1987.

[BSW79]   P.A. Bernstein, D.W. Shipman, and W.S. Wong. "Formal Aspects of
           Serializabiity in Database Concurrency Control." *IEEE Transactions on
           Software Engineering*, SE-5(3):203–216, May 1979.

[CA78]   L. Chen, and A. Avizienis. "N-Version Programming: A Fault Tolerance
           Approach to Reliability of Software Operation."   *8th International
           Symposium on Fault Tolerant Computing Systems*, 1978.

[CAA90a]   S. Y. Cheung, M. Ahamad, and M. H. Ammar. "The Grid Protocol: A
           High Performance Scheme For Maintaining Replicated Data." *6th Inter-
           national Conference on Data Engineering*, pp. 438–445, January 1990.

[CAA90b]   S. Y. Cheung, M. Ahamad, and M. H. Ammar.   "Multi-dimensional
           Voting: A General Method for Implementing Synchronization in
           Distributed Systems."   *10th International Conference on Distributed
           Computing Systems*, pp. 362–369, 1990.

[CAR83]   R. H. Campbell, T. Anderson, and B. Randell. "Practical Fault Tolerant
           Software for Asynchronous Systems." *Proceedings of SAFECOM'83*,
           1983.

[CAS85]   F. Cristian, H. Aghili, and R. Strong.   "Atomic Broadcast: From
           Simple Message Diffusion to Byzantine Agreement." *14th International
           Symposium on Fault Tolerant Computing Systems*, pp. 200–206, 1985.

[CAS86]   F. Cristian, H. Aghili, and R. Strong. "Clock Synchronization in the
           Presence of Omissions and Performance Faults, and Processor Joins."
           16th International Symposium on Fault Tolerant Computing Systems,
           June 1986.

[CBDU75] K. M. Chandy, J. C. Browne, C. W. Dissly, and W. R. Uhrig. "Analytic Models for Rollback and Recovery Strategies in Databases." *IEEE Transactions on Software Engineering*, 1(1):100–110, March 1975.

[CDDS85] B. A. Coan, D. Dolev, C. Dwork, and L. Stockmeyer. "The Distributed Firing Squad Problem." *17th ACM Symposium on Theory of Computation*, pp. 335–345, 1985.

[CHB79] R. H. Campbell, K. H. Horton, and G. G. Belford. "Simulations of a Fault Tolerant Deadline Mechanism." *9th International Symposium on Fault Tolerant Computing Systems*, pp. 95–101, Madison, Wisconsin, June 1979.

[CJ91] F. Cristian, and F. Jahanian. "A Timestamp-Based Checkpointing Protocol for Long-Lived Distributed Computations." *Proceedings of Reliable Distributed Software and Database Systems*, pp. 12–20, 1991.

[CK85] D. Cheung, and T. Kameda. "Site-optimal Termination Protocols for a Distributed Database under Networking Partitioning." *4th ACM SIGACT-SIGOPS Symposium on Principles of Distributed Computing*, pp. 111–121, 1985.

[CL85] K. M. Chandy, and L. Lamport. "Distributed Snapshots: Determining Global States of Distributed Systems." *ACM Transactions on Computer Systems*, 3(1):63–75, 1985.

[CM84] J. Chang, and N. F. Maxemchuk. "Reliable Broadcast Protocols." *ACM Transactions on Computer Systems*, 2(3):251–273, August 1984.

[CMH83] K.M. Chandy, J. Misra, and L.M. Haas. "Distributed Deadlock Detection." *ACM Transactions on Computer Systems*, 1(2):144–156, May 1983.

[CNL89] S. T. Chanson, G. W. Neufeld, and L. Liang. "A Bibliography on Multicast and Group Communication." *ACM Operating Systems Review (SIGOPS)*, pp. 20–25, October 1989.

[Coo84] E. C. Cooper. "Replicated Procedure Call." *3rd ACM Conference on Principles of Distributed Computing*, pp. 44–55, 1984.

[Coo85] E. C. Cooper. "Replicated Distributed Programs." *10th ACM Symposium on Operating Systems*, pp. 63–78, 1985.

[CR83]　F. Chin, and K.V.S. Ramaro. "Optimal Termination Protocols for Network Partitioning." *2nd ACM-SIGACT-SIGMOD Symposium on Principles of Database Systems*, pp. 25–35, Atlanta, March 1983.

[CR86]　R. H. Campbell, and B. Randell. "Error Recovery in Asynchronous Systems." *IEEE Transactions on Software Engineering*, SE-12(8):811–826, August 1986.

[Cri82]　F. Cristian. "Exception Handling and Software Fault Tolerance." *IEEE Transactions on Computers*, C-31(6):531–540, June 1982.

[Cri84]　F. Cristian. "Correct and Robust Programs." *IEEE Transactions on Software Engineering*, SE-10(2):163–174, March 1984.

[Cri89]　F. Cristian. "Probabilistic Clock Synchronization." *Distributed Computing*, 3:146–158, 1989.

[CS68]　W. C. Carter, and P. R. Schneider. "Design of Dynamically Checked Computers." *Proceedings of the IFIP*, pp. 878–883, Edinburgh, August 1968.

[Dah88]　A.T. Dahbura. "System-Level Diagnosis: A Perspective for the Third Decade." In C. S. Tewksbury, B. Dickson, and S. Schwartz, editors, *Concurrent Computations: Algorithms, Architecture, and Technology*. Plenum Press, 1988, Chapter 21, pp. 411–434.

[Dav84]　S. B. Davidson. "Optimism and Consistency in Partitioned Distributed Database Systems." *ACM Transactions on Database Systems*, 9(3):456–481, September 1984.

[Dav89]　D. Davcev. "A Dynamic Voting Scheme in Distributed Systems." *IEEE Transactions on Software Engineering*, 15(1):93–97, January 1989.

[DFF⁺82]　D. Dolev, M. Fischer, R. Fowler, N. Lynch, and H. Strong. "Efficient Byzantine Agreement Without Authentication." *Information and Control*, 52:257–274, 1982.

[DGS85]　S. B. Davidson, H. Garcia-Molina, and D. Skeen. "Consistency in Partitioned Networks." *ACM Computing Surveys*, 17(3):341–370, September 1985.

[DHS84]　D. Dolev, J. Halpern, and R. Strong. "On the Possibility and Impossibility of Achieving Clock Synchronization." *16th ACM Symposium on Theory of Computation*, 1984.

[Dij75]   E. W. Dijkstra. "Guarded Commands, Nondeterminacy, and Formal Derivation of Programs." *Communications of the ACM*, 18(8):453–457, August 1975.

[DM84]   A.T. Dahbura, and G. M. Masson. "An $O(n^{2.5})$ Fault Identification Algorithm for Diagnosable Systems." *IEEE Transactions on Computers*, C-33:486–492, 1984.

[DS83]   D. Dolev, and H. Strong. "Authenticated Algorithms for Byzantine Agreement." *SIAM Journal of Computing*, 12(4):656–666, November 1983.

[EGLT76]   K. P. Eswaran, J. N. Gray, R. A. Lorie, and I. L. Traiger. "The Notions of Consistency and Predicate Locks in a Database System." *Communications of the ACM*, 19(11):624–633, November 1976.

[EL85]   D. E. Eckhardt, and L. D. Lee. "A Theoretical Basis for the Analysis of Multiversion Software Subject to Coincidental Errors." *IEEE Transactions on Software Engineering*, SE-11(12):1511–1517, December 1985.

[ES83]   D. L. Eager, and K. C. Sevcik. "Achieving Robustness in Distributed Database Systems." *ACM Transactions on Database Systems*, 8(3):354–381, September 1983.

[FGL85]   M. Fischer, N. Griffeth, and N. Lynch. "Global States of a Distributed System." *IEEE Transactions on Software Engineering*, pp. 198–202, May 1985.

[FLM86]   M. Fisher, N. Lynch, and M. Merritt. "Easy Impossibility Proofs for Distributed Consensus Problems." *Distributed Computing*, 1:26–39, January 1986.

[FLP85]   M. Fisher, N. Lynch, and M. Paterson. "Impossibility of Distributed Consensus with one Faulty Process." *Journal of the ACM*, 32(2):374–382, April 1985.

[GAA80]   A. Grnarov, J. Arlat, and A. Avizienis. "On the Performance of Software Fault Tolerant Strategies." *10th International Symposium on Fault Tolerant Computing Systems*, pp. 251–253, 1980.

[Gar82]   H. Garcia-Molina. "Elections in a Distributed Computing System." *IEEE Transactions on Computers*, C-31(1):48–59, January 1982.

[GB85]   H. Garcia-Molina, and D. Barbara. "How to Assign Votes in a Distributed System." *Journal of the ACM*, 32(4):841–860, October 1985.

[GD78]   E. Gelenbe, and D. Derochette. "Performance of Rollback Recovery Systems Under Intermittent Failures." *Communications of the ACM*, 21(6):493–499, June 1978.

[Gel79]   E. Gelenbe. "On the Optimum Checkpoint Interval." *Journal of the ACM*, 26(2):259–270, April 1979.

[Gif79]   D. K. Gifford. "Weighted Voting for Replicated Data." *7th ACM Symposium on Operating Systems*, pp. 150–162, December 1979.

[GK85]   S. T. Gregory, and J. C. Knight. "A New Linguistic Approach to Backward Error Recovery." *15th International Symposium on Fault Tolerant Computing Systems*, pp. 404–409, 1985.

[Goo75]   J. B. Goodenough. "Exception Handling: Issues and a Proposed Notation." *Communications of the ACM*, 18(12):683–696, December 1975.

[Gra78]   J. N. Gray. "Notes on Database Operating Systems." In *Operating Systems: An Advanced Course*, Springer-Verlag, 1978.

[Gra85]   J. Gray. *Why Do Computers Stop and What Can Be Done About It?* Technical Report 85.7, Cupertino, CA: Tandem Computers, June 1985.

[GS91]   H. Garcia-Molina, and A. Spauster. "Ordered and Reliable Multicast Communication." *ACM Transactions on Computer Systems*, 9(3):242–271, August 1991.

[H+74]   J. J. Horning et al. "A Program Structure for Error Detection and Recovery." In E. Gelenbe and C. Kaiser, editors, *Lecture Notes in Computer Science, 16*, pp. 171–187. Springer Verlag, 1974.

[HA74]   S.L. Hakimi, and A.T. Amin. "Characterization of the Connection Assignment of Diagnosable Systems." *IEEE Transactions on Computers*, C-23:86–88, 1974.

[HA84]   K. H. Huang, and J. A. Abraham. "Algorithm Based Fault-Tolerance for Matrix Operations." *IEEE Transactions on Computers*, C33:518–528, June 1984.

[HJ89a]   Y. Huang, and P. Jalote. "Analytic Models for the Primary Site Approach for Fault Tolerance." *Acta Informatica*, 26:543–557, 1989.

[HJ89b]   Y. Huang, and P. Jalote. "Availability Analysis of the Primary Site Approach for Fault Tolerance." *8th Symposium on Reliable Distributed Systems*, pp. 130–136, IEEE Computer Society, 1989.

[HJ93]   Y. Huang, and P. Jalote. *Degree of Replication in Voting Systems.* Technical Report TR 93-161, Murray Hill, NJ: AT&T Bell Labs, 1993.

[HKR84]   S.H. Hosseini, J.G. Kuhl, and S.M. Reddy. "A Diagnosis Algorithm for Distributed Computing Systems with Dynamic Failure and Repair." *IEEE Transactions on Computers*, C-33:223–233, 1984.

[HN84]   S.L. Hakimi, and K. Nakajima. "On Adaptive Systems Diagnosis." *IEEE Transactions on Computers*, C-33:234–240, 1984.

[Hoa78]   C. A. R. Hoare. "Communicating Sequential Processes." *Communications of the ACM*, 21(8):666–677, August 1978.

[HR83]   T. Haerder, and A. Reuter. "Principles of Transaction-Oriented Database Recovery." *ACM Computing Surveys*, 15(4):287–317, December 1983.

[JA92]   P. Jalote, and G. Agarwal. "Using Coding to Support Data Resiliency in Distributed Systems." *8th International Conference on Data Engineering*, pp. 192–199, Tempe, Arizona, February 1992.

[Jal89a]   P. Jalote. "Fault Tolerant Processes." *Distributed Computing*, 3:187–195, 1989.

[Jal89b]   P. Jalote. "Resilient Objects in Broadcast Networks." *IEEE Transactions on Software Engineering*, 15(1):68–72, January 1989.

[Jal92a]   P. Jalote. *Efficient Ordered Broadcasting in CSMA/CD Networks.* Technical Report TRCS-92-160, Indian Institute of Technology Kanpur, Department of Computer Science and Engineering, Kanpur, India, 1992.

[Jal92b]   P. Jalote. "Dynamic Reconfiguration of CSP Programs for Fault Tolerance." *22nd International Symposium on Fault Tolerant Computing Systems*, pp. 50–56, Boston, 1992.

[Jal93]   P. Jalote. *Reliable Causal Broadcasting.* Technical Report, Indian Institute of Technology, Department of Computer Science and Engineering, Kanpur, India, 1993.

[JC85]   P. Jalote, and R. H. Campbell. "Atomic Actions in Concurrent Systems." *5th International Conference on Distributed Computing Systems*, pp. 184–191, Denver, 1985.

[JC86]   P. Jalote, and R. H. Campbell. "Atomic Actions for Fault-Tolerance Using CSP." *IEEE Transactions on Software Engineering*, SE-12(1):59–68, January 1986.

[JK90]   N. K. Jha, and S. Kundu. *Testing and Reliable Design of CMOS Circuits.* Norwell, MA: Kluwer Academic Publishers, 1990.

[JM87]   S. Jajodia, and D. Mutchler. "Dynamic Voting." *ACM SIGMOD International Conference on Management of Data*, pp. 227–238, San Francisco, 1987.

[Joh89] B. W. Johnson. *Design and Analysis of Fault Tolerant Digital Systems.* Addison-Wesley, 1989.

[JS91]   P. Jalote, and R. Sriram. *Fault Tolerant Processes in a Network of Workstations.* Technical Report, IIT Kanpur, Department of Computer Science, 1991.

[JV90]   T. T. Y. Juang, and S. Venkatesan. "Efficient Algorithm for Crash Recovery in Distributed Systems." *10th Conference on Foundations of Software Technology and Theoretical Computer Science (LNCS)*, pp. 349–361, 1990.

[JV91]   T. T. Y. Juang, and S. Venkatesan. "Crash Recovery with Little Overhead." *11th International Conference on Distributed Computing Systems*, pp. 454–461, 1991.

[JW91]   N. K. Jha, and S.J. Wang. "Design and Synthesis of Self-checking VLSI Circuits and Systems." *IEEE International Conference on Computer Design*, Cambridge, MA, 1991.

[JZ87]   D. B. Johnson, and W. Zwaenepoel. "Sender-Based Message Logging." *17th International Symposium on Fault Tolerant Computing Systems*, pp. 14–19, 1987.

[JZ90]   D. B. Johnson, and W. Zwaenepoel. "Recovery in Distributed Systems Using Optimistic Message Logging and Checkpointing." *Journal of Algorithms*, 11:462–491, 1990.

[KH87]   S. E. Kreutzer, and S. L. Hakimi. "System-Level Diagnosis: A Survey." *Microprocessing and Microprogramming*, 20:323–330, 1987.

[Kim70]   C.R. Kime. "An Analysis Model for Digital System Diagnosis." *IEEE Transactions on Computers*, C-19:1063–1070, 1970.

[Kim80]   K. H. Kim. "An Implementation of a Programmer Transparent Scheme for Coordinating Concurrent Processes in Recovery." *Proceedings of COMSAC80*, pp. 615–621, 1980.

[Kim83]   K. H. Kim. "Approaches to Mechanization of the Conversation Scheme Based on Monitors." *IEEE Transactions on Software Engineering*, SE-8:189–197, May 1983.

[Kim84]   K. H. Kim. "Distributed Execution of Recovery Blocks: An Approach to Uniform Treatment of Hardware and Software Faults." *4th International Conference on Distributed Computing Systems*, pp. 526–532, San Francisco, CA, May 1984.

[Kim86]   C. R. Kime. "System Diagnosis." In D. K. Pradhan, editor, *Fault-Tolerant Computing Theory and Techniques, Vol II*, Englewood Cliffs, NJ: Prentice Hall, 1986, Chapter 8, pp. 577–632.

[Kim88a] K. H. Kim. "Approaches to Implementation of Repairable Distributed Recovery Block Scheme." *18th International Symposium on Fault Tolerant Computing Systems*, pp. 50–55, Tokyo, Japan, June 1988.

[Kim88b] K. H. Kim. "Programmer-Transparent Coordination of Recovering Concurrent Processes: Philosophy and Rules for Efficient Implementation." *IEEE Transactions on Software Engineering*, 14(6):810–821, June 1988.

[KL86]   J. C. Knight, and N. G. Leveson. "An Experimental Evaluation of the Assumption of Independence in Multiversion Programming." *IEEE Transactions on Software Engineering*, SE-12(1):96–109, January 1986.

[KT87]   R. Koo, and S. Toueg. "Checkpointing and Rollback-Recovery for Distributed Systems." *IEEE Transactions on Software Engineering*, SE-13(1):23–31, January 1987.

[KT91]   M. F. Kaashoek, and A. S. Tanenbaum. "Group Communication in the Amoeba Distributed Operating System." *11th International Conference on Distributed Computing Systems*, pp. 222–230, Arlingon, Texas, 1991.

[KTA75]   T. Kameda, S. Toida, and F.J. Allen. "A Diagnosing Algorithm for Networks." *Information and Control*, 29:141–148, 1975.

[Kum91a]   A. Kumar. "Hierarchical Quorum Consensus: A New Algorithm For Managing Replicated Data." *IEEE Transactions on Computers*, 40(9):996–1004, September 1991.

[Kum91b]   A. Kumar. "A Randomized Voting Algorithm." *11th International Conference on Distributed Computing Systems*, pp. 412–419, 1991.

[Lal85]   P. K. Lala. *Fault Tolerant and Fault Testable Hardware Design*. London: Prentice Hall, 1985.

[Lam78]   L. Lamport. "Time, Clocks, and Ordering of Events." *Communications of the ACM*, 21(7):558–565, July 1978.

[Lam81]   B. W. Lampson. "Atomic Transactions." In B. W. Lampson, M. Paul, and H. J. Siegert, editors, *Distributed Systems — Architecture and Implementation*, Springer-Verlag, 1981, pp. 246–265.

[Lap85]   J. C. Laprie. "Dependable Computing and Fault Tolerance: Concepts and Terminology." *15th International Symposium on Fault Tolerant Computing Systems*, pp. 2–11, Ann Arbor, Michigan, June 1985.

[Lap92]   J. C. Laprie. *Dependability: Basic Concepts and Terminology — In English, French, German, and Japanese*. Vienna: Springer-Verlag, 1992.

[LG85]   K.-J. Lin, and J. D. Gannon. "Atomic Remote Procedure Call." *IEEE Transactions on Software Engineering*, SE-11(10):1126–1135, October 1985.

[LG90]   T. V. Lakshman, and D. Ghoshal. *A new $\sqrt{N}$ Multiple Copy Update Algorithm and its Performance Evaluation*. Technical Report CS-TR-2502, College Park, Maryland: Department of Computer Science, University of Maryland, July 1990.

[LGH80]   P. A. Lee, N. Gehani, and K. Heron. "A Recovery Cache for the PDP-11." *IEEE Transactions on Computers*, C-29(6):546–549, June 1980.

[LL88]   J. Lundelius-Welch, and N. Lynch. "A new Fault-Tolerant Algorithm for Clock Synchronization." *Information and Computation*, 77:1–36, 1988.

[LM85]   L. Lamport, and P. M. Melliar-Smith. "Synchronizing Clocks in the Presence of Faults."

[Lom77]   D. B. Lomet. "Process Structuring, Synchronization, and Recovery Using Atomic Actions." *Proceedings of ACM Conference on Language Design for Reliable Software, SIGPLAN Notices 12, 3*, pp. 128–137, March 1977. *Journal of the ACM*, 32, January 1985.

[LP80]   D. C. Luckham, and W. Polak. "Ada Exception Handling: An Axiomatic Approach." *ACM Transactions on Programming Languages and Systems*, 2(2):225–233, April 1980.

[LS79a]   B. Lampson, and H. Sturgis. *Crash Recovery in a Distributed Database System.* Technical Report, Palo Alto, California: Computer Science Laboratory, Xerox Park, 1979.

[LS79b]   B. H. Liskov, and A. Snyder. "Exception Handling in CLU." *IEEE Transactions on Software Engineering*, SE-5(6):546–558, November 1979.

[LS82]   B. Liskov, and R. Scheifler. "Guardians and Actions: Linguistic Support for Robust, Distributed Programs." *Proceedings of the Ninth Annual Symposium on Principles of Programming Languages And Systems*, pp. 7–19, 1982.

[LS83]   B. Liskov, and R. Scheifler. "Guardians and Actions: Linguistic Support for Robust, Distributed Programs." *ACM Transactions on Programming Languages And Systems*, 5(7):7–19, 1983.

[LSP82]   L. Lamport, R. Shostak, and M. Pease. "The Byzantine Generals Problem." *ACM Transactions on Programming Languages and Systems*, 4(3):382–401, July 1982.

[MB76]   R. M. Metcalfe, and D. R. Boggs. "Ethernet: Distributed Packet Switching for Local Computer Networks." *Communications of the ACM*, 19(6):395–404, July 1976.

[MB76]   R. M. Metcalfe, and D. R. Boggs. "Ethernet: Distributed Packet Switching for Local Computer Networks." *Communications of the ACM*, 19(6):395–404, July 1976.

[MH76]   S. N. Maheshwari, and S. L. Hakimi. "On Models of Diagnosable Systems and Probabilistic Fault Diagnosis." *IEEE Transactions on Computers*, C-25:228–236, 1976.

[MLO86]   C. Mohan, B. Lindsay, and R. Obermarck. "Transaction Management in the R^* Distributed Database Management System." *ACM Transactions on Database Systems*, 11(4):378–396, December 1986.

[MM78]   S. Mallela, and G.M. Masson. "Diagnosable Systems for Intermittent Faults." *IEEE Transactions on Computers*, C-27:560–566, 1978.

[MMA90]   P. M. Melliar-Smith, L. E. Moser, and V. Agrawala. "Broadcast Protocols for Distributed Systems." *IEEE Transactions on Parallel and Distributed Systems*, 1(1):17–25, January 1990.

[MMSA93]   L. E. Moser, P. M. Melliar-Smith, and V. Agrawala. "Asynchronous Fault-Tolerant Total Ordering Algorithms." *SIAM Journal of Computing*, 22(4):727–750, August 1993.

[Mos86]   J. E. B. Moss. *An Introduction to Nested Transactions.* Technical Report 86-41, Amherst, Massachusetts: University of Amherst Massachusetts, COINS, September 1986.

[MPM83]   D. A. Menasce, G. J. Popek, and R. R. Muntz. "A Locking Protocol for Resource Coordination in Distributed Databases." *ACM Transactions on Database Systems*, 5(2):103–138, 1983.

[MR78]   P. E. Merlin, and B. Randell. "State Restoration in Distributed Systems." *8th International Conference on Fault Tolerant Computing Systems*, pp. 129–134, Toulouse, France, 1978.

[MS92]   S. Mishra, and R. D. Schlicthing. *Abstractions for Constructing Dependable Distributed Systems.* Technical Report TR 92-19. Tucson, Arizona: Department of Computer Science, University of Arizona, 1992.

[MSM94]   P. M. Melliar-Smith, and L. E. Moser. "Trans: A Reliable Broadcast Protocol." *IEE Transactions on Communications, Speech, and Vision*, To appear in 1994.

[NCN88]   S. Navaratnam, S. Chanson, and G. Neufeld. "Reliable Group Communication in Distributed Systems." *8th International Conference on Distributed Computing Systems*, pp. 439–445, San Jose, CA, 1988.

[Nel81]   B. J. Nelson. "Remote Procedure Call." Ph.D. Thesis, Department of Computer Science, Carnegie-Mellon University, Pittsburgh, Pennsylvania, 1981.

[NG90]   V. F. Nicola, and A. Goyal. "Modeling of Correlated Failures and Com-
           munity Error Recovery in Multiversion Software." *IEEE Transactions
           on Software Engineering*, 16(3):350–359, March 1990.

[OL82]   S. Owicki, and L. Lamport. "Proving Liveness Properties of Concurrent
           Programs." *ACM Transactions on Programming Language and Systems*,
           4(3):155–495, 1982.

[Pap79]   C.H. Papadimitriou. "The Serializability of Concurrent Database
           Updates." *Journal of the ACM*, 26(4):631–653, October 1979.

[Par86]   J.F. Paris. "Voting with a Variable Number of Copies." *6th International
           Conference on Distributed Computing Systems*, pp. 50–55, 1986.

[PBS89]   L. L. Peterson, N. C. Buchholz, and R. D. Schlicting. "Preserving
           and Using Context Information in Interprocess Communication." *ACM
           Transactions on Computer Systems*, 7(3):217–246, August 1989.

[PGK88]   D. A. Patterson, G. Gibson, and R. H. Katz. "A Case for Redundant
           Arrays of Inexpensive Disks (RAID)." *Proceedings of ACM SIGMOD*,
           pp. 109–116, 1988.

[PJ91]   J. Purtilo, and P. Jalote. "An Environment for Developing Fault Tolerant
           Software." *IEEE Transactions on Software Engineering*, 17(2):153–159,
           February 1991.

[PL79]   R. Pardo, and M. T. Liu. "Multi-Destination Protocols for Distributed
           Systems." In *Proceedings of Computer Networking Symposium*, 1979.

[PMC67]   F.P. Preparata, G. Metze, and R.T. Chien. "On the Connection
           Assignment Problem of Diagnosable Systems." *IEEE Transactions on
           Electronic Computers*, EC16:848–854, 1967.

[PNP88]   C. A. Pu, D. D. Noe, and A. Proudfoot. "Regeneration of Replicated
           Objects: A Technique and its Eden Implementation." *IEEE Transactions
           on Software Engineering*, 14(7):936–945, July 1988.

[PP83]   M. L. Powell, and D. L. Presotto. "Publishing: A Reliable Broadcast
           Communication Mechanism." *9th ACM Symposium on Operating
           Systems, Operating Sys. Rev: 17*, pp. 100–109, 1983.

[Pra86]   D. K. Pradhan. "Fault-Tolerant Multiprocessor and VLSI-Based System
           Communication Architectures." In D. K. Pradhan, editor, *Fault-Tolerant*

Computing Theory and Techniques. Englewood Cliffs, NJ: Prentice Hall, 1986, Chapter 7.

[PS88]   F. Panzieri, and S. K. Shrivastava. "Rajdoot: A Remote Procedure Call Mechanism Supporting Orphan Detection and Killing." *IEEE Transactions on Software Engineering*, 14(1):30–37, January 1988.

[PSL80]   M. Pease, R. Shostak, and L. Lamport. "Reaching Agreement in the Presence of Faults." *Journal of the ACM*, 27(2):228–234, April 1980.

[Rab83]   M. Rabin. "Randomized Byzantine Generals." *Proceedings of the IEEE Symposium on the Foundations of Computer Science*, pp. 403–409. IEEE, 1983.

[Ran75]   B. Randell. "System Structure for Software Fault Tolerance." *IEEE Transactions on Software Engineering*, SE-1:220–232, June 1975.

[RC89]   K. Ravindran, and S. T. Chanson. "Failure Transparency in Remote Procedure Calls." *IEEE Transactions on Computers*, 38(8):1173–1187, August 1989.

[Ree83]   D. P. Reed. "Implementing Atomic Actions on Decentralized Data." *ACM Transactions on Computer Systems*, 1(1):3–23, February 1983.

[RF89]   T. R. N. Rao, and E. Fujiwara. *Error-control Coding for Computer Systems*. Englewood Cliffs, NJ: Prentice Hall, 1989.

[RK75]   J. D. Russell, and C. R. Kime. "System Level Diagnosis, Closure and Diagnosability with Repair." *IEEE Transactions on Computers*, C-24:1078–1089, 1975.

[Rob82]   A. S. Robinson. "A User-oriented Perspective of Fault Tolerant System Models and Terminologies." *12th International Symposium on Fault Tolerant Computing Systems*, pp. 22–28, 1982.

[RT79]   D. L. Russell, and M. J. Tiedeman. "Multiprocess Recovery Using Conversations." *9th International Symposium on Fault Tolerant Computing Systems*, Madison, Wisconsin, 1979.

[RT88]   R. V. Renesse, and A. S. Tanenbaum. "Voting with Ghosts." *8th International Conference on Distributed Computing Systems*, pp. 456–461, 1988.

[Rus80]   D. L. Russell. "State Restoration in Systems of Communicating Processes." *IEEE Transactions on Software Engineering*, SE-6(2):183–194, March 1980.

[S+83]   D. Stott Parker, Jr. et al. "Detection of Mutual Inconsistency in Distributed Systems." *IEEE Transactions on Software Engineering*, 9(3):240–247, May 1983.

[SA83]   A. Segall, and B. Awerbuch. "A Reliable Broadcast Protocol." *IEEE Transactions on Communication*, 31(7):896–901, 1983.

[SA89]   S. H. Son, and A. K. Agarwala. "Distributed Checkpointing for Globally Consistent States of Databases." *IEEE Transactions on Software Engineering*, 3(2):1157–1167, October 1989.

[SC89]   J. W. Stamos, and F. Cristian. "A low-cost Atomic Protocol." Research Report RJ 7185 (67664) 12/5/89, IBM Research Division, IBM Research Division Yorktown Heights, New York, December 1989.

[Sch83]   F. B. Schneider. "Fail-Stop Processors." *Digest of Papers, COMP-CON83*, pp. 66–70, 1983.

[Sch84]   F. B. Schneider. "Byzantine Generals in Action: Implementing Fail-Stop Processors." *ACM Transactions on Computer Systems*, 2(2):145–154, May 1984.

[Sch90]   F. B. Schneider. "Implementing Fault-Tolerant Services Using the State Machine Approach: A Tutorial." *ACM Computing Surveys*, 22(4):299–319, December 1990.

[SDR82]   J. F. Shoch, Y. K. Dalal, and D. D. Redell. "Evolution of the Ethernet Local Computer Network." *IEEE Computer*, pp. 896–901, August 1982.

[SGM87]   R. K. Scott, J. W. Gault, and D. F. McAllistor. "Fault Tolerant Software Reliability Modeling." *IEEE Transactions on Software Engineering*, 13(5):582–592, May 1987.

[SGS84]   F. B. Schneider, D. Gries, and R. D. Schlicting. "Fault-Tolerant Broadcasts." *Science of Computer Programming*, 4:1–15, 1984.

[Sha85]   S. Shatz. "Post Failure Reconfiguration of CSP Programs." *IEEE Transactions on Software Engineering*, 11(10):1193–1202, October 1985.

[Shr78]   S. K. Shrivastava. "Sequential Pascal with Recovery Blocks." *Software Practice and Experience*, 8(2):177–185, 1978.

[Shr79]   S. K. Shrivastava. "Concurrent Pascal with Backward Error Recovery: Implementation." *Software Practice and Experience*, 9:1021–1033, 1979.

[Sil89]   A. Silbershatz. "Communication and Synchronization in Distributed Programs." *IEEE Transactions on Software Engineering*, SE-5:542–546, November 1989.

[Ske81]   D. Skeen. "Nonblocking Commit Protocols." *ACM SIGMOD*, pp. 133–142. ACM SIGMOD, ACM, 1981.

[Ske85]   D. Skeen. "Determining the Last Process to Fail." *ACM Transactions on Computer Systems*, 3(1):15–30, February 1985.

[SM90]   G. F. Sullivan, and G. M. Masson. "Using Certification Trails to Achieve Software Fault Tolerance." *20th International Symposium on Fault Tolerant Computing Systems*, pp. 423–431, 1990.

[SP82]   S. K. Shrivastava, and F. Panzieri. "The Design of a Reliable Remote Procedure Call Mechanism." *IEEE Transactions on Computers*, C-31(7):692–697, July 1982.

[SS83a]   R. D. Schlichting, and F. B. Schneider. "Fail Stop Processors: An Approach to Designing Fault-Tolerant Computing Systems." *ACM Transactions on Computer Systems*, 1(3):222–238, August 1983.

[SS83b]   D. Skeen, and M. Stonebraker. "A Formal Model of Crash Recovery in a Distributed System." *IEEE Transactions on Software Engineering*, SE-9(3):219–228, May 1983.

[Sta87]   W. Stallings. *Local Networks, an Introduction*. MacMillan Publishing Company, 2nd edition, 1987.

[STS87]   K. Perry, S. Toueg, and T. Srikanth. "Fast Distributed Agreement." *SIAM Journal of Computing*, 16(3):445–457, June 1987.

[Svo84]   L. Svobodova. "Resilient Distributed Computing." *IEEE Transactions on Software Engineering*, 10(3):257–268, May 1984.

[SW82]   D. P. Siewiorek, and R. Wsarz. *The Theory and Practice of Reliable System Design*. Bedford, MA: Digital Press, 1982.

[SW89]   A. P. Sistla, and J. L. Welch. "Efficient Distributed Recovery Using Message Logging." *8th ACM Symposium on Principles of Distributed Computing*, August 1989.

[SY84]   R. E. Strom, and S. Yemini. "Optimistic Recovery: An Asynchronous Approach to Fault Tolerance in Distributed Systems." *14th International Symposium of Fault Tolerant Computing Systems*, pp. 374–379, 1984.

[SY85]   R. E. Strom, and S. Yemini. "Optimistic Recovery in Distributed Systems." *ACM Transactions on Computer Systems*, 3(3):204–226, August 1985.

[Tan88]   A. S. Tanenbaum. *Computer Networks*. Englewood Cliffs, NJ: Prentice Hall, 1988.

[Tho79]   R. H. Thomas. "A Majority Consensus Approach to Concurrency Control for Multiple Copy Databases." *ACM Transactions on Database Systems*, 4(2):180–209, June 1979.

[TKT92]   Z. Tong, R. Y. Kain, and W. T. Tsai. "Rollback Recovery in Distributed Systems Using Loosely Synchronized Clocks." *IEEE Transactions on Parallel and Distributed Systems*, 3(2):246–251, March 1992.

[TMB80a]   D. J. Taylor, D. E. Morgan, and J. P. Black. "Redundancy in Data Structures: Improving Software Fault Tolerance." *IEEE Transactions on Software Engineering*, SE-6(6):584–594, November 1980.

[TMB80b]   D. J. Taylor, D. E. Morgan, and J. P. Black. "Redundancy in Data Structures: Some Theoretical Results." *IEEE Transactions on Software Engineering*, SE-6(6):595–602, November 1980.

[Toh86]   Y. Tohma. "Coding Techniques in Fault-Tolerant, Self-checking, and Fail-safe Circuits." In D. K. Pradhan, editor, *Fault-Tolerant Computing Theory and Techniques*. Englewood Cliffs, NJ: Prentice Hall, 1986, pp. 336–415.

[Tri82]   K. S. Trivedi. *Probability and Statistics with Reliability, Queuing, and Computer Science Applications*. Englewood Cliffs, NJ: Prentice Hall, 1982.

[Ven92]   D. Venkaiah. "An Integer Programming Approach for Assigning Votes in a Distributed System." Master's Thesis, Indian Institute of Technology

Kanpur, Department of Computer Science and Engineering, Kanpur, India, March 1992.

[VRB89]   P. Verissimo, L. Rodrigues, and M. Baptista. "Amp: A Highly Parallel Atomic Multicast Protocol." *ACM SIGCOMM'89*, pp. 83–93, Arlingon, Texas, 1989.

[VRL87]   K. Venkatesh, T. Radhakrishnan, and H. F. Li. "Optimal Checkpointing and Local Recording for Domino-Free Rollback Recovery." *Information Processing Letters*, 25:295–303, July 1987.

[Woo81]   W. G. Wood. "A Decentralized Recovery Protocol." *11th International Symposium on Fault Tolerant Computing Systems*, pp. 159–164, Portland, 1981.

[YH86]   R. M. Yanney, and J. P. Hayes. "Distributed Recovery in Fault-Tolerant Multiprocessor Networks." *IEEE Transactions on Computers*, C-35(10):871–878, October 1986.

[YJ89]   S.-M. Yuan, and P. Jalote. "Fault Tolerant Commit Protocols." *Proceedings of Fifth International Conference on DATA ENGINEERING*, pp. 280 – 286, February 1989.

[YJT88]   K. S. Yap, P. Jalote, and S. K. Tripathi. "Fault Tolerant Remote Procedure Call." *8th International Conference on Distributed Computing Systems*, pp. 48–54, June 1988.

[You74]   J. W. Young. "A First Order Approximation to the Optimum Checkpoint Interval." *Communications of the ACM*, 17:530–531, September 1974.

Index